Outside the Apple Macintosh

edited by
Peter Norton, Kevin
Goldstein, and Scott Clark

Brady Publishing

New York   London   Toronto   Sydney   Tokyo   Singapore

Brady Publishing

A Division of Prentice Hall Computer Publishing
15 Columbus Circle, 14th Floor
New York, New York 10023

Manufactured in the United States of America

10 9 8 7 6 5 4 3 2 1

ISBN: 1-56686-015-6

Limits of Liability and Disclaimer of Warranty

Credits

Publisher: Michael Violano

Managing Editor: Kelly D. Dobbs

Editor: Tracy Smith

Production Editor: Bettina A. Versaci

Technical Reviewer: Owen Hartnett

Indexer: Loren Malloy

Book Designer: Scott Cook

Cover Designer: HUB Graphics Corp.

Production Team: Katy Bodenmiller, Lisa Daugherty, Denny Hager,
Carla Hall-Batton, John Kane, Betty Kish, Roger Morgan,
Juli Pavey, Angela Pozdol, Linda Quigley, Susan M. Shepard,
Marcella Thompson

Acknowledgments

A book like this always involves many more people than you think it will, and if we try to thank everyone, we will surely miss someone. So, if you don't find your name here, that doesn't mean we appreciate you any less. We know that your labors of love are still labors and your help and support were—and continue to be—invaluable.

We want, of course, to thank our individual contributors. They are all experts in the various realms of computing, and a good deal of the work that went into putting this book into your hands has been theirs. These are the contributors and their contributions:

David Field	Printing Technologies
Jordan Gold	Graphics Hardware - Output Storage Technologies Networking Technologies (portions)
Clint Hicks	Overview of Graphics Technologies Sound Technologies and MIDI MultiMedia Technologies
Mary Jane Mara	Expansion Technologies
Steve Michel	System 7
Steve Schwartz	Modems Fax Modems
Richard Taha	Networking Technologies
Serge Timacheff	Graphics Hardware - Input with assistance from Antoine Bovard

Sincerest thanks to all of you for your efforts.

Heartfelt thanks also to our agent, Bill Gladstone at Waterside Productions, and his wonderful staff. Matt Wagner was absolutely invaluable in helping us coordinate the project and making sure everyone got paid.

Thanks, as always, to Tracy Smith and Bettina Versaci at Brady Publishing.

Peter Norton
Scott Clark
Kevin Goldstein

Contents

CHAPTER 4. AN OVERVIEW OF GRAPHICS TECHNOLOGIES 101

CHAPTER 9. AN OVERVIEW OF COMMUNICATIONS TECHNOLOGIES 255

CHAPTER 12. NETWORKING TECHNOLOGY   341

CHAPTER 13. COMPUTER SECURITY   391

APPENDIX A. UPGRADING TO SYSTEM 7 AND SYSTEM 7 TECHNOLOGIES   419

Introduction

Back in 1984 when Steve Jobs and all the creative folks at Apple Computer brought us the first Macintosh, the world was young and simple. There was one Macintosh, one word processor, one spreadsheet, one painting program, and one printer. Period. After a little while, the market expanded and there were additional products...one modem and one hard disk.

But it wasn't long after this that the appeal of graphical user interfaces caused the Macintosh market to explode, bringing an array of solutions to every problem, and a variety of options for every solution. As Apple has increased the power of the Macintosh—bringing high-end technologies out of the white towers and down to the desktop—the trend has only accelerated, and it is just as likely as not that when you step into a computer store and ask for a modem, or a hard disk, or a memory upgrade, you will be shown twenty different ways to spend your money...and your time.

These days, even if you were someone who simply "fell in love" with the original 128K Macintosh, it is probable that your primary interest is using your Macintosh to get a job done, and making cost-effective purchases towards that end. The excitement of the original Macintosh still lives, but the bottom line is ever increasingly, the bottom line.

Outside the Apple Macintosh is the first book of its kind: a complete and up-to-date guide for the person who needs to get a job done and wonders exactly what pieces in the giant jigsaw puzzle of peripherals and software to assemble. It is not a "how to" book, like how to use Excel or WordPerfect. It is a "what to" book. In it, you will find everything from what to use if you need to make desktop publications, to what to use if you disseminate daily reports to 25 (or 2,500) satellite locations, to what to do when your critical full-color scanning software overflows the memory you've got crammed into your Macintosh.

You will find comprehensible explanations of the technology behind all of your tools, so you will know what you need and what you don't to get the job done. You will be able to better justify the costs of all you use your computer for by understanding why you are using those tools. You will also save yourself a great deal of money by knowing when you are hearing information that actually tells you, "this will make your job easier."

Which brings us to an important point: Remember that every dollar you spend is a vote. Not only are you determining which hardware and software companies will flourish and which will flounder, you are also supporting the business practices of your retailers and distributors. Today, you should never have to buy any hardware or software product without getting a 30-day money back return policy, and we urge you to support retailers who respect your right to change your mind. With software especially, it is frequently impossible to tell if a program is right for you until you try it. If you buy from a retailer with no return policy, you could easily be out several hundred dollars and have nothing but a lengthening row of "shelfware" to show for it. Be on the watch for return "policies" that only allow you to return a defective product for another copy of the same product. These policies do not give you anything you are not already promised by law.

If you must buy a product from a retailer without a return policy—or if you are buying software in one of the genres that is *notorious* for not supporting returns, even if the retailer normally provides a return policy (MIDI, and other music-related software, is a particularly bad example of this)—ask your salesperson to open the software and let you try it in the store to get a feel for its capabilities. If your retailer will not let you return it and will not let you try it out in the store, find yourself another retailer fast. This should apply to most hardware, too. Beware of retailers who are unable or unwilling to connect hardware to demonstrate it for you. They are basically telling you that your business is not worth their time.

There is a growing number of so-called "Computer Superstores" that promise the best in prices and the best in service; some may, but we can tell you from experience that some definitely don't. All of the problems we mentioned above were encountered at several branches of one such "Superstore," and we now take all of our business elsewhere. If mail-order is an acceptable way for you to purchase items, you will find that many of the Macintosh mail-order houses have very friendly and knowledgeable staff members who are willing to look up answers to your questions; most of them have good return policies, too, but always ask about the *specific* product you're ordering.

That said, *Outside the Apple Macintosh* will allow you to focus on your job and your tools. This book grew out of a recognition of our own needs, and we sincerely hope it fulfills yours. You can write to us at:

Norton, Goldstein & Clark
Post Office Box 91925
Long Beach, CA 90809-1925

or in care of Brady Publishing in New York, and we welcome your comments and recommendations for a second edition. If we did our job right, buying this book will make both you and your Macintosh more productive, will save you money…and maybe even help you have a little more fun in the bargain.

1

Expansion Technologies

At its 1992 Worldwide Developers' Conference, Apple's CEO, John Sculley, announced plans to produce a "steady stream" of improved Macintoshes, with new units scheduled to debut in almost every quarter of the coming year. Included in this vision are additions to Apple's PowerBook and low-cost Mac lines which, among other things, promise to bring built-in color to both Classic and portable platforms. He reiterated an ongoing commitment to increased power and performance in high-end Macs. Attempts to evolve the Mac interface were evident in a preview of a new Finder desktop, sporting drawers and stacks of papers instead of files and folders. The now legendary Apple-IBM alliance is busily engineering a whole new operating system, while cooperative ventures with SONY and Sharp are set to provide us with Mac-like devices called Personal Digital Assistants (PDAs) by early '93.

Meanwhile, third parties are feverishly keeping pace by offering upgrades, accelerators, peripherals, and a multitude of add-ons for every on-the-street, on-the-drawing-board, or off-the-wall Mac product. As predicted in Alvin Toffler's 1970 best-seller, *Future Shock*, "the technology is indeed mutating into higher forms at an exponential rate." The speed of advance has become so frantic that leafing through the trades is like taking a walk with Ridley Scott through his Blade Runner set with mile-high, video images of high-tech turn-ons vying for your mind at every turn. Amidst the onslaught of all this techno-glitter, the cool user maintains equilibrium by chanting the following mantras: "Price...Productivity...Performance."

Questions of which Macintosh to buy and what peripherals, accelerators, and enhancements to add are most easily and adequately answered in light of the tasks you need to perform versus how much you can comfortably spend on optimizing performance. In deciding the latter, don't forget to balance actual out-of-pocket costs against increases in income you can *count on* as a result of higher productivity.

Since knowledge is power, here to help you in your quest are basic explanations of the major expansion paths and products available for the most popular of the currently available Macs. Included are charts to acquaint you with the basic features of each Mac, as well as a breakdown of common tasks and the expansion products that do most to enhance their performance. To begin with, however, let's discuss some of the basic ways in which the Mac communicates with itself and the outside world.

Magic Bus

In their earliest days, computers existed to aid us in our computational chores (thus the name *computer*)—like counting the population via hole-punched cards. Although this technology has since advanced to the threshold of artificial thought, its primordial task remains *data in/data out*.

Like a city needs a transportation system to move workers into the city in the morning and out to the suburbs at night, the computer needs a system to move information in and out. One way to solve both problems is to provide buses. In the case of the computer, buses are channels or pathways between hardware devices. Such devices may be *internal* (a chip on one of the computer's boards), *external* (a desktop scanner hooked to the computer via a connector in its back), or *remote external* (a printer accessed through a network).

When bus architecture is used in a computer, its processor, memory and all peripherals are connected through a dual-channel structure. One channel selects a location for the data and is called the *address bus*. The other transfers data and is called the *data bus*. Unlike some cities, computers often have more than one bus system. Most latter-day Macs have two buses available to users for adding on power and functionality: an *Apple Desktop bus* and a *SCSI bus*. The more powerful machines also have *NuBus*.[1]

Apple Desktop Bus (ADB)

ADB is a serial communications bus designed to accommodate low-speed input devices. It was introduced with the Macintosh SE and II platforms in 1987. Its main impact was to change the type of connector used to hook up the mouse and keyboard, and to allow users to *daisy-chain* up to 16 ADB-compatible devices. Daisy-chaining means hooking an ADB device to one of your Mac's ADB ports, then another ADB device to an ADB port on the back of the first device, and so on...up to 16 devices. In some daisy-chaining schemes, you have to connect devices in an orderly way, carefully assigning numbers to each device (see SCSI Bus). This is not the case with ADB devices that are randomly assigned numbers at start-up and tracked by software.

By the way, if a 16-device allowance seems too generous, degradation of performance gives you a practical limit of three, and Apple does not recommend adding any more. Even if your system has two ADB ports, it still only has *one* ADB bus which can only fully support three devices. Since ADB accommodates *low-speed* input, it is ideally suited to devices like mice, track-balls, graphics tablets, light pens, keyboards, and some smaller modems (such as, the Teleport ADB modem)—all of whose input is slow compared to, say, a SCSI hard drive.

Although the ADB practically supports only three devices, there are a few third-parties whose products use this bus to draw power and aren't counted as part of your ADB chain. For instance, some mass storage companies offer small, pocket-sized hard disks which connect to the SCSI bus for input and output, and to the ADB for power. Examples are La Cie's Pocket-Drive 80 and Mass Microsystems' HitchHiker 80, both of which offer optional ADB power adapters.

NOTE: If you attach or detach an ADB device to an ADB device currently connected to this bus *while the system is on*, all device numbers are reset, causing the system to "forget" addresses. Only the mouse and keyboard may be unaffected. If this happens, restarting your Mac allows the system to re-assign addresses and load them again into its memory.

The ADB port on the Mac connects to a mini-DIN 4-pin ADB connector like the connectors at the end of the mouse and keyboard cables, which are, of course, ADB devices. (See Figure 1.1 for a view of this port.) Current-day Mac keyboards have cables with an ADB connector at both ends, and two ADB ports on either side of the keyboard itself. This allows you to choose which side you wish to connect to your keyboard cable, leaving the other side free for your mouse (quite a convenience for lefties). In systems with only one ADB port, the mouse *must* be connected through the keyboard. In systems with two ADB ports, the mouse can be connected to the back of the Mac or daisy-chained to the keyboard.

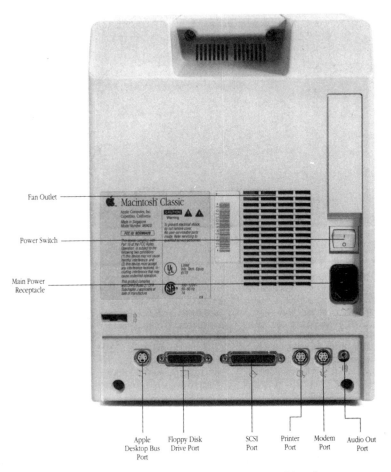

Figure 1.1: A view from the back of the Mac Classic.

SCSI Bus

Apple adopted Small Computer System Interface (SCSI) when it built the Mac Plus, which entered the marketplace in 1986. This interface is based on the ANSI X3T9.2/82-2 proposal by the American National Standards Institute; long recognized as an industry standard for connecting small computers to intelligent peripherals. It consists of a set of mechanical, electrical and functional specifications for effecting a connection between micros and certain peripherals, such as hard disks, optical (CD-ROM) disks, certain types of printers (such as, Apple's Personal LaserWriter SC or line printers), digitizers and scanners. Even the PowerBook 100 may be switched to SCSI mode, attached to the SCSI port of another Mac and assume the behavior of a SCSI hard disk.[2]

Like the ADB, you can daisy-chain peripherals to the SCSI bus (popularly pronounced "scuzzy") via either its external DB-25 or internal 50-pin flat-ribbon SCSI connectors. (See Figure 1.1 or 1.2 for a view of an external SCSI connector.) But only a maximum of seven devices may exist on a given chain. Again like the ADB, although there are two connectors (internal and external), there's still only one SCSI bus capable of supporting a *grand total* of seven devices. However, since a full chain might not cause any degradation in performance,[3] you really *can* add seven devices. Each device needs an ID number between 0 and 6, and no two devices on the same chain may share the same ID. If the Mac comes with an internal SCSI hard drive, it takes "0" as its ID, and the Mac itself takes "7." The remaining six allowable devices are assigned IDs in-between and added to the chain in order, starting with 1 and ending with 6.

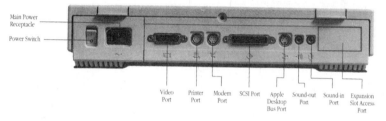

Figure 1.2: A view from the back of the Mac LC.

IDs are assigned using switches (or jumpers) on the SCSI device itself before connecting it to the Mac (see Figure 1.9 for an example of a SCSI ID switch). When the Mac is turned on, its System software checks the bus for peripheral devices starting with the number "6," unless you specify another startup volume via the Startup Control Panel. When a device is found connected to the bus, it's driver is loaded into *main memory*(RAM). If it has a storage device, its icon appears on the Mac desktop. If it's an input device (like a Scanner), you will not know whether it's up and running until you try to use its associated software.

A SCSI device communicates with another SCSI device using a strict initiator-to-target protocol, with the initiator asking the target to perform an action (such as read a block of data). Each SCSI device assumes a fixed role as either target or initiator. Although more than one initiator can exist on the same daisy-chain, only one controls the bus at any given time. If two initiators compete for control, the one with the highest ID gets first dibs, thus assuring that the Mac itself (with its "7" ID) is always first in line for the bus.

NOTE: Any SCSI device you wish to use in a session should be connected and turned on *before* powering up the Mac. Connecting (or disconnecting) a device while the Mac is on may damage your SCSI port. If a device is already connected, but you forgot to turn it on before turning on your Mac, no harm done. Simply turn it on and restart your Mac. If the expected device icon fails to appear on the desktop, or if its software tells you it's not connected, shut-down the Mac, check the connection and restart. If you are still having a problem, open your SCSI Control Panel and check for ID conflicts with any other device. If all else fails, you may need to add one or two *terminators* to your SCSI chain (discussed below).

If any peripherals at all are connected to the SCSI bus, at least one set of *termination resistors* must also be present. Termination resistors may be provided by the SCSI device itself or by a separate device called a *terminator*. A terminator looks like a SCSI connector without a cable. It has a male DB-25 on one side and a female DB-25 on the other, making it possible to connect one side to a SCSI cable and the other directly to a SCSI device.

If there are several devices on the SCSI network—or if more than three feet of total cabling is used—two sets of termination resistors may be required at either end of the network. Since internal hard disks include a set of termination resistors, a Mac with an internal already has termination at the front of its chain. If a second terminator is needed, place it at the physical end of the chain. (The logical end of the chain, #7, is the Mac itself.)

NOTE: Connecting more than two sets of resistors to your chain overloads the Mac's NCR line drivers. Similarly, connecting an RS-232 device to the SCSI port damages the NCR SCSI chip on the Mac's logic board. Although an RS-232 connector has the same number of pins as a SCSI DB-25, the RS-232 draws a higher voltage.

Not all Mac SCSI buses are created equal. Reading and writing data through the Mac Plus, SE, and Classic SCSI ports is slow compared to the SCSI speeds of higher-end and more sophisticated Macs. The most sophisticated Mac platform to-date—the Quadra line—supports maximum SCSI transfer rates of 4 Megabytes (MB) per second (5 in the 950), compared to a maximum rate of 1.2 MB per second in the SE. Additionally, the Quadras offer a gateway into the super-fast world of SCSI-2, capable of supporting a maximum transfer rate of 10 MB per second. The trick is connecting hard disks capable of keeping pace with these higher transfer rates.

Transfer rates not only vary from platform to platform, but are also affected by devices on the chain. Adding devices like scanners, for instance, can slow the whole chain down. For this reason, some modest third-party scanning devices hook into the ADB (which caters to slow input) instead of the SCSI bus. If you've got a standard SCSI scanner (or any other slow SCSI device) and you notice performance degradation when you plug it in, consider plugging it in only when you need it.

SCSI-2

SCSI-2 (aka Fast-SCSI) is a faster, more efficient version of the SCSI standard which—in addition to speedier data transfer—allows you to connect a 14-device chain to a single SCSI bus. Quadra users anticipated built-in SCSI-2 support in the Quadra 950; but the necessary rewrite of the SCSI Manager software wasn't completed by its release date. Nevertheless, the SCSI controller chip used in all Quadra models is SCSI-2 compatible, and Fast-SCSI upgrades from third parties are on the brink of release. Plus, once the necessary supporting cables and hard disks are available, SCSI-2 users can switch to Wide SCSI and enjoy truly mind-numbing transfer rates of 20 MB per second—a consummation devoutly to be wished (sigh).

Mac IIfx owners can join the SCSI-2 party now by upgrading to near-Quadra status with Sixty Eight Thousand's dash 30fx package. Though expensive for an upgrade—yet cheap for a Quadra—the package (which overhauls your fx so completely, it ends up in a different case) includes a SCSI-2 card.

You can also improve SCSI performance in any NuBus Mac (discussed next), thanks to companies like DayStar Digital, which claims its SCSI PowerCard increases transfer rates to 5MB per second and, by creating a second SCSI bus, allows you to connect seven additional devices to your Mac (though, naturally, you'll get slower performance from devices hooked to the original, slower bus). Believe it or not, you can even improve SCSI performance in a Mac Plus, thanks to Brainstorm Products' Brainstorm Accelerator which, the company claims, doubles SCSI disk interface speed and *triples* graphics speed—bringing the vintage Plus all the way up to System 7 snuff.

NuBus

NuBus is a standard bus originally developed at MIT for supporting expansion cards in microcomputers. Rights to the bus were eventually purchased by Texas Instruments, then licensed by Apple in 1989 and adapted for its Mac II line. NuBus is capable of supporting up to six slots for expansion cards[4], though not all NuBus Macs offer all six slots (see Mac Features chart).

The combined width of the NuBus's Address and Data buses is 32-bits, which means it can address and transfer 16-bits of data at a time. NuBus expansion cards plug into the 96-pin Euro-DIN connectors inside your Mac, then the add-on card's own connector is accessed through the expansion slots at the back of your Mac. (See Figure 1.3 for an example of an expansion slot.)

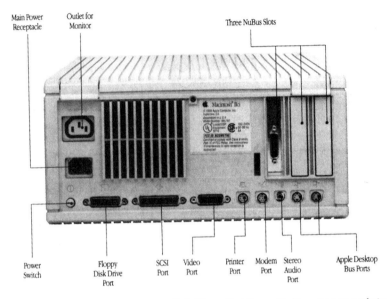

Figure 1.3: Rear view of the Mac IIci. Note the three NuBus access slots, one of which already contains a card.

Among the types of cards supported by NuBus are CPU Accelerator cards, Video Adapter cards, RAM cards, and Network Interface (e.g., EtherNet) cards. Apple has promised that the use of third-party expansion products which adhere to its expansion guidelines and don't physically alter the Mac will not void your Apple warranty. If you wish to insert a noncomplying card or modify the Mac in a way that *does* void the warranty, be sure the third-party covers you for the voided parts of the warranty. (Also make sure the company has been around long enough to gain a good reputation—and has actually done so.)

The array of NuBus-compatible cards available for all manner of NuBus Macs is stunning, and even the Mac industry trades are hard-put to test and report on them all. Recent articles in both *MacWorld* and *Mac User* magazines clocked some of the most popular CPU Accelerators and found diverse results, since it really depends on what kinds of tasks you are benchmarking and which accelerators you choose to include. Further confounding the issue, new accelerators hit the streets even as these reports went to press. Nevertheless, checking into these periodical reports prior to purchase helps *if you understand your needs and the basic features of these cards* (see the "Acceleration Paths" section of this chapter).

You may be surprised to note in the Mac Features chart that the Quadra 900 and 950—Apple's most powerful Macs to-date—have only five NuBus slots each, and that the 700 has just two. Apple explains this by pointing to built-in features of these units which supersede the need for so many add-on cards. Also, each Quadra (along with some of the lower-end Mac IIs) has an additional expansion slot known as a Processor Direct Slot.

Processor Direct Slot (PDS)

Like the NuBus slots, the Processor Direct Slot has 32-bit address and data lines. Instead of a 96-pin connector to NuBus, the PDS provides a 120-pin connector for plugging in expansion cards capable of communicating directly with the Mac's CPU (Central Processing Unit, aka processor). Such direct communication offers obvious advantages in speed, but there is only one PDS to a customer, so choose wisely.

All three Quadras have a PDS, as does the Mac LC. Many users refer to the single expansion slot in the SE/30, Classic II, LC II, and IIsi (and the extra expansion slot in the IIci) as Processor Direct Slots. However, the SE/30's slot connects to its SE bus, while the LC II and IIsi require the purchase of either a PDS Adapter card or a NuBus Adapter card—which *then* allows you to plug in either a PDS card (the LC II is limited to cards made just for it) or a NuBus card, respectively. (Both adapters bonus you with a 68882 *math coprocessor*, discussed in detail later.) The Classic II has no all-purpose expansion slot, just a slot for a math co-processor or expansion ROM—and the IIci's extra port, though it has the requisite 120-pins, supports only high-speed memory cache cards and no other PDS options.

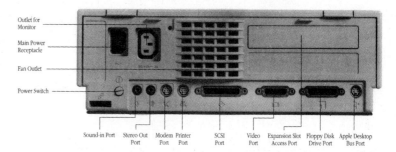

Figure 1.4: The back of the Mac IIsi shows one expansion slot access port. Either a NuBus or PDS adapter card must be added before it's of any use.

Figure 1.5: The IIsi 030 Processor Direct Slot Adapter Card.

Figure 1.6: The IIsi NuBus Adapter Card.

 # Central Processing Unit (CPU)

The terms *Central Processing Unit*, *CPU*, *microprocessor*, and *processor* are used interchangeably to refer to the chip on the main logic or motherboard of a microcomputer that serves as the computer's primary "brain."[5] It consists of a Control Unit that locates, analyzes, and executes instructions, and an Arithmetic Logic Unit (ALU) that calculates and compares. The CPUs used by all Macintoshes derive from Motorola's 68000 family of microprocessors. Apple chose this family because it is high-performing and capable of supporting complex instruction sets.

68000

The original 128K Mac, the 512K, the 512KE, the Mac Plus, the Mac SE, the Mac Classic, the original Portable, and the PowerBook 100 all depend on the 68000 version of Motorola's CPU. Of the four versions of 68000 microprocessors currently available, this is the least powerful.

Although all of these Macs rely on a 68000 CPU, some execute instructions faster than others, due to differences in processor clock speeds. A processor's clock resides in a circuit that uses the fixed vibrations of a quartz crystal to deliver a steady stream of pulses to the processor. These pulses are measured in megahertz (MHz). The higher the MHz, the speedier the CPU's operations and the more information it can handle at once—provided its clock circuit supports the increased speed. Early 68000 Macs have clock speeds of less than 8 MHz (see Features Chart); but the PowerBook 100's 68000 is a hardier version with double the clock speed. Thus, operations in the 100 are faster all the way around than operations in 68000 Macs with lower clock speeds.

Unlike some of its antecedents, the 68000 has no built-in method for dealing with floating point deficiencies, forcing 68000-based Macs to tackle decimal point calculations solely with SANE (Standard Apple Numerics Environment)—a series of software routines stored in ROM (read-only memory chips) and the System software. SANE's performance of such calculations is quite laborious compared to those aided by a math coprocessor or built-in FPU (Floating Point Unit).

Even if your primary computer tasks are heavily supported by decimal-based calculations (e.g., rendering or financial modeling), you don't necessarily need to trade in your 68000 to improve performance. There are plenty of third party accelerators available to upgrade your processor, goose up your clock, and/or provide the necessary math coprocessing. Total Systems, for one, still offers accelerator cards that elevate even 128K Macs to 68020 or even 68030 status. Mobius Technologies offers a 68030 accelerator for the original Classic that snaps onto its system board—and DayStar Digital, Dove Computer Corporation, MacProducts, NewLife, Siclone, Sigma, and Radius are just a few of the available sources for accelerators for all manner of 68000 Macs.

68020

Motorola's first upgrade to its 68000 (don't ask me what happened to the 68010) premiered with the Mac II (since discontinued), and is also the brain of the first Mac LC. The 68020 is said to double the performance of processor-intensive tasks. It is capable of issuing instructions to Motorola's 68881 math coprocessor which, in turn, speeds up the processing of instructions using SANE by 5 to 50 times—and instructions directly accessing the 68881 by 40 to 700 times.

> **NOTE:** Math coprocessors, like CPUs, have internal clock speeds. The clock speed of any math chip added to your system must mimic the speed of the processor's clock. Thus, a 16MHz 68020 requires a 16MHz 68881.

The 68020 also communicates with Motorola's 68851 *Paged Memory Management Unit* (PMMU). Whereas 68000 Macs are only capable of creating a 24-bit Address bus (with addresses from 0 to 23), a *Memory Management Unit* (MMU) offers 24- to 32-bit address mapping (also called memory mapping) and *virtual memory* support. Virtual memory is a means of appropriating portions of a mass storage device to augment the amount of main memory (RAM) available for switching the most current instructions and data in and out of RAM. When such items reside in RAM, operations are significantly faster. Adding virtual memory capabilities relieves you of the need to add (and pay for) additional RAM. (More on this later.) A *Paged* Memory Management Unit (PMMU) further increases the efficiency and functionality of memory management by maintaining a *page table* capable of translating between logical and physical addresses of data in memory—increasing transaction speed.

Finally, the addition of an *instruction cache* capable of storing 256 bytes of the most recently executed instructions speeds performance of oft-repeated tasks even more so than moving them into RAM, since the CPU is saved a visit to RAM to retrieve the address and contents of these instructions.

68030

Apple chose the Mac IIx as a proving ground for the 68030, which incorporates (for the most part) all the features of the 68020 and the 68851 PMMU, but issues coprocessor instructions to a 68882 FPU instead of a 68881. In addition to a 256K instruction cache, the 030 offers a 256K data cache, further improving execution of repetitive tasks.

68040

With the dawn of the Quadra came the 68040—Motorola's most ambitious CPU chip to-date, composed of more than four times the number of transistors used in the 030, and six times the number in the 020. As a result, this single chip draws more power than a PowerBook 140 and requires a *heat sink* to lower its operating temperature. Using a technique called *pipelining*, the 040 can decode and carry out several simultaneous instructions. The chip has a built-in FPU— which means the processor does not have to send instructions to a separate coprocessor chip. However, the 040's FPU eschews transcendental functions (exponential, trigonometric, logarithmic, or hyperbolic) which are handled, instead, by software in the Quadra ROM. Even so, it executes these types of functions every bit as quickly as a 33MHz 68882.

Like its 030 sister, the 040 has both instruction and data caches capable of storing (prepare to be *really* impressed) 4096 bytes *apiece*. Speed and efficiency are gained via the use of *copy-back mode*—a method of updating just the cache when data is written to it, and not main memory (which is then only updated when the cache is instructed to move its contents there).

The bad news is, some third-party applications only look to main memory for instructions and not to the cache—a programming practice which completely violates Apple's long-published developer guidelines. Apple has so far refused to provide an option to revert to *write-through* mode (the mode used by the 68030 which simultaneously writes to both the cache and main memory), but does provide "Cache Control," a Control Panel for disabling the cache in order to run offending software. To do so, you not only have to restart, but you also effectively reduce your Quadra's total performance to that of a mere IIci. Two alternatives are the *Quadra Compatibility* INIT from Alysis and the *Animals* Control Panel from Impulse Technology—both of which allow you to turn off the cache and launch an incompatible application without restarting, then switch it back on when you quit that application. Animals gives you the added option of switching between copy-back and write-through modes. While slower than copy-back, Impulse claims write-through is still three times faster than no cache at all. Meanwhile, most recalcitrant third parties are rewriting their applications to support copy-back.

NOTE: As previously mentioned, a processor's clock speed has something to do with its overall performance. But what is more important: the processor or the clock speed?

continues

continued

Consider this: A July, 1991 *MacWorld* sidebar noted that a 25MHz 68040 is almost twice as fast in *integer performance* (which most applications depend on for their bread-and-butter calculations) than a 50MHz 68030. Conversely, a 5/4/92 *MacWEEK* article claimed that according to users, an 040 25MHz Mac's integer performance is anywhere from merely comparable to slower than that of a Mac with a DayStar 030 50MHz Accelerator. Conflicting reports like these can set a poor user's head spinning; but they also provide important object lessons in reading reviews:

(1) *Consider the date.* The *MacWorld* item appeared *before* the 68040 actually hit the streets and is, therefore, more likely to be based on speculation and manufacturer's promises than fact.

(2) *Consider the source.* Upon what did each writer base the conclusion? Neither claimed to have run an actual test— although the *MacWEEK* reporter did assign findings to actual user feedback.

(3) *Consider the cost.* Where big bucks are involved, better to err on the side of caution. If a review raises doubts about the efficacy of a product—regardless of how sketchy the basis—it cannot hurt to gather more data before taking the plunge.

Serial Ports

Mac's rely on the Zilog Z5380 Serial Communications Controller (SCC) chip to support the connection of serial devices. This chip is a programmable, dual-channel, multiprotocol data communications chip, and a parallel-to-serial and serial-to-parallel converter. It supports the two serial ports found on all Macs, with the exception of the PowerBook 100, which only has one. Both ports use mini 8-pin connectors and are identical except for the fact that Port A, the one with the telephone icon, includes support for synchronous modems. Thus, Port A is for connecting modems; Port B is for connecting printers and may be used to connect to a LocalTalk network—or to a MIDI (Musical Instrument Digital Interface) adapter such as the Apple MIDI Interface, which lets you create musical compositions on the Mac for playback through an external MIDI-equipped synthesizer; or create and edit sequences on the synthesizer and store them on the Mac.

Figure 1.7: The Apple MIDI Interface can be hooked up to any Mac or Apple IIGS—and then to any device that uses the MIDI standard.

Like most Mac attributes, the speed and efficiency of the serial ports vary according to platform. Although the same chip is used to control these ports, they are connected to the *I/O bus*, which is responsible for communications and data transfer. It is the performance of this bus which has become optimized over time, although you are not likely to notice, since most serial devices operate well below I/O speeds. Apple does, however, claim noticeable improvement in EtherNet throughput on the Quadra 950.

Memory

There are three kinds of computer memory: Random Access Memory (RAM), Read-only Memory (ROM), and mass storage media (floppy diskettes, hard disks, optical disks, tapes, etc.).

Random Access Memory (RAM)

Also known as main memory (and, occasionally, working memory), RAM is used to store both data and instructions from a currently in-use application for quick reference as long as the application remains open. It is rather like keeping files associated with a report you are working on at your desk, in lieu of going to the file cabinet each time you need to reference them. Computer applications would run significantly (*unbearably*) slower without RAM, and every application takes advantage of it (including the System software). If multiple applications are opened under MultiFinder, data and instructions associated with each one are moved into RAM. The larger an application, the more space it needs in RAM to run. The more applications you have open at one time, the more RAM you'll need to support them. For instance, to run multiple applications in System 7 (which is quite a RAM *hog*) requires at least 5 MBs of RAM—or you will tear your hair out as you receive one "out of memory" message after the other. If the applications are large (i.e., RAM hogs themselves), you will need commensurately more.

Mac RAM resides in special chips designed for the purpose, of which a maximum of eight and minimum of two sit in a row on a miniature printed circuit board (see Figure 1.5)—called a Single In-line Memory Module (SIMM)— plugged into the main logic board. Either 256Kbit, 1Mbit, 4Mbit, or 16Mbit chips are used (never a mixture in the same row), providing anywhere from 1MB to 16MB of RAM per SIMM.

Figure 1.8: A Single In-line Memory Module (SIMM).

The number of SIMMs you can add to a given Mac dictates the ultimate amount of RAM you can plug into the main logic board. The Mac Features Chart lists the maximum amount of RAM each Mac was built to support. Third parties, however, offer NuBus upgrades, allowing you to expand far beyond such worldly limitations. DayStar, for instance, offers a RAM PowerCard with room for any four-group combination of 1MB, 4MB, or 16MB SIMMs. If that's not enough, you can special order their composite version of 16MB SIMMs, goosing the total to a whopping 256MB per card. If this amount of RAM seems obscene, it may be downright necessary to the performance of some truly large-scale computer operations, such as the creation and manipulation of 16-million color, three-dimensional, animated graphics.

NOTE: To push the outside of your RAM envelope beyond 8 MB, as a rule, you must be running System 7 and you must set your memory Control Panel to 32-bit addressing mode—otherwise, you can't access the additional RAM. However, there *are* software products available for overcoming this limitation, such as Connectix Corporation's Maxima which lets Mac II users access up to 14 MB under System 6.

Increasing the amount of RAM is not the only way to improve RAM-associated performance. You can also replace "slow" RAM with "fast" RAM (i.e., RAM capable of responding more quickly, with response time measured in nanoseconds). The Mac Classic, for example, uses 150ns RAM—while Quadras, on the other hand, use 80ns RAM capable of responding almost twice as fast as the Classic's RAM. Moreover, speeding up RAM response time is not only desirable at times for its own sake, but may also be necessary in order for RAM to keep up with higher processor clock speeds. Let's say you decided to upgrade your 8MHz 68000 Classic to a 16MHz 68030. In the words of *MacWorld* Executive Editor Adrian Mello, "...the 150ns RAM becomes woefully inadequate." Thus, RAM speed can significantly affect the performance of a CPU Accelerator card.

So far, we have been discussing *dynamic* RAM (DRAM), which—like all random access memory—must be periodically refreshed in order to maintain its data, and loses it all if the computer is turned off or power is interrupted (and is, therefore, *volatile*).

A second form of RAM is *static* RAM (SRAM). SRAM can also be used to solve bottlenecks that occur when the faster CPU on an Accelerator card is left tapping its foot, waiting for data from slower main memory. To break up the bottleneck, you can add very fast (20ns) SRAM to the Accelerator to act as a cache between the accelerated CPU and the existing system memory. Data from main memory is then moved into SRAM, to be at the beck and call of the impatient accelerated CPU—providing another (and possibly even better) solution to the slow RAM/fast CPU problem.

A third form of RAM deals strictly with video events and is appropriately dubbed *video* RAM (VRAM). For most Macs, VRAM is added via a Video Accelerator/Adapter card. Quadras, however, come with 1MB of VRAM already installed; the Quadra 950's VRAM is faster than the others (80ns compared to 100ns) and it has room for an extra megabyte.

Read-Only Memory (ROM)

Like RAM, certain program instructions are stored in read-only memory. These instructions are called ROM routines and, unlike RAM, these instructions are actually *burned* into the ROM chip and are permanent. Any actual change of these burned-in routines requires the burning of a new ROM chip which then replaces the old ROM chip on the Mac's motherboard. Alternatively, as Apple has quite regularly done, new System Software can contain *patches* which operate in RAM and replace antiquated ROM routines on-the-fly. Most of the code for the Mac's famous Toolbox is contained in its ROM along with a variety of system routines.

Such routines that provide the meat and potatoes of the Mac Operating System, once stabilized, are moved into ROM, where they can be accessed with all due speed by the CPU without sharing time with any other circuits. Even so, as you might expect by now, ROM size and access rates vary depending on platform. Where the original 128K Mac had a mere 64K of ROM, later versions have graduated to a full megabyte; while ROM access rates have also significantly risen from 3.92 MB to 12.53 MB per second.

Mass Storage Media

The Mac's architecture does not include read-writable media for permanent data storage (that is, storage of the data files that *you* create). Such media is always accessed peripherally, even in the case of internal hard and floppy drives. Such drives are connected, of course, to the computer's I/O bus, but the products themselves are provided by others and consist of an array of options from 3.5-inch floppy diskettes to streaming tape back-up units, to DAT drives, to all manner of hard disk drives.

Storage and retrieval rates not only vary between peripheral types but also between like peripherals. For instance, access times for diskettes in the Mac's internal or external floppy drives is much, much slower than access times for just about any internal or external hard disk drive; and tape is an even slower medium than diskettes. Among the wide variety of available hard disk drives there are also wide variances in disk access time. (For a complete discussion of mass storage media, see the chapter on Storage Technologies.)

Network Connectivity

As already discussed, all Macs (from the Mac Plus forward) can be attached to a LocalTalk network via one of its serial ports. For small workgroup-size networks, LocalTalk is fine, especially if you don't transfer information often but primarily use the network to share devices like printers and modems. However, even a small group may need more network speed if it shares a database on a central server. In these and other cases where speed is of the essence, you will want to look at expanding your network options.

EtherNet

For high speed network, users by-and-large turn to EtherNet. It was developed by Xerox, Digital, and Intel to connect personal computers via coaxial cable. Mac connectivity to EtherNet is accomplished with cabling that comes in three formats: (1) 10Base5 ("thin"), (2) 10Base10 ("thick"), and (3) 10BaseT (unshielded, twisted-pair). To connect any of these cables to most Macs requires the addition of an EtherNet adapter card (or box). Only the Quadras include built-in EtherNet support.

Apple's EtherTalk software interacts with various hardware solutions to hook Macs up to EtherNet. To accomplish this connection, you can use Apple's EtherNet Interface NB (NuBus) card or any of the many third-party Mac-to-EtherNet products. Asanté Technologies offers two adapter boxes for Macs with no internal slot for a network card (such as PowerBooks and Classics), or whose slots are full: (1) the Asanté EN/SC with support for thin, thick and 10BaseT; and (2) the EN/SC-10T with support for 10BaseT only.

Figure 1.9: Rear view of the Asanté EN/SC SCSI, with two SCSI ports for easy daisy-chaining.

To make up for taking an internal slot, EtherNet cards often offer options like Asanté's FriendlyNet card—which has a socket for the 68882 math coprocessor.

Figure 1.10: A 68882 on an Asanté FriendlyNet EtherNet card.

Token Ring

You may also need to hook your Mac up to a Token-Ring network, another act requiring the addition of a network card. Apple offers TokenTalk NB (a NuBus card) for hooking any Mac II to IBM and IBM-compatible Token Ring network environments; Asanté offers MacRing, its series of products for hooking up IIs and SEs to Token Ring. Users of either product can access local area network or mainframe-based services connected to the Token Ring.

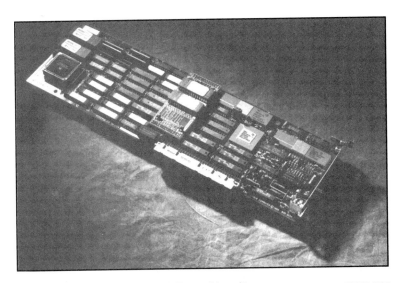

Figure 1.11: Apple Token Ring NB card has its own processor, memory, and multitasking operating system.

SNA

The Mac II family can also be hooked to an IBM SNA (Systems Network Architecture) network and emulate a 3270 Information Display via the Apple Coax/Twinax Card (another NuBus Card)—allowing users to access information from a 3270 mainframe as a dumb terminal. For more details on networking, see the related chapter in this book.

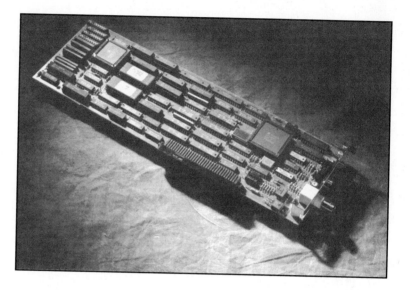

Figure 1.12: Apple Coax/Twinax Card, like the Token Ring NB card, has its own processor, memory, and multitasking operating system.

NOTE: MACs with more than 8M of RAM require 32-bit clean software. The 32-bit compatible software standard has been specified by Apple to its developers since the Mac's inception. Most commercial Mac software developers follow this standard. Be advised, however, that some developers of vertical market or special niche software may not.

Mac Features Chart

Mac Features Chart

	SE/30	Classic	Classic II	Mac LC	Mac LC II	Mac IIcx	Mac IIsi	Mac IIci	Mac IIfx
Processor (68...)	030	000	030	020	030	030	030	030	030
Clock Speed (MHz)	16	8	16	16	16	16	20	25	40
Math Co-Processor (68...)/FPU	882 opt		882 opt	882 opt	882	882	882 opt	882	882
PMMU	✓		✓		✓	✓	✓	✓	✓
ADB Ports	2	1	1	1	1	2	1	2	2
Serial Ports	2	2	2	2	2	2	2	2	2
SCSI Port	✓	✓	✓	✓	✓	✓	✓	✓	✓
Floppy Port	✓	✓	✓			✓	✓		
Video Port				✓	✓		✓	✓	✓
Audio IN		✓		✓	✓		✓		
Audio OUT	✓	✓	✓	✓	✓	✓	✓	✓	✓
NuBus Slots	0	0	0	0	0	3	0	3	6
PD Slots	0	0	0	1	0	0	0	0	0
Other Slots	1	0	1	0	1	0	1	1	0
Maximum RAM	4	4	10	10	10	32	17	32	32
Built-In EtherNet									
On-Board Video				✓	✓	✓	✓	✓	

	PowerBook 100	PowerBook 140	PowerBook 170	Quadra 700	Quadra 900	Quadra 950
Processor (68...)	000	030	030	040	040	040
Clock Speed (MHz)	16	16	25	25	25	33
Math Co-Processor (68...)/FPU			882	FPU	FPU	FPU

	PowerBook 100	PowerBook 140	PowerBook 170	Quadra 700	Quadra 900	Quadra 950
PMMU		✓	✓	✓	✓	✓
ADB Ports	1	1	1	2	2	2
Serial Ports	1	2	2	2	2	2
SCSI Port	✓	✓	✓	✓	✓	✓
Floppy Port	✓					
Video Port				✓	✓	✓
Audio IN		✓	✓	✓	✓	✓
Audio OUT	✓	✓	✓	✓	✓	✓
NuBus Slots	0	0	0	2	5	5
PD Slots	0	0	0	1	1	1
Other Slots	*	*	*	0	0	0
Maximum RAM	8	8	8	20	64	64
Built-In EtherNet			✓	✓	✓	
On-Board Video				✓	✓	✓

*Powerbooks have a pseudo slot for canceling an internal modem. Thanks to third parties, 100 owners have the option of using this slot to hook up a second serial port.

**Apple's maximum RAM limits can be substantially increased. See the section entitled "Random Access Memory" for details.

Acceleration Paths

There are enough accelerator products available for the Macintosh to fill a separate volume. For the most part, however, there are two basic types: CPU Accelerators and accelerated Video Adapters. Each focuses on speeding performance and adding functionality to certain types of repetitive computer tasks. The "Accelerators vs. Tasks" chart lists some of the major features of these cards, and shows which tasks they significantly affect and whether that affect is minor or major.

If you find a familiar task in the chart and discover it may be optimized by one or more accelerator features, remember the "Price... Performance... Productivity" chant that began this chapter. Whether you can profit from an expansion product is not solely based on improved performance of a given task type. It must also be based on *how often* you perform this task versus how much it costs to optimize versus what you have to gain from optimization. If you primarily use the computer for word processing and database retrieval, but also do occasional page layout, springing for a video adapter card so you can plug in a dual-page monitor and view graphics in 16 million colors is probably over kill. On the other hand, if the database is remote (e.g., sitting on a central server in a network), you (and your network group) might very well profit from upgrading to a high-speed EtherNet network.

Ranks of Mac IIsi Accelerators*

Accelerator	Overall Speed	Excel	Illustrator	Photoshop
Sigma Bullet 030	3	3	3	3
DayStar Power Cache	2	2	2	2
Total Magellan 040	1	1	1	1

Ranks of Mac IIci Accelerators

Accelerator	Overall Speed	Excel	Illustrator	Photoshop
Sigma Bullet 030	5	4	5	5
DayStar Power Cache	4	3	4	4
Impulse Performance/ 040	3	1	3	3
Radius Rocket	2	2	2	2
Fusion Data TokaMac ci	1	1	1	1

glossary of Tasks (includes only tasks that aren't self-explanatory)

financial modeling The practice of using series of data elements in equation form to project "what if" scenarios.

rasterization The conversion of graphic objects made up of line segments into dots for output to screens or printers.

ray tracing The creation of reflections, refractions, and shadows on a graphics image.

realtime video A graphic image that can be animated on screen in the same time frame as real life.

rendering Creation of a complex 3-D image, incorporating such simulated lighting effects as shadows and reflections.

screen resolution Clarity and sharpness of a displayed image, based on the number of dots per line times the number of lines. Thus, a screen resolution of 640x480 refers to a dot density of 640 dots per line and a line density of 480 lines per screen. Dots are across; lines are down.

CPU Accelerators

As the name suggests, CPU Accelerators come equipped with their own micro-processor, allowing you to upgrade your existing processor to a later, more powerful version. In addition to upgrading your processor, CPU Accelerators also offer options for math coprocessors, faster clock speeds, and fast static RAM caching.

Naturally, the primary advantage of a CPU Accelerator is enhancing perfor-mance of processor-intensive tasks—like screen redrawing, search and replace operations in word processing applications, or database sorts. It also enhances many video-intensive tasks which depend on frequent screen redraws and disk-intensive tasks which incorporate data retrieval from a hard or floppy disk. The addition of the math coprocessor obviously improves performance of math-intensive tasks like recalculating a spreadsheet, while faster clock speeds enhance everything the processor does and SRAM improves retrieval of data from memory.

In addition, many accelerators displace the main memory (RAM) of the Mac with faster memory, in order to keep up with the faster processor. For instance, NewLife's 33MHz 68030 upgrade for a standard Mac SE replaces the SE's 150ns RAM with 80ns RAM. Then it allows you to turn the older, slower RAM into a *RAM disk*.[6] Finally, key ROM routines are transferred into the accelerator's RAM at start-up so performance really screams.

Which CPU Accelerators are best? Once again, there are too many Macs and too many options for each one to point to "the best" with surety. Additionally, while an 040 CPU Accelerator with 20ns SRAM and a 33MHz clock speed might enhance your current Mac more than an 030 Accelerator with a 25MHz clock and no SRAM cache, the cost might be prohibitive. So at best, "best" is relative to your situation and pocketbook. Suffice it to say that if the product comes from an established company in the Mac community, it is likely to perform according to specifications.

Even though it is difficult to draw any final conclusions, it can be instructive to peruse the results of lab tests conducted periodically by various Mac trade publications. In one such test, MacUser Labs pitted 68030 CPU Accelerators for the Mac IIsi and IIci against their 68040 counterparts and published its findings in the June, 1992 *MacUser*. Each Accelerator was tested for overall increased performance, as well as performance enhancement in three industrial-strength software applications—each of which leans hard on different "parts" of the Mac Operating System.

Not surprisingly, the 040s outperformed the 030s, but also cost more; sometimes a *lot* more. So, when you evaluate laboratory test results, be sure to ask yourself: *Is increase in performance commensurate with increase in price, and how much bang do you need for your buck anyway?* Moreover, fancy options in one accelerator may turn it into a favorite, even if other accelerators are higher performing.

Accelerated Video Adapter Cards

Time for a brain teaser: *When is an accelerated Video card more effective than a CPU Accelerator?*

According to David Ramsey of *MacWEEK*, accelerated Video Adapter cards are even more successful in speeding up scrolling, screen redraws, and things like select-and-drag operations in a paint program than a CPU Accelerator (and this is from the man who wrote Mac Paint II). On the other hand, David further informs us that moving multiple shapes or executing complex fills or curve operations not included in QuickDraw[7] require more computing than drawing and are, therefore, better supported by a faster CPU.

In addition to adding power to pixel management, Video cards also allow you to hook up different types of monitors with options for larger screen displays and NTSC or PAL capabilities[8]—as well as provisions to add more colors, VRAM, and faster QuickDraw.

Adding a Special Monitor

Most Macs, including the original 128K Mac, have a built-in ability to display data on a Cathode Ray Tube (CRT)[9] without the addition of further hardware or software.[10] Since the Mac is a digital device and CRTs or monitors are typically analog devices, the Mac's digital signals regarding screen display must somehow be translated into an analog signal for the monitor to respond. To do this, the Mac's digital signal is sent to a video display circuit on its main logic board which obediently performs the necessary conversion. Depending on the sophistication of this circuit, the Mac is either capable or incapable of working with certain types of monitors. Your basic black and white monitors are no problem but, as you start moving into grayscale and color, the need for additional hardware and software to perform the necessary conversions rears its head. Just lusting after color or grayscale is not enough; you also need to know how much it takes to make you happy. For this, you need to know the following:

2-bits	=	Black and White
4-bits	=	16 colors or shades of gray
8-bits	=	256 colors or shades of gray
24-bits	=	16.7 million colors or shades of gray
32-bits	=	16.7 million colors or shades of gray (and faster QuickDraw)

Figure 1.13: The Apple 2-page Monochrome Monitor provides a 21-inch screen and supports multiple resolutions of 2-, 4-, or 8-bits and a maximum of 256 shades of gray.

A case in point: The Mac IIsi is an 8-bit color machine. This means it has an 8-bit video circuit on its main logic board and, without further ado, can support a color and/or grayscale monitor and display images composed of up to 256 colors or shades of gray, respectively. This is not true of, say, the 128K or 512K Macs—both of which are 2-bit machines (no pun intended) capable of supporting only black and white displays.

While the IIsi is capable of routinely supporting 8-bit color, to take advantage of a monitor's sexier display options like 24-bit color requires something in the order of SuperMac's Thunder/24 Video Adapter card. While 8-bits gets you 256 colors or shades, 24-bits gets you *16.7 million*—making 8-bit color literally pale by comparison. The net effect is a much better picture, but it is going to cost you.

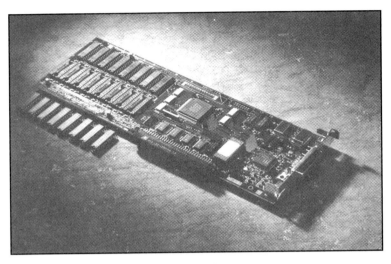

Figure 1.14: The Mac II 2-page Monochrome Video Card is a NuBus card that provides the interface between the 2-page Monitor and a Mac II.

In addition to providing more colors/shades and, thereby, a sharper image, Video Adapters also make it possible for the Mac to map images to larger screen displays. For instance, a Mac Plus is set up to recognize and manage a 9-inch screen with a resolution of 512 pixels (dots) across and 342 pixels down (512x342). In order to hook up and take advantage of larger, higher resolution monitors, you will need to give it the ability to deal with the resulting larger pixel map. There are adapter cards available for allowing most Macs to consort with monitors of almost every size and shape, be they 12, 13, 16, 19, or 21-inches in diameter—or half-page, full-page, or dual-page displays.

How is it done? Once again, by augmenting the Mac's built-in video circuit. Just as this circuit supports a maximum bit-depth for displays, it also supports a maximum screen size. The video circuit in the Mac LC, LC II, IIsi, IIci, and Quadra models supports a screen map of 640x480, common to 13-, 14-, and 15-inch monitors. As you can see, though many users opt for the popular Apple 13-inch RGB monitor, other options are automatically supported without need for an adapter. But to go beyond these limitations, your Mac is going to need help.

One video expansion option gaining popularity is a 16-inch monitor (see Figure 1.15) with a maximum screen resolution of 832x624. E-Machines pioneered this idea, and its ColorPage E16 (like many other monitor manufacturers) offer users multiple resolutions: 640x480, 832x624, or 1024x768. If you are thinking that a 640x480 resolution level only displays a proportionate amount of an image compared to higher resolution, think again. The amount of the image viewed remains the same, but the size of the pixels change, so the whole image becomes slightly larger in 640x480 mode (just as the large-pixel

12-inch LC monitor offers a magnified view of the same screen "real estate" as the 9-inch built-ins). In higher resolution modes, pixels are denser and resolutions should appear more refined, but this is not always the case. The March 1992 *MacWorld* report on monitors noted that the ColorPage display is "... noticeably less sharp than the [other monitors] at 640x480 resolution."

Figure 1.15: The Macintosh 16" Color Display from Apple—for use with the Mac IIsi, IIci, and any Quadra—is based on a Trinitron color picture tube from Sony, and even includes its own built-in ADB ports (though you are still stuck with the 3-device allowance).

Many commonly purchased monitors for PC or Mac hook-up have gained popularity because of their ability to *multisynch* (synchronize with a broad range of video signals). Multisynch monitors, however, cannot be plugged directly into the Mac's video port without a special cable adapter. Many multisynch monitor vendors do not provide this adapter (NEC and Sony are notable exceptions), but a growing number of Mac mail order companies include one as a matter of course when they sell one of these monitors. Nevertheless, be sure to ask.

A final concern when buying a monitor is its level of extremely-low-frequency (ELF) magnetic emissions. Recent concern over the effect of these emissions on the health of users (particularly expectant mothers) has driven concerned manufacturers like Apple to reengineer monitors with an eye toward slashing ELF emissions to a new low. As a result, most monitors now have levels below 1 milligauss (mG)—which is considered too weak in comparison to normal background radiation levels to be a problem. Interestingly, in a recent test of several popular monitors, consumer-conscious Apple showed up with the lowest ELF emissions in its AppleColor High-Res RGB. All monitors tested were shown to emit less than 1 mG of ELF radiation at a distance of 28 inches—the average length of a user's arm and a recommended measure for keeping your distance.

Figure 1.16: The popular AppleColor High-Res RGB Monitor is widely lauded for its high clarity and low ELF rating.

Accelerating Video Performance

In addition to adapting your Mac to communicate with larger, higher resolution monitors capable of supporting more colors and shades of gray, Video Adapter cards offer a number of features for accelerating overall performance of associated video tasks. Like CPU Accelerators, the number of products in this niche are legion. For instance, in a recent lab test (March, 1992), *MacWorld* clocked the performance of 10 Mac II/IIcx cards from the most popular vendors against a set of scroll and zoom tests in Microsoft's Excel and Aldus's PageMaker. The cards ranked as follows:

VIDEO ACCELERATOR	RANK*
Apple Display Card 8•24	4
E-Machines Futura EX	1
Micron MacroColor II	3
Radius PrecisionColor 8x	1
Radius PrecisionColor 8	5

VIDEO ACCELERATOR	RANK*
Radius Direct Color GX	1
RasterOps ColorBoard 24s	6
RasterOps ColorBoard 24si	2
SuperMac Spectrum/8 Series III	6
SuperMac ColorCard/24	6

*Identical rankings in a column indicate a tie.

The three lowest performers were about 20% slower than the three highest performers, with differences in the ratings possibly attributable to the presence or lack of faster QuickDraw. As you may have guessed, prices vary considerably due to similarly variable lists of features per card, with some supporting wider ranges of color, resolution, and again, faster QuickDraw. So, like the CPU Accelerators before them, weigh options against price as well as performance, and remember: what you see is based on what you get, and what you get is based on what you are willing to pay.

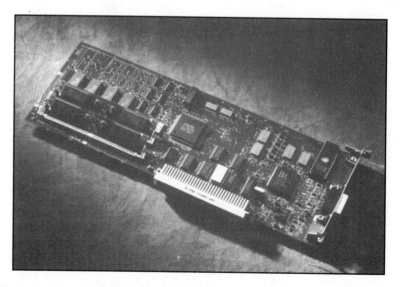

Figure 1.17: Apple's Display Card 8·24 not only received a mediocre ranking in the MacWorld test, but the company has also come under fire for its long-delayed support of the card and System 7.

It wasn't so very long ago that industry mavens were advising users against going too far out on the expansion limb. As recently as August of 1990, a *MacUser* article warned users away from third-party upgrades, in favor of the safer, more reliable, and more easily installed Apple paths. But now it seems enough years have come and gone to bring credibility to the third-party Mac hardware companies who have hung in there. Not only are the products of these surviving firms viewed as more robust than ever, but Apple has thrown open the architecture of the Mac, providing NuBus and other expansion slots that make adding third-party upgrades easier.

Now it looks as if life in the fast lane is only going to get faster as we catapult toward the 21st century and who knows what newer, brighter, faster, and more powerful technologies. If this basic course in expansion helps pave your way and gives you a basis for understanding the add-on options of the here and now, as well as the shape of things to come... this chapter has done its job. But class isn't over yet... not for the wise student who knows that progress never ends and there is always something new under the sun.

 Endnotes

[1] The Mac SE was the first Macintosh with a special bus for external expansion. Called the SE Bus, its supports high-speed direct access to RAM (like NuBus) and allows coprocessors to share the Mac's address and data buses.

[2] To use a PowerBook 100 as a SCSI device, you must hook it (via a special connector) directly to another Mac at the end of that Mac's SCSI chain. It cannot be placed between SCSI devices.

[3] Degradation *can* occur, however, if slow devices like scanners and digitizers are added to the chain.

[4] In the tradition of Apple Computer, the term "board" in this chapter is used to refer to the Mac's basic components (e.g., main logic board), while the term "card" refers to components that may be plugged into one of the system's buses for performance enhancement and additional functionality.

[5] In 1957, the CPU filled a medium-sized closet. Today, a mainframe computer's CPU is still spread out over many printed circuit boards, and a minicomputer's CPU takes up several boards...but a microcomputer's CPU exists on a single chip.

[6] A RAM disk appears on the Finder desktop as a floppy disk icon, and you can copy applications and data into this "virtual" disk—so all subsequent operations related to this data execute at RAM (i.e., very fast) speeds.

[7] The Mac's graphics display system which accepts commands from applications and draws the corresponding objects.

[8] NTSC (National Television Standards Committee) is the U.S. TV standard for transmitting 525 lines of resolution at 60 frames per second—generating a composite signal of red, green, and blue. PAL is the European TV standard, using 625 lines of resolution.

[9] A vacuum tube with a beam capable of shooting electrons at minutely focused sections of a phosphorescent screen.

[10]Notable exceptions are the discontinued II, IIx, IIcx, and IIfx models, all of which (though they have the necessary video circuit on their logic boards) do not have a display card built into the motherboard.

2

Storage Technologies and Hardware

As the speed of computers has grown over the years, so has our appetite for large amounts of storage capacity. Faster computers can process more data and work with larger applications. Today, it's not uncommon for one user to have a hard disk with 200MB of storage, 500 times more than the original Mac offered!

Hard disks for the Mac were not generally available until 1986, when Apple finally released a computer with an SCSI port (more on SCSI later), the Macintosh Plus. The cost was about $50 per megabyte. A hard disk represented a serious investment back then. Today, with a cost of as little as $3 per megabyte, you can buy a lot of storage space for not too much money.

Technically, you could connect a hard disk to your Mac before 1986, but only via its serial modem port. The speed at which it operated left most users practicing primal screams in frustration. Observers considered the Macintosh a toy until the Plus was introduced, largely due to its prior lack of storage capacity.

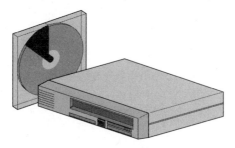

Apple has also beefed up the diskette storage capacity and versatility of the Mac in recent years. Macs purchased since early 1989 include the Apple Floppy Disk High Density (FDHD) SuperDrive. The SuperDrive provides 1.44 MB of storage capacity (more than three times the original Mac's capacity of 400K) and the ability to read and format Apple II, MS-DOS, and OS/2 diskettes in addition to standard Macintosh files. By itself, the SuperDrive makes the Mac much more compatible with other operating systems and environments.

You have a wide variety of storage options available for your Mac. You can forego a hard disk and just use diskettes or you can use a hard disk and one or two diskette drives. You can also add a tape drive, removable cartridge drive, high-capacity diskette drive, optical drive, and/or a CD-ROM player. We'll discuss all of these options in this chapter.

No Hard Disk, Just Diskettes

A diskette-based Mac is the most inexpensive option in terms of cost and the most expensive in terms of time. It's largely impractical because many applications require more than one diskette; inconvenient, because you will often be forced to exchange diskettes while running applications; and exceedingly slow because diskette drives are at least ten times slower than hard disk drives.

We can't overemphasize that you should spend a few dollars and get yourself a hard disk. A hard disk is a convenient place to store your applications and data. As your needs grow, you will likely need more than one hard disk. You might also consider removable hard disks, such as Syquest drives or if you have a serious amount of data to store, consider optical drives.

Conventional Hard Disks

Hard disk drives are a necessary part of your Macintosh system. They are a convenient place to store all of your applications and data. A hard disk-based Mac is much faster than a diskette-based machine. Plus, all of your data and applications are easily found in one place. Organize your hard disk, and your data and applications will be easy to find for years to come.

Technical Details

In the mid-70s, before floppy and hard disks were available for personal computers, people actually used audio cassette tapes to store and retrieve data. This was painfully slow, to say the least. Tapes are still used with computers, although largely for backup purposes, as we'll discuss later in this chapter.

A hard disk is just what its name implies—a fixed, nonremovable device capable of storing large quantities of applications and data. Its function is similar to the way audio and video cassettes are recorded. Floppy diskettes and tape cartridges also use similar methods to encode data. In all cases, information is recorded magnetically onto a specially-coated supporting material. Flexible mylar plastic is used in the case of tape. A hard disk is usually an aluminum platter (glass is being used in some newer drives, especially those designed for laptops).

The *platter* is the "hard" part of a hard disk. It is circular and serves as the base on which data is magnetically stored. The surface of the platter must be defined in such a way so information can be easily stored and retrieved. This is one reason why hard disks must be formatted before they can be used. Hard disks must also be formatted to operate within the constraints of the operating system in which they will be used, whether it be Macintosh, MS-DOS, UNIX, or some other system. Data is written onto the platter via *read/write heads*. These devices magnetically record information onto the platter. When you are ready to access the information, the heads read it off the platter. The device that moves the heads along the platter in both the reading and writing process is called a *head actuator*.

There are several platters in a hard drive. As you increase the number and size of the platters, more data can be stored. There are two sides per platter. What we refer to as "Side 0" of a hard disk for example, is actually platter one, side one. There is usually one head per platter side. However, in an attempt to increase hard disk speed, some vendors have introduced drives with two heads per platter side.

To make the hard disk access your information as quickly as possible, the platter rotates at a fixed rate per minute. Rotation is accomplished via a *spindle motor*. Most hard disks rotate at 3600 rotations per minute. It only takes 1/60 of a second to make one complete revolution allowing the heads to quickly arrive at any platter location. The trend in hard disk design is to increase the rotation speed to as much as 7200 rpm, enabling the heads to access any platter location twice as quickly.

The ability to *randomly* access specific locations on the platter is really the main advantage of disk storage. Video and audio recorders store data *sequentially* on tape. To access the data, you must move sequentially (from beginning to end, in a linear fashion) to the appropriate location on the tape. With hard disks, the heads can be moved quickly and randomly to any location on the platter. No sequential access is necessary, so information is retrieved much quicker. Information is recorded onto a hard disk in a series of unconnected, concentric circles called *tracks*. Tracks are numbered at the edge of the platter starting with zero. The tracks are divided into *sectors*, which is a single storage unit on a drive, usually 512 bytes in size.

While a diskette has two sides and one platter, a hard disk typically has more than one platter, and therefore, more than two sides. A *cylinder* is a set of all tracks, one on each side of each platter, that are equal in circumference from the center of the disk. In other words, all track ones—track one on the top of platter one (side 0), track one on the bottom of platter one (side 1), track one on the top of platter two (side 2), etc.—taken together make up one cylinder. The number of cylinders per hard disk is determined by the number of tracks per platter.

Determining the storage capacity of a disk involves some simple math. Sectors typically hold 512 bytes of data, with 17 sectors per track. A track is capable of storing approximately 8.5 kilobytes of data. Multiplying the number of tracks by 8.5 kilobytes gives you the storage capacity per side. Multiplying that number by the number of sides gives you the storage capacity of the disk. While some of the capacity is occupied by overhead, this is usually within five percent of your overall disk capacity under the Macintosh.

While hard disks have gotten faster over the years, they haven't kept up with the speed increases the Macintosh itself has enjoyed. Older Macs, such as the Mac Plus, simply could not keep up with their hard disks. The hard disks could find data faster than the Mac could process it. To help those Macs keep up, a process where data is not stored sequentially on sectors was used. This process, called *interleaving*, writes data on one sector then allows several more sectors to revolve under the read/write heads (with no recording taking place during that time) before continuing to write data on another sector. For the Macintosh Plus, the interleaving process was typically a 1:3 ratio—for every sector that had related data, there were three that did not. The Mac SE and the Classic use an interleaving of 1:2. With the Mac II series, the SE/30, and the other newer Macs, interleaving is unnecessary, so we say the interleaving factor is 1:1.

As the Mac gets faster and faster, hard disk vendors are pulling out all the stops to make their drives faster than they used to be. Using techniques such as *zone-bit recording*, which places more data at the outer edges of a platter; and tighter *bit densities*, which squeezes data closer together; vendors are making hard disks reach data faster.

Picking a Hard Disk

There are several factors involved in picking a hard disk. The two most obvious are storage capacity and speed. Another consideration is the physical size of the disk. The capacity of your hard disk should be directly related to the amount of data and the kinds of applications you use. Just as you probably wouldn't buy a 12,000 square foot house to live in alone, you may not need a massive hard disk—yet.

At one point, the typical spreadsheet, word processing, and database user could get by with as little as 40MB of disk space. However, with many of today's applications getting more complicated and occupying more space, you are better off having at least 80MB or more of hard disk space available. If you primarily use graphics-intensive applications such as desktop publishing, multimedia, or computer-aided design (CAD) software, the sky's the limit. You probably need at least 200MB; it's not uncommon for a 1 *gigabyte* hard disk to be used by one person in a desktop publishing shop. However, if you are a typical desktop publisher and you supplement your storage needs with a removable hard disk, such as a Syquest or Bernoulli drive, you can probably get by comfortably with 300MB or so.

As a general rule, keep this in mind: *always buy the very best and biggest that you can afford and you won't go wrong.* You may think you are buying useless space today, but remember that people once thought that *nobody* would ever need more than 64K of random-access memory.

Measuring Speed

Even after you decide how much storage space you need (or want), you are not finished. There is more to choosing a hard disk than just capacity. Drives that are identical in appearance and size are often vastly different on the inside. One 80 MB drive may be much slower than another, for example.

One key measure of a hard disk's speed is its *access time*. Access time, measured in milliseconds, defines how fast the disk retrieves the information that you request. Access time is actually the sum of seek time and latency. *Seek time* is how fast the head finds the correct sector where the data is located. *Latency* measures the speed at which the disk spins to get to that location. Older hard disks featured access times of 60 milliseconds or more. Typical hard disks today have access times of 18 milliseconds or less.

The Macintosh offers the option of either internally-installed or externally-connected hard disk drives. If you purchased your Mac with a hard disk, you probably have an internal drive. However, if you add a new drive, you will probably add an external drive. External drives connect to the SCSI port in the back of your Macintosh and come in all shapes and sizes. Some, called "zero footprint" drives, are designed to fit underneath a compact Mac. (Zero Footprint means that the drives don't take up any more space on your desk than your compact Mac is already using.)

External drives are also convenient because you can disconnect them at the end of the day and connect them to your Mac at home. Or, you can lock them in a drawer for security purposes. Plus, external drives are interchangeable; any Macintosh hard drive will work with any Macintosh equipped with an SCSI port (although in some cases you may need to have a special hard disk INIT or startup file present on each machine that will be using the drive).

As vendors learn how to cram more data into smaller spaces, hard disks are getting physically smaller and smaller. Hard disks used to have a 5.25-inch form factor; most now are 3.5-inch drives. Many newer drives are even smaller, at 2.5-inch or even 1.8-inch. Along with size, hard disk weights are also dropping. The benefits these drives offer to users of portable and notebook computers are obvious. In most cases, smaller drives have less storage capacity than larger drives. It's difficult to include 1GB of storage space on a 3.5-inch drive, for example. However, vendors are always getting better at this process, and some amazingly high storage capacities are becoming available for even the smallest (in terms of physical size) drives.

Enter SCSI

All we've measured so far is the ability of your hard disk to get data off its own drives. However, you also need something to get the data from your hard drive to your Mac's central processing unit (CPU), and finally, up on your screen. You need a *disk controller* and a hard disk *interface*.

A disk controller controls head positioning and the other physical operations of your hard drive. An interface is the captain of the ship, indicating how many drives can be connected to a controller, in what way they can be connected, and how instructions—and, ultimately, your data—are sent to the CPU. Without a good drive controller, the fastest hard disk in the world is worthless. A drive controller's performance is measured by the *data transfer rate* it delivers. Data transfer rate measures how fast the data gets from your hard disk to your CPU.

In the MS-DOS world, the process of choosing a controller and interface is fairly complicated, with a myriad of choices available. This is not the case in the Mac world. Only one interface is available for moving data in a Macintosh, and it's the best of the technology—the Small Computer System Interface (SCSI, pronounced "scuzzy"). SCSI, which integrates the drive and controller in one, is the most versatile interface available for personal computers.

Apple chose SCSI as its interface because it's the fastest currently available for small computers, with a data transfer rate of up to 5MB per second. This showed a lot of foresight on the company's part because the Macintosh Plus, the first computer to have a SCSI port, wasn't exactly a speed merchant. In fact, Apple limited the performance of the Plus's SCSI port to approximately 650K per second to help the processor keep up with the data. That's eight times slower than the SCSI port on the Macintosh Quadra, which operates at the maximum 5MB per second (68030-based Macs feature a data transfer rate of about 1.5MB per second).

Keep your Mac's data transfer rate in mind when choosing a hard disk. If you have an older Mac, a fast hard disk that outruns the rest of your system is pointless. Concentrate more on price-per-MegaByte and less on speed when choosing a hard disk for an older Mac.

SCSI is actually not a disk interface, but a system interface. As a result, you can connect up to seven different devices in a daisy chain (one device connected to the back of another device) off of one SCSI port. This is convenient, because you can connect a hard disk, tape drive, CD-ROM drive, scanner and other devices to just one port. In fact, all of the devices mentioned in this chapter connect to your Mac through the SCSI port.

You can even connect a Macintosh PowerBook 100 to another Macintosh via the SCSI port. The PowerBook appears on the desktop of the other Mac as a hard drive. In networked environments, where many drives are often connected together in a drive array, SCSI is the natural choice (and in the specific case of the PowerBook, it is the only choice Apple has given us). When the last device is connected, place a terminating cable (supplied with the device) in the second SCSI port. Some devices are internally terminated. In the case of these devices, you may need to open the case to provide or remove SCSI termination.

Be sure that each device in the daisy chain has its own unique address. You typically set the address by flipping a switch on the back of the device. Use 0 through 6 for each device (zero is reserved for your internal hard drive; if you don't have an internal hard drive, you can use zero for an externally connected device). SCSI address 7 is reserved for the Mac itself. Different devices will allow you to set the SCSI ID address in different ways. Some will provide a small dial or a push button, while others may require that you use a pencil tip to set tiny DIP switches on the back of, or inside the device. If you attempt to put two or more devices with the same SCSI ID into a single chain, you'll have problems. If you *are* having SCSI difficulties, this is the first thing to double-check.

Even when you carefully set SCSI addresses, you can occasionally still run into trouble. SCSI can be complicated. If your cables are too long, not connected properly, or if you haven't used a required SCSI terminator in the last device in the chain, you may run into problems using the devices. If you run into difficulties, don't panic. First, turn off all equipment. Then, turn the devices on in address order, turning on the Macintosh last. If you still run into problems, disconnect each device from the SCSI port, and reconnect them one at a time until the culprit is located. If you're still having difficulty and you have just added a new device to an existing SCSI chain, contact the retailer or distributor from whom you bought the device, or the device's manufacturer for technical assistance.

Making Your Hard Drive Run Faster

As fast as hard disks are, you can always make them run faster. One way to do this is to connect your hard drive to a faster SCSI bus than the standard one that comes with your Mac. This is especially important when working with extremely large files, such as multimedia video files. Called SCSI-2, fast SCSI, or wide SCSI, these interfaces operate at speeds up to eight times faster than traditional SCSI. SCSI-2 uses either a 16- or 32-bit interface rather than SCSI's 8-bit interface. As a result, up to 32 bits of information can travel along the bus at one time. In order to take advantage of this, you'll need a special board in your Mac and a hard drive that supports the faster standard. And, you may encounter address problems with other devices in the chain.

Another way to speed up your hard disk is through the use of *cache memory*. Cache is a temporary memory storage area, where frequently accessed data can be stored. Since it's faster to retrieve data from memory than from a hard disk, a cache can greatly improve performance. Information is loaded onto the cache by using a cache controller. The key, of course, is to determine which data will be accessed and to store it in cache memory. You can't control the data in the cache, only the cache controller can. Typically, files that have been retrieved during the current session are kept in cache memory. The amount of data that can be stored in the cache depends largely on the amount of cache memory available with your hard disk.

Cache sizes vary from 32K all the way up to a few megabytes. Apple recommends 32K of cache memory for each 1MB of RAM memory. The bigger the cache, the more data that can be stored in memory. However, the larger the cache, the more data the Mac must search through to find the data. Set the cache by using the Memory control panel (Figure 2.1).

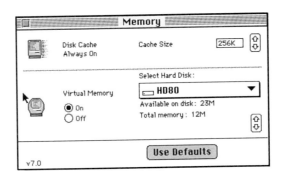

Figure 2.1: Memory Control Panel.

Caches built into the hard disk are called hardware caches. These caches use memory controlled by a cache controller. Hardware caches are the most efficient because they work with memory specifically controlled by your hard disk.

Caches that use your computer's RAM are called software caches. Apple's Disk Cache, which is standard under System 7, is a software cache. These improve the performance of your hard disk but rob available RAM from the rest of your system. It's better to buy a hard disk with a built-in cache, but if your hard disk doesn't have this, a software cache is better than no cache at all.

Organizing Your Hard Disk

A hard disk that isn't organized is like a drawer with everything in it—you know all the information is in there, but you can't find it. A well-organized hard disk is one of the best productivity boosters you can have. Hard disks are organized into *directories* and *subdirectories*. Conveniently—at least for those of us who like real-life metaphors—the Macintosh treats directories and subdirectories as folders. The main directories are in folders at the top level, while subdirectories are folders inside folders. For example, one way to organize your hard disk is to create three main directories — Applications, Data, and System (Figure 2.2). Then, put individual subdirectories inside each main directory—individual applications, data organized by specific subject, and particular system files.

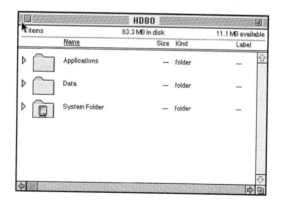

Figure 2.2: Typical Top Level Directory Setup.

You can view directories and subdirectories by double clicking on a folder. If you have System 7, you can click on the arrow next to the folder to see the contents of that folder (Figure 2.3).

You can have as many levels of subdirectories as you want. This file and folder format is so clean that my Macintosh desktop is often much more organized than my own desktop. However, keep in mind that the Macintosh workspace is called the desktop for a very important reason: it's yours and you should organize it in whatever way brings you the greatest productivity.

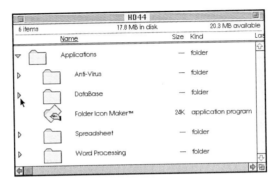

Figure 2.3: Viewing Subdirectories.

Virtual Memory

If you have the luxury of more disk space than you need, consider using System 7's virtual memory feature to give you more RAM. Virtual memory essentially uses hard disk space as RAM memory. While not as fast as actual RAM, this space helps you use more applications at once by increasing the size of available memory to open them. Select virtual memory through the Memory control panel (Figure 2.1). You lose 1MB of disk storage space for each 1MB of RAM you create, but this includes the actual RAM you have installed in your machine. For example, if you have 8MB of actual RAM in your Macintosh, and you create a virtual memory area of another 8MB, giving you a total of 16MB of memory to work with, you will actually lose a full 16MB of disk space...not just the 8MB you have added via virtual memory, so use virtual memory wisely and only as needed.

Using Multiple Hard Disks

You can never really have "enough" memory or storage space. The time may come—if it hasn't already—when you run out of space on your hard disk. When this occurs, you have several options: delete some seldom-used files from your hard disk (a temporary solution at best), compress your files using a compression program (discussed later in this chapter), or add another hard disk.

You could throw your hard disk away and buy a bigger one, but you are better off keeping it and using its data capacity and adding a second hard disk, unless your hard disk is older than your Mac, in which case a newer, faster, larger model might greatly improve your productivity. Adding a hard disk is simply a matter of connecting an external drive to your SCSI port. If you already have an external drive connected, daisy chain it with the first drive (and terminate the last device). In many cases this simply means connecting the new SCSI drive to the back of your first drive and making sure the addresses are different.

If you don't have an internal hard disk, it's fairly easy to install a hard disk inside your Macintosh. The hard disk manufacturer or distributor should provide you with detailed directions, and many computer stores offer free installation. Be aware that opening up a compact (closed) Mac to install a new hard disk is a procedure best left to your authorized Apple dealer—under the strict terms of your Apple warranty, if you open your own compact (closed-box) Macintosh, or make certain kinds of changes to your modular (open-box) Macintosh, your warranty may be invalidated.

Removable Media

Consider a removable hard disk or cartridge drive, if you share a large amount of data with people in other locations; if you are concerned about the security of your data; or if you want to make sure your hard drive never runs out of space. A removable drive is a useful alternative to adding a second hard disk, since removable media is much more flexible than fixed drives.

One of the most popular applications for removable drives is in the desktop publishing world. A typical magazine article, with text, charts, pictures, and graphics can easily take up 40MB or more of data. Sending that information from a magazine's art department to the magazine printer using diskettes is a very difficult task, especially since some individual files are larger than 1.44MB, the typical storage capacity of a diskette. Sending it over a modem at 2,400 or even 9,600 bits per second is not only time consuming, it might also be very expensive, especially if your printer is a toll call away. Many magazines and other desktop publishers copy the information to a high-capacity removable cartridge and send it to the magazine printer via overnight delivery. The main types of removable disks available are high-capacity diskettes and removable cartridges. Optical disks are also an option, as we'll discuss later in this chapter.

High-Capacity Diskettes

As we mentioned, typical diskettes are capable of storing 1.44MB of information. That's enough for most data, but not nearly enough for graphics-intensive applications, such as multimedia, computer-aided design, image and sound storage, and desktop publishing. Enter high-capacity diskette drives, which let you store up to 25MB of information on a diskette that looks very much like a standard 3.5-inch diskette.

The amount of data a diskette drive can store on a diskette is determined by its ability to store data close together. Diskettes are also specially formulated for specific storage capacities, hence the terms *single-sided*, which stores information on just one side of the diskette platter; *double-sided*, which stores information on both sides of the platter; and *high-density*, which stores information closer together than other diskettes. Only drive mechanisms capable of reading and storing information on these types of diskettes can be used. For example, if you have an old single-sided diskette drive in your Mac, you couldn't take advantage of high-density diskettes. In fact, your Mac would only be able to format a high-density diskette to accept 400K of information instead of 1.44MB.

High-capacity diskettes use more precise technology in the diskette drive to enable the drive head to read and write more data in smaller spaces. They place more sectors on each track (27 or so versus 13 or 14 on a conventional diskette) and more tracks per side than conventional diskettes.

Special drives are required to use high-density diskettes, so if you are going to share your data, you have to make sure the person you're sending the diskettes to has the same drive as you do. However, the drives are *downward compatible*, allowing you to read and write to conventional diskettes using high-capacity drives.

In terms of cost, this is an efficient way to store data, since diskettes cost about $20 each. Like traditional diskette drives, however, high-density diskette drives are slower than hard disks. But they are faster than traditional diskette drives thanks to spinning at 720 RPM versus 300 or 360 RPM for lower-capacity diskette drives. Access times are improving, with recent offerings breaking the 40 ms access time mark. Another option when considering these types of diskettes is flopticals, a combination of optical and floppy disk technology developed by InSite Peripherals, of San Jose, CA. We'll look at flopticals later in this chapter.

Removable Cartridge Drives

Combining the durability of diskettes with the speed of hard disks, removable cartridge drives are the most popular type of high-capacity removable media.

A variety of cartridge formats is available, although the most popular by far in the Macintosh world is Syquest, which provides 88MB of capacity on each cartridge. Many vendors offer Syquest-compatible drives for the Mac.

A removable cartridge is essentially just the disk part of a hard disk. The rest of the hard disk's electronics—the heads, actuators, motor, etc.—are included in the cartridge drive. Using one of these cartridges is fairly easy—just copy data from your hard disk to the cartridge. When you fill up the cartridge, remove it and install another one.

Cartridges are rugged, making it easy to send data from one location to another. As long as the party on the other end has the same cartridge format as you, you can share data with them. Cartridges are fairly inexpensive, costing about $150 (or significantly less, if you shop mail order carefully) per 88MB cartridge. You can put the contents of an entire magazine on about five cartridges. Since they are reusable, you can use the same cartridges again and again.

Bernoulli Drives

In the 18th Century, Swiss physicist Daniel Bernoulli observed that when the velocity of a fluid increases over a surface, the pressure on that surface decreases. Little did he know that his theories would be used in computers 200 years later.

In the case of Bernoulli drives, the fluid is air. Aerodynamics moves the disk in a Bernoulli drive close enough to the read/write head to read or write data from the disk. Aerodynamics also keeps the read/write head from touching the surface of the disk by increasing the velocity of the air and causing a decrease in air pressure, making Bernoulli drives virtually immune to head crashes. Bernoulli cartridges flex slightly as the read/write head passes over the disk. As a result, Bernoulli cartridges have a shorter life span than Syquest cartridges. Bernoulli drives are fast; access times can be as fast as 20 ms. With up to 90MB of storage capacity, Bernoulli cartridges are a good choice for removable media.

Syquest Drives

Syquest drives are more like a conventional hard disk than Bernoulli drives. They use the same method of storing and accessing data as hard drives, but the information is stored on a removable cartridge instead of a fixed disk. To make the cartridge more rugged, the disk inside the cartridge is also somewhat thicker than those found on a fixed disk. While Bernoulli cartridges are plagued by a shorter life span than Syquest, Syquest cartridges are more susceptible to dust and other contaminants than Bernoulli. As a result, Syquest cartridges are more prone to data loss and even head crashes. Syquest cartridges also expand and contract with the temperature, which can also result in data loss. Despite these limitations, Syquest cartridges are reliable and an excellent choice for removable cartridges. They offer a capacity of up to 105MB per cartridge.

If you are using a Syquest or Bernoulli drive for desktop publishing purchases and often send the cartridges to service bureaus, make sure to get the same capacity drive as that of the service bureau. Many still use the older 44MB drives, which cannot read the 88MB cartridges from the newer drives.

While not as fast as hard disks, the speed of cartridge drives is improving all the time. They are much faster than diskette drives, and have much more capacity. They are also an excellent media for backup devices, which we'll discuss next.

Backup

In the age of viruses, it always pays to be safe. It's a good idea to always save a copy of your data and applications somewhere off of your hard disk. Popularly called a *backup*, this method protects you from accidentally losing your data.

You have several options when selecting a backup device. You can simply copy your data onto a diskette by "dragging and dropping" on the Desktop; you can use a backup program that quickly copies all or part of your hard disk drive to a series of diskettes; or you can use software and a tape backup device, which lets you copy all of your data and/or applications to one tape cartridge. Your other option is to not back up your data at all. This is a free country, but don't say we didn't warn you. Many people who own backup devices today are victims of a hard disk crash or data loss that cost them time, money, or both. If your hard disk fails and you haven't backed up your data, you can lose *all* of the information on it. Operating on the premise of better safe than sorry, it pays to back up your data.

Backing up your data onto a diskette is probably the most common and convenient way of saving an extra copy of your data. However, this method is close to not backing up your data at all, since it's too cumbersome and time consuming to manually copy all of the data from your hard disk to a series of diskettes by hand. If you use this method, you'll probably save some of your data some of the time, other data other times, and some data not at all. Do yourself a favor: if you are using this method, try one of the next two choices.

Using Backup Software

Backup software and diskettes is the next most common method of backing up your data. Using this method, you get a series of diskettes ready, use an inexpensive backup program of your choice, and start the program. The program typically uses a proprietary method of some kind that saves your data in a compressed format to use fewer diskettes. It also copies data faster to diskettes than your Mac does. The *Norton Utilities for Macintosh, Version 2.0*, for example, provides excellent backup functionality.

The first time you use one of these programs, have a large stack of diskettes ready. A typical 80MB hard disk can use forty 1.44MB diskettes, even when a data compression algorithm is used by the software. After the first backup, however, you won't need as many diskettes. The program "remembers" which data was backed up last time and which is new. Each subsequent backup is called an *incremental* backup, since only new and changed data is backed up. If the idea of storing your hard disk information on a five-inch stack of diskettes seems daunting, read on.

Tape Backup

As hard disk drives have gotten larger, and the process of backing up data to diskette drives more cumbersome, tape backup has caught on. It is much more popular than it used to be, and for good reason. Tape backup is a good choice for efficient data backup. It's also economical: a $15 cartridge can typically back up 40MB of data.

Tape backup devices are very similar to removable cartridges. Like removable cartridges, tape cartridges plug into a drive housing. Also, like removable cartridges, the drive housing can be either externally connected to your computer via a card mounted in an expansion slot, or internally installed and connected to your disk controller. As with removable cartridges, an internal tape drive may be aesthetically more pleasing, but practically is more inconvenient. An external tape drive can be shared and used to backup other Macs in the office and even your Mac at home. An internal tape drive is stuck inside one Mac. However, unlike cartridges, which use a disk to store data, tape cartridges store data on tape. This makes data retrieval more cumbersome, but since you store data on tape cartridges for safety, you aren't likely to be using a tape cartridge to access data, except in an emergency. So the economics of tape win out over the convenience of disks.

Tape backup devices squeeze as much data as possible onto a cartridge. The data from your hard drive can be compressed when it is copied to the tape and decompressed when it is restored back to the hard drive. This allows you to store more data on a tape. The compression ratio is roughly 2 to 1, so a 20MB cartridge can usually hold at least 40MB of data.

There are five major tape formats available for Macs: DC 2000 minicartridge, DC 6000 cartridge, high-speed data cassettes, 4 mm digital audio tape (DAT), and 8 mm helical scan. DC 2000 is used for the smallest capacities

(40MB to 250MB); 8 mm helical scan is used for the largest (2GB or more), on a network. However, these formats do overlap; it won't be long before DC 2000 drives can backup gigabytes of data also.

The higher-capacity formats offer the best performance. However, they are also the most expensive. So, if you have a 120MB hard disk drive, you can choose either DC 2000 or DC 6000. You'll pay more than double the price for a DC 6000 drive, but you'll get much better performance.

With a transfer rate of approximately 2MB per minute, it takes about an hour to back up 120MB of data on a DC 2000 drive. You can do the same job on a DC 6000 in about 25 minutes, which offers transfer rates of 5MB per minute. DAT drives are about 8MB per minute, while 8 mm helical scan drives provide about 10MB per minute. This performance varies widely from drive to drive, depending on the manufacturer, the drive controller card, and the quality of the backup software you are using (most of which comes with the tape drive).

Since tape drives offer sequential, rather than random access, it's important to pick a drive with fast access time in addition to fast transfer rates. Some drives will access any file on a tape within a minute or so, while others can take up to five minutes to access a file. Fast is a relative term here, since an access time of one minute will still seem infinitely slower than that of a typical hard disk.

The backup software for the tape drive is also very important. Good backup software offers data compression, the ability to select particular files to back up, incremental backups—which only back up the information since your last backup, unattended backups—which let you perform backups without having to actually sit through the process, and even background backups which work while you're using your Mac for other things. If you don't like the software that comes with your drive, you can often purchase a third-party package. Make sure that the software package supports your tape drive.

When picking a format and capacity, remember never to get a cartridge format (or cartridge capacity) that results in having to use more than one tape to back up your entire hard disk. If you have to use two or more cartridges, you can't take advantage of unattended backup, and this defeats one of the main purposes of choosing tape in the first place.

DC 2000 is a miniature version of the DC 6000 format, both developed by 3M. Both use quarter-inch tape, but a DC 2000 is the size of a pack of cigarettes, while a DC 6000 is the size of a paperback book. DC 2000 is smaller, slower, and less versatile than DC 6000. For example, because they have only one read/write head, you can't format a DC 2000 cartridge while you're backing up data. You can do this with a DC 6000 cartridge, however. Since it can take up to three hours to format a DC 2000 cartridge, do yourself a favor and spend an extra few bucks to buy preformatted DC 2000 cartridges. Many DC 2000 drives support

Quarter-inch Cartridge (QIC) standards, which theoretically allow cartridges formatted by one drive to be read by another, even if that drive is made by another manufacturer.

The major standards supported by DC 2000 drives include the QIC-40, QIC-80, and/or QIC-380 standards, providing up to 80, 160, and 760MB of storage space (with data compression) on a single cartridge, respectively. Extended length tapes in the QIC-40 and QIC-80 formats increase this to 120 and 250MB.

Except for their larger size, faster speed, higher capacity, and greater versatility, DC 6000 drives are very similar to DC 2000 drives. Both use quarter-inch tape, both have an aluminum base plate for stability, and both use internal rubber drive belts. Many DC 6000 drives support QIC-150, QIC-380, and/or the QIC-1350 standards. DC 6000 drives should have capacities as large as 10 GB within the next few years, placing them squarely in competition with DAT and helical scan drives. DC 6000 drives sidestep the sequential access problems with tape by indexing the information as they write it. This allows you to quickly access a particular file on the tape.

High-speed data cassettes bring our old friends, the audio cassettes, back to the computer world. These are much faster than their 1970s ancestors, and use a higher-quality cassette, available in capacities as high as 600MB. They offer performance on a par with DC 6000 drives.

As DC 2000 and DC 6000 drives are related, so are 4 mm and 8 mm drives. The latter use newer technology borrowed from digital audio cassettes, which provide compact disk (CD) audio quality on cassettes. Recording heads are mounted on a drum that rotates rapidly and transversely to the direction of the tape as it moves past. This forces the recording head to move diagonally across the tape creating slashes of data in its wake. The resulting pattern resembles a helix, hence the name *helical scan*. DAT drives are narrower than 8 mm drives, so less data can be placed on each tape. DAT drives have a capacity of 1.2 to 2GB, while 8 mm helical scan drives store up to 5GB of data.

Tape is the best choice for efficient, cost-effective data backup. Although you can't access backed up information instantly, you can store information on tape cartridges quickly and efficiently while you are off doing more interesting things. But other formats and options do exist.

Other Backup Choices

While it's difficult to beat the convenience of tape, anything that can store data can be used for backup purposes. You can use a spare hard disk, a high-capacity diskette, a cartridge, or an optical drive.

A spare hard disk isn't a bad choice if you have two hard disks that are approximately the same size, one of the disks is older and slower, and you only need the storage capacity afforded by one drive. Use the older, slower drive for your backup device. You're only out of luck if both drives fail at once (highly unlikely) or if your computer and drive perish in a fire. If your data is so valuable that fire can put you out of business, use removable media for backup purposes and store the backup cartridges off site.

High-capacity diskettes are better than regular diskettes because you need fewer of them to back up your hard disk. However, unless you have a hard disk that is less than 25MB, you'll need more than one, so unattended backup is not possible. When this media is available in higher densities, as it will be, it will be a better choice for backup purposes.

Cartridges are useful for backups, but the high cost of media in relation to tape makes them a very expensive choice. In adddition, if your hard disk is 100MB or more, you will need more than one cartridge to store the contents of your hard disk.

In special situations, the best choice for data backup is *disk mirroring*. Disk mirroring essentially writes all information to two separate drives simultaneously. If one of the drives goes bad, no information is lost. While very expensive, disk mirroring is an excellent choice in "mission-critical" applications, such as banks and other financial information. Another common application is telephone companies. Wouldn't it be nice to think that the phone company's computer would go down and we could make all the free calls we wanted? Fat chance. The phone companies are one of the main customers of this technology.

Optical disks are another choice, and are probably the option of the future, as we'll examine in the next section.

 # New Storage Technologies

Just as the compact disk is winning out in the audio world, optical storage is the wave of the future in storage technologies. While audio CDs actually sound better than their older tape and LP cousins (you'll get some arguments on that point from audio purists), optical devices provide more of what computer users crave—storage space. For example, one CD-ROM disk, the exact same size as an audio CD, can store up to 680MB of data, or approximately 500 high-density diskettes worth of information.

All that space opens up a new world of applications to the computer industry; mainly in the form of graphics, video, and sound applications such as multimedia and virtual reality. Storage space, and lots of it, is what's needed to bring computers to life by adding audio and full-motion video to the traditional, staid world of text and pictures we've been used to up until now. Imagine an encyclopedia that provides random access to any information you want, except instead of words and a picture, you get narration and full-motion video. Instead of a 1,000 word description, you'll get a short "movie" on the American Revolution or the Civil War. It is pretty exciting, but we are not there yet. Optical storage has a few kinks to work out before the true majesty and power becomes obvious, but it will be there sometime this decade. Until then, let's look at the current state of the technology.

There are three major areas of optical storage: compact disk read only memory (CD-ROM), write once read many (WORM), and rewritable optical disks. Each type varies considerably, but they all have one thing in common—the optical process. Rather than writing information on a disk with a read/write head, an optical disk uses a laser beam.

In a read-only environment, such as CD-ROM, the laser beam burns microscopic pits into the surface of the disk. Once made, the disk cannot be changed. In a WORM drive, the laser beam evaporates part of the surface of the disk. Once written to, the WORM drive also cannot be changed.

In the most popular form of rewritable optical technology, magneto optical, the laser beam heats the surface of the disk only enough for it to accept changes in magnetic fields. These fields can be changed from negative to positive, so the surface can be changed as readily and as often as a conventional hard drive. Optical drives have no built-in storage media. The actual storage media is a 3.5-inch or 5.25-inch optical disk cartridge, or, in the case of CD-ROM, a compact disk identical to the audio variety.

CD-ROM

Think of a CD-ROM as a disk where the write protect notch is activated and cannot be deactivated. Despite the inability to write to a disk, CD-ROM already provides a wealth of information previously unavailable, since storage space was at a premium before. As we mentioned, one CD-ROM can store information from about 500 diskettes or 300,000 pages of information. Can you imagine receiving an application program that included 500 diskettes? The installation process alone would be a nightmare.

Current CD-ROM applications are heavy on the reference material side, such as encyclopedias, technical manuals, graphics libraries (clip art and photo libraries), font libraries, directories, travel information, almanacs, and dictionaries. They offer much greater flexibility in terms of searching and retrieving information than their paper equivalents. They are attractive to vendors because the cost of paper is much higher than the cost of a single CD (about $1.50). As a result, many vendors of higher-priced computer workstations have started bundling CD-ROM drives along with their computers because the cost of update materials (disks, technical manuals, etc.) is much lower on CD than on paper. Given that an operating system upgrade in the UNIX workstation world can occupy fifty diskettes and thousands of pages of documentation, the cost savings are tremendous.

Because of the superb graphics capabilities of the Mac, vendors are introducing multimedia applications, which combine audio, video, and computer information on CD-ROM. *QuickTime* is a new engine for these applications, providing CD quality digital audio either directly through the Mac or through the CD-ROM drive itself.

The manufacturing process for individual disks is very similar to that for audio CDs, except you get hundreds of megabytes of information instead of 80 minutes of music. CD-ROM drives also work very much like their audio CD cousins—you pop a CD into the drive, much as you would an audio CD. CD-ROM changers, storing up to six CD-ROMs at once, are also available. The technology is so similar that many CD-ROM drives also play audio CDs. However, the cost of CD-ROM drives is substantially higher than that of audio players because of the precision required to read computer data reliably. If an audio CD missed a sound, you wouldn't necessarily notice, and "error correction" is built-in to audio players to help "hide" mistakes made by those components. However, if a CD-ROM drive missed a fragment of computer information, you would be able to tell immediately.

CD-ROM drives are very slow. So slow that an access time of 300 ms is considered good. That's fifteen times slower than a fast hard drive. You have to really want to access the information in order to tolerate waiting for it. In fairness, however, using a CD-ROM with its 300,000 pages of data is a lot more efficient than using a like amount of books and searching for information through all of them.

If you are purchasing a CD-ROM drive to use one application in particular, try it out with your choice of CD-ROM drive. Each application has its own search engine to access data. A *search engine* is typically a database and built-in index that lets you quickly access particular information. The quality of that search engine has a major impact on the speed of the drive. Also, once you find the information that you want from a CD-ROM, you can save it to your hard disk. While you can't write to the CD-ROM, you can write to your hard disk.

The world of CD-ROM will soon change as vendors offer drives that can read CD-ROMs and write to rewritable CDs. Since the late 1980s, Tandy and Sony have been jointly developing rewritable CDs called Tandy High Performance Optical Recording system, or THOR. THOR will employ a type of rewritable technology called dye polymer, which uses a dye on the surface of the disk. When heated by a laser, the dye puts a microscopic bump on the disk surface, representing data. When heated again, the bump relaxes, erasing the data that was recorded. The technology will be here soon, and if access times can be improved dramatically, CDs will give traditional technologies a run for their money.

Full-motion video applications are also on the horizon for CD-ROM. Unfortunately, the current International Standards Organization (ISO) 9660 standard in place for CD-ROM does not offer the ability to support full-motion video. So other standards must be employed. Three have been developed.

The first standard announced for CDs and multimedia was compact disk interactive (CD-I). However, this is designed for use on CD-ROM readers connected to television sets and isn't intended for computers. CD-ROM Extended Architecture (CD-ROM XA) adds audio to the CD-ROM picture. However, video is not included. The really important standard for CD-ROM and full-motion video is CD-ROM Digital Video Interactive (CD-ROM DVI). This allows up to 72 minutes of full-motion video on one CD. This technology will use existing drives but will require a special controller card in your Mac. Assuming the technology comes into play within the next few years and is supported by as many vendors as currently support CD-ROM, CD-ROM DVI has the potential to lead us into the next generation of computing.

WORM

WORM drives have been popular for years in the financial industry. Because you can write information to a disk once and not erase it, the technology is perfect for accounting since it provides an unshakable audit trail for information. Information that has been saved on WORM drives can't be changed.

Unfortunately, while the size of different brands of WORM cartridges is typically the same, WORM is not a standardized technology. International Standards Organization (ISO) and American National Standards Institute (ANSI) standards do exist, but some vendors offer their own incompatible offerings. As a result, a single 5.25-inch WORM cartridge can hold anywhere from 640MB to 1.2GB, depending on what standard it supports or what vendor offers it. There's even a version of WORM for the tape world. Called Digital Optical Tape (DOT), this drive burns holes into tape instead of disk. If you pick a nonstandardized drive, you're essentially locked-in to that vendor. Larger WORM drives, used with networks and large systems, hold up to 6.4GB of information on a single 12-inch cartridge.

WORM is entrenched in certain industries, so it won't be replaced by rewritable technology anytime soon. WORM drives are much less expensive than rewritable optical drives, and their applications are so specialized that being able to write more than once would be a liability.

Rewritable Drives

The technology most interesting to those of us accustomed to traditional storage media is rewritable optical disks, or magneto optical. These disks can read and write information just as a traditional hard disk. However, they have far greater capacity than most hard disks and are better suited for large storage applications. While hard disks can be arranged in an array format for networks and large applications, optical disks are arranged in a jukebox format, with many optical disks working together. An optical jukebox puts gigabytes of information at your fingertips.

Magneto-optical drives are available in both 5.25- and 3.5-inch formats. The 5.25-inch size provides 325MB per side, while 3.5-inch offers 128MB. The smaller drives provide faster access time, as little as 30 ms. This is understandable, because there is less room for the head to travel to reach the information on the disk. Because of its speed and low cost (about $60 for a 128MB cartridge), the 3.5-inch format is a good bet to challenge tape for backup applications and removable cartridges for desktop publishing jobs.

Standards do exist in the rest of the optical world, although they've only been in place for rewritable drives since 1991. The standards have enabled users to share information between drives from different vendors. If you purchase a rewritable optical drive, make sure it supports ISO standards for optical technology.

The 3.5-inch format is also the home of yet another optical technology—OROM, or optical read-only memory. Similar to CD-ROM, O-ROM works with rewritable drives (much as write-protected diskettes work in a rewritable diskette drive). Most importantly, O-ROM disks are as much as ten times faster than CD-ROM.

Multifunction Optical Drives

The ability to read and write data on an optical drive is very useful for a variety of applications. However, the inability to change data once it's written to a WORM drive is also very useful for another set of more specialized applications. Some new drives include the ability to work with both rewritable optical and WORM cartridges. Called multifunction optical drives, these drives cost about the same as single-function rewritable drives. However, like WORM, they are hindered by the fact that three standards exist for them — magneto-optical for rewritable and dye-polymer for WORM; magneto-optical for both; and phase change technology. If you are not concerned with sharing information or using other drives, pick a format you are comfortable with and buy your drives from the same vendor.

The downsides to optical disks at this point are several. Their access times are much slower than a self-contained hard disk (about 100 ms versus less than 20 ms for hard disks). Plus, hard disks can read and write from both sides of a platter at once, while optical disks can only read from one side at a time. In order to read the other side, you have to turn the disk cartridge over and reinsert it in the drive. Optical drives are also very expensive. They provide slower performance at exponentially higher prices than hard disks. However, 3.5-inch optical disks could help the format immensely since they offer more performance at a lower cost.

Optical disks do have some advantages over hard disks. The magneto-optical head does not touch the surface of the disks, so head crashes cannot happen. They are also lighter and stronger than hard disks, so they are less prone to temperature extremes. They are also impervious to electromagnetic information, so a disgruntled employee with a demagnetizer cannot erase information from your optical disks. Optical disks also have advantages over tape backup systems. While cost is a big roadblock to choosing optical for backup purposes, data retrieval is much faster—50 to 100 ms for optical versus 15 seconds or more for magnetic tape. A big advantage is the life of data stored on optical disks. Some vendors will guarantee that your data will be safe for 50 years on an optical disk. In contrast, information stored on magnetic tape can deteriorate after as little as three years.

Optical disks are not ready for the mass market—yet. Unless you have a need for the audit trails provided by WORM drives, or if you are interested in optical's fairly high-speed data retrieval for backups, or need massive amounts of storage space, the optical solution may not be your best bargain. Of the optical technologies currently developed, CD-ROM offers the most to the general user market *today*. The number of CD-ROM applications is increasing dramatically. At the same time, the cost of CD-ROM drives is decreasing. It won't be long before more CD-ROM drives are bundled with Macs.

Optical disks are the storage media of the future. It is inevitable that optical drives will become more affordable, faster, and a staple of Mac storage in the next five years.

Flopticals

A hybrid technology between high-capacity diskette drives and optical disks is the so-called "floptical." This is essentially an optical diskette. Flopticals use optical technology to read and write information to diskette, but instead of using a cartridge, they use a specially formulated diskette with approximately 19MB of storage space. Flopticals have much in common and hence compete with the very-high-density diskette drives mentioned earlier.

Defragmenting and Compressing Your Hard Disk

Running out of room on your current hard disk? Does it seem to run slower than it used to? Before you run out and buy another hard drive, tune up your hard disk to maximum performance and give it all the space you can. To make it run faster, *defragment* your hard disk by putting all related data closer together. To give yourself more space, compress the data on your hard disk using any of a number of available compression utilities.

Defragmentation

The Mac scatters your data all over your hard disk. It stores part of a file here, another part over there, and the rest off in a corner somewhere. When it retrieves this information, it obviously takes longer than if it had just stored it all in one place to begin with.

When you format your hard disk, the Mac allocates a minimum amount of space for each file, no matter how small it is. This space contains approximately 512 bytes, or one sector, of disk space. When you first start using your hard disk, the Mac stores files contiguously from the beginning of the disk to the end. However, things start to disintegrate in due course. Once you start erasing information, the Mac puts new data in previously erased locations. This puts part of a file in one location and other parts in other locations. Each contiguous unit of data is called an *extent*.

The only reason you see a contiguous file when you retrieve it is because of the Mac's volume bit map, which keeps track of all of the disk space on your hard disk. Meanwhile, your poor read/write head on your hard disk is forced to race to all locations of the disk to access the file. Needless to say, this slows things down quite a bit.

Defragmenting programs, like the *Speed Disk* program that is part of the *Norton Utilities for Macintosh*, aim to help the Mac with its messy inclinations by storing all of a file in one place. These defragmenting programs can dramatically improve the performance of your hard disk, and as a result, your entire system. An off-the-shelf package temporarily copies data from one area of a disk to another in order to free up space. When enough space has been freed up for one file, the program puts it there. It continues the process until all files have been copied to the hard disk in contiguous locations. You have two choices when defragmenting your hard disk. You can either use an off-the-shelf disk optimization package, as we mentioned before, or you can backup and restore your hard disk.

Backup software automatically copies files sequentially to the tape cartridge. Once you do this, make another backup, just in case. Then reformat your hard disk so your tape cartridge has a clean disk to copy to. Finally, restore the backup to your hard disk using the file-by-file option (rather than the disk image option). This restores the data to a fully optimized hard disk.

The problem with the backup-and-restore option is obvious— defragmenting programs can do in ten minutes what it might take your backup-and-restore software an hour or more to achieve, depending on the various speed factors we discussed earlier when we talked about backups. A defragmenter is probably one of the most inexpensive, most intelligent purchases you can make.

Data Compression

Data compression products perform essentially the same task that backup compression products do—they compress your data by approximately a 2 to 1 margin to store more on your hard disk. If you have a 40MB hard disk, you can compress all of your data and wind up with the equivalent of an 80MB hard disk.

Compression programs also eliminate redundant data by storing it once per file, then storing all other occurrences on a token. Tokens are substituted for words, strings of words, and numbers. If you use a word, such as "word," 100 times in a document, it's only stored once. A token marks the spot of each additional occurrence. In this way, spreadsheet, word processing, and database files can be compressed up to 80 percent.

Typically, compression programs employ loss-less compression techniques which ensure that your data is not lost or changed in any way during the compression process. The most popular loss-less technique is called the Lempel-Ziv compression algorithm, named after its two Israeli mathematician inventors. Most vendors modify this technique somewhat to make their own method proprietary and incompatible with the competition. Graphics, by the way, are usually stored using lossy compression, which changes the image somewhat in exchange for dramatic savings in space of up to 40 to 1 in some cases.

Compression programs work in real time. They compress data as you store it and decompress data as you request it. Compressed data is stored in a proprietary format on your hard disk. This takes somewhat longer than using uncompressed data and can be inconvenient. However, some compression products include hardware boards with coprocessors dedicated to the decompression process. This makes performance nearly as good as your hard disk without decompression built in. In addition, these products also include defragmenting software to make your hard disk run more efficiently.

3

Printing Technologies

There are as many types of printers as there are types of Mac users. There is the small office manager, still cranking out forms on an ImageWriter; the fledgling desktop publisher, running an inkjet printer off her Mac Classic; the Mac network users, relying on high speed lasers; and the graphic designer, proofing his designs on a color printer. And, of course, there is *you*. What kind of printer is best for you? You can get an idea by answering three questions:

- How good do you want your work to look?

- How fast do you want your work to print?

- How much do you want to pay?

The answer to the third question is governed by the first two. We would all like to have high-quality output flying from the printer, but that comes at a price. So we cut a compromise and try to work within our budget. You can pick up a Mac printer for under four hundred dollars, or pay something between ten and twenty thousand for some color models. You can wait up to ten minutes for a page, or have a new sheet appear every few seconds. You can have print which is charitably called "legible," or you can have text and illustrations that look sharp and color-perfect. You can choose one of three technologies for single-color printing, or weigh which of the rapidly-changing full-color printer

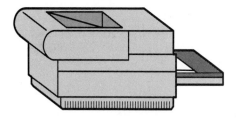

technologies to employ. When you have finally made up your mind, it will all change by the next week.

To make things even more confusing, you can't just pick any printer. The Mac was designed as a graphical computer; from day one the intent was that what you saw on the screen would be as close as possible to what you got on your printer. Your PC cousins could choose between dozens of printers to hook up to their DOS machines. Better resolution and performance of Mac printers cost users in more limited choices and higher prices.

Today, the situation is better for the Mac user. Only at the low end, in the fast-vanishing world of dot-matrix printers, is the Mac user at an obvious disadvantage. Almost all printers nowadays can be used with a Mac; at worst, you may have to spend a couple of hundred dollars for a Mac printer interface; at best, the printer will cost no more in a Mac version than in an IBM-compatible version.

Technology

What every printer does is put an image on a sheet of paper. The earliest printers were dot-matrix; although Apple has ceased to manufacture its dot-matrix ImageWriter, many of them still survive. The next step up is the inkjet printer; Apple replaced the ImageWriter with the StyleWriter. Finally, at least for single-color printing, there are laser printers, like Apple's LaserWriter series. There are several technologies for color printing; we will talk about these later in this chapter.

Dot-Matrix Printers

If you are looking to buy a printer, this section is only of historical interest. If you could even find a new dot-matrix printer, it would probably be a bad deal. If you are offered one second-hand, it had better be dirt cheap for you to consider it. Look for an inkjet printer instead.

What's so bad about dot-matrix printers? The trouble is that they are slow, noisy, and they produce the worst-looking output of any printer technology. So why would anyone use them? Because they are cheap. For most of the Mac's life, they've been the only way to get a printer for under a thousand dollars. Now that inkjets compete with them in price, there is only one reason to keep using them. That use is for multi-part forms. Another term for dot-matrix printers is impact printers; and, like your typewriter (remember them?) with carbons, the dot-matrix is the only printer technology that can print on several sheets at the same time.

The way they work is by pushing pins onto an ink ribbon which transfers dots of ink onto the page. What happens is that each time a character is sent to the printer, the printer decides which pins should be pushed to make the shape of the letter. Some printers have nine pins; better ones have twenty-four. Just as an LCD watch can make all the numbers with seven segments on its display, so any letter can be created from a combination of nine dots. But as you can imagine, a letter formed in this way is a pretty poor representation. As personal computers became more common in the mid-eighties, such "computer type" was all too widespread.

There were several attempts to improve the quality of dot-matrix output. Instead of making a line in one pass of the print head, the paper was moved up slightly and another pass was made. This effectively doubled the resolution to eighteen pin positions for each character, and was optimistically called "near-letter quality." However, this double pass meant that it took twice as long to print every line.

Another method to improve resolution was the introduction of twenty-four pin printers. This didn't help Mac users, because the ImageWriter was meant to work with the supplied fonts, like Geneva, Chicago, and the other "city" fonts (so-named because they were named after cities). These were designed to use the same resolution on the screen as the printer. Apple's response was to introduce a twenty-seven pin ImageWriter, called the LQ.

Because the PC printers of the day used even less legible fonts than those of the ImageWriter, Apple felt justified in using a nonstandard printer connection. When even the most basic computers cost several thousand dollars, this was not such a hardship; but as printer prices for DOS machines dropped, Mac users looked for cost-effective alternatives to the ImageWriter. They found these alternatives in a few Apple-standard printers like the Seikosha SP-1000AP and the Olympia NP30APL. Although these printers are hard to find (and have probably been discontinued), you may come across them secondhand. One holdout is GCC's WriteImpact, a $599 dot-matrix printer that's still in their product line. Another alternative to using the ImageWriter was by purchasing products like Orange Micro's Grappler, a software/cable combination which let you connect a Mac to a PC printer.

One feature of the ImageWriter was color printing; you could buy a four color-ribbon for it which used the basic colors separately and in combination to produce multicolor output. Compared to present-day printers, the output was crude, but in its day it was the only way to get color output. As prices for other printer technologies dropped, the ImageWriter had few advantages, and eventually Apple discontinued it.

PostScript and TrueType

With the newer kinds of printers, all kinds of possibilities open up, but there is more to understand. Because inkjet and laser printers are capable of typeset-quality printing, the technology has been developed to give quality results from them. Users demand more choices, more speed, less money.

One given with printers is that you should be able to print a font at any size. This luxury, unknown to the printing trade at any price until 1950, makes a lot of work for your equipment. To understand this you will have to look at the way fonts and illustrations were represented on computers (and in some cases, still are).

Dot-matrix printers made characters from a 72-dots-per-inch grid, so all fonts and illustrations were represented in this way. Even though laser printers have become widespread, many of them still cannot scale a drawing or font without outside assistance. The idea of bitmapping, that is, deciding which of the dots on the grid should be printed black to make up the character, seems simple and logical. So it is until you come to scale your font or artwork.

A font or typeface (there *is* a difference, but we'll go along with the world and use the terms interchangeably) is a very small piece of artwork. Everything we read is made up of characters, and all these characters are drawn to a similar design called a typeface. There are thousands of typefaces, and though you may not be able to name many of them, you are probably aware of the differences between them. If type of the same design is made smaller, you expect it to look the same. Any differences stick out like a sore thumb.

If you make a letter at twelve points (or one-sixth of an inch), you will have roughly fifty dots to play with (three hundred dots per inch on a printer, divided by six). That figure covers from the top of capital letters to the bottom of letters that go below the line, like *g* or *j*. So a letter *a*, for instance, is only about sixteen dots high. Let's suppose you design a letter *a*, using a grid of sixteen by about fourteen dots. You will make a reasonable job which you can check by looking closely at this letter printed out on a laser.

But what happens if, instead of making the letter at twelve points you now want to change it to eleven? The drawing program that you used to create it will try to fit it in a smaller grid, but drawing programs have real problems making the slightly smaller character look anything like a letter *a*. The nicely curved lines become a jagged mess; you will be lucky if you can even identify which character it is, let alone which typeface it's supposed to be.

Bitmapped fonts were created in several sizes, each drawn individually to get the best representation of the character. Just one size of a bit-mapped font takes up a lot of memory. To get a reasonable selection of sizes meant allocating vast amounts of RAM and hard disk space, at a time when these cost considerably more than they do now. And illustrations? You had to take what you were given, because any change of size rendered the artwork illegible.

This was the situation when Adobe introduced PostScript in 1982. What they did not only allowed you to size fonts and artwork by any amount, they also introduced the idea of device independence, or reproduction of artwork at the highest resolution that each printer would allow. This revolutionized printing, but back then, the benefits outweighed the costs for only select users.

Figure 3.1: A Mac IIsi and an Apple LaserWriter IIg. The LaserWriter has eight page per minute output and PostScript Level 2. Print and picture quality is enhanced by FinePrint, a resolution enhancement feature, and Photograde for better gray-scale images. The IIg also includes an EtherNet connector for network use.

When Apple introduced the LaserWriter a few years later, it cost $5,000, and came with PostScript built-in. At the time only Adobe made the fonts. These have become known as the "PostScript thirty-five." Even today, when you buy a PostScript printer, you will get these fonts supplied. Adobe took a hefty license fee (which was understandable, given the smallness of the market), and the printer required extra circuitry to work with PostScript. However, one font could be scaled to any size, and the process was also suitable for illustrations. One major advantage which launched desktop publishing was that a page could be made and printed on the computer at three hundred dots per inch; then it was taken to a new operation called a service bureau where it would be printed out at twelve hundred dots per inch. This resolution was good enough for text to look as though it had been professionally typeset on a machine costing tens of thousands of dollars.

How does PostScript work? Instead of representing characters by dots, they are represented by describing their outline. This is done by saying "go up for x units, turn right and make half a circle with a radius of y units," and so on until the character is fully described. The amount of "one unit" is controlled by the point size you want the character to be. When the outline is fully described, the inside is filled. This outline cannot be printed, but it can be scaled to any size and lose nothing of its shape.

The second part of the process occurs in a PostScript interpreter attached to your printer. This may be part of the original circuitry, or it could be an add-on cartridge that plugs into the printer. What the interpreter does is compare the outlines to a grid of square dots and change the dots from white to black if the outline fills more than half of any square. The size of the dot varies according to the resolution of the printer. While the final output is still bit-mapped, the intervening steps have preserved the shape of the character.

The extra cost of a PostScript interpreter first hindered their acceptance, although the difference is generally now less than a few hundred dollars. If laser printers cost less than a thousand dollars, this difference could be vital to some buyers. This has led to lower-cost solutions which provide some of PostScript's capabilities. These include PostScript "clone" interpreters, which are functionally equivalent to Adobe's designs but are made by other manufacturers at a lower price; software interpreters that use the power of the Mac itself to change PostScript into a bitmap; and Adobe's own Adobe Type Manager, which allows non-PostScript printers to print Adobe format fonts.

The PostScript interpreter, or to give it its technical name, the Raster Image Processor (RIP) or rasterizer, has a program in it written by Adobe to convert PostScript to a bit-map. Several manufacturers have copied the functionality of this program without copying the code, using a process known as "reverse engineering." The programming team knows what has to be achieved, so they write their own code without reference to the Adobe solution. Each step is thoroughly documented, so that if the team inadvertently creates the same code as Adobe, it can be shown that this was coincidental and not deliberate copying. Adobe claims that no clone can do all that their own program can do, while the clone makers say that there is no difference.

Another way of achieving printing of PostScript on a non-PostScript printer is by using a PostScript emulation program. This takes PostScript information as it is sent to the printer and converts it to information your printer can understand. Programs of this sort include QMS's UltraScript Plus and Custom Applications' Freedom of Press. The drawback of this approach is that the Mac is slowed up while printing as the PostScript instructions are converted, and this is most noticeable on the least powerful Macs.

The final method of printing on non-PostScript printers is Adobe Type Manager (ATM), a low-cost text-only software solution. This program not only lets you print PostScript fonts, it also improves the appearance of the characters on-screen. This last feature is so useful that many PostScript printer owners have installed ATM. It also makes it easier to load fonts onto the system. Because ATM costs well under a hundred dollars (and has been given away free with some products), it is in wide use.

Why should Adobe make it easier for you to do without a PostScript printer? The reason is in the introduction of TrueType, a rival font format developed by Apple and Microsoft. A TrueType interpreter, similar to ATM, is part of System 7 on the Mac and Windows 3.1 on DOS machines.

In a series of astute marketing moves, Adobe took steps to ensure that their format would be dominant by the time TrueType was introduced. First, they published details of the Adobe font format; the secrecy that had surrounded this had prevented other manufacturers from producing fonts in this format. Then they introduced Adobe Type Manager, which let non-PostScript users employ Adobe-format fonts in their system. Finally they pressed ahead with developments like Multiple Masters, which would let users modify fonts to any degree of width and line stroke.

This meant that by 1992, just about every user of a Graphical User Interface (GUI) had some Adobe fonts installed on their machine. Adobe's own font catalog numbered over 1,000 designs; there were 5,000 Adobe-standard fonts in total. When TrueType was introduced, it was fully compatible with ATM, and finally Apple announced that future versions of its operating system would incorporate ATM technology. Today the two systems coexist freely and it is possible to mix and match TrueType and Adobe format fonts on a page with few problems. However, many people find that the quality of TrueType fonts is not as good as PostScript designs.

One definite advantage that PostScript has over other systems is its ability to control artwork as well as type. With its recognizable designs at small sizes, type is most vulnerable to distortion; illustrations similarly need the ability to be scaled without alteration. Adobe invented the Encapsulated PostScript (EPS) format for drawings, and the highest quality artwork is produced to this standard. If you have certain drawing programs, you can convert bitmapped originals to PostScript, using a part of the program called autotrace, and scale them within the program. Then you convert back to bitmaps, if that's all your printer can deal with. However, it's not advisable to scale these images once they are exported to a page layout program because the same problems will arise.

PostScript is described as a vector-based system, because it relies on direction and distance instructions. It is also a page description language because it carries all the information in its files on how to lay out a page. In fact, PostScript can be used as a programming language and skilled programmers can create numerous special effects with it; however, average users will let their application programs do the work. PostScript programming is not reckoned to be an easy skill to pick up, and it is not necessary to know it to get your work printed.

PostScript's device-independence shines in the production of work that will be reproduced at the service bureau on an imagesetter, usually a Linotronic machine. This is a high-resolution printer; it prints sixteen times more accurately than a laser printer by using a laser beam to draw outlines on photographic paper or film, which is then processed chemically to reveal the outline.

The whole setup costs over a hundred thousand dollars and is usually outside the budget of the user, who pays a service bureau by the page. The PostScript interpreters for these machines are often sold separately. Because of the detail in each page, they manipulate many megabytes of information. However, they still use the same principles as the PostScript interpreter on your laser printer, only this time each square inch can hold up to a million and a half dots instead of the ninety thousand of a laser.

This detail means that the characters look perfectly formed to the naked eye. The jagged character edges that afflict laser output are gone and the letters appear to have perfect circles and diagonal lines. Compare a page of laser output with the same page output on an imagesetter; the imageset page has a certain "snap" and sharpness missing from the laser output. But one thing is certain, if the correct fonts have been used, the laser page design and the imageset page will be exactly the same. The PostScript process assures this.

One drawback to the PostScript process of creating a bitmap to print is that the thinnest lines of a small-sized font may not always cover the required fifty percent or more of a square in a three-hundred-dots-per-inch grid. This means that a stroke of a letter may disappear in places. To counteract this effect Adobe added "hints" to their fonts, which overrode the rasterizer to ensure that the letter would print completely. Some vendors of Adobe-standard fonts do not include hints and this means that the characters do not look good at small sizes. Hints are not necessary when outputting from imagesetters because of their high resolution.

You may hear of Adobe-standard fonts being called "Type One." This stems from the days when Adobe kept its standard for its best fonts to itself—the Type One fonts—but released a format that would work with PostScript called "Type Three." Type Three fonts are noticeably inferior to Type One fonts, and with the disclosure of the Type One format they were no longer produced. Type Three fonts did not support hinting.

In 1991 Adobe announced PostScript Level 2. The main advantages of this are in color work (so that's where they are covered) but the new standard uses caching and file compression to speed up page drawing. Because all the enhancements in Level 2 do not alter the format, it's possible to use the original PostScript and Level 2 interchangeably. You can run both at once, but only when you have a level 2-equipped printer will you see a speed increase.

Hardware—Not Always What It Seems

One point you will notice when you start looking at printers, both inkjet and laser, is that many of them have similar specifications. This is not an accident. Like many consumer products, the important parts of the printer are often made by one of only a few manufacturers. Canon, for instance, makes most of the inkjet machinery and quite a lot of the laser printing mechanisms. The mechanical part of a printer is often referred to as the engine.

This isn't to say that it doesn't matter which printer you buy. The circuitry is usually made by the company whose name appears on the box and this can vary considerably. It is possible to make a laser printer controlled by a slow Motorola 68000 chip (the same as the CPU for the Mac Plus, SE, and original Classic); it is much better to use a chip optimized for the purpose, like the AMD 29000 RISC chip. The result is faster printing and PostScript interpreting.

Figure 3.2: Texas Instruments makes a range of laser printers. The MicroLaser XL Turbo features an up-to-date specification, including PostScript Level 2, sixteen pages per minute, and a RISC processor.

Another variation is the resolution of the printer. Apple, like several manufacturers, has a process that gives an apparent six hundred dots per inch resolution. Apple also has a process that improves the appearance of photographs; both of these enhancements are in the controlling circuitry. Given that there are many parts to a printer, you might expect them to be one of the most troublesome parts of a computer system. In fact, they are generally built strong and are unlikely to go wrong. Keep them clean and cool, do not try to run the wrong kind of paper through them, and they'll reward you with many years of trouble-free service.

Inkjet Printers

Although inkjet printers are cheaper than laser printers, they are a more recent technology. They have many of the advantages of laser printers and cost less. Apple, Hewlett-Packard, and Canon are the main suppliers, but it seems the list grows daily.

The products work by heating ink in an open-ended tube. The heating is so fast that it causes a microscopic bubble of ink to fly out of the open end of the tube toward the paper. The bubble is less than one three-hundredth of an inch across and can, in theory, give the resolution of a laser printer. In fact the image is slightly degraded as the ink spreads a little as it hits the paper. However, improvements in ink technology have all but eliminated this spread, and you may find that you cannot tell the difference between output from an inkjet or a laser. At one time you had to use special paper so that the ink was not absorbed too much, but newer inks make this unnecessary.

Inkjet printers come in four varieties. There are the low-cost workhorses, like the Apple StyleWriter and the Hewlett-Packard DeskWriter, selling for half the cost of a laser (see figs. 3.3 and 3.4). For just under $500, you will find some portable printers to connect to your PowerBook. At around $1500-$2000, there are inkjets that print on paper up to 22 inches by 17. Finally, there are the ever-growing number of color inkjets, from under a thousand dollars up to fifty thousand. We will cover them in the color printer section.

What can a low-cost inkjet do for you? A great deal, surprisingly. Their text quality satisfies many people; they deliver a page every one or two minutes; slow page production for long print jobs; and the cost of ink is slightly greater than the cost of toner for a laser printer to print the same number of copies. The low-cost inkjets do not have a PostScript interpreter and there are no PostScript cartridges available. The quality of solid areas of ink can vary more than a laser, and may lead to banding of different areas of density. The typical inkjet user is perhaps producing short documents, and is most interested in spending very little to get set up. For some people, the inkjet printer is the only printer they will ever use; for others, it merely serves as a cheap proofing printer to check that all is well before they send their files to a service bureau.

Figure 3.3: The Apple StyleWriter is Apple's lowest priced printer. Paper flows from top to bottom on this ink-jet printer. The StyleWriter is a QuickDraw printer, so you will probably want to use System 7 for TrueType fonts or Adobe Type Manager for PostScript fonts.

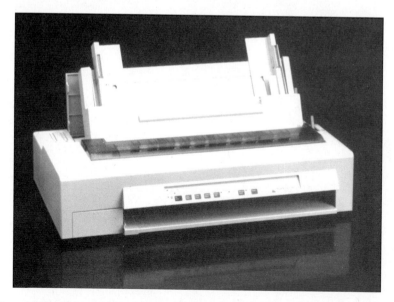

Figure 3.4: GCC makes a range of laser printers; also the WideWriter 300 that uses paper up to 22 x 17 inches. The WideWriter is an ink-printer.

To make up for the lack of PostScript, most inkjet owners use Adobe Type Manager and the TrueType rasterizer in System 7. Of course, this cuts you off from illustrations in EPS format but most people's work is text-intensive and there is no need for special illustration handling. Another drawback is that some inkjet printers cannot be put on an AppleTalk network. Users get around this by putting their Mac on the network and receive files which they print out on the inkjet.

The extra cost of materials comes from the higher price you pay for ink cartridges. This only becomes significant if you print vast amounts of pages. Given the inkjet's typical printing speed, it's unlikely that you will ever worry about ink costs as a major expense. Some companies have kits that allow you to refill an ink cartridge. If you're watching every penny this is an economical (if potentially messy) way to go.

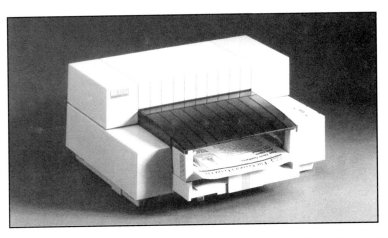

Figure 3.5: The Hewlett-Packard Deskwriter is a low-cost alternative to the Apple StyleWriter. Both models use the Canon ink-jet print engine. You will get typeset quality output for only a few hundred dollars; if cash is tight it is a good alternative to a laser printer.

Laser Printers

Ever since Apple introduced the LaserWriter in 1985, it has been the printer of choice for the Macintosh. With rapidly falling prices, it is possible to get a third-party laser for your Mac for under a thousand dollars. There are plenty of manufacturers and if that makes choosing difficult, it means that price competition keeps lasers affordable.

How does a laser printer work? It's a marriage of copier technology with computer control. An office copier comprises two parts: the scanner picks up light reflected by your original document, and the printer takes the scanner's electronic output and recreates the document using toner on plain paper.

In a laser printer, the information about the page comes from your Mac, and the image is created electronically in the printer's circuitry. But just as in the copier, the light source (a laser, in the case of your laser printer) draws an image on the printer's drum, by putting an electrical charge in areas that are to be printed. As the drum revolves, it passes a toner compartment, and toner is attracted to the surface of the drum by the electrical charge. In the meantime, paper has been brought into the print area. As the paper picks up the toner from the drum, a wire behind the paper attracts toner to aid the process. The paper continues past a discharge brush where any electrical charge is removed; then the paper continues through heated rollers that fuse the toner to the page. The drum, meanwhile, continues to revolve past a cleaning blade where any toner that failed to adhere to the paper is removed. The drum also passes under a wire that neutralizes any electrical charge. The printer is now ready to print the next page.

All the processes that take place in the laser printer also take place in a copier; but copiers run much faster than laser printers. Why is this? It is because much of the time spent printing a page on a laser printer is actually spent creating the image in the circuitry. The drum can be stationary for long periods while the next page is being imaged. This is why the controller circuitry is vital. While many laser printers are rated at eight pages a minute, you rarely see more than four or five. The printing mechanism can run at this speed, but the electronics can only keep up with the drum when they run a simple document; typically, a few words in a font that's resident in the printer.

You may only be doing eight-page newsletters where speed is not important to you but for a person producing two-hundred page books, the hour and a half that a "four pages per minute" printer takes to do the job will be far too long. That is assuming that there are no complex graphics or multiple fonts involved which can slow down the printer even further.

Another figure that may concern you is the "duty cycle." Printers are built to sustain certain levels of use; many people never come close to driving them very hard. If your expected use runs into thousands of pages a month, then check that the printer of your choice can sustain this kind of output.

A figure that might mean nothing or everything is the capacity of the paper trays. Some printers hold as few as fifty sheets of paper, others have multiple paper trays that each hold two hundred sheets or more. These printers can hold different types of paper as well as envelopes. However, if you are restricted to a fifty-sheet machine, you may find it irksome to have to constantly check and refill the paper tray.

If you share an office with an IBM-compatible machine, you may have to think about how you will share your printer. IBM compatibles use a parallel port printer, and most of the mid- and high-priced lasers come with a parallel port as well as AppleTalk. Many printers of this kind have autosensing so you can connect both the Mac and the PC to the printer, and have the printer determine how to treat the incoming information. Other printers may require you to manually switch between inputs, and a few, noticeably most of Apple's LaserWriters, have no parallel port at all.

Figure 3.6: QMS makes a range of laser printers, including heavy-duty models suitable for fast network printing.

You may think that you are not interested in networking, that your printer is for your exclusive use—but if you use an AppleTalk connection to your Mac, you are already networking. The way Apple designed the laser-to-Mac connection was with AppleTalk, the same networking that lets Macs share files and programs. Every printer-Mac connection is a mini-network, and that has advantages if you work in a situation where there are several Macs. Because the average printer is used for around twenty minutes a day, the advantages to networking are obvious. Several Macs can easily share one printer with a minimum of fuss in wiring or software. If you happen to be unlucky and try to print when someone else is printing, AppleTalk simply puts your job in a queue and starts it as soon as the printer is free. You can even equip an IBM-PC compatible with an AppleTalk card to put it on the network.

Lower-cost lasers, like Apple's Personal LaserWriters, don't use AppleTalk. This means that they cannot sit on the network to take printing from anyone who sends it, but instead must be connected to one Mac and print only from that. The Mac is equipped with AppleTalk and can take information from other Macs on the network; no matter where it gets its print files from, the Mac must dedicate itself to printing out the file. This means that the lucky person who has a non-AppleTalk printer on an otherwise printerless AppleTalk network will have to stop everything from time to time to print out files sent by another Mac.

Apple seems to be moving away from AppleTalk with their most recent range of computers and printers. The Quadra 950 and LaserWriter IIg come with an EtherNet card as standard. While AppleTalk is cheap or free, it is far slower than most networks and is not found outside the Apple world. EtherNet is a commonly-used standard in networking and adoption of EtherNet makes the LaserWriter IIg network-ready for both Mac and PC networks.

There is a wide range of laser printers which will only work with a PC in their basic configuration. Many of these printers, however, can be fitted with an AppleTalk adapter manufactured by the printer company. This approach looks inviting, but it is generally not great. You will probably want to add on PostScript and will need the two or three megabytes of memory that PostScript requires. By the time you tally up the costs, you probably could buy a better performing Mac-ready printer for less. PostScript cartridges usually don't work as fast as built-in PostScript. Even if you buy printer memory cheaply from one of the third-party suppliers, you will still pay more than a printer aimed at the Mac.

Because your printer is really just a single-function computer, it needs some of the things your computer needs. A simple control panel and LCD panel take care of the input of controls and output of messages, but the big item of expense is memory. Some Macs are less powerful than the printers they are connected to, and it's not unusual to find a Mac with two Megabytes of RAM driving a printer with three Megabytes.

This is because a PostScript printer needs sufficient memory to keep a whole page in memory; an entire three hundred-dots-per-inch, letter size page. This requires a Megabyte and a half, and the remaining memory is used for computation and storing fonts that have been downloaded from the printer. You may find that the printer you are considering doesn't have enough memory to run PostScript unaided; even if you don't want to run PostScript, you might want to put graphics on your pages. This also requires two or three Megabytes, so having only one Megabyte or half a Megabyte soon cramps your style.

Figure 3.7: Here's a group of Hewlett-Packard laser printers. (Back, left to right) The LaserJet IIID and LaserJet III for printing eight pages a minute; (front, left to right) the LaserJet IIIP and IIP, which print at four pages a minute. You can buy these with the necessary AppleTalk interface and PostScript cartridge already installed.

If you need to add memory, you may have two choices; you can go to the manufacturer (or his dealer) and buy the same brand of memory as your printer; or you can go to one of the third-party memory suppliers and pay a lot less for the same thing. Unfortunately, third-party suppliers only make memory for the more popular printers. Memory for your printer is not the same as memory for your Mac, in most cases; the chips come on special circuit boards, which do nothing but add to the memory's cost.

Even if your printer can be fitted with memory from a third-party supplier, the costs are not the same for all printers. For his most expensive items, one supplier charges a hundred and fifty percent more than his cheapest memory. Memory for the most popular printers is usually the cheapest. All this makes it very difficult to assess a printer's final cost. Is printer A cheaper than printer B, when you take into account the extra cost of memory? You will have to check your math carefully.

Some printers even have a SCSI port that lets you can connect a hard drive to the printer itself. A hard drive can be used to replace RAM, but it is a very slow way of keeping page information in memory. The major use of a printer hard disk is to store fonts, so that you are not kept waiting while the computer downloads them to the printer. A hard drive is only worthwhile if you have many fonts and you are trying to squeeze the maximum performance from your printer.

Another point to look at when buying a printer is how many fonts come supplied with the machine, although this is less important than it once was. Having fonts resident makes printing slightly faster, and obviously you do not have to buy them. A disk containing screen fonts is loaded onto your computer when you install the printer driver.

Most printers come with Times Roman and Helvetica, along with Courier (the typewriter font) and a Symbol font. PostScript printers add Helvetica Condensed, Avant Garde, Bookman, Century Schoolbook, Palatino, and Zapf Chancery (a script face) and Zapf Dingbats (decorative symbols). All but Symbol and the two Zapf fonts come in four variations—Normal (or Roman), Italic, Bold, and Bold Italic. This gives you thirty-five fonts.

These specs give you the basics for evaluating a three-hundred-dots-per-minute laser, but more and more models are now offering some kind of enhancement of print quality. Many models now sport resolution enhancement, where the definition of the letters is increased, and recent Apple LaserWriters have the ability to improve photographs as well.

Resolution enhancement (or whatever your printer manufacturer calls it) is a cheap way of giving an apparent six hundred dots per inch output. Just like the old dot-matrix printers moved the paper slightly so that the print head did a double pass over the same area, newer laser do an electronic "double pass," by filling in curves with slightly offset toner dots, so that diagonal and curved lines don't show so many jagged edges.

The controller circuitry looks for instances where a character could be badly formed and adds toner dots to fill in the spaces inside the character's outline to give a smoother outline. This procedure is not limited to any kind of font or illustration, and the added time to enhance the fonts is minimal.

Apple has added a new type of resolution enhancement to the LaserWriter IIg. It enhances continuous-tone (photographic) images. If you look closely at a photograph in a newspaper, you will see that it is made up of a series of dots. The dots are absent in white areas, but as the image gets darker they gradually get bigger, so that in the end black areas are made up of continuous overlapping dots. How can this be achieved on a laser printer, where the dots are the same size? Apple manages this by having the image made up of small squares, which are themselves made up of tiny dots. Depending on the darkness of the area, the small squares are made up of more or less of the tiny dots, to give the impression of smaller and larger dots like those of the newspaper.

One use that the laser printer can be put to is to act like a fax machine; Hewlett-Packard makes an add-on that sits on top of its LaserJet models and works like a plain paper fax. Don't confuse this with computer fax modems; the computer plays no part in the fax transmission and receiving. It might be that this combination suits your needs.

The next step up from the standard laser printer is the high-resolution laser printer, capable of results of up to twelve hundred-dots-per-inch, depending on the model. These can cost into five figures, but their output is much improved over the three-hundred-dots-per-inch models. Because high-resolution laser printers are dealing with large amounts of memory, their controllers run at high speeds, so that the claimed four or eight pages a minute output is often approached, and graphics do not slow the printer down.

These printers are aimed at people who might normally use a service bureau. Their advantages are that they give output within a minute, rather than sending out pages for next-day delivery. They use plain paper, so there is no need for any of the chemical processing associated with the photographic methods of the service bureau. The cost per page is very low; just a few cents compared with the six dollars a service bureau would charge for a long job.

Yet in spite of all the advantages of a high-definition laser printer, many people still prefer to go to the imagesetter. They do not produce huge amounts of pages, so they can afford to wait a day for output. They do not use an imagesetter in-house, so the disposal of chemicals is not a problem. The per page cost is passed on to the client. But most of all, a page from a high-resolution laser printer does not have the sharpness that an imageset page possesses, even if the resolution is the same. This may be due to the photographic nature of the imagesetting process, but whatever the reason, the laser print looks "soft."

But some people feel that there are advantages to high-resolution laser printers that makes them worth working with. If they produce technical manuals, for instance, where the last degree of quality in output is not necessary, they will produce their pages on a laser and save money. Some books have been produced on a laser and the quality is passable. One producer of computer books went with high-resolution laser originals, but went back to imageset output after complaints that their books looked cheap.

You should explore the high-resolution option, but make sure you see three samples of the same page; from a three hundred dots per inch laser, from a high-resolution laser, and from an imagesetter. Some companies show examples of their printers reproducing text at thirty-six points and larger; that's not a good example. What you need to see are originals that show several paragraphs of type at body text sizes; around ten or twelve point. That is where quality shows up.

Apart from paper, the laser requires very little else to keep it running. The major consumable is toner in toner cartridges. Time was when people used to throw empty cartridges into the trash when they bought a new one, until someone had the bright idea of refilling them. The major manufacturers pooh-poohed the idea, but in spite of some disasters the idea caught on, and environmentalists pointed out that used toner cartridges didn't do much for landfills.

So are refilled cartridges a bad idea? Every Mac guru seems to have the same answer. "You might get ripped off, but I have had good results from . . . ," and the name of a local recycler. While the toner cartridge recycling service was sold as a get-rich-quick idea to entrepreneurs, most of the corner-cutters have left in search of more lucrative schemes. The principal dodge was to "drill and fill"; the cartridge was drilled, toner was inserted, and a bung sealed the hole. Present-day recyclers dismantle and clean the cartridge, and seem to put slightly more toner than the original manufacturers do. You should ask if you can have your own cartridges refilled, so that you will not be using a cartridge more than three or four times.

You have several options open to you when it is time for a new cartridge. If you are uncertain about refills, you can salve your ecological conscience and help your local refiller improve their act by selling them your empty cartridge for a few dollars. Or you can just go the refill route, and save about 50 percent over new. Your cartridge manufacturer will take your old cartridge off your hands and melt it down to create new cartridges. Whatever you do, don't throw it in the trash! Also, remember to replace the other parts that come with a new cartridge. These pieces keep your images bright and clear.

Care and Feeding of Your Printer

These three types of printers—dot-matrix, inkjet, and laser—are the printers most Mac users connect to their computer. While they all run very well, a little care can make your printing trouble-free. There are also papers that vary from mild to wild, which can spruce up your output.

Like most computer equipment, printers do not like extremes of temperature and humidity. A dusty atmosphere will make life difficult, and if a page comes out with a piece torn off, you had better retrieve the errant scrap before it derails every other sheet you try to print on.

One major danger is the sticky label. If you run a sheet of these through your printer—especially a laser—you could end up finding that you are one or two labels short. These labels are probably now orbiting on the printer drum, essentially making your printer useless. That is not to say that all sticky labels will do this; just make sure you have those that are designed for printer use, and cross your fingers.

If you do find that you seem to have eleven labels out when twelve went in, hope and pray that the missing piece has attached itself to some less vital part of the machine. Wherever the label landed, you will probably find that it deposited adhesive which will attempt to pick up everything you now want to run through. Use Isopropyl (denatured) alcohol and cotton buds to remove the unwanted deposit.

Another no-no to put through your printer is embossed note paper, especially the kind that has a raised part that is a different color from the paper. This part is made out of plastic and can melt as the paper passes the heated rollers of a laser. At best, you will get a smear. If you are not so lucky, some of the plastic will have deposited itself on the rollers to smear all succeeding sheets. It goes without saying (almost) to follow your printer manufacturer's instructions on keeping the inside of your printer clean by preventative maintenance. This is rarely arduous, and it saves you the embarrassment of printing a sixty-page report with a gray streak down every page.

Different printers can cope with different weights and types of paper. While the dot-matrix is the only kind that can create multi-copy forms, this isn't such a problem if you have an inkjet or laser. Multi-part forms were a quick way of getting an office record of a payslip, for instance; today's inkjets and lasers simply print separate reports that put the relevant information into a much more useful format. By the time you have printed another report, you will still have taken less time than the dot-matrix did.

Dot-matrix printers run with continuous paper; this usually has a green backing on every alternate line, and is perforated so that it can be stored accordion-fashion. On either side are tractor holes; pins in the platen of the printer engage these to pull the paper through. If you want, you can tear off the edges of this kind of paper. This kind of computer paper has been used since the nineteen-sixties, and suppliers are easy to find. It is also easy to discover companies who will produce the specialized multipart continuous forms your business may require. Some dot-matrix printers came with single sheet feeders, so that they could print on company notepaper.

The supplier's manual will tell you what weights of paper you can run through your printer; this is most important for inkjet and laser users. Many of these printers come with an opening flap on the side opposite to the paper tray; this lets you use heavier paper that cannot be bent around the paper path that lighter paper takes. Note, however, that pages printed this way will come out in reverse order to normal; many applications allow you to print back-to-front to compensate.

If you are using a laser, or a recent inkjet printer, you will get perfect results with ordinary copy paper from an office-supply store. Older inkjets needed special coated paper, which could be quite expensive. If you have newer ink cartridges, you may be able to use an old inkjet with copy paper; try a few sheets to see.

Some people claim to get better results from their laser using coated paper which is a brighter white; they create proof copies on copy paper, then load up with expensive paper for the final run. If what comes out of your printer goes to a print shop, you may find you get better results with this kind of paper; try it and see.

There is a huge range of specialty papers from companies like Paper Direct and Queblo. These companies will send you a catalog, and for a small amount, a sample box of their papers. The range covers everything from normal output paper to preprinted sheets that can cost nearly twenty cents each. Most of these papers are aimed at people who use their lasers and inkjets for producing documents singly, or in only a few copies.

These documents are created in runs too short to print at a print shop; for example, a personalized brochure for a small consulting company. Describing the company's services in a letter would be too dull; instead, they are desktop published onto a preprinted double-sided sheet with three panels on each side, in typical brochure style. The sheets have an abstract, multicolor design, which is printed to the edge; to design and print this for one application would cost thousands. But if you do not mind the outside chance that the design will be recognized, you can put your text on the sheets and look like a million dollars.

Other types of paper include sheets with colored edges to make an eye-catching press release, papers with a color gradation across them, and heavy sheets with a perforated area so that the recipient can store name and address details in a Rolodex.

You'll Never Own the Best Printer for Your Mac

You will really appreciate the power of PostScript when you go to a service bureau with your first document on disk, and return with high-quality pages that put a laser to shame. The letters appear lighter and better-formed, shaded backgrounds are colored gray, instead of obviously looking like an area of dots, and photographs show an astounding amount of detail. This is as it should be, because the imagesetter used to create your pages costs around $50,000-$100,000.

Because of the high price of imagesetters, very few end-users have them. Yet thanks to PostScript, you do not need any extra hardware to take advantage of them. You probably will not need extra software either; so for about nine dollars a page, depending on the number of pages, you can get high resolution output.

It is very hard to make a case for *not* using imageset output. An eight-page newsletter, for instance, will cost well under a hundred dollars to imageset, yet the improvement in quality will be dramatic. The quality, in fact, will be identical to all the other printed pieces we see around us; if you use laser output for the print shop, the result will look shoddy.

What is sad is that many people are not aware of imagesetting, or feel they cannot justify the cost. But what are they producing? Often, it is a document designed to change an opinion; a sales brochure, or an environmental group's newsletter. Part of changing an opinion is the image you give with your printed materials. If you produce shoddy-looking work, it implies an unprofessional organization and that makes it harder to get the message across.

So how do you go about using a service bureau? The first thing is to shop around (look in the yellow pages under "Desktop Publishing"). Do not walk in the door with your first job and expect it to be ready half an hour later. You should be looking for a service bureau that is friendly and concerned about your output. There are some bureau clients who run dozens of pages a week; you may not be at that stage yet, but a good bureau will try to treat you as though you might.

Discuss the hardware and software that you are using; a good bureau will have had experience with most equipment and programs, and can probably give you hints and tips that will save time for both of you. What they will probably suggest is that you produce some sample pages so that any potential problems can be eradicated. Also, they will advise as to whether you should make a PostScript file or bring in the document saved in your page layout program format.

At this point you may have a nasty surprise if you have been buying fonts on the cheap. That low-cost "Garamond" may have been indistinguishable from the real thing on your laser, but "Garamundo" will be replaced by a genuine PostScript Garamond font to make it print on the service bureau's machine. What this means is that the knock-off may well have different widths than the equivalent characters in the real thing. That means that the text in your document may end up being a line extra; not a good thing to happen when it runs outside the margins. Even worse, that snazzy headline could suddenly run to a line plus a few characters when the last word needs to hyphenate to fit.

Of course, the service bureau has done nothing wrong. Now you have to redo the offending pages; you may even have to replace the offending font all the way through your document. Naturally you have to pay the cost to rerun the job. So, if you are taking work to a service bureau, always use fonts from major makers like Adobe and Monotype. If you bought your fonts in a huge package for a low cost, especially if the names are similar to well-known typefaces, you are asking for trouble.

Your service bureau may suggest that you send them your files by modem, and this will save you time. Always agree on the compression utility and always use it. There is no point in tying up the modem line for other users while your mammoth file downloads. Again, don't leave anything to chance. Arrange to send a test file to sort out any bugs.

If you submit your work by disk, you will need to follow some rules to make sure that everything runs smoothly. First of all, write your name and phone number on every disk you submit. There is nothing worse for the bureau than to have a disk with no identification and a single file called "newsletter." If you free-lance, imagine your shame when your client contacts you to say that the service bureau called them because theirs was the only name that appeared on the document.

While there is a great temptation to pick up the nearest floppy to save your work, don't let the disk out the door with a jumble of files on it. By the time the service bureau gets to work on it, you may be unsure of the name of the file you want processed; and if you make the wrong choice, you will get back another copy of the file you sent two weeks ago. So make sure there is only one file on the disk.

The service bureau needs a list of fonts that you have used in the document. Thankfully recent versions of page layout programs have decided to add features which tell you which fonts have been used. You should check this before you take the file to the bureau, because there may be fonts in the document that you have forgotten. Characters like a period and even a space have font information. By changing these characters to a font you have used elsewhere, you will save time at the service bureau.

Be certain you understand how your bureau defines a rush job. You will save yourself money if you can give them a longer turnaround time. It is also a good idea to specify exactly when you want your output. You may know what you mean when you say "as soon as possible," but your service bureau wants to prioritize jobs so that everybody gets their work on time. If your work is getting behind, and you realize that you will need a rush job on the document you will finish tomorrow morning, call the bureau and let them know ahead of time.

Finally, be certain that you submit all the files to make the job print. Some page layout programs do not store illustrations in the files, so make sure you have submitted everything the bureau will need. What it boils down to is setting things up ahead of time and taking your bureau's advice. Whatever problem you have, it is likely they have had it before and can fix it with a minimum of fuss.

One last potential problem is caused by the high resolution of the imagesetter. If you are used to laser output, you will have a preconceived notion of how wide a hairline rule is. What you may not realize is that the width of this rule varies according to the device it is imaged on and is the thinnest rule the printer can image. A laser will make the line one three hundredths of an inch; an imagesetter will make the line one twelve hundredths of an inch. This can affect your design because rules which looked great on the laser proof fade into nothing on the imageset output.

When you see your favorite fonts output on an imagesetter, you will notice that they are slightly lighter than on a laser. This is because lasers tend to make character strokes wider rather than cause them to drop out altogether. One useful byproduct of imagesetting is that you will notice that some fonts improve considerably when imageset. The strokes of the Optima font have a gentle flare which lasers are unable to reproduce. The ITC Eras font comes in two versions: high-resolution output has a five degree slope to the verticals and laser output has verticals that go straight up and down. Even that hoary old chestnut, Times Roman, looks far better imageset than laser printed.

How does an imagesetter work? By using a laser beam to etch out the shapes of letters. The characters are imaged on photographic paper or film, which has a resolution far greater than is necessary. Twelve hundred and seventy-five dots per inch is the minimum resolution for a Linotronic, the most popular imagesetter (hence the terms Lino output and Lino bureau). Some models image at 2540 and 3386 dots per inch. The paper or film is developed using the photographic method of developing and fixing (which stabilizes the image).

Twelve hundred and seventy-five dots per inch is sufficient for text work. It's virtually impossible to see any improvement at higher resolutions. Where the extra resolution of the higher-standard imagesetters pays off is in areas with gray screening and with photographs. Your service bureau will have sample pages output at each resolution, to give you an idea of the quality. Remember, of course, that what you see as imagesetter output will be degraded by the printing process; it may look alright in the bureau, but the printed pieces turn out to be not good enough. This logic applies to laser output as well; it will never look as good as the laser original.

Why use film instead of paper? When your print shop gets your camera-ready art, they shoot an image of it and use the resulting film to make a printing plate. By using film in the imagesetter, one stage is removed from the process, with some cost saving and improved image. However, you will have more trouble manipulating film if you have to add other images, such as camera-ready advertisements.

While service bureaus are generally helpful, they sometimes get behind through no fault of their own. It is possible to make PostScript illustrations that are so complex that they print slowly, if at all. Some people are so new to illustration programs that they submit work with errors covered by other parts of the drawing. If these errors are not deleted, they have to be rasterized along with the visible part of the illustration, so an apparently simple job can end up taking a long time. That is in addition to the faults mentioned above.

Other Output Devices

There are a few other output devices you will come across. They don't have a big sale, but for some people they can prove invaluable. The most common of these are label printers. These print low-resolution labels for addressing or labelling, and most can print a bar code as well. If you print dozens of address labels, this could be an option for you but these printers typically sell for about two-thirds the cost of an inkjet, which is far more versatile and can print labels on sheets.

If you are involved with CAD (Computer-Aided Design), you will have seen flatbed plotters that take the output from CAD programs. These will interface with the Mac, but the growth of printers with a large paper size which work by inkjet or laser may make plotters unneccessary. Another "printer" you might find is an add-on to the Mac which lets you cut letters and shapes in vinyl to make signs.

There is a whole group of output devices that let you take the output from an illustration or presentation software program and make a 35 mm slide. This is an alternative to putting special tranparency film through your laser or inkjet printer to get a large overhead projector slide. Sometimes a presentation may need to run unattended, or maybe the presenter may need to be some way from the projector and has to change slides by remote control. In both cases a 35mm slide projector is necessary. These devices are dealt with in more detail in the section on color printers.

There is a new type of hybrid printer/duplicator that is showing up in some large companies where printing is done in-house. Instead of printing pages on your laser, taking them to the copier, and then collating and binding the results, these machines do everything for you. An interface connects to your Mac; the results are as good as straightforward copying, but the speed of the machines makes it easy to produce short and medium runs of documents.

Color Printers

The fastest-changing and most complicated area of printing is in color printing. New products are introduced weekly, and many of them redefine the cost you have to pay for color printers. Yet the whole area is full of uncertainty. Many people ask two questions: Why should I be concerned with color? Why should I buy a color printer?

Why Should I Be Concerned with Color?

Many people think that color is extravagant. These people will be wondering what hit them in about two or three years' time when color becomes a part of almost every computer user's life, especially the desktop publishers.

What is happening now is that the makers of printers and other equipment are designing and selling products that reduce the price of color to such a degree that its widespread adoption is not a case of *if* so much as *when*. Within a few years the cost and ease of color will rival black and white.

The pressure from this is not just in the realms of the equipment that sits on your desk. Two developments that occur largely outside your home or business will make color much more affordable. The first of these is the color imagesetting systems such as Kodak's Prophecy and others. The second is the advent of the computer-controlled press, pioneered by PressTek and Heidelberg.

The Prophecy system lets you create full-color pages from photographs and slides without any special hardware or software; in fact, as long as you have a color monitor, you can use this system. Let's suppose you are producing a catalog. You have shots of the products which are expected to look exactly the same as the products themselves in that there can be no changes in hue (that is, the colors must match perfectly). You take your work to a Prophecy-equipped service bureau. They scan the photographs (or better still, slides) at high resolution. These scans would be far too large to fit into your program and your monitor could not show the detail. So you receive a second set of image files which have a 300-dots-per-inch resolution. You take these back to your computer and import them into a Quark or PageMaker file. This file holds the text of the catalog, and you place the images into the document. You can size them, scale them, and crop them to fit the publication.

In the meantime, the bureau has been color-correcting the scans. They check the color of the product against the color on their screen, which is calibrated against their output devices so that what they see is truly what they get. They may need to correct for skin tones if there is no need to show the exact color of the product, and if you need it, they can use a product like Adobe PhotoShop to manipulate the images. If you want, you can sit in on this process, but most people leave it to the expertise of the service bureau staff.

Now comes the magic. You take your PageMaker or Quark file to the service bureau. As your file is fed into the Prophecy system, the low-res scans you used are automatically replaced with the high-res scans, exactly sized, scaled and cropped to the dimensions that you gave them in your own computer. A proof print is produced if necessary, and then the pages are split into color separations ready for the print shop.

If you are used to single-color work, the average of two hundred dollars a page for this service may seem excessive, but to anyone who has worked with color, the price is a bargain. The exact cost will depend on how many photographs you have on a page and how much work each one needs.

One of the main barriers to cheap color printing has been the extra work color needs in the print shop. Because there have to be many adjustments to the press before a single page is produced, this extra time has added significantly to the cost; because a color image is made up of four separate images, each one of these has to have a press unit to itself and each color image has to be correctly inked and in exactly the same position on the page. Sometimes hundreds of test sheets need to be run off before the press operator is satisfied that all is well; then, with a touch of a button, the press produces thousands of copies an hour.

No matter how long or short the job, this process called "make-ready," has to be gone through. Naturally, the cost is passed on to the customer. If the job requires many thousands of copies, the cost of make-ready is an insignificant part of the price. But if the customer wants a run of a thousand, the make-ready charge pushes the cost per item up to uneconomical levels.

The computer-controlled press, developed by PressTek and manufactured by Hiedelberg, aims to cut down make-ready time. It achieves this by doing away with printing plates and using the computer to control the amount of ink. Instead of making a metal plate for each color, the image is laser-etched on a cylinder so that the alignment (or register) of the image is consistent on each press unit. By making the computer do the work, make-ready time is reduced to the degree that only a couple of dozen test sheets are required.

Although these presses cost over a million dollars and would crush your desk, they have important implications for computer users. The presses have been installed under a pilot program in quick-print shops where the majority of work is short run. While the pricing of color printing is still settling down, expect big savings on this work, especially if the job is for around a thousand copies.

What is especially important is that neither the Prophecy system nor the computer-controlled press are projected; they are available now, and at a price that does not prevent you from taking advantage of them. These are just the first of a flood of color-related products that will change the way that you think about color. If you feel that you can happily carry on producing the publications you already do in black and white, wait until an organization like yours starts producing a color newsletter or similar document. So, the point is to keep abreast of developments in color printing. You may not need to buy anything yet; but when the time comes, you will have the advantage over anyone who thought that it wasn't for them.

Why Buy a Color Printer?

Having realized that color is the coming thing, you may well be intent on running out to buy the latest and greatest in color printers. Don't. Surprisingly, a color printer has fewer uses than a black and white printer.

This may sound crazy until you think what you do with a black and white printer. You produce original work straight off the printer in its final form; a report, perhaps, or an overhead transparency. You produce work that is an original to be duplicated by a copy machine or sent to a print shop. Lastly, you use the printer as a proofing device to check that your work is OK before you send it to the service bureau.

Now look at the same applications with a color printer. Yes, you can make overheads and nice color work for reports. Yes, you can use it as a proofing device for a service bureau. But unless you can afford output from a color copier, there is not much use there. And if you send pages to a print shop, they'll scan them and separate the results. You would be better off sending them the program file on disk.

So you may well decide that you will output from the color printer at the service bureau, rather than spending thousands of dollars on your own machine. If you need to see *something* on paper, you could do no worse than to buy a cheap color inkjet for under a thousand dollars. The quality of output may not be as good as you would like, but the low equipment cost and low cost per copy may well decide the matter.

So How Do They Get Sixteen Million Colors from One Printer?

Color theory is complicated, but if you want to work in color you will need to understand all of it eventually. Much of the work on color has come from academic and scientific circles, or has been adopted from the traditional color prepress industry, where million-dollar machines were the norm, and highly-trained staff operated them. Do not be concerned if you find the whole business confusing.

You may wonder how we move from one color—black—to the sixteen million colors some printers can manage, without the whole business becoming incredibly complex. Do we need sixteen million inks? Luckily, the answer is no. Thanks to four-color printing we can reproduce most colors in the spectrum. Notice the word *most*; color printing is not as perfect as we would like it to be.

If you remember back to when you first got your hands on a set of paints, you will probably remember how two colors mixed together made another color. Red and yellow made orange, red and blue made purple, and blue and yellow made green. If you were wild, you mixed all the colors together to get a rather muddy brown. That pretty much explains the four-color principle; any color can be made up from a mix of three colors, but to get black it is best to have a black ink just for that purpose, rather than the dark brown which is the best three colors can manage. The printing industry uses the CMYK system, with *C*yan, *M*agenta, *Y*ellow, and Blac*k* inks. Your color monitor uses the RGB system; it has three color guns of *R*ed, *G*reen, and *B*lue, and gets a pretty nifty black by not aiming any light at that spot.

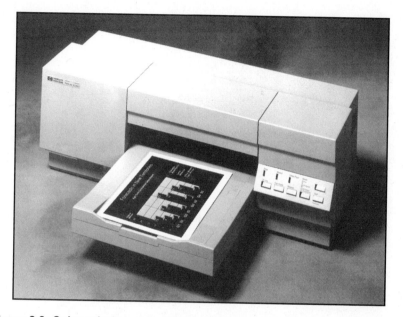

Figure 3.8: Color printing at an affordable price is the hallmark of the Hewlett-Packard PaintJet XL300. This ink-jet printer can reproduce over 16 million colors on plain paper. Depending on the illustration, print time can be from 1 1/2 to 6 minutes.

You may be a little concerned here, and you have every right to be, if you wonder how we can represent a color one way on the screen and another way on the printing press. Welcome to the world of WYSAWYG, or What You See Ain't What You Get. The two systems (or to give them their technical term, color *models*) don't show the same color exactly alike.

The RGB process in your monitor works by using a property of projected light: red, green, and blue light, shone on the same spot, give white light; red light and blue light give yellow; red light and green light give cyan. By varying the amount of light from each color gun, a wide range of colors can be produced. Just to make the situation muddier, this process is called additive color, while the CMYK process is called subtractive color. The reason for this is that when you mix all the colors in the CYMK process, you tend toward black, which is the condition where no light is reflected. With additive color, the more you add, the more the color tends toward white, where all light is reflected.

The CMYK and RGB are the two color models you will come across in your equipment, but in order to describe color more accurately, several other models have been developed. These other models are necessary so that color can be described without having to take into account the way it is produced; if you remember the discussion of PostScript earlier in this chapter, you will recall the advantages of a device-independent method, even if it does introduce an extra level of complexity.

In fact, PostScript Level 2 uses the CIE model. This has conversions to RGB and CMYK, and it means that color information travels with the color document file in a purely perceptual form; that is, without it being related to the way any device would produce the color. This is even more important when you realize that most devices cannot reproduce all colors; the range of colors a device can reproduce is called a color gamut.

Let's move away from this theme to talk about the ultimate arbiter of color— the human eye. After all, if we can't see it, there is no point in trying to print it. If you produce a range of values between black and white using 256 steps of gray, this is enough to show every shade that the human eye can distinguish. With color, we can distinguish the same 256 steps on each of the three colors, so we need to be able to reproduce 16.7 million colors. Because 256 steps can be described by eight bits on the computer, 16.7 million colors can be produced by three of these eight-bit steps, giving 24-bit color. Because 24-bit color covers every shade the eye can distinguish, it's often called true color, or photorealistic color.

Therefore, all we need in a color printer is the ability to accurately convert color information into a CMYK model, and reproduce it at 24-bit level. And while we are at it, at as high a resolution as possible. Of course, we also have the constraints of low initial cost and low cost per copy. You have probably guessed by now that printers like this do not exist—yet.

Every color printer is a series of compromises, with a variety of different methods being employed to get the color onto the page and to make up for the printer's deficiencies. Currently, new color printers and new printing methods are flooding on to the market, and the price for each type is constantly being redefined. While the color printer of your dreams becomes steadily more affordable, the best color reproduction comes from imagesetters, and we'll look at those later.

Spot Color and Process Color

There is an easy way to get into color which does not require lots of knowledge or expense. If you are doing a newsletter, for example, judicious use of color can make it look much more attractive. Maybe you will have a horizontal line across the top of a page in the second color (black is the first). Provided that your second color does not come too close to the rest of the text and graphics, this is an easy job for your print shop.

This type of work is called spot color. The color is the same shade throughout and does not mix with any other ink. You can define a spot color by using color systems like PANTONE, which is a collection of inks which every print shop has available. You have a swatch of colors and you pick your color from these. If all you want is some color contrast, you will probably be better off not being exact; it is easier and probably cheaper to specify "red" or "blue." This gives your print shop the freedom to use whatever inks they happen to have around; all you need to do is check that the actual color is near enough to what you had in mind.

PANTONE and similar systems shine when you want to create an image for your organization. You may decide that every printed piece you put out must have the company's logo in a particular color, and by specifying that color with PANTONE you will get a consistent result wherever the work is printed. Potential customers tend to collect printed pieces like brochures, and a common look gives a much more professional look for your organization.

The cost of spot color is low compared to four color or process color. It simply means that what you do requires another trip through the printing press. If you start trying to integrate a second color into the original text and graphics, problems of alignment arise. This means the print shop must check the print register, and there are usually more sheets to be discarded—all of which you pay for.

If you are prepared to take this a step further, you can ring the changes most effectively with tricks like using black on a screened color background, black on a solid color background, or white on a solid color background. However, some of these effects need careful control so that the ink of one color fits into the space left for it in another color. You will be talking to your print shop about knockouts, traps, and chokes, so check with them first before you incorporate these color effects into your publications.

Process color or four color work is done by separations. Most professional-level page layout programs have a basic color separation program built-in. These programs analyze the color at any given point and define it in percentages of cyan, magenta, yellow, and black. The next step is to make four images in one color which can be used to make the printing plates for each of the four process colors. Because the color of the ink on the press defines the print color, the image used for the plates is always in black.

You can also buy color separation software in a package by itself. These packages give more control to the operator, but also require more technical skill. Some of the programs allow you to link directly to high-end prepress systems. Most users still prefer to let the service bureau handle separations, but this may be another skill you have to master in the coming months.

Which Color Printer for You?

The volatile color printer market has nevertheless thrown up some guidemarks. From the method used to get the color on the paper, it is often possible to guess how good the result will be and what the cost is. There are lasers and inkjets here, but there are also thermal wax, phase-change, and dye sublimation models. In some categories, there may be only one or two examples.

Color inkjet printers are available at the bottom, lower-mid, and top price points. They work like a single-color machine, but they have three jets—one for each of the CYM colors. You can also fit a single black jet. The problem with the low-end inkjets is that they have no way of varying the amount of ink that falls on the page, so there is a very small range of colors available. Like other low-end color printers, inkjets get around this problem by dithering.

Dithering means taking an area of several pixels and putting in a pre-determined pattern of colored dots. For instance, to make a dark yellow, in every block of eight pixels five would be black and three yellow. Pink could be created by having four magenta pixels and four blank pixels (i.e., white pixels). This makes for a huge range of colors, but there is an obvious drawback. The blocks of pixels appear to clump and give a much poorer resolution than colors that change with every pixel. Low-cost inkjets also don't have very good color saturation, giving a washed-out look to your work, but if all you want is a rough indication of how the job will look, they could be for you. The price of under a thousand dollars in the stores may well be the thing that sways you.

If your budget goes over $50,000, you should be looking at the Iris SmartJet printer which has up to 256 levels of each color, and thus qualifies for photorealistic output. While the Iris has the same 300- to 400-dots-per-inch resolution as other inkjets, the fact that each pixel can change color independently has led some people to claim that it has an apparent resolution of 1600 dots per inch.

Canon, the copier manufacturer, also supplies the laser engine for Apple's LaserWriters and Hewlett-Packard's Laserjets. They also manufacture an inkjet copier that can interface with your Mac to provide a scanner and printer. The

CJ10 has up to 256 levels in each color, so image quality is high, and the price is only $6,000, plus the cost of the computer interface.

The current leader in the low-cost photorealism market is Hewlett-Packard's PaintJet XL300, which has a list price of $3,495. It qualifies by reason of its 256 color levels, giving twenty-four bit color at an incredibly low price. The XL300 has Mac and PC compatibility, and prints on plain paper as well as transparency material.

Like all color printers, inkjets should be judged not only on their specifications but also on the quality of output. The only true way to determine how good a printer can be is to see output from it, preferably of a color photograph. Another point to check is how much each page will cost in consumables. This can be from as little as fifteen cents to as much as five dollars a page. Inkjets generally have the lowest cost per page, but some models may require coated paper. The cheaper models do not have PostScript.

PostScript color printers can cost considerably more than low-cost inkjets. Thermal wax transfer printers use a large ribbon the size of your page and use heat to transfer the wax to the paper. The ribbon has a cyan, magenta, and yellow section; some models also have black. The saturation of the colors is much improved, but this only shows up problems with dithering. Like inkjets, each page takes about two minutes to produce. There are numerous thermal-wax printer manufacturers, with prices ranging from $5,000 to $10,000, and a page will cost you around fifty cents.

A cross between thermal-wax and inkjets, phase-change printers melt wax and spray it onto the page. This results in a slightly sharper image and a better rendition of red tones, but colors still are dithered. The image is produced in one pass, so the time per page is somewhat reduced from thermal wax printers. Because phase-change printers can print onto plain paper, their cost per page is around twenty-five cents. You will pay from $5,000 to $10,000 for a printer of this kind.

If you have over $10,000, you can look at dye-sublimation printers. These use a heating element to change dye from solid to gas when heated. The great advantage of this kind of printer is that the amount of heat can be controlled in 256-step increments to give photorealistic output. The cost per page is around five dollars and printing times are slow because the cost of the dye is high and the printer must use special paper.

Color laser printers are usually too expensive for individuals, yet there are plenty of them around. They are found in copy centers: the most common is the Canon CLC 500. This can be fitted with a computer interface. The copy shop pays twenty-five cents a copy in consumables, and offers printing up to 11×17 inches. The quality of these machines is exceedingly high and can be good enough to duplicate color photographs.

No book chapter or magazine article can accurately describe what is available on the color printer market. The Canon CJ10 and the Hewlett-Packard XL300 were introduced within a month of each other while this book was being written. No doubt there will be other low-cost inkjet printers, and it may be that thermal wax, phase-change, and dye-sublimation printers will disappear, unable to compete. Perhaps there is a new, low-cost version of one or more of these technologies on its way. Whatever happens, there is always a risk that the expensive printer you just bought will be sadly outdated a few weeks after you buy it. Stay tuned.

Film Recorders

We have already identified the laser and inkjet printer as suitable for producing letter-size transparencies for presentations with an overhead projector. But if you are doing presentations with 35 mm slides, you have the option of using remote control, photographs, and other slick touches. You can even set up a self-running presentation for trade shows. No wonder people prefer the smaller sized slides.

Getting the slides produced is another matter. Most presentation software packages have a link with a national slide-producing service; you modem the file to the company, and an overnight delivery service delivers the slides the next day. Alternatively, you can use a local service the same way you would use a service bureau; you take or modem the file to them, and either collect the slides or have them delivered.

For many people this is fast enough, but the fact remains that once the file leaves your Mac you have no chance to change anything. It is possible that when you get the slides back there may be something wrong with them; perhaps a typo, or a mistake in the figures. For these reasons companies are investing in their own film recorder to produce slides as soon as possible.

Film recorders basically consist of a box with a monitor screen at one end and a camera at the other. The associated electronics color separate the image, then expose each separation through a colored filter onto the same slide. This means that the monitor can be black-and-white, which saves money and avoids complications from having multiple color guns.

Because film is such a high-quality medium for recording images, the film recorder has to have a higher color resolution than most other devices. Twenty-four-bit color is adequate for screens and imagesetting, but the eye can detect steps in a color blend, even at this resolution. In a presentation, we can be twelve feet away from an eight-foot high image; the equivalent in normal reading distances would be a sixteen-inch square. For this reason, film recorders use 33-bit color, so that there are 2,048 levels of color which provide for smooth transitions.

To get the sharpest image on a slide, the exposure should be as long as possible. Because there are four exposures per slide, the time to image each one is measured in minutes, not seconds or fractions of a second. It is also possible to control the resolution of the monitor which is measured in the number of horizontal pixels. Thus a 4K resolution means that the monitor is set to display 4,096 by 2,730 pixels. The higher the resolution, the sharper the slide, and many recorders have 2, 4, and even 8K settings. However, the higher the monitor resolution, the longer the time to generate the slide.

You can load the camera with standard 35 mm slide film, in which case you may process it yourself or get it processed nearby. Another option is to use instant slide film, made by Polaroid. Using this film gives you slides in a matter of a few minutes.

Manufacturers of film recorders point to the cost of slide film production from a modemed file—typically, $10 to $12 per slide, with a $50 minimum order—and claim that a company producing ten slides a week can save money buying a slide recorder. That's in addition to the time savings and the possible security risk of sending confidential company information out of the business.

Color and Your Service Bureau

The major trend in service bureaus in the last two or three years has been their ability to produce color work that rivals traditional prepress houses. While the newcomer may find dealing with a color service bureau confusing and inexact, the fact remains that just a few years ago traditional prepress, with its expensive equipment and skilled staff, would have priced these jobs out of the designer's reach. Currently, service bureaus are trying to deal with work by designers using programs they themselves don't understand, and bureau staff are trying to cope with new equipment and software all the time. Because color prepress is on the "bleeding edge" of computer technology, the pioneers of this process can't expect a smooth ride. What they can expect is significantly lower prices than at any time in the history of color prepress.

This isn't to say that your work will not print. What you should be prepared for is the possiblity that there could be complications. You should definitely not expect an instant turnaround. You should take into account the instructions for dealing with a service bureau earlier in this chapter, but now it is even more vital to get the bureau involved in your plans as soon as possible. This is because the bureau is aware of ways that a badly set up illustration can take far too long to image. Your bureau can give you useful tips on exactly how to set up a blend, for instance, so that the job will take far less time than a badly-composed version that looks identical.

The problem is aggravated by the fact that the equipment used by the Mac designer is in some ways primitive compared to that used in the service bureau.

Your monitor may not give a very accurate rendering of a color; your printer almost certainly won't. A page of text sent to a service bureau will be enhanced compared to laser output; but a color illustration may appear in a different color to that which the designer intended, and this could ruin an illustration.

So visit your service bureau as soon as possible; get them to explain things to you, and don't be afraid to ask for clarification of anything you do not understand. Far better to appear a little uneducated at this point, rather than when you are facing a bill for imagesetting that turned out nothing like you intended it to be. You will be told a lot; some of it will be bad news about problems you did not know existed, but at least you will be aware.

What are the complications in color imagesetting? Most of them occur because you are printing the same subject in four colors on the same sheet. There are many practices in single-color printing that are impossible in four-color print work. There is also the obvious problem of getting the color right, and there are problems because of the large size of files involved. Many of these problems are the service bureau's responsibilty, but some of them will have to be fixed by you.

One problem with color files is their bulk. There are ways of compressing files like the JPEG method, but many people dealing with color end up with files that are far too large to be easily moved by floppy. If your files reach this kind of size, you should be looking at the large removable hard disks like those made by SyQuest or Bernoulli. These hold either 45 or 90 megabytes of data. Obviously, you will need to be compatible with your service bureau's system, so this is another point to ask them.

First, let's look at the progress of work that you submit to the service bureau. If there are any photographs or nonelectronic artwork, the bureau will scan them using a drum scanner. This typically has a resolution of around twelve hundred dots per inch (although some scanners can operate at four thousand dots per inch and more), and can take several minutes for one scan.

This scanner, like all the equipment in a color service bureau, is color-calibrated. Calibration is essential in the bureau so that output is predictable. Sensors are put in front of monitors, output is compared to input, and all the devices are adjusted until everything matches. This calibration is the main reason why service bureaus will always reproduce better results than individual designers, but look for calibration to be introduced to more and more Mac peripherals.

The computer workstations in a bureau use very high-power machines. This is where you will find computers like the Mac Quadras and Fx, although some bureaus get even more power by using UNIX workstations like Sun computers. The monitors are large, and often the room has no windows, so that daylight won't affect the operator's color manipulation.

If you have entrusted your color separations to the bureau, they will work on them here. Color separations are not the automatic operation they might seem to be. A skilled operator can improve the contrast and definition of a photograph, and may suggest ways that specialized programs like Adobe Photoshop can improve the process further. At this point, a proof print may be necessary to check that all is well.

Finally, the separations are sent to the imagesetters. The registration of each pass must be perfect, so imagesetters for color have a precision transfer system to move the film in front of the laser. The margin of error is less than one hundredth of an inch. The old methods of running film from a roll to a takeup spool have given way to laying film on the surface of a drum.

Then the film is developed in a deep tank system. This is to ensure that each part of the film gets exactly the same amount of development so that there are no unwanted changes in color. Just adjusting the temperature and composition of the chemicals can affect the color image here. Then the film is yours to take to the print shop.

Much effort has been expended on what seems to the newcomer to be an abstruse subject—dot screens. When a solid area of a color is printed, it is made up of four screens, one of each process color, of varying density. These screens are made up of rows of dots, and they are normally invisible to the naked eye. The angles of the rows of dots are varied for each color and unless this is carried out with precision, the lines of dots interact causing moire patterns. These are clearly visible and look something like a dithered cross-hatch pattern. There have been several attempts to provide the definitive set of screen angles, mainly led by Adobe. Their newest technology has been incorporated into PostScript level 2, and it is hoped that from now on problems of moire will have been overcome.

Making Your Printer Choice

When the Apple Macintosh was introduced, it was a revolutionary happening in the computer world. Whatever computer you were planning to buy, you had to take the Mac into account. Similarly, the arrival of the Mac Classic was a revolution of another kind. This signalled Apple's intention to stop charging premium prices for Macs and let them compete on price.

Mainly, though, the computer world has become evolutionary. We know that next year's computers will offer more power for less outlay than this year's; and it is almost possible to predict by how much. In fact, people's expectations increase with the increased power; some classes of Mac user will always be looking at machines that cost around $2,500, for instance.

In the world of printers, some of it is evolutionary and some is revolutionary. In 1991 photorealistic color printers cost $15,000 for one-hundred-and-fifty-dots-per-inch models; a three-hundred-dots-per-inch model cost $45,000. By early 1992, there were a few three-hundred-dots-per-inch models at $15,000-$20,000, and two manufacturers brought out models at $10,000. Then, less than a month later, the Canon CJ10 scanner/printer/copier was released at $6,000, and within a month or so, the Hewlett-Packard PaintJet XL300 was announced at $3,495. The 1992 product cost eight percent of the 1991 product.

This revolutionary drop in prices—like real revolutions—has winners and losers. The winners are the people who buy the product at the new low price; the losers have an expensive piece of machinery that has a resale value nowhere near the cost they paid for it. The 1991 model may have some advantages over the newer model, but hardly enough to justify its high price. When you come to select your printer you should be aware of possible changes in the market. It may be that we've seen the end of color printer price drops—or maybe there are competing technologies that will offer better printers at the same price.

So with that warning, let's look at the choices for different budgets. At the bottom end of the market, Apple's StyleWriter and the Hewlett-Packard DeskWriter are the two main choices. They will cost you under $400, print a reasonable page quietly and slowly. With Adobe Type Manager or the TrueType manager in System 7 in your Mac, you will produce text and simple graphics at about a page every couple of minutes. New printers that let you use large paper (up to seventeen by twenty-two inches) have come onto the market at a fully configured price of around two thousand dollars. The prices on the smaller machines fall steadily, but the big price drops are probably gone.

The same is true for lasers, at least in the bottom and mid-range of the market. You will pick up a basic model for under a thousand dollars; PostScript compatibility costs a little more. The cheapest printers give you a page every fifteen seconds; the mid-range, eight pages a minute; and some of the dearer models print ten or sixteen pages a minute. Of course, that is the rated speed; expect about sixty percent of this performance on real-world jobs.

One trend you will see more of is resolution enhancement in one form or another. You will either be offered "apparent" six hundred dots per inch or the real thing, if you are prepared to pay a little more. If some printer manufacturers don't offer this feature, they will do so shortly. There also are some printer manufacturers, like Apple, who offer enhanced photographic reproduction; look for this feature to become more common.

What do you get from a laser that you do not get from an inkjet? Faster performance, a slightly better image, and you give it less attention. If you produce fifty pages every business day, you will only have to change the toner cartridge two or three times a year.

A trend that will probably become much more important is the add-in card for speedy, high-resolution PostScript printing. These cards fit in your Mac (if it can accept cards) and add PostScript capability, six-hundred-dots-per-inch resolution, and high-speed printing, typically at the rated speed of your printer. These cards use the Mac's processor and work with specific laser printer models. Expect to see them at under a thousand dollars.

The higher end of the laser printer market is still volatile. Because the cost of an AppleTalk card is a small proportion of the total cost, and because many of these printers will be used in a mixed Mac/PC environment, just about every higher-end printer is available for the Mac. Many of these machines will be connected to a network. Because the market is large and growing, expect significant improvements in the price/performance ratio as companies strive to win market share. Currently, the $3,000 and up range has plenty of machines with multiple paper trays, speeds of up to sixteen pages a minute, and the ability to print on both sides of the paper. Like all sections of the laser market, there are plenty of companies involved.

As to the color printers, the situation is changing every day. There appears to be no sign yet to show that the market is stabilizing. At the bottom end, the only current contender is the Hewlett-Packard PaintJet, which produces basic color pages, with dithering, at the rate of one every two or three minutes. It will cost you under eight hundred dollars. If the $3,495 Hewlett-Packard PaintJet XL300 lives up to its promise, then the rest of the color offerings may well be irrelevant. But if there are shortcomings in this model (and there are no signs of that yet), then the next step up is the group of machines in the $5,000 to $10,000 range; the Tektonix Phaser models have made news for their low cost. You may have special needs like wanting to print on large sheets of paper, and only a model from this price range will satisfy you.

Imageset output is criminally underused. Only total poverty should prevent you from imagesetting anything that might affect people's opinion of your organization. It may be complex, but with a little help from your friends at the bureau you will get results that will make you smile.

In fact, whatever printer or printing method you use to produce your Mac's output, there is no mistaking the thrill when you see that first page roll off the press. There is nothing to beat it.

An Overview of Graphics Technologies

The Macintosh started the revolution in personal computer graphics. It's true that computers had been harnessed for graphics applications long before the Macintosh debuted (the first computer graphics applications were demonstrated in the early 1960s); however, it was the Mac that moved this capability out of the realm of expensive mainframes and monster workstations and onto the desks of people like you and me. Since then, the graphics powers of the Macintosh have been used in publishing, in scientific research, and even in motion pictures. For many such applications the Macintosh is considered the premier graphics production tool.

In this chapter, we are going to take a close look at graphics on the Macintosh. We will start with an examination of how computers in general work with graphics images. We will discuss the three fundamental ways that image data are stored: as *text*, as *rasters*, and as *vectors*. After defining and explaining each of these three *imaging models*, we'll talk about the advantages and limitations of each. From there, we'll move on to a discussion of system-level support software used to create graphics images. After a side trip through the realm of fonts (they are among the most important graphics developments of the last 10 years), we'll take a look at the kinds of graphics software available: the *imaging models* they use, the *system support software* they rely on, the *file formats* they employ, and the ways in which they *optimize the storing* of graphics images.

How Computers Work with Graphics

At a fundamental level of operation, computers (the Macintosh included) do not work with image data *per se*; rather, they manipulate numbers according to the rules of arithmetic and logic. Thus, all the graphics operations possible with a modern computer are built-up out of thousands of additions, subtractions, multiplications, divisions, and comparisons. In addition, computers don't work with numbers (or, in computerese, *data*) quite like you and I do. Instead of the decimal format (using the digits "0" through "9") that we commonly use, computers use *binary code* to store and work with data.

Binary Code and Working with Text

A single binary digit, or *bit*, represents one of two possibilities: "on" or "off," "yes" or "no," "1" or "0." Clearly we want to work with bigger numbers than that. Larger numbers are represented by sequences of ones and zeroes. Each position in such a sequence has a value twice that of its predecessor. For example, the number 5 is represented by the binary sequence 101 $(1 \times 2^2 + 0 \times 2^1 + 1 \times 2^0)$. Using this scheme, any number that can be represented by the ten decimal digits can be represented using the two binary digits.

So much for numbers. But suppose we want to work with characters, what then? Since, ultimately, computers only work with numbers, we need some sort of code that assigns a unique number value to each character we want to use. The number of bits we use to represent each character depends on the total number of characters we want to use: to represent 256 different characters, we must use 8 binary digits, representing the binary numbers 0000000 through 11111111 (0 through 255 in decimal notation).

Such combinations of binary bits, or *bytes*, are used in a now-standard coding scheme for all the characters you can enter from the keyboard. By convention, this *ASCII code* (American Standard Code for Information Interchange) assigns the most commonly used characters into a 7-bit byte. For example, in standard-ASCII the values 32 to 127 (more properly, the values 0100000 through 1111111 in binary notation) are used for letters and numbers. Any personal computer can read and interpret a file made of these 7-bit ASCII character assignments. We call such a file a *text file*.

Seven-bit, or *lower ASCII* was a holdover from the days of CP/M (Control Program for Microprocessors). This was a 7-bit operating system from Digital Research that predates Microsoft DOS. However, the number of characters possible with seven bits was not enough, so with the introduction of more modern operating systems an 8th bit was added to ASCII. That doubled the number of characters available. These additional characters are called *upper-* or *extended-ASCII*. The new characters are not standard between computer systems, making it a bit of a problem to translate eight-bit ASCII text files from one computer system to another. On the Macintosh, the extra characters are used for special symbols, particularly ones useful in representing foreign languages. Although most of the extended characters are standard, you'll find some differences between fonts (more on fonts in a bit).

Keyfinder, one of Symantec's Norton Utilities for the Macintosh, can be used to show the ASCII value of any character you can enter from the keyboard. The value is given in decimal, hex, and octal notation. Hex and octal are based on 16 and 8 respectively. They are used by programmers as a convenient shorthand for representing binary numbers; it takes only two hex digits to represent the ASCII value of a character.

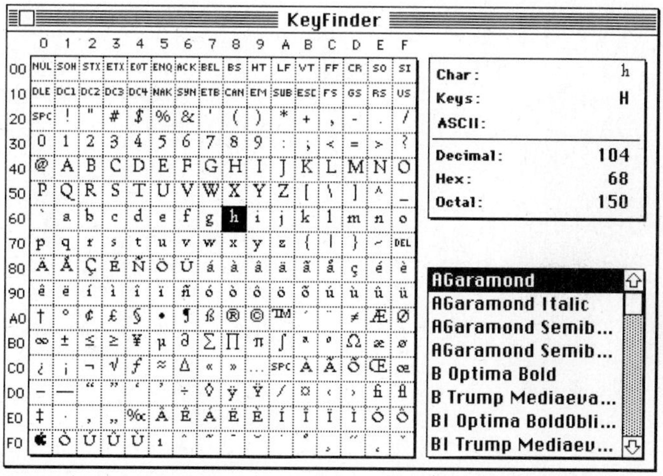

Figure 4.1: The Keyfinder window set to show ASCII values. The decimal code for the small letter "h" in the Adobe Garamond font is "104."

You can see how the strings of numbers within a computer can be used to represent letters and numerals. But what if we want to draw pictures? Some computer systems used (in fact, still use) characters to do just that. Some versions of ASCII assign many of the extended ASCII codes to special picture-drawing characters. When assembled in order on a grid, these characters can be used to draw very simple graphics such as squares and rectangles. Actually, you don't have to use special characters to draw pictures. This writer remembers taking a tour of a university computing center back in the late 1960s. Their powerful mainframe computer (32K of RAM, 1MB of disk storage) spit out a calendar, topped by a picture of the Peanuts' character, Snoopy, on his dog house. Looking closely, you could see that Snoopy was composed of row after row of the letters S N O P and Y, with some blank spaces in strategic spots. Was this calendar simply a curiosity of another, simpler era? Not really. In fact, the principles underlying the structure of the Snoopy calendar are used by just about every modern computer graphics system, including that of the Apple Macintosh. How can this be? In the next section we'll find out.

Representing Graphics with Numbers: Introducing the Bit Map

Let's consider a simpler example of the Snoopy computer graphic described above. How might we go about representing a square using only the binary digits 1 and 0? Supposing we confine ourselves to a grid, we could "draw" such a square using 1's for the lines in the square itself, and 0's for the blank spaces. Like so:

```
0000000000000000
0000111111110000
0000100000010000
0000100000010000
0000111111110000
0000000000000000
```

Figure 4.2: Drawing a "square" using ones and zeroes.

The above square is sort of difficult to see, isn't it? It would be easier if the blank spaces represented by zeroes really were blank, wouldn't it? Then we'd have this:

```
11111111
1        1
1        1
11111111
```

Figure 4.3: Drawing a "square" using ones and zeroes; the zeroes left blank.

Better, but it could still be better. Suppose we use dots instead of ones? That way, we can use the same number of dots across as we do down, forming a better square. The graphic becomes:

Figure 4.4: A square of ones and zeroes: the zeroes blank, the ones turned into dots.

With some modifications, this is exactly the process used to create Macintosh computer graphics. The simplest graphics files consists of strings of ones and zeroes that are mapped onto the screen by a rule that says "zeroes mean blanks and ones mean dots." When we say "mapped," we mean that each one or zero corresponds to a certain exact position on the screen. The file used to generate such a graphic is called a *bit map*. Graphics generated via bit maps are sometimes called *raster* graphics.

Why are bit maps sometimes referred to as raster images? Because the images they create are built up out of horizontal lines of pixels; these lines are called *rasters*. The same process is used by your video display, or by your TV set, for that matter. In a CRT (cathode ray tube) monitor the electron beam is swept across the inner surface of your screen, turning on when a pixel is required to be lit, and off when a pixel is required to be dark. A bit map in your computer is used to control the electron beam, determining which pixels are on, which are off, and what colors they all have.

You could think of the electron beam actually "painting" the image on the inside of your display, according to instructions from the bit map. Each line swept out by the electron beam is a raster. When one raster has been painted, the beam returns to the opposite edge of the screen and begins sweeping out the next one immediately below the first. The rasters are "stacked up" to form the complete image.

The binary digits in a bit map describe the attributes of each individual piece of the rasters in an image. (In the above example, the only attributes that exist are "blank" and "dot.") We call these "image pieces" *picture elements* or *pixels*. Each pixel is a single dot on the printed page or on your computer screen. (Look closely at your screen or at a newspaper photograph to see such dots.) On most Macintoshes, there are 72 pixels per inch. (Other values such as 55ppi and 87ppi are possible.) The size of a Macintosh pixel is roughly equal to a single printers point, the smallest vertical measurement commonly used in traditional publishing. The size of a pixel defines the *resolution* of your bit map. The smaller the pixel, the higher the resolution; however, more data is needed to describe the picture.

Bit map images are *resolution dependent*; that is, the data describing a bit map has an intrinsic pixel size. If you save bit mapped data at the typical Macintosh resolution of 72 dots per inch (dpi, same as ppi) and try to print on a 300 dpi laser printer, you will often see large chunky pixels (a phenomenon called *image degradation*). Many graphics programs will interpolate data and smooth the image somewhat. Going the other way, compressing a bit map to a lower resolution generally gives an image enhancement.

If our computer hardware can handle it, we don't have to limit ourselves to a single bit per pixel. (See the chapter on Monitors for more information about the relevant hardware.) On a color Macintosh, several numbers are used to represent the intensity of the color components of each pixel as well. The amount of information—how many numbers—used to describe each pixel's brightness and color is referred to as the *depth* of an image. The most common pixel depths on a Macintosh are 1, 8, and 24 bits. Compact Macintoshes are limited to a single bit per pixel, giving strictly black-and-white images; the newest Macs as well as Macs with special hardware can handle 24 bits per pixel, making realistic color images possible.

Raster versus Vector Graphics

All graphics programs ultimately generate bit maps. The bit maps so generated are used by your computer to create the ultimate screen image. We have to ask ourselves, "Are bit maps the most efficient way to represent an image within a computer?" Not necessarily. Consider a two-inch diameter circle. Using the Mac, we need a lot of numbers to complete such a circle's bit map. Because there are 72 pixels per inch and we need two inches, we need 144 bits in each raster, and 144 rasters. This gives 144 x 144 = 20736 bits, only a few of which are actually "on."

You may remember from your high school algebra, however, that a circle on a grid (such as a bit map) can be represented by a simple formula. The formula is $X^2 + Y^2 = r^2$, where X and Y are the coordinates of each point on the circle's circumference, and r is the circle's radius. Using such a formula, we only need four numbers to represent the circle: two for the location of its origin (center), one for its radius (half the diameter), and one for the thickness of the line around it. Even using sixteen bits (two bytes) for each number, we only need 64 bits to describe the circle, rather than 20,000. The same 64 bits could be used to describe a circle of any size, up to the largest one that would fit on the monitor. The bit map for such a large circle would be huge.

Graphics that rely on descriptive formulas such as the one described above are sometimes called *vector* graphics. In this sense, a vector is just an ordered collection of numbers. For example, (0,0,72,1) is a vector. We could interpret the vector as "horizontal position of circle origin," "vertical position of circle origin," "size of circle radius in pixels," and "width of circle boundary in pixels." There are, of course, all kinds of shapes that can be specified using mathematical formulas. A vector graphics system generally has an entire repertoire of such shapes: circles, ellipses, rectangles, complex curves, and so on. We refer to the different entities that a vector system can draw as objects. For this reason, vector systems are more commonly called *object-oriented* graphics systems.

Object-oriented images are built up out of geometric parts such as lines, circles, polygons, and other curves. Lines have end points, each of which may be described by a vector. Lines may also have strokes or widths which could contain fill patterns. These are also specified by vectors. (Fills are created by a mathematical algorithm for dot placement.) It's up to the program creating the object to determine which parts of the vector correspond to the different parts of an object-oriented circle, or to any such graphic.

Even more complex shapes can be described with vectors. Some techniques use the so-called Bézier curves. These are nonuniform curves that have both endpoints and inflection points; the inflection points describe how the curves twist. All the points in such a curve are specified with vector. Images may also be filled in a more complex way using halftones; these are screened patterns of dots used to simulate smooth grays. (The term "screen" is a holdover from commercial printing. Formerly, photographs intended for publication were re-shot through a uniformly spaced wire screen to yield an image made of dots. Although the dots could be of different sizes, their centers were evenly spaced. You can see halftones in any image in a newspaper: take a low-powered magnifying glass to one of the lighter shades in the picture to get a good look at the halftone screen.)

Object-oriented graphics have a number of advantages compared with raster graphics. For one thing, object-oriented graphics can also be sized or scaled perfectly without distortion or loss of resolution because its data description is conceptual. Thus, a circle with a given fill and bounding pattern can be made any size without changing the size of the pattern or the width of the line bounding it. This property makes vector graphics ideal for technical illustration like CAD/CAM where precision is required.

Vector graphics also has the property of being *device independent*: the quality of the image displayed is as good as the given device and its driver software can make it, using the original description. Remember that we said a 72dpi circle that looks good on your Mac monitor will appear chunky when printed on a laser printer. An object-oriented circle made of 72 dpi pixels on a monitor can be constructed of 300 dpi pixels on a laser printer, appearing smooth in the process.

One other feature clearly differentiates raster images from vector images. A raster image is formed in a single two-dimensional plane with each pixel having a single value or description. You can simulate the third dimension by shading objects, just as is done by many programs to create the illusions of buttons on your screen. But the description of a bit map has no underlying structure; it is just a 2-D matrix of numerical values. So if you put something "on top of" a part of a bit map, the region underneath is lost. Vector objects, on the other hand, can retain their mathematical identity whether they are displayed or not. In a vector or object representation, layers of objects are created and their appearance depends on whether anything is "in front" or "on top" of them. Objects in a layer behind another can even show through if the object on top is somewhat transparent.

This difference in the dimensionality of raster and vector images has consequences in the way graphic images are handled. When you select an area in a bit mapped program, say an image or a painted program, and move that selection, you expose a blank canvas. Most paint or image programs let you define a background color, so that when you move your selection it's the background color that shows through. By contrast, when you select an object in a draw program, that entire object is defined and selected. Select a partially hidden circle; if you move it so that no other object is on top of it, the entire circle will show through. It doesn't matter what layer that circle was created in. Typically, draw programs offer commands that let you manipulate object layers, such as Send To Back, Bring Forward, etc.

Since vector (object-oriented) graphics are compactly described by sets of mathematical instructions, they can be conveniently and compactly represented—most of the time. Often, the resulting descriptions take the form of simple text files. The compact descriptions resulting mean that object-oriented or vector graphics files don't need much space. Simple drawings can be only a few KB in size, whereas complex bit map images are normally in the 100KB range depending on the complexity.

Vector graphics have a lot of advantages: small file sizes and device independence among them. You might think that, given these advantages, vector graphics is the way to go for all image types. That isn't necessarily so. For example, if you attempt to image a natural photographic image with a vector representation, the changes in shading, complex shapes, and other features in that image would create a description that would soon choke your computer with computations. The files created would also be enormous.

Because of the limitations inherent in each kind of graphics setup—raster versus object-oriented—the best strategy would seem to incorporate both into one ultimate graphics system. This is just what the Macintosh does. The basic system software of the Macintosh is designed to take full advantage of both raster and vector graphics. It uses a special computer programming language (a special code for writing instructions to tell a computer what to do) that draws graphics on the Mac screen, and can also be made to image graphics on a printer. There are other such programming languages in addition to the one used internally by the Macintosh, yet only one other is important to Macintosh graphics. We'll talk about both languages in the next section, after we discuss the fundamentals of such graphics programming languages.

Doing the Drawing: Page Description Languages

The description of raster and vector graphics you have just read paints only the broad outlines of both types of graphic systems. It should be clear that, as far as the details are concerned, there are any number of ways of implementing a graphics system in hardware and software. For a number of reasons, however, we do not want to leave the job of deciding all the details up to every software manufacturer who wants to sell a graphics program. For one thing, there would be a lot of wasted effort as each team of designers had to "reinvent the wheel." For another thing, since each solution is bound to be different, the graphics files created by one such graphics application are not likely to be useable by others. This is, more or less, exactly what happened with the IBM PC. The resulting mess only really began to be straightened out about the time the Windows operating environment appeared on the scene.

The makers of the Macintosh avoided this problem and did their software developers a favor. The fundamental operating software of the Macintosh (its *system* software) contains a wide range of basic commands that can be used to draw graphics on the Mac screen. Taken together, these commands constitute a fundmental graphics programming language. Because this language is used to create a single screen image or (in the case of certain printers including the ImageWriter and the StyleWriter) an entire printed page, we consider it to be an example of a *page description language*.

A page description language (PDL) is a graphics programming language that specifies the output of text, objects, and images on a page in a device-independent set of commands. There are several important PDLs in use, PostScript is probably the best known. Another PDL called PCL (for Printer Control Language) is used in the Hewlett-Packard LaserJet series, which are mainly used by IBM PCs although there are a few hooked up to Macs. The PDL we referred to in the first part of this section is the QuickDraw language, which as we say is built into the operating system of Macintosh computers. In some cases a PDL can also be used as the source of video imaging commands in addition to being used to drive printers. QuickDraw is used for that purpose on the Macintosh. As you might expect, having a unified imaging language for both display and output has compelling advantages, although not all Macintosh setups offer this capability, as we will see. In particular, most laser printers are based on PostScript, rather than QuickDraw. Apple tried to address this shortcoming with the introduction of TrueType (a printer-supporting part of QuickDraw). Apple is now moving to incorporate features of PostScript into QuickDraw. More on this later on. Whether it's PostScript, QuickDraw, or something else, a typical PDL has commands that:

- Display and modify type. "Type" is a printer's term referring to different styles of printed or displayed characters. Since vector descriptions of text are required, PDLs use outline or stroke representations for characters. The process by which characters are converted from outlines to bit maps is an essential ingredient of a PDL. The ability to work with a wide range of type styles (fonts, in Macintosh parlance) was one of the things that set the Mac—and its QuickDraw operating software—apart right from the beginning.

- Create objects. Commands called graphics primitives describe lines, fills, etc.

- Group objects. PDLs let you manipulate sets of objects in logical layers.

- Describe color values or gray scales. A PDL also contains algorithms for creating the patterns used by a printer to simulate halftones. These algorithms are proprietary and patented.

- Provide Special features. The are many additional features built into PDLs like file compression, special transformation, and other graphics operators.

Page description languages are among the most complex programming languages used in modern computing. Whereas procedural programming languages might use 50 major commands, a PDL like PostScript contains over 250 commonly used commands.

QuickDraw may be at the heart of the Macintosh, but in many ways it isn't the important PDL in Macdom. That honor belongs to PostScript, the PDL first introduced to the public in the Apple LaserWriter in 1985, that went on to revolutionize the industry and helped launch desktop publishing to boot. It is worth talking about in more detail.

PostScript

The PostScript page description language was introduced by Adobe Systems (Mt. View, CA) in the early 1980s. In 1985 it became the key component in the Macintosh desktop publishing system. It was the glue that connected page layout programs like Aldus PageMaker, a Macintosh, the LaserWriter, and a Linotronic image setter together to create medium quality (then high quality) output. In the intervening years it has become the *de facto* industry standard, appearing on most computer platforms, in dozens of printers, and in many other output devices.

PostScript is still undergoing revision. In 1991, Adobe released PostScript Level 2 to address deficiencies in the way the language treats complex half-tones and color images. PostScript Level 2 printers have just begun to appear in the marketplace. Level 2 is a *superset* of the original PostScript, meaning that in addition to all the original commands, it adds speed enhancement for work with digital images, new composite fonts (called Multiple Masters), data compression routines (ways to squeeze large files into small storage spaces), improved memory management, forms and halftone caching, better halftone screening algorithms, device-independent color, and support for printer-specific features like mixed print jobs and sorters, and more.

PostScript, Level 1 or Level 2, is probably the richest and most complete PDL available. It is noted for one of the largest electronic type libraries available, and for its advanced routines for converting type outlines to bit maps.

Adobe uses fonts based on Bézier curves, and encrypts the fonts with *hints* (see the section on Fonts in this chapter) so that rasterization is improved in small type sizes (generally below 12 points in size). Adobe is also pioneering the use of Multiple Master fonts, where a single font description allows you to construct fonts of different weights and styles. That is, using a single description you could construct condensed, normal, and bolded versions of the font. This technology allows type to be *optically scaled*, something that was done before digital typesetting. With optical scaling, a character's shape is altered based on its size. This makes type more readable at smaller sizes. The first two Multiple Master fonts—Myriad and Minion—ship in both the Roman and Italic forms. They were scheduled to be released in mid-1992.

The implementation of variable weight fonts has opened up the possibility of a universal cross-platform (i.e., between computer systems, like from Mac to PC and back) electronic document file format based on PostScript. When you open a document created by another program or computer, unless you have the same set of fonts and the same PDL, your line and page breaks will not be preserved. By using the *font metrics* (specifications for how to compose text in the font, more on this later) from the original font, a program using Multiple Masters can instead construct a new set of fonts. These will replace the originals, while preserving the appearance of pages. The resulting

"Interchange PostScript" also would specify electronic documents with "hot buttons," much like the hypertext links found in some applications. Buttons let you navigate to other parts of your document, or to other documents on a network, even to a different kind of computer. A chapter entry in a table of contents would be linked to that chapter, or to other related topics, and thumbnail page views could be shown.

Adobe has code-named the "Interchange PostScript" project "Carousel." Introduction is expected sometime in 1992. Since PostScript is well supported on the Macintosh, DOS/Windows, and on UNIX operating systems, Adobe hopes that this portable PostScript will become the industry standard. The concept of an interchange format based on PostScript is a promising one. Given PostScript's position and Adobe's past track record, it stands a chance of success. Still, PostScript is not the only game in town. As we said earlier, Apple had a go at PostScript by introducing its own type and font technology to complement its QuickDraw PDL. We'll talk about it next.

TrueType and TrueImage

Since PDLs are at the heart of computer display and output technology, they comprise one of the most competitive areas of technology. Vendors like Apple and Microsoft have been reluctant to license such a core part of their system software to an outside source like Adobe, and have introduced their own scalable outline font formats. Called TrueType, and developed at Apple (originally called Royal fonts), the technology has been cross-licensed by Microsoft.

TrueType appears in Macintosh System 7 and in Microsoft Windows 3.1. Based on quadratic outlines, TrueType fonts are rasterized by a Font Manager in the system software giving results judged—by a select few—to be competitive with PostScript fonts. There is only a small library of TrueType fonts available now, but good conversion tools have been created to create this format. In 1992-3, TrueType fonts that will appear may create a viable alternative to PostScript fonts.

As part of the original announcement of TrueType, Microsoft cross-licensed to Apple a PostScript clone called TrueImage developed by Bauer, a company purchased by Microsoft. TrueImage has not been aggressively pursued by either Microsoft or Apple, but has appeared in several printers. Notably LaserMaster (Eden Prairie, MN) and Microtek have introduced TrueImage printers, with the former company turning into the prime TrueImage developer. At this time it is unclear just how much impact TrueImage will have in the marketplace, if any. Apple continues to make and sell PostScript printers, and to support PostScript fonts. Recently, Microsoft has indicated that it will continue to develop TrueImage.

In 1988-90, when TrueType and TrueImage were announced, they created what were called in the trade press the "font wars." Adobe was compelled to open up the specification of PostScript's proprietary "Type 1" font file format, creating an explosion in the number of "true" PostScript fonts in the marketplace. Previously only the unhinted, Type 3 font format was fully described. (We'll talk about Type 1 and 3 fonts, hinting, and font metrics later in this chapter.) Adobe also lowered their licensing fees, making PostScript printers more affordable. At this moment PostScript printers and fonts still offer better compatibility with output devices and software, a much larger typeface library, and wider cross-platform (PC, Mac, UNIX, etc.) compatibility.

Adobe also responded to the failure of Apple and Microsoft to license Display PostScript, Adobe's scalable outline font display technology. In 1989-90 Adobe released the Adobe Type Manager (both Mac and Windows versions exist) that is a subset of Display PostScript. ATM scales and rasterizes PostScript type to your display and allows print output to non-PostScript printers like a DeskJet. PostScript graphics are not handled by ATM. ATM is one of the most significant product introductions of the last several years.

As of this writing it appears that ATM has already won the "font war." Apple is expected to incorporate ATM into the next release version of System 7. At the present time, they're distributing the existing ATM free.

PDLs and Printers

Most commonly, page description languages are used to output to a printer or some other peripheral device. Using a PDL for this purpose offers a compelling technological advantage over software that sends ASCII characters to a printer. Since the PDL creates text files to describe pages, it is possible to send these files directly to the printer memory (downloading), where they are processed and interpreted. This frees up your computer, by shifting the burden of creating the actual page from your CPU to the printer. A file in a PDL like PostScript must be interpreted before it can be output or displayed. An *interpreter* is a program that takes the vector commands of a PDL and converts them to the bit map required by a printer or display. Normally there is a great deal of specialized graphics calculations required to create the bit map. For that reason, most printers encode the PDL in ROM inside the printer and use a dedicated microprocessor to free your computer for other tasks. The interpretation of your file is called raster-image processing, or RIPing. Not all printers use a separate microprocessor to RIP files. So-called "Personal laser printers" are often cheaper because they use your computer's own microprocessor to RIP and drive the printer.

For PostScript printers, the interpreter is encoded in ROM. The printer manufacturer must pay a licensing fee to Adobe Systems to do so. The fee used to be considerable, prompting the development of PostScript clones. Raster Image Processing Systems (Boulder, CO) was the first to break the PostScript type description code, followed soon thereafter by the largest PC type foundry, Bitstream (Cambridge, MA). Several other clones have followed. These clones, like Custom Applications' Freedom of the Press, are emulations or *reverse engineered* interpreters. They are used to make non-PostScript printers like the HP DeskJet or LaserJet series PostScript compatible. There are also PostScript clone printers available, as well. Although PostScript clones can be very close to perfect, small differences between them and the PostScript interpreter licensed by Adobe can be detected.

RIPing a PostScript file can be slow, even with a dedicated microprocessor and instructions encoded in ROM. There has been a trend in advanced printer technology to incorporate high speed *RISC* (Reduced Instruction Set Computer) controllers. RISC technology deals with fewer commands, and is thus much faster than conventional technology. For example, Adobe has developed and is licensing the Adobe Type 1 Coprocessor with PostScript Level 2 support. This custom microprocessor is 25 times faster than even most RISC-based printer controllers, because the Adobe design does not require software intervention to manage PostScript processing. It's all done directly on the processor.

Programming with a PDL

No matter how they end up being processed, most PDLs like PostScript describe graphics on a page in a set of procedural, text-based instructions. When you create a drawing using a program like Adobe Illustrator or Aldus Freehand, what that program is actually doing is writing the "code" that describes your drawing. You are actually being a PostScript programmer. Your programs are actually shielding you from knowing how to program your graphic image in PostScript itself, although the results are the same. If you take a file created by one of these applications and open it up as a text file in a word processor, you can see your drawing described in a series of PostScript commands.

You might want to try this experiment, supposing you have a PostScript drawing program on your computer. Create a file with a drawn rectangle, and perhaps some text, and save that file. Use your word processor to open that file as text, and scroll through the description. A lot of the file is overhead. If you search for the text string of the text object you created, you will find its description in the file, along with properties like what font it is, the font size, style, and so on. Nearby should be the instructions on how to create the rectangle, including the endpoints of each of the four lines that comprise the rectangle.

While it may be enlightening to examine a PostScript file in this manner, there is a point to this exercise. If you know the PostScript commands and their syntax, you can create many useful effects that may not be possible using your regular, PostScript application. Say, for example, that you wish to create a graduated, blended fill inside an object, but your program doesn't offer that feature. By adding the appropriate PostScript commands in the section describing the object you wish filled, you could accomplish the task within your word processor. When you print the PostScript file, the description you created is sent to the PostScript interpreter (which is normally contained in ROM within your printer), and the effect is printed.

Many word processors like Microsoft Word also allow you to embed a PostScript text file within a document, to achieve graphics capabilities like fills or halftones. The procedure is often quite simple. With Word, you just add some PostScript code in front of the paragraph you wish to alter. Since the code is a PostScript command, you won't be able to see it or its effect on your screen, even in Preview or WYSIWYG mode. But when it goes through the PostScript interpreter, the effect appears on your printed output. Knowledge of PostScript for special effects is probably of most interest to graphic artists or designers. It's generally not for the average user. The subject of the PostScript language and its commands is a book unto itself, and falls outside the scope of this discussion. However, if you are interested in knowing more about PostScript, the following should be of assistance:

> Adobe Systems, *PostScript Language Tutorial and Cookbook*, 1985, Addison-Wesley, Reading, MA.

> Braswell, Frank, *Inside PostScript, 1989*, Peachpit Press, Berkeley, CA.

> Kunkel, Gerald, *Graphic Design with PostScript*, 1990, Scott Foresman, Glenwood, IL.

> Roth, Stephen, ed., *Real World PostScript*, 1989, Addison-Wesley, Reading, MA.

> Smith, Ross, *Learning PostScript: A Visual Approach*, 1989, Peachpit Press, Berkeley, CA.

> Thomas, Barry, *A PostScript Cookbook*, 1988, Van Nostrand Reinhold, New York, NY.

The books by Smith and Roth are particularly recommended. They include good basic introductions, but came out before the PostScript Level 2 specification was introduced in 1991. A recent volume, the *PostScript Language Reference Manual*, 2nd Edition from Addison-Wesley, describes the additional Level 2 functionality. From the preceding, it should be clear that one of the most important aspects of a page description language is the way it handles different styles of characters, or fonts. In fact, the subject of fonts on the Macintosh is so important it warrants discussion in a section of its own, to whit, the next one.

Font Technologies

In the early days of personal computers, lack of available memory and processing power required that characters be represented by patterns of bits in a 9 X 7 pixel cell, such as that found in the original IBM PC. These *bit-mapped* or *raster* fonts displayed well on your screen. At printing time, they even looked good at the resolution they were designed for. Often, the print quality exceeded the display quality. That isn't always desirable; you want to see on your screen more or less exactly what you get out of your printer. So, in order that a font's print quality and display quality be equally as good, two font descriptions were stored: a *screen font* and a *printer font*.

If you decided to scale a bit-map font up to a larger size, then you saw the same kind of distortion you would for any bit map. Worse yet, although you could apply an algorithm to bold, italicize, outline, or style a font, bit-mapped fonts still had to be designed for a particular resolution. That led to the storage of several weights and styles of a font. Having the two different descriptions of each font—for the printer and the screen—also ate up disk storage space. Large font sizes represented by large bit maps gave large file sizes. In order to print high quality bit maps, manufacturers stored fonts in large point sizes, and scaled down to smaller point sizes. (If you remember, reducing a bit-mapped font yields a resolution enhancement.) Take it altogether, and it was not uncommon to have multimegabyte font libraries.

Now, bit-map fonts actually have several advantages. Because they are designed for a particular resolution and size, they look good when printed or displayed under those conditions. They can look better, in fact, than the results of a rasterized outline font (more on these in a bit) because a human's trained eye can still out perform the routines used to fit pixels to an outline. For this reason, it is still common to use bit-mapped fonts as system fonts in most computers. Little processing is needed to work with bit-mapped fonts, so although they can be memory hogs, they are actually quite efficient performers.

A second font description, but one not that commonly used in typographic applications, is the stroke font. A *stroke* is a form created by the movement of a conceptual "pen" of a certain width along a path. As long as a letter can be written with the pen touching the page, and different widths are not required for parts of the characters, strokes are fine. Stroke fonts have also been called *vector* fonts. They are resolution independent, about 50 percent smaller than outline font files (described below), and faster to process than outline fonts. Strokes are most successfully applied to san serif fonts. Describing the small serifs (flourishes) of letterforms would add considerably to their description. If you have seen the kind of characters that can be written using a pen plotter, then you know what stroke characters are. In fact, strokes are almost always used in plotter applications. They are part of the Hewlett-Packard Graphic Language (HPGL), the most commonly used plotter format.

The third, and most popular font format description is that of the outline font. An outline font is an object-oriented description of a set of characters. Different outline font formats exist; we discussed some of them earlier in this chapter when we talked about page description languages. In one case, PostScript, the outlines are based on Bézier cubic spline curves; alternatively, in the case of TrueType, the outlines are based on B-cubic splines. All you need to know about these jaw-breakers is that both descriptions give equally good results.

In order to display or print an outline font, the outline has to be converted to a bit map. The process involves placing the outline on a grid and turning the right pixels on and off so that the letterform is best represented. This is referred to as *grid fitting*. The overall process of creating the entire font at a particular size from an outline is referred to as *building* a font. Software for this purpose is called a *rasterizer*. When the rasterizer for display on the screen is the same rasterizer used for printing, then only one outline description need be stored. This is the case for TrueType, found in System 7. Using a font rasterizer for video display purposes means that type has a smooth appearance at any size.

> **NOTE:** Where the rasterizer is placed has some interesting system design implications. With Adobe's approach the rasterizer is placed in the printer, and when technology improves you have to buy a new printer to take advantage of it. The TrueType approach puts the rasterizer in system software. Therefore, using PostScript means more expensive printers, but printers that are independent of the computer; whereas TrueType favors cheaper printers that are dependent on computer processing.

Fitting a letterform to a fine grid gives good results, and a rasterized character that is fairly close to the outline. However, when the grid is large compared to the character outline, the bit map can be a crude representation of the outline. Depending on what pixels get turned on or off, the bit map might not even look like the outline at all. For example, if the letter has thin portions, then a rasterizing routine might drop these portions out, most especially at very small sizes.

A more sophisticated approach based on AI routines can be used to preserve details at small sizes. This technique is called *hinting*. Hinting is only really effective in outline fonts at point sizes below 9 points, and is rarely used above 12 points. Hinting is part of the proprietary technology font developers create to enhance their product, and it has been jealously guarded. Hinted PostScript fonts are in a format called PostScript Type 1. An unhinted version of these fonts is called PostScript Type 3. Any outline can be used as a Type 3 character, an EPS graphics file, for example. For this reason, Type 3 fonts have been called user-defined fonts, since anyone can develop such a font from PostScript outlines. Fonts are also normally encrypted (data are scrambled according to some key); encryption serves as a barrier to piracy. Adobe uses the Data Encryption Standard (DES) algorithm. A compression algorithm is usually also applied to save space.

For many years the full specification of Type 3 fonts have been published, whereas Type 1 fonts were unpublished. Due to competition from TrueType fonts, which were published as an open standard, Adobe released the specification for Type 1 fonts in 1990, also publishing their encryption scheme. However, their hinting technology remains proprietary. Other vendors have implemented their own hinting schemes to conform to the Type 1 specification. TrueType fonts also use a hinting scheme to improve readability at small point sizes.

There are utilities currently available commercially that allow the conversion of various font formats, as well as medium-priced utilities for the creation of fonts from scratch. Although it takes hard work and artistry, anyone can be in the digital typeface business, and many people are. This is one of the gifts of the personal computer to individuals. These topics are best discussed in books dedicated to typography, and they make fascinating reading. For further information you may want to look at the following books:

> Collier, David, *Collier's Rules for Desktop Design and Typography*, 1991, Addison-Wesley, Reading, MA.

> Sosinsky, Barrie, *Beyond the Desktop: Tools and Technology for Computer Publishing*, Bantam Computer Publishing, New York, NY.

> Labuz, Ronald, *Typography and Typesetting: Type Design and Manipulation Using Today's Technology*, 1988, Van Nostrand Reinhold, New York, NY.

> Efert Fenton, *The Macintosh Font Book*, 2nd Edition, 1991, Peachpit Press, Berkeley, CA.

Outline fonts have another advantage over bit-map fonts, they can be edited. Several programs let you convert font formats to editable outlines. Adobe Illustrator and Aldus Freehand are notable examples. This area of technology is still undergoing rapid transformation, even though the actual font formats have remained largely the same for several years. You may wish to read about more current developments in the trade press.

In addition to the shapes of the characters, a fully developed font also has a set of intercharacter spacings, scaling factors, line spacing, and other variables called a font's *metrics*. Font metrics tables (which are a database) for PostScript come in Adobe Font Metric (*filename*.AFM) files. Font metrics adjusts *kerned pairs*, those special letter combinations like "AV,""AW," and "To" which look better condensed. *Kerning* adjusts the spacing between certain letter pairs so that they look better; for example, the small letter "o" needs to be moved slightly under the crossbar on the capital "T" to look best. Kerning is particularly important in display type, which is usually displayed in large sizes where spacing problems are more apparent. A PostScript font might have from 150 to 500 kerning pairs.

Font metrics also includes information on changing the spacing of proportional characters based on the adjacent characters. Proportional fonts are those with variably-spaced characters; contrast them with monospaced fonts that use fixed space characters. Courier and other typewriter fonts are monospaced fonts. Scale factors and placements for sub- and superscripts, line spacings, and small caps are also part of a font's metrics. Some programs that manipulate type, such as page layout programs, font editors, and type modification programs, let you modify font metrics.

Up to this point, we've mainly been concerned with the general features of Macintosh graphics technology. The specifics depend on the exact implementation of the tools available (e.g., QuickDraw and PostScript) to Mac software developers. There are a number of graphics software packages available, each with its own way of doing things. These idiosyncrasies have implications for how graphics files are stored, in addition to constraining what they can contain and how they're constructed. We'll look at all these issues in the last part of the this chapter, coming up.

Graphics Software and Graphics Files

Unless you go to the trouble of buying a reference book and researching the subject, you may never encounter a page description language directly, be it QuickDraw, PostScript, or something else. However, if you use a Macintosh at all (and we must assume you do, or why did you buy this book?), you encounter the effects of a PDL on a daily basis. In particular, the graphics software you use employs QuickDraw (at least) to render images on the screen. We haven't yet discussed graphics software, but it's time we did. We will look at how the tools relied upon by a particular graphics software program constrain what it can do. We'll also look at some specifics regarding how graphics files are stored, and how they can be stored in less disk space than usual.

About Graphics Software:
"Paint" versus "Draw" Programs

Perhaps the most important distinction that can be drawn between graphics software is whether a given program relies on raster or vector graphics; that is, whether it is bit-map or object-oriented. On the Macintosh, we generally refer to the former as paint-style programs (after the original such program, MacPaint), and the latter as draw-style programs (MacDraw was an early example). The difference is an important one.

Paint programs rely entirely on bit maps. Generally, a paint-type image is stored as a single bit map. A paint image can approach a level of realism not possible with an object image, but this capability comes at a price: it is usually quite difficult to make significant changes to individual parts of a paint image. On the other hand, paint programs offer subtlety in line, shading, and color that's impossible to achieve using draw programs.

Paint Programs: Palettes for a Digital Seurat

Among the best-known paint programs is the very first to appear: MacPaint. The original version of MacPaint shipped with the first Macintosh in 1984. As neat as it was (we played with it for hours on end that year), it had serious limitations. Because the first Mac was itself a monochrome (black-and-white) machine, MacPaint didn't know about color. The area you could paint upon was limited in size: it was about 8 by 10 inches, with no way to resize it. There was a limited set of tools and fill patterns.

Naturally, Mac software developers noticed these shortcomings (as did Apple), and set about designing paint applications of their own to address them. MacPaint, too, underwent considerable revision, especially after Apple gave it to its software spinoff, Claris Corporation. What's more, as the Macintosh itself has evolved in the last decade or so, paint programs of all kinds have sprung up to take advantage of the latest capabilities. Surveying the current state of the art, we notice several areas in which advances have been made. Some of the most important are summarized below:

Color:

Color graphics became possible when Apple introduced the Mac II series in 1986. Color paint programs were not far behind. (Actually, limited color was possible before this time, although you couldn't see your results on screen. Programs such as FullPaint took advantage of the color capabilities of the ImageWrite printer, which could print in color when equipped with the right ribbon.) At first, the number of colors you could use was limited to 256 at a time.

Macs equipped with 8-bit graphics adaptors (again, see the chapter on Monitors) can still only handle this many colors.

The advent of 32-bit color QuickDraw opened up a new realm of color on the Mac. With the right hardware, a Mac can now display literally millions of colors; more, in fact, than the human eye can actually distinguish clearly. Studio/32 and Fractal Design Painter are two programs noted for their implementation of 32-bit color, although there are many other such programs available.

Advanced Tools

All paint programs have traditionally offered tools that imitate typical artists' implements, such as paint brushes, pencils, and even paint buckets (cf. Jackson Pollock). The latest paint programs are known for the additional tools they provide. Some even allow "extra" tools to be plugged directly into the application. As System 7—which makes such add-ons easier to program—catches on, expect to see more of this sort of thing.

There are now tools that let you mask off certain areas of a painting, so that special effects can be applied to other areas only. Fractal Design's Painter (winner of the 1991 MacUser Eddy award for Best Paint Program) even offers brushes that paint in the style of famous artists: particularly the pointillist Seurat (that seems appropriate) and the post-Impressionist Van Gogh. The program also lets you simulate the effect of different painting surfaces. You can make your Mac screen behave like canvas, rice paper, and so on.

Figure 4.5: A typical tool palette from a newer paint program (Color It). Different tool palettes can be selected using the pop-up menu at the top. Note the Smudge tool (hand icon, upper right), the technical pen, the airbrush, and the stamp.

Special-Focus Applications:

Specialized applications have sprung up to handle certain types of work. Adobe Photoshop, for instance, is intended to work with scanned photographic images. (A scanned image is one that has been fed into a Mac using a special device called a scanner; see the chapter on Graphics Input Technologies.) It offers tools for retouching, cropping, sizing, printing and otherwise playing with photographic images. Broderbund's Kid Pix, on the other hand, is a staggeringly popular, simple paint program for children. One writer's two-year-old daughter especially likes the alphabet stamp. When you stamp a letter onto the screen, the computer "pronounces" the letter's name, using one of a number of different voices. It'll even talk in Spanish.

The preceding is just a small indication of what's out there. Indeed, the array of choices can be bewildering to even an experienced buyer, to say nothing of a first-timer. When investigating paint programs, however, there are but a few things to keep in mind. Don't buy more paint program than your Mac can handle: you can't run Studio/32 on a Mac Classic, for instance. Eschew programs with lots of fancy tools, unless you're a serious artist, or mean to be. Do you need (and can you display) 32-bit color, or will 8-bit do?

Professional graphics artists may want to check out advanced programs such as Studio/32 and Fractal Design Painter. The latter program, in particular, has been getting good notices. On the other hand, if you work mainly with scanned or canned (pre-drawn) images, you might want to consider Adobe Photoshop. If you're just doodling around, KidPix might be enough. Not only is it a decent 8-bit program; the kids like it, and it's very inexpensive, too.

Draw Programs: The Mac as Drafting Table

There are many applications for which a paint program simply won't do. Technical illustrations, for instance. Such work requires precise lines and exact geometric shapes. Although you can achieve such shapes with a paint program, woe be unto you if you should need to change part of the drawing, say to change the size of some element. It just cannot be done.

Draw programs, on the other hand, are designed specifically to do this sort of work. Because they're object-oriented, such programs make it easy to create and modify simple geometric shapes. What's more, you can move shapes behind or in front of each other without obliterating them. Even an object that's been totally hidden can be moved forward and modified. It's also possible to group a number of objects into a larger object. This lets you apply certain operations (resizing, e.g.) to the group as a whole, without having to apply the operation individually to each component object.

Draw programs are well suited to such applications as architectural or engineering drafting and preparation of technical illustrations. (You could never imitate Van Gogh's Starry Night with such a program, however.) Existing draw programs fall into three broad categories, one of which has a special focus.

General Draw Programs: These include MacDraw II and MacDraft. They offer fairly standard tools and capabilities.

CAD Programs: CAD is an acronym for Computer-Aided Design. It has been all the rage in architecture and engineering for years now. CAD programs are supposed to make it easy to draw (and more importantly, modify) blueprints, architectural plans, and the like. The best known Mac CAD programs are AutoCAD (the industry leader, though most of its business is on the IBM PC and compatibles), VersaCAD and ClarisCAD. These programs tend to be difficult to learn.

PostScript-based Illustration Programs: These programs, such as Adobe Illustrator and Aldus FreeHand, use PostScript to create images. (Of course, they must use QuickDraw to render images on your Mac screen.) Because they work closely with PostScript, they can be quirky and bizarre. However, they can be used to create complex curved shapes that aren't possible in other draw programs. They are also good at modifying PostScript text.

Of all the programs named above, Adobe Illustrator is perhaps the most popular. It is not suitable for blueprints or house plans, but it is good for technical illustration. The cubic spline curves used by Illustrator are difficult to manage at first, but you tend to get the hang of it in time. If you are only creating very simple graphics, however, it would be best to stick with a general purpose draw program like MacDraw.

We ought to mention that there are hybrid programs in existence that incorporate both raster and vector graphics into one application. *SuperPaint* from Aldus is a notable example. SuperPaint has two layers; a draw layer and a paint layer. The final drawing is a composite of the two layers. Neither part of SuperPaint is as full-featured as a typical paint or draw program, but if you only need moderate capabilities in both areas, it's an excellent choice.

Now you might think that your choice of a drawing or painting program will lock you into a certain product forever since you'll want to work with your existing files well into the future. Fortunately, this isn't necessarily true. These days, there aren't nearly as many ways of storing graphics files as there are applications to produce them. Many (in fact, most) graphics applications can read and work with each other's files. The exact way that an application stores a file is called its file format. It's an important topic; one we'll discuss next.

Graphics File Formats

All programs save files in standard or specified manners; otherwise, the files could never be looked at again, because nothing would be able to interpret the data within them. Such a standard way of saving a file is called a *file format*. Programs can either save or write, and open or read a format. Most of the time programs create data files. A data file is just that: data only. Data files rely on applications to provide the programming needed for their use.

Image file formats use various schemes to describe images. In addition to being based either on bit maps or object graphics, many file formats also specify file compression schemes (more on compression at chapter's end).

On some computer systems (notoriously, on the IBM PC), graphics file formats have proliferated to the extent that they have almost turned into a night-l mare topic. Fortunately, this isn't the case on the Mac. However, there are still a number of file formats out there, and it isn't always easy to choose the right one. (Most applications let you choose what format to save under.) Hopefully, the following information will help you in selecting and using one format type rather than another.

Bit-Mapped Formats

TIFF

TIFF, or the Tagged Image File Format, is a widely used bit mapped file format. TIFF is frequently used in digital imaging application such as scanning. Developed by Aldus and Microsoft, TIFF is now at Version 5.0. This specification can contain 8-bit gray scale (256 shades of gray), up to 24-bit color images, and of course black and white. TIFF files are normally quite large: an 8 1/2" X 11" in 24-bit color can be 6 to 12MB in size.

Several versions of TIFF exist. There's Monochrome TIFF (black & white), Gray scale TIFF (8-bit or 256 gray levels supported), and Color TIFF. The latter supports 32-bit color images. Just to make things even more confusing, the TIFF standard allows for the use of proprietary compression algorithms. (Compression is a technique for squeezing a large file into a smaller disk space. We'll talk more about it at the end of the chapter.)

TIFF has a reputation for introducing subtle changes in image quality and tone, and should be used carefully and with caution. Some applications, like Adobe Photoshop, will save in PC TIFF format directly.

Paint

MacPaint format is the original standard Macintosh black-and-white file format. Images are limited to a crude 72 dpi, the resolution of the Macintosh screen. There is also a nominal 8" X 10" limit to a PNT image; larger images are cropped to size. The format is really just a holdover from the days in which there was a large library of *clip art* (ready-drawn artwork that can be copied and used to spice up dull documents) drawn with MacPaint.

Object-Oriented Formats

PostScript

Many programs let you create a pure PostScript text file as an option. Adobe Illustrator creates PostScript files routinely. PostScript files can be opened and printed by any program that can read text and can work with the PostScript language.

DXF

This is AutoDesk's proprietary format for its AutoCAD program. Most CAD programs support DXF; almost nobody else does.

Combination Bit-Map and Object Formats

EPSF

Encapsulated Postscript (EPS or EPSF) format is a PostScript (text) description of a graphic image, with an accompanying low-resolution representation used for display of the image. The low-resolution image lets you see the approximate effect of a transformation without requiring that the object representation be calculated. This speeds up work on complex images immensely, which is a good thing, since EPS is noted for large file sizes and long processing times.

Two flavors of EPS are used: ASCII EPS, which is a text description, and Binary EPS, which is a hexadecimal representation. Draw programs most commonly save files in ASCII EPS, while image editing programs save in Binary EPS. The low-resolution image for preview is normally in TIFF format, but Macintosh versions of EPS can save their preview image in either QuickDraw or TIFF. It is this bit-mapped representation that adds to the file size. Binary EPS files are normally about half the size of ASCII EPS.

In many cases the displayed low-resolution bit map can be distorted, while the true file is output perfectly. Without fully understanding the nature of the EPS file format, it is easy to get confused and believe that the underlying high-resolution graphic image has been distorted by the transformation.

EPS was developed by the Altsys Corporation (Richardson, TX), the developers of Freehand and several font creation and modification programs. Since EPS is supported by several PostScript graphics programs found on the Macintosh, it is one of the favored object file formats. Programs like Adobe Illustrator will convert EPS files. You should be aware, however, that EPS is normally opened and written completely and correctly only by the creator application, and not by anyone else. This can make it a pain to attempt to use the same EPS file in different applications. Many times even the creator application can open an EPS file, but cannot edit it. Worse still, only certain transformations—like scaling—are available. Still EPS is popular and definitely has its place.

PICT

PICT files are the standard Macintosh vector or draw format, encoded as QuickDraw commands, the graphics language of the Macintosh. The original specification was a black-and-white format, but eight standard colors could also be assigned. A newer version of PICT called PICT2 can save images in 8-bit gray scale or up to 32-bit color. Unlike the PNT format based on MacPaint, PICT can save both low- and medium-resolution images. PICT is probably the most common Macintosh graphics file format; virtually all programs can save and open PICT files.

Format Conversions

From time to time, you may wish to translate one file format into another. You may even want to translate a file created on your Mac into a file useable by a PC. Knowing one arcane file format type from another is useful in determining how successful a file translation can be. Converting a bit-map file to another bit-map file, or an object-oriented file to another object-oriented file, is likely to be successful. However, when you convert between raster and vector graphics you can get unpleasant results. Consider that converting an object circle (perfectly defined) will give you a bit-mapped circle where each pixel is defined at the resolution of the bit map. Once converted, that file is locked into that resolution, unless you reconvert the object file again.

Raster-to-vector graphic file translations are even more problematical. Translators for this purpose use edge-detection algorithms to define line segments, resulting in a set of Bézier curves. When you convert a natural image to a line drawing (vector) you can end up with collection of shapes of tremendous complexity, with a large file size to boot. Most such programs, called autotracing programs (e.g., Adobe Streamline), allow you to set the sensitivity of the algorithm, and the number of inflection points (places where curves change direction) that the curves can have. We have found that watching a drawing emerge from an autotraced image is quite interesting. The results can range from fair to quite good.

Since file formats often come in slightly different flavors, it is common for a program to incompletely read or write a file based on the available data, even when it appears that a single format is used. This occurs most often when using the same file format with different programs on the same computer platform.

For example, if one version of a format specifies additional color values, but a program uses a version with fewer colors, there will be a problem with color mapping that will distort your image. For example, color mapping from 32-bit color to monochrome black and white can give hideous results. Going the other way, from a format with fewer colors to one with more colors often works well. Usually the colors are mapped exactly.

Often some data loss is fine, but not always. If you don't keep an original copy of the file, you may lose the additional information; information that you may find you need. Sometimes the problems in a file format conversion are obvious, and other times they are subtle. Worse yet, if it was someone else's file that you were using, you may have no idea what the original should have looked like, so you may not know what was lost. You need to be on your toes.

One way of judging how well a graphic format has been translated is to create a test pattern. In one file format create all of the fine details that you need to translate. For example, create a series of gray boxes from white to black (such a transition is called a *ramp*). Create some test colors, indicating the color values in RGB along with the overall intensity. Many graphics packages let you indicate what color you want to specify in RGB, or will tell you a color's RGB value when you select it. Create some other important details: sample text, some sample lines, etc. Then save the file. Use the file to make test translations between graphics formats. Then, you will know whether the translation has been successful. Sounds like work, doesn't it? Here you were wondering when you were going to get the time to back up your hard drive.

When a format has both bit-mapped and object components, you often run into trouble trying to convert to another format that is solely one or the other. The PICT format is one example. PICT uses the Macintosh QuickDraw PDL to write descriptions of the file, using both data types depending on the file's contents. Opening a PageMaker Mac file that contains an embedded PICT graphic in the PC version of PageMaker will result in a blank box where the image should be. Clearly, a conversion problem. However, it may be just a display problem, and you should try to print the file to see whether the graphic is still there. The problem of the disappearing graphic can also occur in file translations that use the IBM PC native format of PageMaker going to the Macintosh.

EPS is another format that can cause such problems. Some (not all) Macintosh EPS files use a PICT (QuickDraw) representation for their low-resolution component, whereas all PC programs use TIFF. If a PC program tries to read a Macintosh EPS file with the wrong low-resolution description, you might have problems similar to those described in the previous paragraph. A gray box may appear; or, some programs will display a box with a cross through it where the graphic should be. This isn't a common problem, and you should try and print the page to see if the graphic is there. Adobe Illustrator on the Macintosh allows you to save files in an IBM PC option to create TIFF viewers in EPS, and you should always take that option when offered, as it causes fewer problems.

Some of the bigger software packages are also some of the best at file format translation. Desktop publishing packages like PageMaker can use image format types from a variety of sources. These programs have developed or licensed numerous translators for that purpose, and users like you have heavily tested these packages in real world production assignments. Adobe Photoshop is also notable for file translation. Both these programs are expensive, and no one would buy them for their file translation capabilities alone. However, if you own them, they are the best place to start when attempting to translate file formats.

Moving Images between Platforms

There are two separate steps in moving a file across computer platforms: file transfer, and file translation. Some people refer to file translation routines as *filters*. You can transfer files using:

(1) SneakerNet (e.g., walking a disk from one machine to another).

(2) A network. They often translate files.

(3) By a direct asynchronous, modem-to-modem connection using telecommunications software.

(4) With a null modem connection, that is, direct serial port connection.

Many programs have translators so that they can read other program's file formats, but that is not always the case. Understanding file formats allows you to accomplish multiprogram projects using the best tool for the job. Some file formats have become *de facto* standards, and if a program does not read or write to a standard format that is a critical defect. Fortunately most programs have this capability, and there are fine stand-alone translator programs that you can purchase for this purpose. Many major programs also come with an extensive set of translators built-in, or with a system that allows for additional or update translators to be added. In any case, without testing you can never be sure if that translation has been correctly and completely accomplished.

Perhaps the best way to convert images between computers is by using a program that works on both systems. For example, Aldus PageMaker running on Windows can read TIFF or EPS files created by its Macintosh cousin. When you make the conversion (in either direction) you are assured that the same versions of these file formats have been used, and that the developers have tested these conversions to see that they are precisely implemented. Undoubtedly, this represents the best approach to file transfers between computers.

PC to Mac, Mac to PC

There are several solutions to transferring a disk written on a Mac so that it might be read on a PC, and vice versa. To read a Macintosh disk on a PC, use a program like PLI's MAC-to-DOS Transfer. It allows you to read and write to Macintosh formatted 1.44 MB disks.

If you try to read a disk formatted for the PC on a Mac, you get an error message asking you if you want to format that disk. (Doing so would erase your data.) The process of having the disk show up on the Macintosh desktop without such messages is called *mounting* the disk. You must have additional software to recognize the PC disk's formatting. You can use the new Apple Computer software, *Macintosh PC Exchange*, to allow you to mount a DOS diskette graphically on the Desktop, just like you do with every Mac diskette and hard disk. The software is highly customizable and quick. This is probably the most-direct and quickest solution available. The software is also *very* inexpensive, with a street price of as little as $70.00 at the time of this writing.

Two products that allow you to do PC-to-Mac file transfers by serial cable are MacLinkPlus/PC from Dataviz's (Trumbull, CT) or Traveling Software's (Bothell, WA) LapLinkMac (Release III). The PC version of LapLink for Mac-to-PC file transfers is called LapLink III. These products come with file translation filters built-in, and they generally work quite well. Compatible Systems sells a product called QuickShare that connects a PC and a Mac using an AT expansion board on the PC and the SCSI port on the Mac.

One of the peculiarities of doing file conversions between the Macintosh and the PC has to do with the different file format naming conventions. The Mac uses two four-letter codes to mark files: a file type that specifies the associated (or creator) application, and a creator type which can be anything the developer desires.

When going from the PC to the Macintosh, three-letter file extensions are used to map to appropriate four-letter file types. Utilities are used to make the correct translation. DOS Mounter is such a utility, it also aids in reading disks formatted by a PC. The process is similar to using the File Associate command in DOS or

Windows to mark extensions as belonging to a particular application. A Word .DOC file would get mapped to the Macintosh Word file type specification of WBDN. The PageMaker .PUB file extension is mapped to ALD4. You could also choose to map a Lotus 1-2-3.WKS file to the Excel XCEL file type to open 1-2-3 files automatically in Excel. The actual executable file for Word, or any application on the Macintosh for that matter, is given the four-letter code APPL. File types are registered by Apple.

The second half of the file transfer process involves the translation of files. The MacLinkPlus/PC package contains a set of translators (they can be purchased separately) that will work with the Apple File Exchange or with the MacLinkPlus/PC program. MacLinkPlus/PC Version 6.0 offers over 400 conversions: Mac/NeXT, Mac/Sun, Mac/Wang, as well as Mac/PC translations are supported. The program is well regarded. Additional translators (380) for the Apple File Exchange are offered by System Compatibility's Software Bridge.

Compatible Systems' AnyPC uses a unique system for transferring files between the Mac and the PC. Most PC programs can write a print-to-disk file in the format of the IBM Graphics Printer. The created file *filename*.ANY is then transferred to a Mac and translated by a companion program. What AnyPC does is convert that disk file to the MacPaint format. A text transfer utility called AnyText can translate character output in the print file format on the Mac.

Emulators are another approach to file transfer and translation. An emulator is a program that simulates an operating system on another computer. This can be done either through hardware or software. As a hardware solution, Orange Micro offers the Mac86, Mac286, and Orange386 coprocessor NuBus expansion cards for the Macintosh II family of computers. They operate and feel just like PCs, except the PC volume appears as a disk, while PC programs appear in a window on the Macintosh desktop. PC file formats are the same; printing to Macintosh printers is supported. In software (without coprocessors), the experience of emulation is different. You take a performance hit while software instructions are interpreted. SoftPC and SoftPC AT are two software versions of DOS that run as Macintosh volumes.

Two programs are available that let you control a PC from a Mac screen. Both use serial cable connections to communicate. They are MacChuck, and Argosy Software's (New York, NY) RunPC. DOS programs run in a window on the Macintosh, with the connected IBM PC responsible for actually processing the information and passing the video to the Macintosh for display. Files can be written in either direction. The programs come with a set of file translators (the previously mentioned Software Bridge) that can be used with the Apple File Exchange. Of the two, RunPC is newer, better supported, and well reviewed.

Format Summary Time

We have but a few closing thoughts regarding Macintosh graphics file formats, ones gleaned from our years of work. For one thing, we've noticed that TIFF files print much faster than PICT files. We don't know why. Still, given a choice, save a file in TIFF before printing it. We've seen a PICT file that took 1 1/2 hours to print on a LaserWriter II NTX, take ten minutes when converted to TIFF. The time you save may be your own. When converting files, or modifying them in any way, never throw away original data files. Always work on copies. If you screw up the original file, you can't go back again. If you mess up a copy, you can just go back to original and copy it again.

Working with 32-bit color images is much slower than working in eight-bit land. Keep this in mind. If you don't need all those colors, don't waste your Mac's processor power trying to produce them. You can use your monitor's control panel to set the number of colors to display: 256 is for eight-bit, "Millions" is for 32-bit. Even a Quadra is slowed down annoyingly when working in full color, which is only useful for photo realism anyway. When in doubt, save as PICT if you can. This format stands a much greater chance of being useful to other applications than does some application-specific file format.

This sums up *some* of the issues involved in working with image files, but not all. There's also the question of all the space that image files—especially bit-mapped ones—can take up on your disks. Fortunately, there are ways to reduce this burden, as we'll see in the next and last section.

Image Compression

It's kind of hard to believe now, but back in 1984, both the System software and MacPaint fit onto one 400K diskette, with room left over for a few Paint files. These days, a single color image can easily surpass 400K on its own. True, we have more storage space than we used to: 80 and even 120 megabyte hard disk drives are now considered "small," and you can get more storage if you have the bucks. Some of us don't. And some of us work with lots of graphics files, which take a lot of space. More than 80 megabytes even.

There is a potential solution to the problem of storing lots of massive files. It is possible to compress a large file into smaller spaces, sometimes without even losing any information. The process of reducing a file is called compression. There are two basic types of file compression: lossless, which preserves all original information, and lossy, which discards the least important information in a file, while achieving greater compression. We'll talk about both types of compression.

Lossless Compression

Lossless file compression involves representing the same file data in a smaller space, by encoding redundant or unnecessary information. Most popular file formats are using, or will be using some form of file compression to improve performance. PostScript fonts, for example, are stored in a condensed format. There is also a condensed version of TIFF.

You are perhaps familiar with compression utilities like Compact Pro and StuffIt. Some are used on electronic networks to lower the time taken to transfer files. They do this by applying standard and proprietary algorithms to compact files. Some of these algorithms are over 20 years old and were developed by the phone companies and military research agencies for these purposes. These programs as a class are reliable. Some are nearly bullet-proof. Good compression software will even make the operation transparent for you by selecting the optimum compression, the best performance, or some mix thereof.

Data compression programs operating on ASCII require that every byte of information be preserved. You don't want characters to drop out of a word processor document. An algorithm that fulfills this requirement is called *lossless*. Data can be compressed at a 2:1 or 3:1 ratio, hence names like DiskDoubler and the basis for the claim in the preceding paragraph. Image compression works even better than data compression: Using lossless algorithms you can achieve from a 5:1 to a 20:1 compression depending on the file format used and on the algorithm applied. Less complicated TIFF files often compress down to 5 percent.

There are numerous schemes for achieving compression, where redundancy in text or images is eliminated by replacement with shorter data coding schemes. Huffman encoding is one of the more commonly used algorithms. In this format the file to be compressed is examined, and a lookup table with the frequency of use of characters is created. A common character like the letter "a" or "e" receives the shortest ASCII byte, replacing an 8-bit representation with a 3-bit code. This is how you get the 2:1 or 3:1 compression. Faster Huffman routines use a preassigned lookup table based on a particular spoken language, but these methods give up some compression efficiency. PostScript fonts are Huffman encoded. Huffman is lossless and solid, but slow.

Lempel-Ziv (LZ), also called Lempel-Ziv-Welch (LZW), is another common algorithm. Here the statistical codes used in the lookup table are based on a set of character strings rather than letters. Common words like "the," "on," "as," etc. get the shortest assignments. Uncommon words like "aardvark" and "zoetrope" are left unchanged. LZW can also create a statistical table, or use a standard language table for its compression. You can apply Huffman and LZW algorithms to image files, which are binary coded. A repeating color value like the blue of a sky, or a spot color will compress well with these schemes, perhaps to 20 percent. However, natural images with many colors or tones will not.

There are more efficient algorithms that can be applied to images. One scheme called *Run Length Encoding* (RLE) examines an image line by line from start to finish. If it finds a repeated value—say, many blue pixels—it records the value and then records a number that describes how long that value repeats. If the next line contains the same value, there is a short code for that as well. This is the scheme that FAX files use to describe a rasterized page and limit file size.

The format also describes the frequencies of white-and-black lengths in place of characters and character strings. An 80-character line might have 160 transitions from white to black. This is described in place of its alternate description of 1728 pixels. This compression scheme yields a 10:1 savings ratio. If a look ahead feature is used that has a short code to indicate that the next scan line, or set of scan lines, is the same, then some files can be compressed up to 60:1 with no loss of data.

Lossy Compression

Lossless data compression is quite slow and inefficient. You can achieve faster compression if you use dedicated coprocessors for that purpose, especially if they are specially designed for compression. (Coprocessors for compression in computer devices, even on system motherboards, is an industry trend.) However, lossless compression really is an unnecessary luxury with most image files, and many applications can tolerate some amount of data loss. Programs that use *lossy* algorithms will often allow you to specify the amount of loss you'll tolerate, the so-called *Q-factor*. Such compression products can give compression up to and beyond 100:1.

The losses you accept in an image file compression routine are normally in the number of colors supported or in the apparent overall resolution of the image. Boundaries become fuzzier and detail is lost. How much loss is acceptable depends on the application you are using. Small format 35mm slides—where no enlargement is used—can tolerate high Q-factors. On the other hand, large format work like movie films cannot accept any loss at all.

RLE compression of colors by lines has already been described. Another technique is called *region coding* where an area (as opposed to a line) of color is described by a single value. Yet another technique, called Differential Code Modulations (DCM), measures differences in the color values between pixels and their nearest neighbors, and codes those numbers. An RGB value described by three, three-digit decimal numbers (and a number for the intensity value) drops to considerably smaller numbers when looking at only the differences, resulting in large compression ratios.

Another similar scheme looks at a set of pixels, taking the most common value. Called Block Pixel Replication, this process will reduce the number of apparent colors. Since 24-bits of color contains 16.8 million colors (the eye can perceive only tens of thousands of colors), this is normally acceptable. Similarly, gray scale can be reduced even further, as only about 256 shades of gray can be differentiated by the human eye.

A number of other standards are appearing for lossy compression, but the most prominent is the international standard based on the Joint Photographic Experts Group or JPEG. JPEG specifies three algorithms, two of which are lossy. (The third is lossless.) JPEG algorithms are symmetrical: The same software and hardware used to compress files are also used to decompress them.

The JPEG algorithms are based on a technique called Discrete Cosine Transformations (DCT). (For you buttonheads out there, DCTs are similar to the Fourier transform, but only the cosine part of the function is used. The rest of us need not worry about such arcana.) Using DCT, a 64 square (8 x 8) pixel region is assigned a color and light intensity. The DCT measures variance across the region and breaks it into a set of coefficients. Only the middle range coefficients are used. Outer range coefficients are tossed out, leading to the data reduction.

DCT converts color to the YUV (luminance, brightness, and chrominance) perceptual color model, the same used on color TV transmissions. The DCT process also achieves data reduction by throwing away every other pixel's *chrominance* value (a measure of color intensity). This works because the human eye does not differentiate chrominance well. DCT values are then quantified to give relative values, and finally run-length and Huffman encoding are applied.

JPEG routines are also being built into system software. They are part of Apple's QuickTime extension to the Macintosh system software. (More on QuickTime— much more—in the chapter on Multimedia.) Image compression will be even more important to future versions of system software.

From ASCII files to fonts to compression, we have covered a lot in this chapter. We hope you find it useful, whether you attempt to transfer files across different computers, or you just try to print a document that looks good. Hopefully, the knowledge you have gained about how Macs work with graphics data will help you, no matter what.

Graphics-Output Hardware—Monitors

Buying a computer is a difficult process. There are so many decisions to make. What size hard disk do you want? For that matter, which Macintosh to buy? What peripherals do you want? One peripheral that you can't do without is a monitor. Unless you have a Macintosh with a built-in monitor, such as a Classic or PowerBook, you'll have to select a monitor to use with your Mac. Arguably, it's the most important choice you'll make in the buying process.

While a fast processor or a large hard disk are important parts of your system, you don't have to *look* at them all day. To your eyes, the monitor *is* the computer. When choosing a monitor, then, it is very important to make the right choice. If you choose a bad monitor, you won't like your computer. Not only that, but the resulting eyestrain could cause some serious health problems.

This chapter will discuss monitors and the choices available to you in the Macintosh world. It will also discuss video adapters—which work with your Mac to get an image on your monitor's screen—and new technologies, which allow you to display other images on screen, such as television signals and video information. It is important to select a monitor and graphics adapter that are compatible with each other. There would be little reason to use a low-resolution monitor with a high resolution video card, for example.

How They Work

Most Macs use a cathode ray tube (CRT) to display images on the screen (we will discuss other display types later in this chapter). In fact, many computer users call their monitor a CRT. A CRT is basically a vacuum tube with a flat screen on one end and an electron gun on the other. This technology is anything but new. J.J. Thomson built the first tube in 1897. Of course, it's much improved since then.

The flat screen is what you see when you look at your computer monitor. The electron gun includes several parts: a heating element, a cathode, a control grid, an anode, and an electrode. The heating element causes the cathode to produce a cloud of electrons. The control grid determines how many electrons can pass; the more electrons, the brighter the image. The anode accelerates the electrons, while the electrode focuses and shoots them, in the form of an *electron beam*, from one end of the tube to the other. A focusing cylinder makes each beam focus on a fine point when it reaches the screen. The gun actually produces a series of beams simultaneously; each beam collides with the screen and causes the *phosphor* coating on the screen to glow.

Phosphors only glow for a short period of time. Therefore, a deflection system moves the beam vertically and horizontally around the screen, drawing the image you see on screen and causing it to strike the screen as many as 100 times per second. The number of times each beam strikes a phosphor is known as the screen's *refresh rate*. This is also called a screen's vertical refresh rate or vertical scanning frequency because a screen is scanned from the top to the bottom.

Another specification related to this is *horizontal scanning frequency*, which refers to how fast the monitor draws each line across the screen. This is typically 30KHz or better. For high-end graphics applications, such as computer-aided design (CAD), special monitors offer a horizontal scanning frequency of 65KHz or more.

The way that a monitor refreshes the screen has a direct impact on picture quality. For example, some screens are *interlaced*. The monitor redraws half the lines on the screen in one pass (say, the even-numbered lines) and the other half of the lines on the next pass. While this may seem hardly noticeable to some people, it can result in screen flicker, particularly with certain applications. Even if you don't consciously notice it, your eyes do, resulting in eyestrain or headaches after extended use. A slow refresh rate can also cause screen flicker. Anything less than 65 times per second (or 65Hz), causes a noticeable and irritating flicker on-screen. Most monitors have a refresh rate of 75Hz. Avoid monitors with a refresh rate below 65Hz.

Screen flicker can be so annoying it may result in your not being able to tolerate the monitor. Therefore, select a monitor that is *noninterlaced*. These monitors redraw the screen in one pass. By drawing only half the lines per pass, interlaced monitors can have a slower electron beam than noninterlaced monitors. As a result, noninterlaced monitors are more expensive than interlaced monitors. But you'll find they're well worth the extra cost. Don't buy an interlaced monitor.

Monochrome Monitors

Images are displayed on-screen in either color or monochrome. On a monochrome monitor, phosphors are typically made out of a mixture of silver-activated zinc sulfide and silver-activated zinc cadmium sulfide. This mixture is designed to create a white background on-screen. Not all white screens are the same, however. Some are yellowish, resembling paper viewed under incandescent light. These are referred to as "warm" phosphor screens. Others use "cool" phosphors, employing a brighter white, which is actually bluish in tone. The tone of the phosphor is directly related to the exact amount of each chemical in the phosphor.

Two types of monochrome monitors are available for your Macintosh—black-and-white and gray-scale. Gray-scale monitors are sophisticated devices able to display up to 256 shades of gray. They work similarly to color monitors, except instead of displaying colors, gray-scale monitors produce shades of gray. Black-and-white monitors—by far the most common type of monochrome monitor—are able to display only two shades, black or white. Black-and-white monitors are appropriate for most applications, such as word processing, spreadsheets, and even most music-related applications, while gray-scale monitors are appropriate for sophisticated graphics applications, especially when you're dealing with a number of scanned images or photographs.

Color Monitors

Color screens contain many groups of red, green, and blue phosphors (called *triads*), arranged triangularly. Many color monitors also include three electron guns, one for each color (these monitors are also known as RGB monitors for Red-Green-Blue). A colored dot on the screen is created by striking each of the three phosphors with electrons of different intensities—defined by voltage levels. This is similar to mixing paint colors. A lot of red will give you a more red color; a lot of blue more blue; etc.

Because there are three guns, color screens need some way to align the beams for the sharpest possible dot. To this end, RGB monitor makers employ *shadow masking*. A shadow mask is a metal plate with precisely placed holes located between the electron guns and the screen. Shadow masks ensure that only thin beams hit the screen and that the beams are aligned correctly and strike the correct location on the screen. One flaw in shadow masking technology is that the metal plate tends to heat up as it is used. When it heats up, the metal expands, resulting in a distorted image hitting the screen. This phenomenon, known as *doming*, may cause discoloration and blotches on the screen.

Some color monitor makers bypass shadow masking in favor of *slot masking*. Patented by Sony, and popularized in the company's Trinitron picture tube, slot masking is actually more prevalent in the Macintosh world than shadow masking. This is due in large part to the fact that Sony makes most of Apple's color monitors.

Slot masking solves many of the problems inherent in shadow masking. It employs an aperture grill, which is essentially an array of vertically aligned wires that separate the electron beams before they hit the phosphors. The aperture grill lets more of the electrons strike the phosphors than a shadow mask, so the picture is brighter. An aperture grill is also more resistant to doming than the thicker shadow mask. Also, slot masking uses a single-gun, single-lens approach, so the electron beams are more aligned, reducing the chances of any one beam losing focus or alignment. Finally, slot masking only restricts the beams horizontally, so more of the beam can strike the monitor screen, resulting in a better picture.

Don't necessarily give up on shadow masking, however. Some vendors, Hitachi in particular, have introduced monitors employing a new type of metal alloy, called Invar (a combination of nickel, iron and manganese), as the shadow mask. Invar is resistant to doming; hence shadow mask monitors using Invar tend to have bright colors and a sharp picture rivaling that of slot masking monitors.

Factors Affecting Picture Quality

You obviously want the best possible picture on your computer screen. Not only is a good picture pleasing to look at, it is also easy on the eyes. The easier a picture is on your eyes, the longer you're willing to look at the screen; the longer you're willing to look at the screen, the more work you will accomplish.

While we all can't agree on which is the best picture (if we did, we would all have the same monitors, assuming money was no object), we can certainly discuss the technical factors affecting picture quality. We can also agree on the qualities we'd like to see in a good picture.

Several factors influence picture quality, including brightness, contrast, convergence, distortion, focus, glare, linearity, resolution, sharpness, and screen geometry. A good monitor displays a picture clearly, brightly and with a minimum of glare. A monitor should have good *screen geometry*; that is, circles should be round, lines should be straight, and squares should be square. Poor screen geometry is often the result of a poor *aspect ratio*, which is the ratio of the monitor's width to its height. This is typically 4:3, the same as for broadcast television. This is also why pixel resolution (discussed later in this chapter) tends to be at a 4:3 ratio (640 by 480, 1,024 by 768). Your Mac's QuickDraw system is set up to work with this aspect ratio, and a monitor that does not or cannot be made to conform to that ratio will have poor screen geometry—and very distorted images.

In a good monitor, distortion should be at a minimum, even at the edges of the screen where the potential for distortion is greatest. Focus should also be sharp, since sharp focus minimizes eyestrain. However, not all factors can be maximized. It is necessary for monitor vendors to make a number of compromises while designing a monitor. For example, monitor designers walk a fine line when trying to maximize brightness while making focus as precise as possible. The brighter the picture desired, the more intense the electron beams creating the picture must be. As the beams get more intense, their focusing becomes less precise. Monitor designers must work to find a happy medium; making the picture as bright as possible without sacrificing focus.

Another problem monitor designers face is reducing glare and reflections while maintaining a sharp picture. Glare is typically reduced by placing a special coating, such as silica, on the screen. Unfortunately, placing anything on the screen allows less light to be transmitted to your eyes and reduces sharpness and brightness. Glare is, in fact, one of the most difficult problems to control. This is largely the result of the shape of a monitor screen. Because it is difficult to reach the edges of the screen with the electron beam, monitor designers curve the screen, thereby making it easier for the electron beam to reach all parts of the screen and keeping distortion to a minimum. The greater the curve, the more of a problem caused by reflected light. The flatter the screen, the less the glare. Flat screens, by the way, also have better screen geometry.

You can also reduce glare by keeping your monitor away from fluorescent lights or bright windows. These are two of the worst causes of glare. The best way to reduce glare is to purchase a monitor with as flat a screen as possible and place it in an area away from fluorescent lights or bright windows. You can also purchase a third-party, anti-glare screen that fits over your monitor. These reduce glare markedly, even in areas of bright lights. However, always preview a glare screen before you purchase it. Some do such a good job of reducing glare that they block light and make the screen appear dark or even fuzzy. Some glare screens also double as anti-radiation devices, blocking potentially dangerous electromagnetic emissions (discussed later in this chapter).

Sharpness, at least on a color monitor, is directly related to a monitor's *dot pitch*, or the distance between the holes in a shadow mask or slots in a slot mask (this is sometimes called *slot pitch* on slot masking monitors). The higher the dot pitch, the less sharp and focused the image. A lower dot pitch results in a sharper image. A good dot pitch for most monitors is .28mm or lower. With larger monitors, acceptable dot pitch can be higher, as much as .31mm. However, as resolution gets higher, dot pitch should be lower, so 1,024 by 768 resolution monitors need a dot pitch of .26mm or lower. Dot pitch is not important on monochrome monitors, since they do not employ shadow or slot masks.

Two other factors important to color monitor users are *convergence* and *color tracking*. Convergence refers to the correct alignment of a monitor's red, blue, and green electron beams. The symptoms of poor convergence, or *misconvergence*, are shadows, colored halos around white objects, or bleeding between adjacent colors. Misconvergence is typically a result of incorrect factory settings or magnetic fields from other electronic equipment. Many monitors have convergence controls, so you can eliminate most of this problem yourself. Some monitors even have *degaussing* controls, which eliminate convergence problems caused by external magnetic fields. By the way, since slot masking monitors have only one electron beam, they typically have the best convergence.

Color tracking is a measure of how well all three electron beams deliver the proper intensity on-screen, and *gray linearity* is related to this. These terms refer to a monitor's ability to display the correct shade of gray or the correct color density as the intensity of the color increases.

Controls

The ability of your monitor to control the quality of the picture on-screen is extremely important. If you can adjust the screen to give the best possible picture (remember, this is subjective), you can use your monitor productively. Therefore, all monitors include controls for the two most important technical factors—brightness and contrast.

Contrast is the relative difference between the lightest and darkest areas on-screen. This is very important for readability, as poor contrast between text and background can cause eyestrain and good contrast makes a monitor more appealing to look at.

Be cautious when using brightness controls. As a monitor ages, the screen's phosphors deteriorate. If brightness is kept too high, the phosphors deteriorate faster. When a monitor completely deteriorates, you need a new picture tube, which is an expensive proposition. Plus brightness reduces sharpness. Turning it up actually increases the width of the electron beam, which could cause an image to bleed into adjacent pixels if turned up too high.

Monitors also include a variety of other controls to help you manipulate the screen image. As mentioned, some monitors include controls for convergence and degaussing. Others include controls to change the active image area or adjust the horizontal and vertical screen size; black/white reverse controls let you display white text on a black background, or a reset switch automatically sets the monitor back to its factory settings, in case you get too carried away when making adjustments. Other controls correct pin-cushioning, which is caused when an image is distorted by bending inward around the edges of the screen (a problem primarily on flatter screens); barrel cushioning (caused when an image is distorted by bending outward towards the edges of the screen); color controls, which let you change individual colors on screen; and many more. All of these controls are intended to give you the best possible mastery over the screen image.

One factor overlooked by some users is the *location* of the controls. A control is only useful if it is easy to use. If a control is on the back of the screen, you're less likely to use it. Look for monitors that place most of the controls on the front of the screen, or at least on the side towards the front. Some monitors now offer digital push-button controls, which you may find easier to use.

A word of caution: Some users want even more control over their monitors and attempt to adjust them by changing internal switches and settings. **DO NOT DO THIS!!**

A CRT is essentially a very large capacitor; as such, it retains a very high-voltage electrical charge long after it has been turned off (sometimes for days). Let qualified repair people adjust your monitor internally.

Another control factor is tilt and swivel adjustments. Many monitors include a tilt and swivel base, which let you vertically and horizontally set the monitor to your liking. This is very handy, particularly if you work in an environment where glare is a problem. Often, tilting the monitor at just the right angle can eliminate much of the glare. You should also adjust the vertical height of the monitor so it is at eye level. This way, you don't have to tilt your head to read the monitor.

Some larger monitors—too big and heavy for the top of your Macintosh—now include Apple Desktop Bus (ADB) ports on the back of the monitor. These let you connect your keyboard and mouse to the back of the monitor and put your Mac on the floor, saving you precious desktop space. The signals from your mouse and keyboard are sent to your Mac via the monitor.

One of the best ways to keep an image sharp is to make sure your monitor screen is clean. CRTs are often covered with fingerprints, dust, smudges and other nuisances that obscure your view of the images on-screen. To clean your monitor, use any glass cleaning fluid and a paper towel or soft cloth. Spray the fluid on the cloth, not the monitor, since excess fluid can stain a monitor casing, or worse, seep inside the monitor or computer below and cause damage.

Color Matching

If you are using your color monitor to produce color output, realize that it's very difficult for any monitor to match its color with that of the final output. Color is affected by a number of factors. For example, lighting and the location of the image on the screen can change your perception of colors. As a result, you can usually only approximate colors from their on-screen appearances to their printed ones. The color-separation process you use affects the final colors. So does the printing process. Documents printed on a web press are not as sharp as those printed on a sheet-fed press. You may have to change colors after you've seen a color proof, which also doesn't exactly match the final version. This process can drive you crazy if you let it.

As a result, if you're selecting colors on the monitor, realize that the final colors in the printed document will almost always be somewhat different. This is not a reflection of the quality of your monitor. You'll get better with experience and your on-screen colors will more closely match your printed ones. For the best results, compare your monitor's colors with a Pantone color book, which shows standard colors used in the printing process. Also, look for a monitor with controls that let you adjust on-screen color to more closely match final output.

Decisions, Decisions

When selecting a monitor for your Mac, you have a variety of decisions to make: How big should the monitor be? Should it be color, black and white, or grayscale? What resolution should it be? What kind of display adapter should you use? Let's discuss these factors one at a time:

Screen Size

A variety of monitor sizes are available for the Macintosh. The original Macintosh and its direct descendants (the Plus, SE, SE/30, Classic, and Classic II) use a built-in nine-inch monitor (as with television screens, screen size is measured diagonally, from one corner to the other). Typical external monitors for these and other Macs are available in sizes from 12 inches to 21 inches or more.

Screen size, as with televisions, is measured diagonally from one corner of the screen to the opposite corner. Note that there is a difference between screen size and *active image area*. Because images distort as they reach the edge of the screen, most monitor makers leave the outer edges black. The active image area is the part of the screen that is used.

Depending on the monitor's resolution (more about that later), a 12- or 13-inch monitor shows about half of a typical 8.5 by 11-inch page, a 16-inch monitor shows a full page and a 21-inch monitor shows nearly two pages side by side. The compact 9-inch Mac monitor shows less than half a page. The size that you choose should be directly dependent on the applications you use.

If you use your Mac mainly for word processing and small spreadsheets, stick with a standard-size 12- or 13-inch monitor. If you do some desktop publishing or heavy word processing, consider a full-page display. And if you are a heavy desktop publisher or spreadsheet user, or you like to have several applications open simultaneously, select a two-page display. If you opt for a classic Mac design, be sure the screen size is not a problem for you. Many Mac users quickly tire of its small screen size.

If you use both wide spreadsheets and word processing software, consider a monitor such as the Radius Pivot, which includes a switch that automatically changes the monitor's perspective depending on the way the monitor is turned. In landscape (wide) mode, the monitor is good for spreadsheets. In portrait (long) mode, the monitor is an excellent full-page display. The monitor can be rotated while in use.

As the size of a monitor increases, so does the size of its CRT. As a result, a 21-inch monitor can easily include a tube that is two feet deep and weighs more than 50 pounds. Most 21-inch monitors are much too heavy to put on top of a Macintosh and can take up most of your desktop. Make sure that you have the space for a large monitor before you buy one. Consider more than just the top of your desk—also consider the space behind it. If you are concerned about electromagnetic emissions (discussed below), you also have to keep people behind your monitor in mind, since they are affected by the emissions generated by a monitor. The larger the monitor, the more emissions are generated and the more other people may be affected.

Resolution

Resolution is a confusing term in the Macintosh world. It actually refers to two things: the total number of dots, or *pixels*, on-screen, such as 640 by 480; and the number of dots per inch, or how tightly packed together the pixels are. In theory, the tighter the pixels are packed together, the sharper the image. Also, the greater the number of pixels on-screen, the more information that can be displayed.

In the Macintosh world, conventional wisdom says the best monitor is one that faithfully represents screen images at their printed size. These monitors have a resolution of 72 dots per inch (dpi). This resolution is based on the printer's standard measurement of 72 points, or dots, per inch. Monitors that have 72 dpi of resolution are known as WYSIWYG (pronounced "wizzy-wig") monitors, for What You See Is What You Get. In other words, one inch on the screen is equal to one inch on the printed page. These monitors provide the most accurate image for desktop publishing and other applications.

If dot-per-inch resolution is too high, you may have to make adjustments when printing an item to compensate for the higher resolution. Higher resolution monitors force you to recalculate the size of an image from its on-screen size to its printed size. If you don't find yourself needing to make these calculations, this is not critical, but if you do, it is.

This argument is controversial, especially among graphics artists, who tend to be more interested in graphics than text. The higher the resolution, the closer together the pixels. As a result, images tend to be sharper than they would be with a lower resolution display. This is particularly important when editing photographic images.

Some vendors have eliminated the need to adjust for high dot-per-inch resolution by offering adjustable resolution monitors. For example, Radius recently introduced the Precision ColorDisplay/20, a monitor with switchable resolution between higher resolution for photo retouching, and 72 dpi for desktop publishing. Expect other vendors to follow suit soon.

You can calculate the dpi of a monitor by dividing the number of pixels (measured horizontally) by the horizontal size of the active display area. This is not the same as the width of the monitor since most monitor makers blacken out a portion of the edges to reduce distortion. (It is very difficult to have accurate focus and color convergence on the entire front of a monitor.) Therefore, a 8.8-inch wide active display area with 640 pixels of horizontal resolution results in 72 dots per inch.

The pixel resolution of your monitor is not necessarily an indication of readability. The higher the pixel resolution on a smaller monitor, the sharper the image, but the smaller the objects. At 1,024 by 768 resolution, a 13-inch monitor has too many pixels on the screen for its size. The pixels are smaller than they would be at 640 by 480; as a result, more of the page fits onto the screen, and text is shrunk—too small to be read easily. By the same token, 640 by 480 resolution on a 21-inch monitor results in too few pixels on-screen. The pixels are much larger than they should be and dots are visible. While text is very readable, the result is an ugly image.

If you are comfortable with the size of the text, higher pixel resolution lets you put more information on-screen. Your word processor displays more text, your spreadsheet displays more cells, and your database displays more records. One negative factor in this is that more pixels require your Mac to process data faster in order to refresh the screen adequately. Some Macs cannot write to the screen fast enough to keep up with large-screen displays. They need the help of a video accelerator to take care of this (discussed later in this chapter).

By the way, pixels are not directly related to the phosphor dots on the screen's surface. The size of the pixels depends directly on the resolution of the graphics adapter that you're using. As a result, most monitors are capable of handling a number of different resolutions, from 640 by 480 to 1,024 by 768. To get that higher resolution, you need a video display card that can provide it. We'll discuss video display cards later in this chapter.

Color or Not

Most of us do not need a color monitor. Most of us don't have color output devices, such as color printers or image recorders. We see things in color on screen and then print in black and white on our laser printers. Still, most of us *want* a color monitor. Color is psychologically more pleasing and gives us a better feeling about our monitor and our computer.

Color monitors have long provided a dilemma for MS-DOS users, since they have had to use word processing software on a monitor with a black background with text in glorious green—not the most readable or pleasant combination. On the other hand, Macintosh users have long enjoyed a paper-white background and black text on a color monitor. This has now come to the fore in the DOS world with the popularity of Microsoft Windows and its paper-white background for text. The result is less eyestrain for everyone.

If cost is a consideration, consider a monochrome monitor. They are much less expensive than color and offer a sharper image. If you mainly use your Mac for word processing and spreadsheets, and foresee no future interest in color applications, monochrome monitors are definitely an economical choice. On the other hand, you obviously need color if you are producing color output, such as color slides, color desktop publishing files, color charts or color graphs. If this is the case, spring for the extra bucks and buy a color monitor. The Macintosh offers a wide variety of color applications, and serves as an excellent color platform. Apple includes a number of features in its System software that take advantage of color, such as color-coded folders, a color desktop pattern, the ability to customize menu, highlight and window colors, and much more.

The fact that most Mac software packages take advantage of color is striking, considering that color is a relative newcomer to the Macintosh world. Until the Macintosh II was introduced in 1987, it was very difficult and very expensive to connect a color monitor to a Macintosh, so little software supported it. The Mac's own 9-inch display was, basically, all that was available. Even today, it's very expensive to connect a color monitor to a Macintosh Classic, because its system ROMs are designed for black-and-white. The Classic II and SE/30, on the other hand, do accept color monitors cost-effectively.

Don't think that you will be in the minority if you opt for monochrome. There are still a lot of 9-inch black-and-white Macs out there, plus new machines, such as the PowerBook, that are primarily black and white (although you can hook up a color monitor to a PowerBook). Even the LC, which debuted as the lowest-cost color Mac in 1990, is used by many with a monochrome monitor. You won't be deserted if you decide on a monochrome Mac. Software developers make sure that their applications work well with monochrome screens. Monochrome monitors also offer some advantages over color. Since they use only one electron gun and have no need for masking technology, monochrome monitors tend to produce sharper text. Convergence and eyestrain are less of a problem.

Display Adapters

Without a display adapter, there is no way for your Macintosh to send video information to your monitor. The display adapter is one of the four items that get information from your computer to your screen in the following order: software, QuickDraw, the display adapter, and the monitor. The display adapter, either part of your Mac's motherboard (as on the LC, LC II, IIsi, IIci and Quadra), is mounted in a NuBus slot or is connected to a processor direct slot (PDS) in your Macintosh.

The software and QuickDraw create the instructions for putting an image on the screen. QuickDraw, which is part of Apple's system software, sends image instructions to the display adapter, via either Apple's NuBus architecture or your Mac's motherboard or processor direct slot (PDS), depending on where the display adapter is located. This communication is controlled by firmware in ROM on the video card. A frame buffer chip on the display adapter holds this data and writes it to video RAM (VRAM) on the display adapter. A timing crystal on the display adapter generates the sync (syncronization) timing, which controls the speed at which data is sent from the buffer in the display adapter to the monitor.

With an 8-bit video card, image data is stored as a bit map of index values (consisting of 8-bits each) in VRAM. A color-lookup table (CLUT) containing three 8-bit channels converts these index values into the proper amounts of red, green, and blue and sends these instructions to the Random Access Memory Digital to Analog Converter (RAMDAC) chip at rates determined by the frame-buffer controller and the timing crystal. The RAMDAC chip converts the digital signals from your computer to analog signals that your monitor can work with. It then sends this information to the monitor, which places the image on the screen using the technology described earlier in this chapter.

No matter how capable the monitor is, it can only display the images on-screen according to the instructions it has been given by the display adapter. So, if a monitor is capable of displaying images at 1,024 by 768 resolution, but the display adapter can only handle 640 by 480, the image will be at 640 by 480. By the same token, if a display adapter can handle 1,024 by 768 but the monitor can only handle 640 by 480, the image will be at 640 by 480. Also, if the software can only display images in black and white, you won't get a color image on-screen.

Choosing a display adapter can be a complicated process. In most cases, it is much less complicated in the Macintosh world than in the IBM world, however. Many vendors sell their monitors and display adapters together, as a *display system*. The choice of a display adapter is made for you.

As we also mentioned, many Macs include video capabilities on-board, eliminating the need for a display card and saving precious expansion slots. Monitors from Apple and other select vendors are compatible with this on-board circuitry, making your choice of monitors much easier. When selecting a monitor, take care that it uses the full extent of Apple's video circuitry. On the LC and IIsi, some monitors provide four-bit video with Apple's built-in circuitry and eight-bit video with their own cards, which must be bought separately and are mounted in the PDS.

The choice of display adapters has a crucial impact on the quality of the image you see on-screen. The amount of VRAM a display adapter has directly affects how many colors you can place on-screen. VRAM typically limits the number of colors, while the palette is limited by the display's digital-to-analog converter. Many Mac display adapters can be upgraded with more VRAM to display more colors. And the speed of the adapter directly affects how fast you see those colors.

Bits and Bits

Once you've decided on a color system, you have to decide how much color you want. This is directly related to the *bit depth* you select. Several color options are available on the Macintosh. There is 2-bit color, which provides four simultaneous colors on-screen; 4-bit, which provides sixteen; 8-bit, which provides 256; 16-bit, which provides 32,000; and 24-bit, which provides 16.7 million. The most common options are 4-bit, 8-bit, and 24-bit color.

With only four colors on-screen, your Macintosh will operate much faster than at greater color capability. Unfortunately, the colors look very dull and few options are available to you to change them. 16 colors look grainy, but are fairly recognizable; 256 colors look much better; and 16.7 million look "real."

If your computer cannot display a color properly, it uses a process called *dithering* to approximate it. Dithering is a mixing process that approximates the color you want, but the results are somewhat grainy, and you can often see the differently-colored dots mixed together. With only 16 colors available, the Mac will do a lot of dithering. If you try to create an image with a color that is different from the 16 available, the Mac will try to approximate it. With 256 available, colors are much smoother with considerably less dithering necessary. Images look closer to photographic quality than they did with only 16 colors. At full 24-bit mode, images look like they possess true photographic quality.

The choice you make has a big impact on the apparent speed of your Mac. The more colors you display on-screen, the longer it takes your Mac to process them and the more storage space they take up. With 4-bit color, you can only display 16 colors on-screen, and each pixel needs only four bits to describe it. Four bits can be used to create sixteen numbers—0000, 0001, 0010, 0011, 0100, 0101, etc.—with each number representing a different color (see Table 5.1).

To display 256 colors, the Mac needs 8 bits (or one byte) per pixel. Hence the name, 8-bit color. Eight bits can create 256 numbers—00000000, 00000001, 00000010, 00000011, etc. To display 16.7 million colors, the Mac needs 24-bits per pixel, as 24 bits can create 16,777,216 different numbers. There are 8 bits in one byte, so 24 bits are actually three bytes. To create 24-bit color, each byte is assigned to one of the three primary colors (red, green, or blue). 256 shades of each color can be created, and mixing these colors results in our 16.7 million total.

Table 5.1. 4-Bit Color Assignments.

Binary Number	Color Number
0000	1
0001	2
0010	3
0011	4
0100	5
0101	6
0110	7
0111	8
1000	9
1001	10
1010	11
1011	12
1100	13
1101	14
1110	15
1111	16

Video adapters take this information—which is in digital form—and convert it into analog signals for use by the monitor. This tells the monitor what color each pixel should be. By the way, just because you're limited to 16 or 256 colors on-screen at one time, your color *palette*, or the total number of colors available to you, is much larger. This is because of the Mac's use of CLUTs. With 8-bit color, the CLUT includes three 8-bit channels, which result in a palette of 16.7 million colors, the same as for 24-bit video. However, it's limited to using 256 of these colors at a time. For most uses, 8-bit color is just fine. However, if you have specialized high-end needs for your Mac, consider 24-bit video. But realize there are minuses along with the plusses.

24-Bit Color

24-bit boards open a new world to you. While 8-bit color boards provide you with "only" 256 colors on screen, 24-bit color boards offer you 16.7 million colors. This limit corresponds directly to the number of hues a display can create by using one byte for each of the three primary colors. This plethora of color riches provides you with more versatility than you may need. In fact, if your first thought was "what do I need that for?" you probably don't need it. However, if you are a serious desktop publisher, who often sends files to be color-separated or who makes a lot of slides, consider 24-bit color.

If you do make the move up to 24-bit-color programs, make sure you have the storage space to deal with the enormous data files that result. You need half a byte per pixel for 16 colors, one byte per pixel for 256 colors, and three bytes per pixel for 16.7 million colors. A 256 color image at 640 by 480 resolution takes up about 154K of storage space. The same image in 24-bit color at 1,024 by 768 resolution takes up 2.5MB of space.

To save disk space, you can compress video images. Several software products, such as Kodak's ColorSqueeze, use the Joint Photographic Expert Group (JPEG) standard to compress images. Compression can be an incredible space saver, reducing a 5MB picture file to less than 100K of disk space. The more you compress the image, the greater the chance of a loss in image quality, which may or may not be noticeable. Because these methods of compression actually remove information for the image as they compress, they are referred to as "lossy" compression techniques. The other negative aspect of image compression products is that they can be slow, especially when compressing large files. Vendors are working around this and expect to release hardware compression products soon. These products will be much faster than their software-only cousins. (Keep in mind that images—like all files on the Mac—can also be compressed with "non-lossy" compression. Any of the file compressors on the market will reduce image files as well as text and applications, but they may not achieve the degree of compression that dedicated image-compressors (lossy compressors, that is) achieve. A benefit of non-lossy compression—as the name implies—is that you lose *no* image quality from the compression process.

It's helpful to have a removable hard disk drive to store large graphics files. That way, instead of taking up space on your hard drive, particularly large data files can be stored on their own removable cartridge. You also need VRAM. 8-bit color systems can get by with 512K to 1 MB of VRAM. 24-bit systems, however need at least 1.5MB, and in most cases, 2MB. As usual, more is better.

Besides more storage space and VRAM, 24-bit systems also require more horsepower. While 24-bit colors look a lot better than 8-bit, you may find yourself gnashing your teeth waiting for your Mac to process the data. It takes a lot longer to display 24-bits of color on-screen than it does 8-bit. For black-and-white images, the Mac has to process one bit per pixel to get the image on-screen. For 8-bit images, it has to process 8 bits per pixel, making it eight times slower. For 24-bit images, the Mac has to process 32 bits per pixel. The extra eight bits, known as the *alpha channel*, are currently used for special effects by some programs. There are two ways to get around the frustration posed by waiting for the Mac to process your data—get a video accelerator board, or lower the bit depth and only use 24-bit color when necessary.

Video Accelerators

Accelerated video cards make your Mac process data faster through the use of an on-board microprocessor that exclusively handles graphics tasks. The graphics microprocessor is as much as 100 times faster than your Mac's CPU at executing graphics tasks. As a result, instead of having QuickDraw (the Mac's built-in drawing manager) handle a task, your video accelerator handles it. Instead of waiting for the graphics to be processed, your Mac's CPU can continue with other work immediately.

Video accelerators also include RAM on-board. Storing video in RAM on the accelerator card means graphics can be processed on the card instead of through the Mac's NuBus or PDS architecture. This again reduces the amount of time the Mac spends processing information and increases the rate at which graphics are processed.

To get the most out of a video accelerator, make sure you are using the correct applications. If your application doesn't support QuickDraw, you won't gain anything from an accelerator. In addition, while some video boards support GWorld memory—which processes off-screen video data to increase scrolling speed—most *applications* don't support GWorld yet. Select one that does or ask your vendor to start supporting it in the next version of your favorite application.

Be careful when you purchase an accelerator to ensure that it is compatible with your monitor. The easiest—though by no means the least expensive—way to do this is to purchase an accelerator, monitor, and video card at the same time. Also make sure that your power supply can handle the added load a 24-bit color card and accelerator add to your system. Moreover, the large power draw of these boards results in extra heat, so make sure your Mac is well ventilated. When it comes to processing 24-bit video, every edge helps. Even with a video accelerator, most Macs can process 24-bit video only about as fast as a Mac using 8-bit video without an accelerator.

Using Bit Depth To Improve Processing

You can also improve your processing speed by lowering the bit depth. Do you really need to see the best possible colors during the entire editing process? Do you really need 24-bit video when you're using a word processor?

The monitor's control panel (Figure 5.1) lets you change the bit depth by selecting a different number of displayable colors on screen. (A 24-bit capable Mac has an additional selection called "millions.") The lower the bit depth, the faster the processing speed. At the end, return to 24-bit mode to make your final corrections.

There are also a number of "freeware" utilities that let you switch between video modes at a keystroke, rather than using the monitor's control panel. For example, Switch-A-Roo, available on CompuServe and other on-line services, lets you toggle between any two screen depths (for example, between 8-bit and 24-bit) by pressing Command-Shift-9.

Changing Colors on the Macintosh

Many programs on the Mac include an editor to let you create colors on the fly. Figure 5.2 shows the editor in the Color control panel. This particular editor is used to change the color for highlighted text, but most color Macintosh applications let you change colors of various items via a similar menu. The selected option is purple, which is made up of equal amounts of red and green with full intensity blue, the maximum amount of brightness, a lot of hue, and some, but not much saturation. The Mac lets you adjust all of these options.

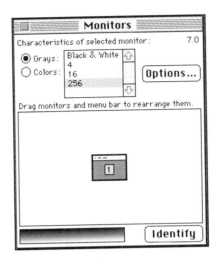

Figure 5.1: Monitor's Control Panel.

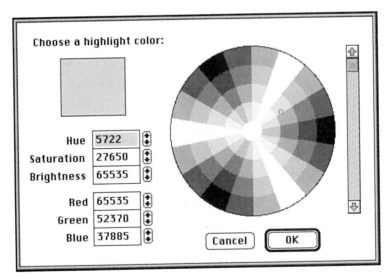

Figure 5.2: Editing Colors on the Mac.

Software

Most monitors now come with software intended to help you get the most out of your display system. One of the most important software packages for your monitor is a screen saver. These nifty devices help prevent *burn in*, which results when the same image is displayed on-screen for too long. A burned in monitor literally has the guilty image burned into the screen. Screen savers also lengthen phosphor life by blanking out the screen after a preset period of time (usually fifteen minutes). In the old days, a screen saver just blanked out the screen. Not any more! Now most screen savers are fun packages that include a variety of patterns and images running across the screen. This fun is not without aim; by moving images across the screen, no one color or shade of the screen's phosphors is depleted.

Other software utilities included with some monitors let you tear-off or expand menus, change the menu fonts, change cursor size, test monitor performance, capture screen images, or find the cursor (useful on a large screen). One especially useful feature lets you turn the monitor into a virtual screen, which effectively lets you make the screen size as large as you like, regardless of the size of the monitor. You then pan to the location of your choice. An even better approach is to use extra VRAM in your display adapter for virtual screens. The VRAM is more stable than a software screen allowing for smoother panning.

Using More Than One Monitor

One advantage of the Macintosh is its ability to use more than one monitor at a time. This lets you display a great deal of information simultaneously. You can display a gigantic image on two screens, for example, or, you can display several applications at once. This is especially useful when using a Macintosh with a 9-inch monitor. You can put menus, icons, and open file windows on the small screen leaving the large screen for work. It's also good when building an in-store or trade show display, as you can literally create a wall of monitors.

You can adjust your applications to compensate for more than one monitor through the Monitor's control panel (Figure 5.1). This control panel lets you change the orientation of each screen, using monitor one for some images and monitor two for others. For example, you can move menus to one screen and the display area to the other.

Emissions

Just as you should never sit too close to your TV screen, you should never sit too close to your monitor. Monitors emit a variety of radiation from the front, sides, and back of the screen. The farther you are away from the monitor, the better. There is some controversy associated with this issue, and several researchers have stated that there are no health risks associated with monitor radiation. However, others have found that monitors may cause health problems such as miscarriages, birth defects, and even cancer. Although there are no conclusive studies of this issue, it's better to be safe than sorry.

Many types of electronic equipment emit electromagnetic radiation. Typically, they do this over a wide range of frequencies. Monitors and televisions are among the worst offenders. Some emissions, such as x-rays, are known to be dangerous, so they are regulated by law. Most color monitors and TVs emit very low levels of x-radiation, but special shielding and the glass in the screen absorbs it. Other emissions at the lower frequencies have been getting attention for some time. The FCC routinely seized computing equipment in the early '80s, for example, because it emitted low-frequencies that frequently interfered with broadcast signals. You could tell if a computer was being used by your next door neighbor when your TV signal went out. These emissions are tightly regulated, so they aren't noticeable anymore.

Even *lower* frequency emissions are now in the spotlight. VLF (very low-frequency, in the range of 2 KHz to 400 KHz) and ELF (extremely low-frequency, in the range of 5 Hz to 2 KHz) emissions are not radiation, per se, since radiation actually ionizes molecules. These emissions are electromagnetic. Rather than ionizing molecules, these magnetic fields interact with the natural electric activity of cells, modifying ion balances across cell membranes, growth rates, and nerve-cell behavior. ELF has been more in the news than VLF lately, as research has shown it to be harmful. Monitors are one source of ELF emissions, but even more powerful sources are electric blankets and power lines.

In 1987, the first recommendations of The Swedish National Board for Measurement and Testing (the MPR) for monitor levels covered VLF only. Since recent ELF research has indicated that ELF is more dangerous than VLF, MPR released a stricter set of standards, called SWEDAC MPR 1990:8, in 1990. Because it is so complete, organizations around the world, including the U.S.-based Institute of Electronic and Electrical Engineers (IEEE) have adopted it. As a result of these and other factors, monitor makers have started introducing low-emission versions of their monitors. These monitors have been popular in Europe in general and Sweden in particular over the last few years. If you decide to purchase a low-emission monitor, make sure the monitor complies with the Swedish standard for emissions. There are some so-called low-emission monitors that don't. In particular, make sure the monitor complies at the ELF level.

But what if you already have a monitor? What should you do then? You have a few choices. There are many anti-radiation glare screens on the market that limit emissions through the front of the monitor. Keep in mind, however, that the strongest emissions are through the back and sides of the monitor. Take care not to place yourself or others directly behind or to the sides of monitors. These emissions can also go through walls. Even if you decide to do nothing, you can limit your risk of exposure by staying at least 28 inches from the front of your monitor. This is about arm's length. Electromagnetic fields diminish in strength dramatically at that distance. Stay at least three feet away from the sides and backs of monitors. If you sit in cubicles, try to arrange the monitors so they all back into a common corner. Also ensure that people are at least three feet from the sides or back of the screen. Finally, make sure monitors are far enough apart so that their ELF emission does not interfere with the picture on other monitors. Also remember to turn off your monitor when you aren't using it. If you just dim the screen, emissions continue.

Putting It All Together

So what are the most important factors to consider when purchasing a monitor? First, realize that you are not just purchasing a monitor, you are buying a *display system*, which includes the monitor, video card, and if necessary, the graphics accelerator. Also realize that the monitor is the computer to your eyes, neck, and mind. You're going to be spending thousands of hours staring at it so you better get the most for your money.

Don't skimp on features such as dot pitch and interlacing; get a noninterlaced monitor with a tight dot pitch. To that end, if you decide to purchase a color monitor, consider an 8-bit video system. This offers 256 colors, more than enough for most applications. Don't get a 4-bit system; 16 colors are barely better than none. Unless you are using your Mac for high-end graphics or multimedia applications, don't get a 24-bit system. The high overhead a 24-bit system exacts on your system is not worth the extra money, again, unless you need it.

The key issue when purchasing a display system is the applications for which you will be using your Mac. If you're typically a spreadsheet user, for example, decide whether you need a wide display to show more cells on-screen at once. Don't just think about what you're using today; if you plan to consider desktop publishing or add multimedia capabilities in the next year or two, get a display system capable of meeting those needs as well. If you can't afford the best display system right now, get a monitor capable of handling high resolutions and get a display adapter than can be upgraded or traded in for a more capable one in the future.

Other Technologies

The CRT is fine as a display choice, but it's really only suitable for desktop environments. As a result, other technologies have come along for portables and notebooks. The one currently used in the Macintosh world is LCD. Others available in the world of general computing are gas plasma and electroluminiscent displays.

Liquid Crystal Displays

LCDs were developed in the early 1970s when researchers found that a thin layer of liquid crystal changes from transparency to opacity when an electric current is applied to it. LCDs are made by sandwiching a thin layer of liquid crystal between two plates of glass, the inside surfaces of which are coated with transparent electrodes.

LCDs use a light background. Images are formed by creating dark images on that background. This happens by blocking light through the use of polarizing filters. Because they are suspended in an oily fluid, the crystals naturally form a helix. As light travels through the helix, it is prevented from reaching the screen, thereby creating a dark pixel. The more light that is blocked, the darker the pixel. Light pixels are created by applying a charge to crystals, which forces them to become parallel to the light, allowing more light to pass through.

LCD technology is much better than it used to be. The screens are lighter and offer higher contrast. Resolution has improved, and users are able to view the screen at much wider angles than before. In the old days, if you weren't directly in front of the screen (and we mean directly in front), you couldn't read it. The result is a much more readable screen. As LCD technology has improved, sales of notebook computers has gone up. Notebooks rely on liquid crystal technology because LCDs are lighter and consume less power than any other screen technology.

The PowerBook 100 and 140 use supertwist technology to display images. Supertwist refers to the orientation of the liquid crystals. The greater the twist, the higher the contrast and hence the better the readability. LCDs require supplemental lighting for display purposes. Two methods, sidelighting and backlighting are currently in use. All PowerBooks provide backlit screens, which provide the most light. Sidelit screens are not as bright, but they can be thinner than backlit. In supertwist screens, light passes through a polarizing filter. LCDs, controlled by the computer, either pass light at a given pixel or don't, producing light or dark areas.

Active matrix screens, like those in the PowerBook 170 and Macintosh Portable, produce the best possible LCD displays. They use thin-film transistors, repainting the screen much faster than other LCD screens and offering a wider viewing angle, up to 60 degrees. Up to 32 shades of gray can be produced on LCD screens. This is accomplished by varying the speed at which a pixel is turned on or off. The faster they're turned on, the darker the gray. LCD's are much lighter, require less power, last longer and cost less than CRTs. LCDs also have a flat surface; compared to the curved surface on most CRTs, glare has been effectively eliminated on LCDs.

Color LCDs

Although Apple doesn't offer color portables yet, they are gaining popularity in the MS-DOS world. Currently, the best color displays for portables are TFT-active LED matrix screens. These use a technology similar to color CRTs, employing a triad of red, green, and blue liquid crystals for each pixel. Each liquid crystal is paired with a transistor. When a transistor is turned on, the associated crystal lights. Just as with a CRT, different colors can be created by varying the intensity of the three colors. Color is created in much the same way shades of gray are; by varying the number of times the liquid crystal turns on and off.

Field Emission Displays

A new technology, FEDs take the best of CRTs and the best of LCD technology. They resemble a flattened CRT and include millions of tiny, individual emitters between two thin, glass layers. When available, FEDs will offer lighter screens using less power than LCDs.

Other Forms of Video

With multimedia becoming a burgeoning application, your Mac is already capable of displaying more than just text and graphics on-screen. It can now display full-motion video, captured images, even television signals on screen. This capability generally has little to do with your monitor; it is strictly the result of the capabilities of the display adapters inside your Macintosh. There are two ways this happens—the Mac captures video information from broadcast sources, or the Mac sends video signals to broadcast sources. In either case, this is called desktop video, or DTV.

Sending information from your Mac to a VCR is especially useful for multi-media presentations and training videos, since you can record the presentation or class on video. The recipient doesn't need a Macintosh to view the video. Since almost everyone has a VCR, more people can view it. Plus, the video cassette can include video, music and voice in addition to Macintosh output. This makes a compelling presentation. Receiving information from a VCR or a TV to your Mac is useful for a variety of applications as well, such as creating presentations or building a library of snapshots. You'll find significant discussions of these and related topics in both the Graphics Input and Multimedia chapters, elsewhere in this book.

6

Graphic Input Devices

Today's Macintosh is blessed with a variety of "eyes," or hardware options giving the computer visual senses. These products, such as *scanners* and cameras, provide a way for you to acquire graphical data into the Mac. The data may be photographs, drawings, or text scanned as an image to be converted into a text file. These graphical input devices greatly expand the capabilities of the computer by essentially allowing you to include anything you can "see" in a document.

The best carpenter knows when a job requires a saw, a router, or a drill. All are tools that cut, but each has a specialized application; for each, there's an abundance of hardware and price options. Likewise, the key to acquiring graphical data is knowing what tools to use for the job, and it is best to try to find the right tool for the job. Cameras, for example, allow "three-dimensional" image capture—in other words, a photo of a "live person," an object (such as a house or a car), or anything else you might photograph with a conventional camera. Scanners are meant to scan "two-dimensional" data, such as a photograph, printed data (text or images), or slides. For special needs or effects, you can even scan cloth patterns or something as offbeat as food placed under glass! If you need to acquire text from sheets of paper but you don't want to fall victim

to the drudgery of retyping, you can use *optical character recognition (OCR)* software that turns your scanned "image" of text into an actual text file you can use in a word processing or other document. For people such as attorneys, OCR software is a tremendous productivity tool. Bar code scanners, such as those you see in a grocery store, are highly specialized tools that allow the computer to read a printed series of lines representing a number (code) for inventory and database use.

Finally, yet another type of graphic input device provides the ability to capture video images for still or animated use. These *frame grabbers* and *video digitizers* can attach to video cameras, VCRs, and other video acquisition sources, and then digitize the images for use in the Macintosh.

Just like a carpenter, once you've determined what the correct tools are for the graphic input you want to do, you have more choices to make. Within each of the broad divisions of categories there are a variety of types of hardware alternatives and prices. The acquisition of graphic data can be immensely pleasing and fun; it can also be tedious and frustrating. The key to making a cost-conscious, useful, and effective decision is defining the task at hand as carefully as possible.

In this chapter, you'll find descriptions of all the various hardware devices for the Macintosh and their uses. Additionally, a number of new advances in technology are described, ranging from digital photography to new compression algorithms. The carpenter building the best-looking cabinet is the one who not only has skills, but who also knows the right tools for the right job.

Scanners

A scanner is actually like a common office copier. Using a *light source,* it passes light over paper, and using a special *receptor,* it captures the image it has "seen." While a copier then prints the image onto another sheet of paper, the computer *digitizes* the image and stores it onto a disk. In this way, it has converted the image into a digital format that the computer can store and retrieve: you can then manipulate.

Most people are interested in two basic functions of scanners: acquiring images and acquiring text. To the scanner, whatever it sees is just another image to be digitized—whether it's a photograph or a typed letter. A common misunderstanding is that the scanner can distinguish between text and graphics—this is not true; the initially scanned image is the same to the scanner, and specialized software deals with text or graphics. *Optical character recognition* (OCR) software takes a scanned image of text, looks for patterns of letters and numbers it recognizes and turns them into text. *Image manipulation software* allows you to work with a scanned image and make a variety of changes to it.

What Scanner Is Right for Me?

As with all graphic input devices, your needs dictate what type of a scanner to buy and use. For example, if you're an attorney and you have to turn multiple contracts and letters into text but you really won't need to use many images, then you will want a *sheetfed* scanner, which is essentially a *flatbed* (desktop) scanner with an automatic sheet feed capability. You don't need support for color or even a high degree of gray scaling, because the scanner views text as "line art," or black and white images without gradations of color.

Conversely, if you are a designer and you want to acquire colored logos clients have given to you to modify, you will want a scanner that supports color. If you are desktop publishing a company newsletter—presumably not in color—then you will want a scanner that is powerful enough to acquire detailed images with gray-scale support, not color.

Another choice is between a desktop scanner (flatbed or sheetfed) or a *hand-held* scanner. The desktop scanners are more expensive and are suitable for scanning large quantities of images or text. The hand-held scanner today can offer the same level of quality, but is primarily used by people who don't need to scan multiple pages daily and who want to save some money. It's also a great choice if you want to affordably provide scanners for people at their desks without having to rely on a shared flatbed unit.

Scanner Technology

Every scanner needs a source of light to illuminate what it is scanning, and a receptor to allow the scanner to "acquire" the image. In combination with specialized analog and digital chips, the light and receptor work to convert an "analog" image (such as a printed photograph) into a digital format.

Commonly, the light source is a fluorescent tube or an LED (light-emitting diode) array. While black/white and gray-scale scanners can have a red or green light, the best color is white because it allows for no dropout of color in the scanning process (for most gray-scale applications, however, a green or red light is acceptable). Color scanners, however, must acquire all colors; thus, they must have white lights.

The light spectrum defines the scanner's characteristics; fluorescent light generates a broader light spectrum than LEDs. A color scanner needs a continuous light spectrum. The light receptor also needs to match the characteristics of the document to scan and the light source. The light is projected over the document (or across, in case of a slide scanner), generally reflects onto one or more mirrors, and then is focused by a lens to end over the receptor (also called a photosensor). It is then converted into digital format and transmitted to the computer.

The Mechanics of Scanners

Desktop scanners are composed of moving parts. Flatbed scanners move the entire optical system assembly over the document, while overhead scanners rotate a mirror to cover the surface of the original. The "motor" of the hand-held scanner is the user's hand, which guides the scanner over the document being scanned. The need to pass the photosensor over the document is required so that the image of the document can be "cut" into fine slices, or lines composed of a fixed or arbitrary amount of points (pixels) used by the computer.

Flatbed scanners use a *stepping motor* to move the scanner head, generally under a piece of glass, in a manner similar to a copier. The steps of the motor define the vertical resolution of the ultimate scanned image. You set the resolution you want (e.g., 100, 200, 300, or 400 dpi) before scanning. The higher the resolution, the slower the scan.

Sheet-fed scanners move the paper onto a glass plate where it can be scanned just as by the flatbed (and also like an automatic feeder on a copier). The hand-held scanner uses a friction roller that transmits displacement and assures a straight scan trajectory.

Scanner Electronics

A common electronic component to scanners is the CCD, or *charge-coupled device*. The CCD works like a row of little buckets that fill depending on the amount of light sent over them. The electronics then read the content of each bucket while emptying it. The result is a series of analogic values that are transformed into digital data.

The number of cells in a row determines the maximum hardware resolution possible; however, using computational algorithms called interpolation, the resolution can be artificially increased by calculating the value of added pixels depending on the value of adjacent ones. This can give a lower-resolution image the appearance of being higher. The true physical resolution is determined by dividing the width of the scan area by the number of CCD elements.

In the case of a gray-scale scanner, the analogic value (the amount of photons) is sent to an *analog-to-digital (A/D) converter* which translates into 4, 8 (gray-scale), or 24 (color) bits of data. In the case of black and white, the analog value is compared with a reference number stored in the scanner, and the corresponding bit is set accordingly. The sequence of lines is then sent to the host using the SCSI, serial, or NuBus interface.

Scanner Types

Hand-Held Scanners

Once considered mere toys, hand-held scanners are rapidly gaining some success and user recognition. They have long suffered a poor reputation because of their relatively low performance and their narrow width (typically about four inches) compared to their flatbed cousins. Ease of use has always been a factor of their success, together with affordability. In the last few years, however, this reputation has changed with dramatic increases in image quality—comparable with flatbeds—combined with the ability to *stitch* large images together as well as continued low prices.

There is nothing like a hand-held scanner for quickly acquiring a magazine article or photograph into a document. In the computer-peripheral rally for desk space, each square inch is accountable for quality of life. You don't need to ask for a free time slot on the company's flatbed to get the job done. Hand-held scanners are available, affordable (typically less than $500), and easy to use.

Choosing a hand-held scanner means deciding between black and white, gray-scale, or color. Black and white scanners simply transmit only one bit of information per pixel—either black or white. These units are appropriate for simple OCR work or acquiring line-art original documents. Almost every one-bit scanner is also capable of generating "artificial" gray-scale information using "clusters" of pixels to simulate an analog value of a larger pixel. This translates into a reduction of the true resolution, since pixel squares of 4-by-4 (16 grays), 6-by-6 (36 grays), or 8-by-8 (64 grays) are used to create one larger, gray-scale pixel. Fortunately, this limitation may not be as dramatic as it appears if the printer used to output the result has 300 or less dpi resolution; this is a common maximum basic laser printer resolution.

Here's an example: A hand-held scanner has a maximum resolution of 400 dpi, and uses a 6-by-6 matrix to generate 36 grays (37 counting the white). The software averages the matrix value and creates a pixel that has 37 possible values at 66.66dpi (400/6). A laser printer with 300 dpi will need a similar matrix to print 37 grays. This means that the actual gray-scale resolution of the printer is only 50 dpi (300/6). The image in the computer's memory carries still a little more information than the printer can output (66.6 x 37=2468 versus 50 x 37= 1850). This problem is common to all printers, and is the main reason for disappointment and frustration from users expecting great results and blaming the scanner while their printer may actually be at fault!

The hand-held scanner's vertical movement across the image is detected using a friction roller that uses a series of wheels to rotate a slotted disk in front of an optical sensor. This process is very similar to what happens in your mouse, except that in the scanner only the Y-axis displacement is taken into account, while a mouse uses a ball to track X-and-Y-axis movement.

The multiplication ratio between the roller and the slotted wheel as well as the number of slots in the wheel determines the vertical resolution. When the hand-held scanner is set to a lower resolution than maximum, the electronics knows to skip one line every so often to match the horizontal settings.

Gray-scale, hand-held scanners are more sophisticated devices that have all the functionality of their big flatbed brothers. Their A/D converter translates the value of each pixel into 8-bit digital data, which is sent to the computer. Since the amount of information to be sent to the host is much bigger (eight bits instead of one), selecting the right resolution to match the real needs of the output is critical to achieve an acceptable scanning speed. Contrary to a flatbed scanner, which can interrupt its displacement at any time to send the data from the memory to the hard disk, a hand-held scanner needs to keep a full pass in memory.

> **NOTE:** Most hand-held scanners use the SCSI interface to feed the data to the Macintosh, and the hard disk uses the same interface. The SCSI implementation in the Macintosh does not allow simultaneous transfers to various targets.

To go around the perceived limitation of the narrow width of the hand-held scanner, software solutions provide help for *stitching* together two or more passes of a large image. ThunderWorks offers the "skoogy" tool, which, provided a small overlap between the two passes is available, allows you to manually stretch the right half of the image to achieve a "perfect" stitch.

Another more sophisticated and emerging technology is called *virtual-page scanning*, which is a fully automatic software solution for merging as many stripes as your memory permits. Autostitching functionality will hopefully migrate to the Macintosh platform in the future.

To help achieve a straight scan, one of the hand-held scanner's biggest drawbacks, several vendors offer plastic pieces that attach to the scanner head, making it easier to slide against a ruler. Some devices even offer templates with rails that guide the scanner head and assure optimal results. Scans can also be straightened once the image has been scanned and is loaded into the software, using what is commonly called a "deskew" tool.

Flatbed Scanners

Black-and-white flatbed scanners have become largely obsolete. They were the pioneers of the desktop digital image technology, but have been progressively replaced by higher-quality gray-scale units that have become increasingly affordable. The only reason for purchasing a black-and-white unit today would be if you plan to use the scanner for extensive (and exclusive) OCR applications. In that case, you would want the unit to be equipped with a fast scanning unit and a large sheet-feeder, as well as a powerful and accurate OCR software package.

Gray-scale scanners are the most common desktop devices in use today. Color printed output is still a sophisticated technology requiring expensive equipment and a lot of know-how, or used in specific applications, such as desktop publishing.

Apple has always played a low-profile game with scanners, providing the fan of the multicolored logo with a disappointing 4-bit unit. Recently, however, the release of the excellent 8-bit OneScanner finally matches the expectations and needs of the professional. OneScanner is combined with one of the best scanning software of the market (LightSource). Virtually every other scanner manufacturer has been offering an 8-bit unit typically sporting maximum resolutions ranging from 300 to 600 dpi.

Another important flatbed issue is the size of the scan area. While all flatbed scanners accept a standard letter-size page, some units support up to 11-by-14 inch paper. Bear in mind, however, the required desktop space taken by these large units. To operate, they need to be close to your Macintosh, and you can't stack piles of books on top of them.

Color scanning is the latest rage. Although few casual users have color printers, the price difference between an 8-bit gray-scale unit and a full 24-bit color scanner have become negligible enough that buyers increasingly select color—even though gray-scale jobs are by far the most common applications.

Color scanners operate much as a gray-scale scanner that generates and mixes three color planes (like a TV). Red, green, and blue planes are superimposed to generate true color. Each color has eight bits of data per pixel, resulting in very large files. Two basic technologies exist for creating these three color planes: one pass and three pass. The reflected light is sent to three separate CCDs, one each for red, green, and blue. The scanner transmits the RGB data for each line, before moving to the following one.

A three-pass scanner uses only one CCD, and moves three times over the original using a colored filter to acquire each color. This approach is generally slower simply because of the time and repetition the scanning unit needs to move for three passes.

A critical issue with color images is fidelity. WYSIWYG images are not easily attained, primarily because of the physics of color: the difference in nature between color on a printed document and color on-screen. A computer screen uses an *additive* process to render an image. Beams of electrons of red, green, and blue converge on the surface to generate red, green, and blue light for each screen pixel.

A printout uses a *subtractive* process. The ambient light is absorbed by the colored dots on the surface of the paper, and only a fraction of the light is then reflected to the eye. In a traditional printing process, colored dots on the paper are complementary colors of red, green, and blue—cyan, magenta, and yellow. Black is added to provide better control over contrast. This requires a translation from a three-color additive process to a four-color subtractive process. Additional variables include type and quality of paper and inks, as well as ambient light.

To achieve perfect color matching requires calibrated screens and iterative corrections that comprehensively control all elements in the chain. A professional will print a sample document, scan it, and compare the results, perform necessary corrections, and print again, repeating the process until satisfactory results are obtained.

Scanner vendors are working with software and printer companies to provide software-based calibration parameters that help ease the problem. These files (PPDs) are loaded into the image editing software and adjust the values of the image components to match a specific printer. The recent release of PostScript level 2 printers and standardization of the different color models in use will certainly bring WYSIWYG color to the desktop in the near future.

Sheet-Fed Scanners

A sheet feeder is a built-in or add-on mechanism identical to that of a copy machine or printer, which moves the pages to the scanning area automatically. It is particularly useful for large OCR jobs. Before selecting a sheet feeder, make sure the software you are using will support its operation!

The sheet-fed scanner is basically a flatbed scanner with a sheet-feeding mechanism added to it. Just as with a copier, there is a variety of basic methods for feeding paper. These have virtually no bearing on scanner operation or image quality. The main thing to keep in mind when choosing a sheet feeder is that it has a good reputation for resisting paper jams and accurately places paper on the face of the scanner so your documents are perfectly positioned for high-quality scans.

Overhead

An overhead scanner might be described as an upside-down flatbed scanner. The original lies face-up on the digitizing table, and the optical system assembly moves over the table to cover its entire surface. The biggest advantage of this approach is to let the scanner pass over nonflat objects, giving it a 3-D or camera-like capability. In particular, small objects like coins can be scanned without the need for an intermediate photograph.

The Truvel unit is a very high-end, expensive performer. It uses a standard camera lens to achieve up to 900 dpi and can scan an original as large as 12-by-17 inches. This 24-bit color unit moves the entire optical and lighting assembly over the area being scanned. Since it uses standard 35mm lenses, you can zoom-in and adjust the F-stop value to achieve optimal results.

However, this high-end scanner is not without drawbacks. For example, it requires a calibration procedure, a time-consuming process, each time you power-up. Also, scanning at 900 dpi is extremely slow and generates huge files: a 4-by-6-inch original scanned at 900 dpi in 24-bit color totals approximately 58 megabytes of data! Obviously, a large hard disk is in order if you plan to generate images such as this.

The Mirror VisionScan exists in two versions: 200 and 300 dpi; there is even a color version. The sensor is fixed and a rotating mirror covers the entire page. Because the scanner connects to the computer's serial port, scanning time is very slow (up to 20 minutes for a full-page color document!), which makes them inappropriate for volume scanning. The scanner has a distinct price advantage, however.

Printheads

One of the first and more innovative methods for inputting images was marketed in 1985 by ThunderWare, called *ThunderScan*. This inexpensive device was designed to replace the ribbon cartridge in an ImageWriter printer, which then provided horizontal and vertical displacements. The original image was fed through the printer like a regular sheet, while the optical assembly moved across the page like a printhead. A very fine spot of light was sent from the ThunderScan towards the image. The reflected beam was converted into digital data capable of up to 64 shades of gray.

The most significant drawback was its slothful speed because it relied on the serial interface and was only able to read one line at a time at the printer's resolution. It also necessitated the original to be a thin piece of paper, preventing the scanning of pages in books or thick originals; the possibility of your artwork jamming and being destroyed was a frequent danger. Nevertheless, the ThunderScan affordably and uniquely helped bring the concept and capability of scanning to the mainstream user.

Slide Scanners

When it comes to achieving magazine-quality or professional image quality, nothing tops a slide scanner. Professional photographers always work with slide film instead of paper because the color fidelity and subtlety of the material is so much higher. But there is definitely a cost for this level of quality. A slide scanner can ring the register anywhere from 3 to 100 thousand dollars, depending on the models and performance. Typically, the higher the price tag, the higher the quality.

Virtually all slide scanners provide 24 bits of color, although some of them internally use even more. To achieve high-quality "gamma" correction in images, some of the high-end models work with 12 bits of data per channel, then reduce that amount to the 8-bit per color channel common to most 24-bit models. Slide scanner resolutions can achieve as much as 2400 dpi. As you might expect, these images are huge and can take anywhere from several minutes to a few hours to scan.

Two main technologies are used in slide scanners: *drum* and *flat*. A drum scanner consists of a transparent cylinder of glass onto which the slide is taped. Inside the tube is the light source, which is generally in a fixed position. Outside is the optical assembly, which moves in parallel with the cylinder axis in very small increments. The cylinder rotates to expose the surface of the slide to the optical system, resulting in a series of lines being analyzed. The flat approach is similar to a regular flatbed scanner, where the original lies on a piece of transparent material, although the light source is positioned across the CCD unit.

The size of the original slide the scanner will support varies with different models. Professional photographers commonly use medium-format film (4-by-6 inch), which is not accepted by every unit—most of the entry-level machines accept only 35mm slides. Some common lower-end units are the Nikon LS-3500, Eikonix 1435, and Array Technologies Slide Scanner.

RasterOps offers an interesting option if you're on a budget: The Espresso, so named because of its resemblance to an espresso machine, is a low-cost slide scanner that uses a video-camera type of CCD to acquire images. However, the video technology, relatively limited resolution, and need for a video digitizer of some sort makes it unsuitable for high-end, press-printed output.

Some recent flatbed units offer an option for transparency (slide) scanning, in the form of an accessory kit that attaches to the flatbed, providing the flexibility of transparent and opaque originals support.

The very high-end slide scanners operate with CMYK color space instead of the traditional RGB method, allowing for highly accurate calibration and color correction to take place in the scanner electronics itself, rather than in the host.

Connection to Your Macintosh

No matter what type of scanner you use, you will have to feed all this newly acquired data into your Macintosh. There are several ways to connect a scanner to your system.

SCSI

The SCSI port is the fastest and most convenient way to connect to the Mac, although a few rules apply. Each device on a SCSI chain needs to have a unique ID, and almost every SCSI interface allows you to select a free ID for your scanner to be connected. Some scanners ship with software that automatically determines a free ID from which to select. *Termination* is also an issue. In particular, some hand-held scanners require being first in the chain (ScanMan, LightningScan), while some require being last (Typist).

Most hand-held scanners come with a SCSI interface box; for the most part, the only inconvenience of this is the box's size. They need to have a provision for a second connector, and get their power from a wall plug, which can generate a cable mess. Although the manual specifies it is better to shut them down when not in use, rarely—if ever—will you experience problems keeping your SCSI box continuously powered on.

Flatbed units are typically quite bulky, with the SCSI interface circuitry built-in, therefore requiring no additional dedicated desk space.

Hardware Compatibility

The Macintosh uses the SCSI port to access other peripherals as well, external or internal. Some external storage devices require the operating system to regularly (every 500 ms.) question the drive if any cartridge has been inserted. This disables the SCSI port for a short time, and can result in data loss (this problem has been reported with Bernoulli storage systems). As a result, you should take care to discuss with your dealer or MIS representative any potential hardware incompatibilities before investing in your scanner.

Floppy Interface

A recent and innovative way to connect a hand-held scanner to a Macintosh uses the external floppy port. (Of course, not all Macs are equipped with this peripheral device.) This method, developed by ThunderWare, offers a low-cost means for entering a large amount of data, therefore offering a good speed/price performance (LightningScan Compact) for a one-bit hand-held scanner. A notable drawback to this method, however, is its dependency on specific Macintosh models. If you change your machine, you may lose the usage of your scanner.

Serial Connections

A serial port is relatively slow, compared to a SCSI port (up to 115 Kbits/second compared to 1 megabyte/second or higher). There may be a future in serial connections, however, when compression takes place in the scanner itself, and the bandwidth is significantly lower (these developments are currently in the works).

The only real benefit to a serial interface today is its universality. Every computer ever made—Mac, IBM PC, work station, etc.—has a serial input. This allows manufacturers to develop an identical product on various hardware platforms while writing software specific to each of them.

NuBus

Some gray-scale and color hand-held scanners use a NuBus card (e.g., Mouse System's PageBrush or Asuka's Nuscan Gray-Scale scanner) and a few flatbed units (e.g., the Sharp JX-450). This is the best approach if you have a free NuBus slot; they are fast and may contain additional dedicated hardware, such as compression optimized processors, which can be used to speed up other applications.

Video Digitizers and Frame Grabbers

A frame grabber differs from a scanner like a still-life painting differs from a portrait. A frame grabber can import "live" images into your Macintosh, sometimes compressing and decompressing them on-the-fly, finally giving some true meaning to the much-hyped "multimedia" trend.

This kind of sport, however, requires a hefty hardware setup to play the game. Much of the video processing takes place in the host CPU, requiring the fastest machine you can afford, all the RAM you can stuff into it, and a very large hard disk. In addition, a bunch of removable optic and magnetic media, and a few other indispensable gadgets.

But the results are stunning. Looking at a movie on a Macintosh, in a resizeable window on top of the finder or in the middle of your favorite word processor or mail software is an unforgettable experience. Twenty-four-bit accelerated screen cards are offered by three major manufacturers.Numerous lesser-known brands are also available, and provide an inexpensive source of images for education, desktop publishing, and all sorts of other applications. Their prices range from below a thousand dollars to significantly higher prices.

Standards

In order to better understand video capture, a brief word about the underlying technology will help. The world is divided into three major video standards, true of any common VCR: *NTSC* in the USA and Japan; *PAL* in most of Europe; *SECAM* for France and eastern Europe. Most Americans are unaware that the video tapes so commonly available at video stores will not run on European machines.

Each of theses standards carry a common characteristic: interlaced video (a term you may have run into when studying different types of monitors). Interlacing means the electron beam projected from the cathode of the picture tube begins its travel at the left-hand top corner, draws the first line, and continues on all odd lines down to the right bottom. It then goes back to the top to draw all the even lines. It does this for each "frame."

In an NTSC picture, there are 525 lines that pictured in two halves called *fields* to form a frame. There are 30 frames displayed per second, allowing for smooth animation.

There are also two types of video signals: Composite video, most commonly found in consumer products; and component video, a higher quality method. Composite video mixes the red, green, and blue components of the signal (chrominance) with the black and white (luminance) into one signal. The component video, also called S-video, keeps the two parts separate and provides a higher color quality.

Another important part of the video signal is synchronization, called *sync* for short. It indicates the start of the frame and keeps the image in position when using the pause function in your VCR. It is recommended you test your VCR for a good sync output if you expect to use it to grab single frames from a videotape. This feature is also called *genlock*.

As mentioned earlier, the NTSC standard is made of 525 lines. This resolution is achieved only with professional equipment, consumer electronic products being far behind. A video laser disc player, for example, is capable only of outputting between 425 and 450 lines of resolution. An S-VHS player may reach 400 lines, while standard VHS will rarely give you anything better than 240 lines. A good-quality consumer video camera outputs between 300 and 350 lines.

Live Video

QuickTime

The central component of live video in your Macintosh is *QuickTime*. QuickTime is a set of routines that provides standard mechanisms and interfaces for synchronizing video and audio, handling on-the-fly compression and decompression, and isolating the software from the hardware by providing a well-designed "toolbox." It is similar to how Quickdraw opened the door to static images.

QuickTime can—providing you have the right hardware—display full-motion video on your Macintosh, 30 frames per second of 24-bit video on a 640-by-480-pixel screen. However, to date there is no digitizer board capable of sustaining this bandwidth. A more realistic image size is 160-by-120 pixels, which still means almost 60K bytes for a single frame—meaning 10 seconds of animation will stack up to nearly 18 megabytes of data! This is why compression has become such an important and driving issue in the computer industry today.

QuickTime provides support for hardware and software compression, with replaceable codes (coder/decoder) to allow future implementation of powerful algorithms or dedicated hardware fully accessible from any application using QuickTime. In fact, QuickTime is good enough in its design and implementation to interest other platforms, and it has plenty of chances to become a multimedia standard over various types of hardware (for example, Intel- and UNIX-based platforms).

Once you've got the animation in the computer, you'll most likely want to edit and correct the raw data to suit your needs. The software adapted to these new applications is just emerging; Adobe's Premiere and Diva's VideoShop are the pioneers in this area.

Frame Grabbers

The hardware that facilitates the acquisition of a single frame of video is called a *frame grabber*. Choosing a frame grabber requires you to thoroughly analyze your needs and financial resources. Additionally, frames per second and size of the output, as well as prospective sources of data, should be taken into consideration.

At the low-end, The Koala MacVision Color Video Digitizer offers video capture to NuBusless Macs using the SCSI port. This approach prevents motion capture, due to speed and design limitations. The MacVision digitizes the incoming image in three passes, requiring several seconds for each. Consequently, the source needs to be static, which is not always easy with a VCR in pause mode. Substantial blurring and other visual defects are often the result of this low-cost ($799) and now rather obsolete technology. Another digitizer carries the same limitations, although using a NuBus slot. Digital Vision's ComputerEyes/Pro ($399) is also somewhat slow in acquiring a frame and requires an absolutely stable source.

Frame grabbers that can digitize an image in less than 1/30 of a second are *Processor Direct Slot* (PDS) or NuBus-based cards. Some of them are combined with other functions, such as a 24-bit display (RasterOps' popular 364 at $1099; the 24STV at $1799; the 24XLTV at $3999; and the recent MediaTime at $2799; as well as TrueVision's NuVista at $ 3595) which work as a video input and display card, requiring only one slot for this dual functionality. Other hardware on the digitizer includes compression/decompression- specialized processors (such as the ComputerFriends' ColorSnap 32+, 24STV, and 24XLTV, as well as the MediaTime). Yet others offer a TV tuner for direct connection to cable TV and display of a live window that will still let you watch the SuperBowl while finishing up that last-minute report for your boss.

A newcomer is the VideoSpigot, from SuperMac Technologies. For $500 or $600, depending on the host model, you can have direct input of QuickTime movies at a bargain price. This board is optimized for its task and support following resolutions: 160-by-120, 240-by-180, 320-by-240 in NTSC format; and 192-by-144 and 388-by-288 in PAL format, with sound input. Its supporting software lets you review and correct the aspect of the display, then save the result on disk or in RAM.

Still Video

The easy to use Canon Mavica or XapShot cameras use an approach similar to video capture, and can store up to fifty photographs on a built-in 2.5 inch diskette drive. These relatively inexpensive cameras (usually under $1000) use a video CCD to produce an analog signal that is recorded as-is, with the additional capability of recording ten seconds of sound at the expense of half of the storage capacity. These cameras provide 16 bits of usable color output in a 24-bit format

The composite video output signal is similar to that of a VHS camera in pause mode, requiring a frame grabber (often the bundled ComputerFriends ColorSnap digitizer), which ups (often doubles) the price.

Color-still video has become an accepted, relatively inexpensive way to acquire single images from video. Ultimately, however, the still-young digital photography market will overtake still video in quality, value, ease of use, and performance.

Digital Photography

Digital photography is an emerging technology with a bright future. Not to be confused with the still video Xapshot approach, a digital camera converts directly the analog signal collected at the output of the CCD into digital data in the camera.

As with most other graphics hardware categories, pricing and image quality span quite a spectrum of options suited for a variety of needs and applications. For simple, lower resolution and inexpensive cameras, users get the advantage of speed for some of the following reasons: putting someone's photo onto a network immediately after the photo was taken (say for security reasons); for transmitting images over a modem immediately after they were taken (such as industrial or intelligence applications) so others can see them without delay; or even for the real estate agent who wants to take photos of properties, store them into a database, and send them over the network, modem to other agents, or desktop publish them into a flyer. Immediacy is the primary advantage; if you have the luxury of time, taking a photograph with a conventional camera, having it developed, and then scanning it will produce a higher quality image (given digital camera capabilities today, that is). However, if you need to use the image immediately, there is nothing better than a digital camera because you immediately have a digitized image with simple, limited hardware demands.

At one end of the spectrum is the Logitech FotoMan, based on the Dycam Model 1 Digital Camera (Logitech purchased the technology from Dycam and then improved the hardware and software). Using a black-and-white video CCD, FotoMan can store up to 32 pictures in 256 gray-scales into its built-in dynamic RAM memory, under a compressed form, without any other media (such as the floppy disk required in the Canon XapShot). The camera connects to any serial port and uses a PhotoShop plug-in module to bring the images into your Macintosh. This simple connection approach provides maximum flexibility by letting you use any Macintosh available without a frame grabber. FotoMan's primary drawback is the image transfer speed inherent to a serial communication, limited to 19,200 bits per second to 57,600 bps (depending on the Macintosh model). Most images take about 20 to 30 seconds each to download, although the software allows you to view a thumbnail versions of the images before downloading.

The camera's fixed focus and aperture optics, with built-in automatic strobe flash, makes it an ideal point-and-shoot tool if you need to bring real-life images into an application without using extra time, hardware, or money. The camera sells for $699. As always, if you spend more money, you get more quality and power. Aimed at professionals in need of a fast and high-quality option for transmitting pictures over wires is the Kodak's digital camera, which replaces the original back of a Nikon F3 35mm camera and offers a 24-bit megapixel image (working much like the Polaroid option many pro photographers use to generate quick Polaroids before shooting on film). This state-of-the-art camera is bundled with a portable 300 megabyte hard disk for picture storage in the field. Since it attaches to the photographer's 35mm camera, the digital "base" lets the pro feel at home with his own equipment, but is nevertheless benefiting from a high-end optical system. The cost of this setup starts around $20,000.

Photo CD

Kodak has firmly announced its plan to replace chemical photo-processing by digital photography within a few years. Upon bringing film into a lab for processing, any 35mm camera user will have the option of either receiving standard negatives, or a CD-ROM filled with high-quality, high-resolution digital versions of his photographs in addition to traditional paper copies. With a CD-ROM drive and a personal computer, photographers can view and store images on CD, and use them in a variety of ways. This process is called Photo-CD and, according to Kodak, can store as many as 100 pictures on a single disk. The CD-ROM contains multiple versions of the originals at different resolutions. The lowest resolution is useful for screen display on a computer using the CD-ROM. You can display the images on a TV using a specially developed multifunction player manufactured initially by Philips. Philips invented the audio cassette and coinvented the CD player (with Sony). This multifunction player can also play regular audio CDs.

The higher resolutions will be used for subsequent printed output, and the cost to the user should not increase significantly, if at all.

Digitizing Tablets

A *digitizing tablet,* also called *digitizer,* is a flat-surface peripheral device and working area. The tablet contains electronics which can detect the *absolute* position of a pointing device located on its top, and transmit this position with great precision to your Macintosh.

Designers and architects have known about digitizing tablets for years, using them to enter existing drawings accurately into the Mac. People using the computer for extensive drawings and designs are still the most significant consumers of digitizers; most business and home users really do not have great need for such devices. Digitizers are readily available for Macintosh-based systems because so many designers choose this platform to answer their computing needs.

Most tablets use an electromagnetic field to sense the position of the *pointing device* or pen. The field is emitted by the pointing device through the surface of the tablet to a network of wire loops beneath the work surface. The system scans once vertically and once horizontally to determine the X and Y position of the pen, establishing an absolute position.

Digitizer pointing devices come in a variety of configurations. One common type is a mouse-shaped tool generally called a *puck*, that can have up to 16 colored buttons to perform specific predefined functions. The puck sports a cross-hair visor for precise positioning, and is generally attached to the tablet with a cord. Pen-based pointing devices have also become very popular, both in corded and cordless versions; the pens feature fewer buttons. For some, the pens are the most natural way in which to work.

Probably the most well-known member of the digitizer family is the Wacom SC 510 tablet, which provides a cordless pen and a pressure-sensitive tablet. This device, with its 6-by-9 inches of active surface, has become especially popular by the arrival of painting software (Fractal Design's *Painter*, Time Arts' *Oasis*, *PhotoShop*, *ColorStudio*, etc.) that takes advantage of the pressure information to simulate real-world tools.

Tablets trace their origin to the CAD world, where they are extremely useful for tracing data in a paper form, such as plans and maps, with a precision as high as a thousandth of an inch. The tablets can be as small as 6-by-6 inches, and as large as a full drawing board (6-by-4 feet)! Most popular models range between 12-by-12 inches and 12-by-17 inches. One of the age-old problems of draftspersons and architects is how to keep drawings stationary while working on them; an interesting solution to holding paper for work *or* to print upon is used by some tablets as well as some pen plotters, with an electrostatic field that retains the sheet flat and immobile on the surface. The larger units can also take advantage of preprinted or custom templates to directly access the program's functions, performing in this case a pointing device job rather than inputting coordinates.

Bar-Code Readers

A very quick, easy, and accurate way of inputting digital data into the Macintosh is with a bar-code reader. Essentially the same technology as that used by grocery checkers in the supermarket, bar codes are read using a combination of light source and receptor, and the patterns of black and white lines are translated into ASCII codes depending on their width and position.

Some bar-code readers require contact with the label, while some can read at a distance, using a laser beam to illuminate the code. Some can store data to be downloaded later, useful for doing field or warehouse inventories remotely. Most, however, require a serial port and power supply.

Image Types

Resolution

The resolution of an image is defined by the amount of dots per inch distributed in every direction. The dot, or pixel (which stands for *picture element),* is the smallest indivisible element of the picture. Most pictures use an identical resolution for vertical and horizontal, and therefore their resolution is qualified using a single number. Each pixel can contain a different amount of information resulting in different image types.

Black-and-White (Line Art) Images

In a black-and-white image, such as that used for OCR or bar-code applications, pixel can be either white or black. Technical drawings and schematics are drawn as line art.

Most printers can only print in black and white: a black dot, or no dot. The vast majority of laser, ink-jet, and dot-matrix printers simulate gray-scale output using a process called *dithering,* necessary to translate gray values into a certain amount of black pixels per square unit. The simplest half-tone algorithm consists of assembling a square number of pixels (25, 36, 64, 100, or more), at the resolution of the output device, and then filling these squares with black pixels proportional to the darkness of the corresponding gray pixel. This translates into a dramatic reduction of the effective resolution of the printer, which renders a 300 dpi laser ineffective and disappointing when it comes to producing quality output. More advanced algorithms use a random value to rotate the patterns, or to fill the squares, resulting in less visible lines in the final result. It is also possible to define other shapes (lines, ovals, circles) to produce various results.

A PostScript printer can accept any gray-scale image and dither it before printing, isolating the user from these complicated issues. A dithered image cannot be scaled since it would change its resolution and would not print correctly (vertical and horizontal black or white lines would appear across the printout). The black-and-white image is the most compact, since it carries only one bit per pixel.

The resolution of a black-and-white file should match the resolution of the output device at the final scale. There is no need to manipulate and store a 400 dpi file if it is intended for laser output (typically 300 dpi) or screen display (typically 72 dpi).

OCR generally requires a black-and-white file to recognize text most accurately. Some recent programs, however, perform a gray-scale to black-and-white translation before performing the actual recognition. There is a tradeoff between resolution, accuracy, and memory requirements: A 400 dpi page is nearly double the size of its 300 dpi counterpart (i.e., 300 x 300 = 90,000 dots per square inch; 400 x 400 = 160,000 dots per square inch) Additionally, recognition time usually increases due to the difference in size.

Gray-Scale Images

The most common scanner image format is a *gray-scale* image, which provides black-and-white photographic quality output. Taking color, gray scale, and line art into consideration, the gray-scale image is the best tradeoff between size and amount of information carried. Gray-scale images vary from four to eight bits per pixel, resulting in images featuring a range of 16 to 256 shades of gray. The more shades of gray, the more detailed and accurate your image will appear. Here again, the resolution should be synchronized with the target output device.

Many scanner users ultimately print their images to a service bureau or company photo-typesetter such as a Linotronic. This is definitely the best way to get the most out of your scanned image, but it also presents some specific considerations. If you plan to use a Linotronic or any other photo-typesetter with a very high resolution (e.g., 2,540 dots per inch), here is what to do.

Most experts agree the human eye cannot distinguish more than a hundred or so different gray values. For simplicity, let's use 144 as a round number. This translates into a 12-by-12 cell to reproduce the 144 grays and translates into a "gray resolution" of 2,540/12, or 211 dpi. These units are defined in the printer's language as "lines" and are referred to as "frequency." The quality of output is then calculated in lines per inch and varies between 50 lines, for newspaper quality; 150 lines, for high-quality books; and 120 to 133 lines, for producing excellent flyers and magazine quality. Check your printer's capabilities to assure optimum results.

A good rule of thumb for calculating the optimal resolution based on the printer's frequency is to double it to obtain the original's resolution. For example, 133-line output will require a 266 dpi gray-scale file to maintain its quality. Since the scanner cannot always provide the exact resolution, this can be achieved typically with the image editing software, after scanning at the immediate higher resolution available, and once all corrections have been performed.

Another important parameter is the *gamma* factor of both the display and the printer. Since the printed dots of a laser are larger than the white spaces left, generally a 50-percent-gray image will output much darker, and everything above 75 percent gray will output as black. A PostScript printer will take this factor into account, according to the characteristics of the print engine, and most page layout software provides a set of files (PPDs) to correct for appropriate and more linear results.

Color

Color is sexy, and the Macintosh is a great machine with which to manipulate color images. But *true color* image manipulation doesn't come cheap. The 8-bit video common to most Macs is not appropriate for displaying the subtleties and delicate nuances found in real world color. It can only display 256 colors at a time, and uses dithering to simulate more colors (thanks to Color QuickDraw, this masterpiece of software is found in ROM on the newest CPUs).

To work with true colors, you really need a 24-bit video card, which is capable of more than 16 million colors (that's right, 16 *million!*). This is more than the human eye can see, and much more than even your 21-inch screen can display simultaneously. Yet, it gives the monitor enough color to generate very good quality images that look very life-like.

Color files can be found in many different formats and bit depths, with 8-, 16-, 24-, and 32-bit files the most common. An 8-bit file requires no more space than a gray-scale image and can carry a lot more emotional content. Overall, a 256-color image will also contain a "color look-up table" or palette, which is a listing of the colors drawn from a 24-bit set. The standard Mac palette is typically overridden by a custom palette generated by the software when the 24- to 8-bit reduction is made.

A 24-bit file is regarded as the industry standard, and virtually every color scanner can output to it. Mostly they are stored as three 8-bit planes, each carrying one channel of red, blue, and green data. An optional additional 8-bit layer is used to keep track of additional information such as selection masks or transparency, often resulting in a monstrous 32-bit-per-pixel image.

 File Formats

The Macintosh has plenty of graphics file formats, but some are more useful than others. The early MacPaint format still lingers, but carries significant limitations: It has only one bit per pixel and a fixed resolution of 72 dpi, with a fixed size.

The native PICT format is more flexible and can represent both objects and bit maps at any resolution, but also is limited to one bit per pixel. Furthermore, it is a compressed format, with Quickdraw providing routines for its manipulation.

PICT2 took the stage with the introduction of the color Macs, and was freed of these limitations: up to 32 bits-per-pixel, with any size, resolution, and possibility of integration of custom color lookup tables. But it still is a Macintosh-only format due to its proprietary compression schemes.

TIFF (tagged image file format) was defined by Aldus Corporation to provide a multiplatform standard for virtually every type of bitmapped image. Its definitions have evolved and improved with time, the most recent update at this writing being version 5. TIFF files also can be compressed with a variety of schemes, including a special format for electronic faxing purposes. TIFF is a packrat, and thus is a very safe bet when you save your pictures and do not know where they will end up—it carries all available information with each file, and every desktop publishing program can import them on multiple platforms.

Encapsulated PostScript (EPS) is another popular text-based format. An EPS file generated by a Macintosh application such as PhotoShop actually consists of two embedded files, the high resolution image itself plus a preview at 72 dpi used for placement in a desktop publishing program. To achieve full control over the way a color picture is being printed, EPS5 is used. This format comprises five discrete files generated by the color separation program and which contain a text file for each of the primary printing colors (cyan, magenta, yellow, and black), with the angle and frequency information included and ready to be sent to the typesetter. In addition, the PICT color preview for placement in FrameMaker, Quark X-Press, or PageMaker is attached.

It's no surprise, then, that these files are huge, since no compression is used; multimegabyte files are common and easily attainable for even a small 3-by-4-inch picture. Other more exotic file formats, most of them coming from other platforms, can also be found supported in a variety of applications today:

GIF, the CompuServe standard

PIXAR, TGA from high-end workstations

SCITEX from high-end scanners

Many other file formats specific to various hardware platforms exist and occur frequently as optional export/import formats in various applications.

Data Compression

We've seen how color images generate huge files when stored as simple bit maps where every dot is listed and described. Even though hard drives get continually larger and storage options have made amazing advances recently, large files nevertheless remain a problem and an irritation. To circumvent the problem of the available space on your hard disk and offer reasonable ways of archiving these images, the computer industry is constantly expending great energy pursuing more efficient and accurate compression algorithms.

There are two common types of compression: *lossy* and *lossless*. A lossy compression will throw away a certain amount of information (typically, but not always, unnecessary data or blank space) that cannot be recovered by the decompression scheme. A lossless compression reduces the size of the file without this inconvenience, so multiple compression decompressions can be achieved without degradations of the picture.

Lossless Compression

These schemes are mostly used with black-and-white images, such as for OCR purposes. It is critical in an OCR file that the decompressed image be identical to the original for optimal character recognition. Fax files also use these types of compressions, which have names like CCITT, LZW (Lempel-Ziv-Welch), and others.

The simplest way to achieve these types of compressions is to count the number of consecutive pixels of the same color, and store this number instead of each pixel. This works well with line-art images, and can achieve reductions of up to 60 percent in text files since all the white space between lines is reduced to a single number. Conversely, it does not work well at all with dithered files where constant changes are common, and the resulting files may well be bigger than the original (which rather defeats the purpose!). All the compression algorithms derive from a strategy similar to this one, and "smart" applications select the most appropriate one depending on the content of the image.

Lossy Compression

To achieve even more dramatic reduction in size, and when the result is only to be seen (as opposed to being read and converted, as with OCR), lossy compression is the way to go. Most of the algorithms in use today derive from early efforts of European workers looking for a way to transmit images over phone lines with the best efficiency. Later, the algorithms became more or less standardized into a format known as JPEG (Joint Photographic Expert Group). Digital cameras and other graphics hardware commonly use this type of compression internally; compressions of up to 100:1 are within reach for color images.

The principle of JPEG compression is following: The software divides the image into blocks of variable size (8-by-8 pixels, for example) and attributes an average value to this block for each of the color planes. Large areas of similar colors can then be defined as a label to this color instead of the computer having to list each pixel. When more detailed information is needed to describe a detail, the selected blocks are chosen in a smaller size to keep track of the changes. The result depends on the compression factor, which is user-selectable and determines the final image quality. Although most commercial products claim JPEG compatibility, they are mostly incompatible among each other. Each supplier has different subtle proprietary solutions for achieving the best quality for a defined compression ratio, and these "hints" are rarely publicized.

When saving JPEG compressed files for distribution, make sure that anyone else using the files has the same software to be able to read your files. The most common problem with JPEG compression is that it is very computation intensive: Squeezing 20 megabytes at a ratio of 20:1 is a process of several minutes, particularly if you don't have a dedicated compression board in your Macintosh. Decompression by the file recipient will usually be equally as long. Many manufacturers now offer JPEG compression hardware, but this approach tends to tie the user to one vendor because of the differences in the various incarnations of JPEG. Multiple compressions/decompressions of a file can produce distracting and unwanted artifacts and can render the image unusable.

QuickTime has built-in support for replaceable compression/decompression engines that can support specific hardware to speed-up the sluggish process. In fact, speed gains of one hundred-fold are possible, and once they are generalized among the Macintosh community, will help to solve compatibility problems currently plaguing many users.

An evolution of the JPEG standard is called MPEG, used for animations. It compresses the information by analyzing the difference between frames and keeping track of the changes. This process requires even more processing power, since decompression has to take place on-the-fly to keep the animation smooth. Digital animation requires this type of high-speed, high-compression factor to be accepted by and useful for the general public.

Intellectual Property Rights

Although the many graphics hardware and software tools described in this chapter make it apparently easy to bring any artwork into your Macintosh, the image does not necessarily belong to you. While it's common to scan images in magazines or books, or to scan text, it is no more legal to do so than to copy the pages using an office copier. Again, while this is common, it is not legal if the work being copied is copyrighted. In particular, it is not legal if the work is being used for republication or distribution.

This should be kept in mind, particularly, with images, where it is very tempting to scan attractive images and include them in a newsletter or other graphics/text document. A plethora of public-domain images and clip-art files have come to market as a result of this, and these are the best source of images for newsletters or other documents rather than scanning copyrighted works. Of course, it is perfectly legal to scan images you own, have created, or have photographed, or ones that someone has given you permission to use. However, scanning or in any way copying any images or text that are potentially copyrighted is illegal and should be emphasized by your company policies, just as those that prohibit software piracy.

 # Evolution

Pen Input

The future of personal computing, as described by many industry analysts, will at least in part move from keyboard and mouse as the primary interaction devices with the computer to more ergonomic, intuitive, and direct methods based on pen and voice. While perhaps not everyone will want to emigrate from the keyboard in the near future, these hardware innovations certainly will have increasing importance as computing technology advances.

Apple has announced and promised a series of new devices broadly known as PDA (Personal Digital Assistant), which feature among other characteristics voice and pen support, as well as a large amount of cordless peripheral support. *Newton,* the first of the family, will become available in 1993, and has the potential to replace your phone, fax, mail system, agenda, and address book, and is small enough to be carried in a shirt pocket.

As mentioned earlier in the discussion of digitizers, the pen as a pointing device is based on the technologies currently used for graphic tablets, and the most powerful of these units will recognize your handwriting and store it as ASCII characters, for later retrieval and sort capabilities. A great number of exciting technological opportunities are looming on the horizon!

The Macintosh has commanded a revolution in the use of graphics on personal computers. The integration of graphics and text in desktop publishing became a significant force on the Mac, and Mac users without second thought accepted graphics as a natural part of the computing process. To be sure, in an age of computer "senses" with sound, sight, and even touch (such as with pen input or pointing devices), it is the *humans* who benefit from a machine that has adapted to their needs instead of the reverse.

It is important that hardware and software developers provide a variety of options filling the needs of consumers with all levels of applications and budgets. It is also critical that even the lowest-cost products maintain a high degree of reliability, quality, and design. For the user wishing to explore the capabilities of graphic input devices, the choice has never been more fruitful.

Sound Technologies

From the beginning, the Macintosh line of personal computers has been well suited for working with sound. Apple saw to that when they included sound generation circuitry as part of the computer itself. Since then, the capability has been expanded so that the most recent additions to the Mac family can process sound into digital information and then play it back. This capability has been harnessed for tasks ranging from managing musical performances to generating humorous voices; from sampling existing sounds for inclusion in multimedia presentations, to operating software via your spoken commands.

In this chapter we will look at all of these developments. We will start with a discussion of the physical nature of sound. We will show how sound can be converted into information that a computer can store and manipulate. We will look at the software and hardware that makes sound capture and generation possible on the Mac, including software that recognizes your voice. We will also look at the Macintosh in music, paying particular attention to the world of MIDI, a network standard for electronic instruments and software that makes it possible for one Macintosh to control an entire ensemble of electronic musical instruments.

The Physics of Sound

What is sound? Hoary clichés about falling trees and unoccupied forests aside, what we perceive as sound is a relatively simple phenomenon. Sound consists of vibrations in a medium of some kind: the medium is usually air, although water can carry sound, too. Sound vibrations are usually called waves.

Waves are an extremely important class of physical phenomena. The dictionary defines a wave as "any of a series of advancing impulses set up by a vibration, pulsation, or disturbance in air or some other medium." Think of dropping a pebble into a pond. The momentary disturbance caused by the pebble's breaking through the water sets up a series of ripples that radiate outward from the point of impact. These ripples are water waves.

Acoustic Fundamentals

Sound waves are different from water waves, the only kind of wave that most of us have had any direct experience with. Water waves are *transverse* waves—the medium (water) is displaced perpendicular to the direction of the wave's travel. Think about it for a moment: a water wave causes the surface of the water to rise to a crest and fall to a trough, as the wave itself moves across the water surface. Although the water rises and falls, it does not move along with the wave.

Sound waves are different. Sound displaces its carrier medium in the same direction in which it travels. Sound waves are thus *compression* waves. The crests in a sound wave correspond to areas where the air (or other medium) is compressed more densely than normal; troughs in such a wave correspond to areas of relatively rarified air. Although the air tends to move back and forth along the sound wave's direction of travel, the air itself does not accompany the wave on its travels.

All waves have a characteristic velocity in each medium through which they move. In air, a sound wave moves about a mile in six seconds, roughly 700MPH. Light waves travel much faster. This is why you almost always see a flash of lightening many seconds before you hear the crack of thunder. The two events occur at the same moment, but it takes sound longer than light to travel the distance from the event to you.

Sound waves are generated by a vibration or disturbance, usually in the air. The head of a drum, a violin string, or the paper cone of a loudspeaker are all examples of vibrating objects that generate sound. The speed with which the object vibrates determines an important characteristic of its sound—*pitch*. The faster something vibrates, the higher we perceive its pitch to be.

Physically, we say that a higher pitch sound has a higher *frequency* (see Figure 7.1). Frequency refers to the number of complete sound waves that pass a fixed point in one second. A typical musical tone has a frequency of about 440 waves per second (this unit is called a Herz, after a famous German physicist who studied wave phenomena). Most of us humans can perceive sounds with frequencies as low as 50Hz and as high as 20,000Hz.

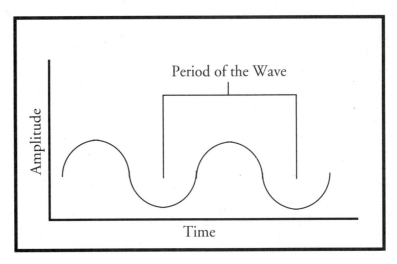

Figure 7.1: The Frequency of a wave is calculated by using the formula; Frequency = 1/Period. Frequency is measured in Cycles-per-second, or Hz.

Another important characteristic of a sound wave is its amplitude. This is a measure of how strongly the sound source is vibrating. Sources with a high amplitude are "loud," those with a small amplitude are "soft." It takes more power to drive a low frequency sound than it does to drive a high one. That is why it takes a powerful audio amplifier to generate good bass tones; bass comprises the lowest freqency sounds, which need the most power to be produced accurately. It is also no accident that you can "feel" really strong bass, such as that produced by those pernicious car stereos. A strong-enough bass tone can crack glass or topple masonry. (In fact, we could view an earthquake as an extremly low frequency sound wave moving through earth as its medium.)

Using these two important charactersistics of sound—frequency and amplitude—we can draw a picture of a sound. Physicists and acousticians (acoustics is the name given to the science of sound) call such a picture a graph. Frequency is usually shown on the horizontal axis of such a graph; the more closely the waves are bunched together, the higher the frequency. Amplitude is shown on the vertical axis. The higher the peak, the greater the amplitude.

You will notice from the graph in Figure 7.2 that the sound shown isn't uniform; some parts have greater amplitude, others have greater frequency. Most sounds vary through time in this way. A sound with a uniform (non-varying) amplitude and frequency is called a *tone*. Introduce some variation and you have a sound.

Figure 7.2: A graph of a sound (from Adobe Premier).

There are very few pure tones in the world. Most of the time, a fundamental tone (usually called a *fundamental*) is accompanied by other tones of higher frequencies. These higher-frequency tones are called *harmonics*. The frequency of a harmonic is some integer (non-fractional) multiple of the fundamental tone. As a rule, harmonics have lower amplitude than the fundamental tone, although this isn't always true. The number and power of individual harmonics determines the quality of a sound.

Ultimately, the design of a musical instrument determines what harmonics will accompany its fundamental tones, and how strong each harmonic will be. The body of a violin, for example, reinforces certain harmonics and dampens others, giving the violin its own tone "color." Add to this tone color the noise (random vibrations with no set frequency or amplitude) from the bow scraping the string, and you have the sound of the violin.

Computer Acoustics

It is a triumph of technology that a computer can be harnessed to imitate the sound of a violin, even imperfectly. (Give the computer credit, though; there is considerable variation among violins themselves, and not even the greatest modern violin maker has been able to reproduce the instruments made by Stradivari or Guanari.) How does it happen? First, the sound has to be converted into a form that a computer can handle.

Modern computers such as the Macintosh work with information in digital form. Each bit in a computer's memory represents a single binary digit. Taken together, a series of bits can represent a number of discrete values. For example, 8 bits (one byte) can represent one of 256 possible values. The more bits you have, the more values you can represent. Actually, each time you add a bit you double the number of possible values than can be represented.

Sound isn't all digital. For practical purposes, a sound wave can have any one of an infinite number of possible frequencies as well as one of an infinite number of amplitudes. (Note for the scientifically hip: The preceding isn't strictly true in this era of quantum mechanics. Like any other varying phenomenon, sound can only change frequency or amplitude in discrete steps. The aggregate nature of sound makes the number of steps so vast, however, as to be practically infinite.) Sound is, for all intents and purposes, a smoothly varying or *analog* phenomenon.

An analog phenomenon can be represented by *analogy* with some other smoothly-varying quantity. Electric voltage is one example. We could represent the sound's amplitude by the voltage of an electric circuit. (think of voltage as a measure of electrical "pressure"). In this way, sound information is "stored" by analogy with another quantity. The ratio of a sound's voltage to some standard voltage gives a measure of its intensity. This intensity measurement is given in deciBels, or *dB*, a unit named for the famous acoustician and inventor Alexander Graham Bell.

Clearly, the first step in getting sound into a computer is to change it from a pressure wave into an electrical signal. This is done through a transducer of some kind. A transducer is a physical device that changes one type of signal into another. A microphone is an example. Part of a microphone vibrates as sound waves strike it. This vibration causes changes in the electrical properties of the mike. These changes cause variation in the current flowing through the mike's circuitry. In this way, a sound wave is converted into an analog electrical signal.

Formerly, there were analog computers that could add, subtract, multiply, and divide numbers that were represented by discrete voltages. It was even possible to design analog circuitry to perform calculus (this writer did just that in a freshman physics laboratory course in the late '70s). These circuits aren't very flexible, and they also tend to be slow and expensive. These are among the reasons that current computers are digital rather than analog.

If we want to work with analog information in a digital computer, clearly we need to convert that information into digital form. We can use a special piece of circuitry called an *analog to digital converter* (A-D) to do just that. In practice, an A-to-D converter takes the entire range of possible analog signals and matches them to discrete digital values.

Consider a very simple example: an 8-bit converter designed to work with voltages from 0 to 8 volts. This 8 bit converter can represent 256 possible values. Voltage values from 0 to 1 are presented by digital values 0-31, voltages from 1 to 2 are represented by digital values from 32-63, and so on. It would appear that some information is lost. The voltage values 0.01 and 0.02 must both be represented by the digital value "0," for example.

Although an A-D converter cannot capture exactly the right values of a smooth varying signal, in practice it can get very close. So much for capturing a sound's amplitude. What about it's frequency? How often would you guess that a sound must be measured in order to perfectly capture its frequency?

As it turns out, a very important piece of scientific work called the *sampling theorem* states uncatagorically, that we need only measure sound at twice the rate of its highest frequency in order to capture it perfectly. In fact, the theorem further says that sampling at this rate will also perfectly capture the way the sound's amplitude changes. (In practice, the limited number of values given by an A-D converter will introduce some error into the sound amplitude.)

High-fidelity sound is usually measured at 44.1KHZ (44,100 cycles per second), because the highest harmonic that we humans can perceive is a little over 22KHZ. Thus, 44,100 times per second, a sound must be measured and its amplitude recorded. The resulting strings of digital numbers can be used to recreate the sound. Quite a lot of nifty mathematics is involved.

On the other side, a device called a *digital to analog converter* (D-A) can take digital values and recreate an analog signal from them. These devices are at the heart of a lot of modern gear, including the now ubiquitous compact disc (CD) player. There is D-A circuitry inside the Macintosh; it is used to convert sounds stored on a Mac disk into signals that can be played on the Mac's internal speaker, or on an external speaker if one is hooked up. A speaker works in the opposite way that a microphone does: a varying analog electric signal causes a diaphram to vibrate, in turn exciting vibrations in the air that constitute sound.

You can see that it takes quite a lot of information—and a lot of disk space— to represent sound accurately. If you allocate two bytes (sixteen bits) to represent each sound value as a CD does, then you need about 88KB of storage for each second of sound on each of the two stereo channels (left and right). When you consider that a compact disk can hold a maximum of about 72 minutes of music, you can see why CDs are such a prodigious storage medium; factor in stereo, and the result is it takes over 750MB of storage to archive 72 minutes at 16 bits per sample. CDs store extra information that brings the total somewhat higher.

The Mac's internal circuitry doesn't process nearly the amount of data that a CD does, but it still handles a lot. The Mac uses 8 bits per sample rather than 16 and generally samples at a maxiumum rate of 22KHZ rather than 44.1. This gives an effective rate of 22KB per second per channel of audio, which is still a large number. You can buy equipment to let some Macs sample at the CD rate of 16 bits per sample; we will talk about them a bit later.

So that's how a computer stores sound data: as strings of digital values representing the amplitude of the sound signal at each moment in time. The Macintosh stores sounds in just this way. However, there's much more to the Macintosh sound equation than just strings of numbers, as we will see in the next section.

Capturing and Playing Sounds on the Mac

All Macintoshes can generate sound from digital information, although it hasn't always been possible to "pour" pure sound into a Mac. It wasn't long, however, before manufacturers saw this deficiency and began working to correct it. Today, there are products on the market that make it relatively easy to record sound on a Mac. You can also manipulate this sound after you record it. The newest Macintoshes have sound-recording capability built in, although you must buy software to record long sound segments, or to edit any sound at all.

The Macintosh sound universe is not limited to buzzes, squawks, and boings, however. For a long while it has been possible to generate realistic human speech on a Mac. This capability has been incorporated into a number of programs, including at least one amusing little application that does little more than make periodic wisecracks.

In this section, we are going to look at all these capabilities—and the software/hardware that makes them possible. We will start with the basic parts of the Mac that support sound. Then we will look at moving sound into a Macintosh, working with it there, and then reproducing it.

Macintosh Sound Support

Like we say: all Macs can generate sound. The simple "beep" that frequently accompanies a mistake is a vivid example. This capability has been harnessed to add sound effects to games and to give custom beeps and chimes to applications. In order to do much more than that, however, you have traditionally needed additional software and possibly hardware.

The first Macs supported 8-bit audio sampled at a rate of 22KHZ through one channel. Unfortunately, the circuitry used at that time required the Mac CPU's full attention. (The CPU is the main computing "brain" of the computer.) This made it hard for the Mac to play sounds at the same time it was performing other tasks. These early Macs had an internal speaker for audio output, but they had no built-in equipment to handle sound input.

Later on, Apple started to include a special sound chip in all Macintoshes. This circuitry could work independently of the CPU to generate sound. This scheme has two advantages over the old one: the CPU itself is not burdened by extra calculations, thus increasing the system's overall speed. Second, sounds can be played back at the same time other system events are taking place, without degrading sound quality. The new sound chip also supports stereo output.

New hardware needs new software to run it, so Apple created an addition to the system software to handle the new sound chip. The Sound Manager takes care of all the necessary housekeeping. Included in the Sound Manager are software tools to reduce the amount of space that sounds occupy on disk. We call such reduction compression; it involves throwing out unnecessary or redundant data. Apple calls their scheme Macintosh Audio Compression/Expansion, or MACE. At the highest level, MACE can achieve a 6:1 savings in disk space. You should note that highly compressed sound suffers a loss of quality.

Before the Mac's LC and SI were introduced, all Macs needed special hardware in order to convert sound into data they could work with. We call such equipment a *sound digitizer*. It does the hard work of listening to a sound, sampling its amplitude, converting the amplitude from analog into digital form, and then sending the information back to the Macintosh. A sound digitizer has special software to manage its operation; this software is used to record digitized sound data onto a disk.

The newest Macs have much of this capability built in. The LC and LC II, the IIsi, the Classic II, the Powerbooks 140 and 170, and the Quadras 700, 900, and 950 all have built-in hardware that digitizes sound. Each of these Macs comes equipped with a microphone, although you can also connect other sound sources (such as tape recorders and CD players) through a special adaptor. These Macs use an expanded version of the Sound Manager. You, the user, can get to Sound Manager capabilities through the *Sound* control panel. In System 7, it looks like Figure 7.3.

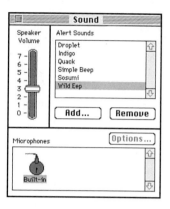

Figure 7.3: The Sound control panel.

On a Mac that can digitize sound, you will find a choice of input devices under the heading "microphones." Only one—the Mac's own internal mike—is shown on the preceding figure. You click a microphone's icon to select it. Only one input device is active at a time. To record a new sound with the selected mike, you click **Add...** This brings up the sound recording dialog box, as shown in Figure 7.4.

Figure 7.4: Recording a sound on a newer Mac.

The speaker icon at the top center shows the current sound intensity (the sound shown was fairly loud). It is active even when you are not currently recording. To record a sound, click the Record button at the far left. Click Stop when you are finished. You can play back the sound over your Mac's internal speaker by clicking Play.

When you have finished recording a sound, you must click Save to store it permanently. At this point, you must give it a name. The named sound is then added to the list shown in Figure 7.3. You can make the sound into your "system beep" (the sound you hear when you make a mistake or when your Mac wants your attention) by clicking its name to select it.

There are products out there that let you assign sounds to events beyond just the System beep. For example, *SoundMaster*, a shareware program available over several online services (e.g., America Online), lets you assign sounds to a number of different events (see Figure 7.5).

Figure 7.5: The SoundMaster Shareware program

In this example, we have assigned a sound to the "Shut Down" event. When yours truly shuts down the old Mac, it says "Goodbye." (By the way, we got hold of *SoundMaster* and the sounds shown in the figure in a nifty book, *Cool Mac Sounds*, from Hayden.

Generally, recorded sounds are stored directly within your System file as sound resources. A Macintosh resource is a piece of unchanging data that's available for use by different programs and files. Fonts are resources, for example. In System 7, you can see all the resources stored in your System by double-clicking the System file's icon (See Figure 7.6).

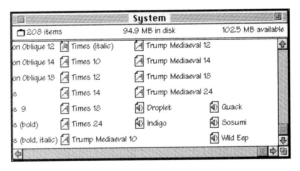

Figure 7.6: Sounds (SNDs) and other resources in the System file.

To hear any of these sounds, you just double-click its icon. Users of System 6 don't have this capability, although whether it is worth upgrading just to be able to "open" the System file is purely a matter of taste. Anybody can examine a sound resource more closely with the right software. Using a resource editor such as Apple's own *ResEdit* (*ReSourcerer* is another such program) you can peek directly into any resource file (See Figure 7.7).

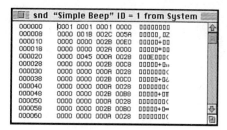

Figure 7.7: The contents of an SND resource.

The data is not presented in a very friendly format. Especially not if we want to make changes to the sound represented. There is another annoying limit to sound on the Mac as it's shipped from the factory. Check out Figure 7.3 again. You will see that you can only record ten seconds of sound at a time.

So that is the basics of sound on a standard Macintosh. Today's Macs have a sound chip that creates sound independent of the CPU and is controlled by the Sound Manager. They also have microphones to convert ambient sound into digital information. The resulting data are stored in SND resources, which tend to live within the System itself. They can exist as separate entities, however.

With regard to sound, today's Macs can do a lot on their own. However, to record more than ten seconds worth of sound, or to edit sound in any way, you need separate software. And if your Mac doesn't have a built-in microphone, you need separate hardware to digitize sound. You may also want to add speaker to take over from your Mac's small, internal speaker. Indeed, you *have* to add a speaker if you want to hear stereo, Fortunately, there are several such products out there on the market. We will discuss a couple of them.

Sound Digitizing, Editing, and Generation

Before you go rushing out to buy sound hardware and software for your Mac, you have to know what you need, what is available, and how the two line up. This is especially true in the case of hardware. If you have a newer Mac (and LC or LC II, IIsi, Powerbook 140 or 170, or any Quadra) then you don't need to buy sound digitizing hardware; your Mac has that capability built in. Otherwise, you need some simple hardware along with the software to run it. The good news is that you can acquire such a setup for less than $100.

We are going to talk about a number of products in this section. We will start with some software to support the sound digitizing capabilities of current Macs. Then we will move on to software/hardware combinations that let you record and edit sound. From there, we will move on to the kinds of speakers you can hook up to get better sound from your Mac.

Sound Editing and Recording Software: *Voice Record* and *SoundEdit*

If you already have the right hardware and just want to work with sound in ways the *Sound* control panel doesn't support, you should consider adding a software package such as Articulate Systems' *Voice Record* to your Macintosh System (see Figure 7.8). *Voice Record* is a relatively inexpensive (<$100) application that lets you record and edit sounds on any sound-capable Mac. The software is designed to work with sound-aware applications, including *Microsoft Word 5.0* and *QuickMail*. In fact, *Word* already contains a smaller version of *Voice Record* that lets you annotate your documents with the built-in microphone.

Figure 7.8: Voice Record within Microsoft Word 5.0.

This "pony" version of *Voice Record* lets you record annotations, although you cannot edit them afterward. For that you need the real thing. The commercial version of *Voice Record* includes *SoundWave*, a separate program with which you can modify existing sounds. This software lets you apply filters and special effects to sounds you have previously recorded.

Voice Record supports Apple's standard file format for audio information, the AIFF format. You should look for this feature in any product you contemplate buying. You want your sound applications to store sound data in a standard way; this lets you work with the same data in all your applications. Idiosyncratic ways of storing data are tedious and unnecessary. Fortunately, just about every product available supports AIFF.

There are other sound editing software packages available. Not long ago, Macromedia unleashed *SoundEdit*, which used to be available only as part of their *MacRecorder* digitizer product. This software has all kinds of nifty effects. You can add reverb (echo) to existing sounds, make them louder, add noise, change pitch, and so on.

Sound Digitizing Hardware

If you own an older Mac (Mac Plus, Mac SE, SE/30, Mac II, IIx, IIcx, IIci, IIfx), you need to add some hardware to your system before you can record sound into it. Both Macromedia and Articulate systems offer hardware to complement their audio recording/editing software.

Voice Impact and Voice Impact Pro

Both these Articulate Systems (AS) products are packed into sleek little boxes that sit next to your Mac and plug into a serial port. Those who own a modem and printer will sense an immediate disadvantage: your Mac has only two serial ports, both occupied. You are going to have to get used to swapping cables. You will likely want to buy a simple box called an "A-B switch" that lets you connect two devices to the same port. You switch between them with a selector dial.

Like the sound recording hardware on newer Macs, these products rely on 8-bit sampling. This is fine for voice but unsuitable for high-fi music. Microphones are built directly into the boxes. AS makes much of their "Auto Gain Control" feature. This supposedly suppresses background noise, making voice recordings clearer. The *Voice Impact Pro* has fancier hardware, and comes with AS's *SoundWave* editing software, which the standard *Voice Impact* lacks. Both include the *Voice Record* operating software and support inclusion of sound in *Hypercard* stacks.

MacRecorder

This is the old standard; it seems like it has been around since the Diety was a teenager. Formerly offered by Farallon, it's now part of the Macromedia stable of multimedia products. Like the *Voice Impact* products, the *MacRecorder* plugs into a serial port. Well, you can't have everything.

The *MacRecorder* comes with *SoundEdit* and with *HyperSound*; the latter lets you incorporate sound into *Hypercard* stacks. We talked about *MacRecorder* earlier. You can cut material from sounds and paste sounds together, and you can also mix sounds down into single channels.

The preceding products are for average-quality audio only. If you want to work with CD quality audio on any Macintosh (even one with sound input), you need to look at other hardware.

Digidesign's Audiomedia and Sound Tools

Basic Macintosh audio uses 8-bit samples. That's okay for voice and simple music applications, but it isn't nearly enough for professional audio. Remember: 8 bits gives you only 256 values for each sample of sound. Think of it this way: at every instant in a recorded sound, the "volume" can be set to one of only 256 different positions. Not only does this allow less difference between sounds, it also compresses the range of intensities possible. You need as wide a dynamic range as possible so that quiet sounds are truly hard to hear, and very loud ones are almost unbearable. Otherwise, it all sounds the same.

CDs and other digital media use 16 bits per sample, which gives over 65,000 different values to each sample. To add such capability to a Mac, you need to add a special add-in card with special software. Digidesign offers two such packages: *Audiomedia* and *Sound Tools*. The latter is much more expensive than the former, although both are pricey. Each card fits into a NuBus slot within your Macintosh (see the chapter on Expansion for more info on NuBus.)

Sound Tools is evidently used by studios, music producers, and motion picture sound effects editors. It comes with Digidesigns *Sound Designer II* software, which is just about the last word in sound editing software. A big enough hard disk could record all the audio needed for a 60-minute CD with this set up. It should not surprise you that it sells for several thousands of dollars.

Audiomedia is a less advanced version of *Sound Tools*, targeted more toward multimedia productions. It has a less advanced version of *Sound Designer II* as well. It also doesn't have all the input options that *Sound Tools* provides. However, it weighs in at less than a grand.

Another high-end option to consider is Opcode's *Studio Vision*, which includes their *Audiomedia* digital audio card. The accompanying software offers digital audio recording and synchronization to the SMPTE standard (SMPTE stands for *Society of Motion Picture and Television Engineers*. It is a time-code standard used to synchronize sound with film or video.) It is also MIDI capable. (More on MIDI in the last section of this chapter.) This package gives you a complete multimedia sound editing and playback extravaganza in a box.

Sound Playback

Once you get sound into your Macintosh, and you have edited it to your heart's content, naturally you will want to hear the results. You could rely on your Mac's internal speaker (all Macs have one), but the results will be less than they could be. Your speaker is just a little 3 or 4 inch affair with a limited amount of amplification. What's more, you have only got one. Newer Macs support stereo output, but you will never hear it if you rely on your internal speaker.

Fortunately, there is a whole range of external speakers you can buy from fairly inexpensive to quite costly. (This is a common occurence when dealing with audio gear; you can spend anything from a few bucks to a king's ransom. At the upper end, you pay a lot more money for ever a little more improvement.) We will talk about several options. We will even throw in a little bit on generating voices with your Mac, paying homage to a neat but pesky application that has been around for ages.

Mac Speakers: Inexpensive

First of all, no matter what speaker you buy, you want to make sure they are *self-powered*. This means you won't need an external amplifier. You see, the Mac provides but a weak signal at its audio output ports. To hear that signal, you must boost its strength, or *amplify* it. Your average speakers need a fully-amplified signal before they will even think about reproducing music. In tradional audio land, you buy a separate piece of equipment to do just that.

You can buy speakers that have amplifiers build into them. They will save you connection and setup headaches, as well as a little money. Probably the most common of these speakers are the MacSpeakers from Monster Design. The amplifiers in these speakers produce 10 watts per stereo channel. That is not nearly enough for thumping bass, but you can hear them plenty loud enough from where you are sitting.

The speakers are sold in sets of two (convenient for stereo, no?) Each inclosure has two sub-speakers: one for high frequencies (a tweeter) and one for bass (a woofer). The woofer isn't very large, so again you cannot expect really good bass response. We have seen the set advertised for less than $200. You can find them in the catalog listings of just about every Macintosh mail order house.

Koss makes very small powered speakers: their SA-30 model runs on batteries and sells for less than $50. Sony also makes powered speakers, ostensibly for use with their Walkman series of portable audio equipment. They offer model numbers SRS-55, SRS-57, SRS-67, and SRS-77G, from around $100 on up. You can find these speakers at your local electronics store.

Mac Speakers: Expensive

If you want to really hear the music and you are less concerned about price, you might consider spending a little more for your powered Macintosh speakers. This is especially true if you mean to play back musical compositions directly over your Mac's speakers, and you need or want them to sound accurate. (More on the Mac and music in the last section of this chapter.) Two well-respected names in audio pop out at us: Bose and Acoustic Research. Bose offers the RoomMate series of speakers, at around $500. Acoustic Research offers the Powered Partner 570 speakers at about $500. The latter are serious speakers, with plenty of power (35 watts per channel), and plenty of size.

More Audio Output: Music and Conversation

While talking about audio editing and output, we would be remisss if we didn't point out that you can play CD music directly over your Macintosh IF you have the right equipment. The right equipment is a CD ROM drive. For our purposes here, we will say that a CD-ROM lets you access prodigious amounts of information stored on a specially formatted CD. These CDs are called "ROMs" (read only memories) because you can only retrieve information from them; you can't write new information onto them. Most all CD ROM drives let you play conventional audio CDs, however. You can play them back directly through your Mac's internal speaker. Yet another reason to acquire powered external speakers.

Finally, we feel obliged to mention an old friend in this space. Years ago, Apple introduced a System Extension called *Macintalk*. Macintalk brought speech synthesis to the Macintosh, on the quality level of the old Speak and Spell toy offered by Texas Instruments.

You may wonder why extra software is useful, since speech is just another form of sound that can be recorded digitally as can any other. Well, remember how much information it takes to store one second of sound: about 22KB. If you want your Mac to be able to say lots of things, you have to store each phrase individually by taking up acres of disk space.

A better way is to store a "script" that your computer "reads," rather than sounds it reproduces. The space required to save a paragraph of text is miniscule compared with the space required to store the sound of someone reading it. This is the approach Apple took with *Macintalk*.

Macintalk sound files looked superficially like English. Each letter had a particular sound value. There were special symbols for pauses and the like. Stringing the symbols together could create a plausible imitation of a male speaking voice. In addition, if you know enough about language, you can get your Mac to speak French, Russian, or any other non-tonal language.

Macintalk never really caught fire. The only "application" we ever saw was a System Extension that brought the *Talking Moose* to your screen. When active, the *Talking Moose* extension would "wait" until your Mac had been idle for a certain period of time (say, five minutes). It would then appear in a little window: a cartoon moosehead that looked somewhat like Bullwinkle. He would voice some wiseacre remark ("How come we never go out anymore?) and disappear. The *Talking Moose* was quite a novelty. Before long, folks discovered that you could use a resource editor to change the phrases in his repertoire. In fact, we have two developer friends who made the moose into their telephone answering machine message. Something about holding the two of them hostage, but still taking their calls...

We are actually happy to say that the *Talking Moose* is alive and well and selling for under $40.00, list. The "*Talking Moose* and His Cartoon Carnival" is available from Baseline Publishing. He and his friends know about 1000 jokes; you can add more. He's System 7 compatible. He won MacUsers 1991 Eddy award for "Best Desktop Diversion." He may never leave us alone.

All kidding aside, the Moose points out an interesting new area of Macintosh sound research. We have seen that it's been possible for years to get a Mac to "talk." (At times, it is easier than getting it to shut up.) But what about talking to your Mac? Only recently has it become possible. The technology has not been perfected, but it merits attention. It is the subject of our next section.

What Is That You Said?: Macintosh Voice Recognition

A dream that many of us have had for years is to be able to talk to our computers. Perhaps we want a less malicious companion than HAL, with which David Bowman conversed in the movie *2001: A Space Odyssey*, but we still wanted someone digital to talk to. Lots of scientists and researches have had the same dream. The technology of voice recognition—equipping a computer to listen to, "understand," and act upon human speech—has been a hot area of research for decades. It has launched and sustained entire careers in the field of linguistics, the study of languages. It has not gotten very far.

In the last thirty years we have learned what a difficult problem speech presents. Consider this: the word "return," it is sound graphed and displayed; looks only superficially similar when spoken by a six year old girl or a forty five year old man. We would be justified in calling them two different sounds. Yet any speaker of English hears the same word no matter who speaks.

Linguists have been trying for years to isolate the distinctive "features" within human speech that make a word the same no matter who says it. The work has progressed quite far. Scientists have been able to isolate the feature that makes an "s" different from a "z," and a "t" different from a "d." (The feature is called voicing.) They can even create an image of this feature, and have been working on getting a computer to recognize it. However, the computation required to isolate all the features from just one sentence spoken at normal speed still overwhelms even large computer systems.

We have a colleague who worked at a speech-recognition software development firm. They were trying to develop a system to allow radiologists to control x-ray equipment by talking to it. Their system occupied many hundreds of megabytes of disk storage; it required hours to recompile every time a change was made and employed dozens of programmers, editors, and linguists. In the end, it didn't really work.

There is a way to circumvent the difficulties of working with speech analytically, at the expense of creating a less flexible system. We do away with the problem of trying to recognize the same word spoken by anybody and concentrate on the speech of a single invidual. We then 'train' the system to recognize words spoken by this person. This approach has been bearing fruit as of late, even in the Macintosh realm.

You can now buy hardware (and its associated software) to recognize verbal commands and implement them. *Microsoft Word 5.0*, for example, can be run using this hardware. To make a selection into bold text, for example, you need only highlight it and say the word "Bold." You must train the system to recognize your voice. Although it isn't inexpensive it can be quite useful.

Articulate Systems, the people who brought us *Voice Record* and *Voice Impact*, are now selling the *Voice Navigator* speech recognition software/hardware package. The product comes in two versions: a software-only package (*Voice Navigator SW*) that works with Macintosh built-in microphones (LC & LC II, IIsi, Quadras, Classic II, Powerbooks 140 & 170), and a software/hardware combination (*Voice Navigator II*) for Macs without built in sound digitizing capability. You must "train" the *Voice Navigator* to recognize each individual that will be using it. More than one person can use the system; you change "voices" via the Control Panel. The software features a prompted training regime: You are asked to "say" a number of commands as their names appear on the screen. *Voice Navigator* "listens" to you, recording what it sounds like when you say "Cut," Open," "Show Clipboard," etc. There is one good thing about having to train the software: it can be made to recognize commands in any language, spoken with any accent.

The controlling part of *Voice Navigator* runs in the background; it is loaded as a startup document. You have a separate language "template" file for each application that you use the software with. There is a special, automatic command to recognize all the menu items in an application, although you must still train the software to recognize the spoken equivalent of commands it has not yet "heard." Included with the package is Articulate Systems' *Voice Record* software, which we talked about earlier. An improved microphone (compared with the Mac's standard mike) is included as well. The retail price is less than $400.

The *Voice Navigator II* comes with a sound digitizer box that plugs into your Mac's SCSI port, a big improvement over systems that use the serial ports. You can have up to six external SCSI devices connected at once—assuming you have an internal hard disk, which uses one SCSI link—as opposed to two serial devices. Using the *Voice Record* software provided, you can use the system as a sound digitizer in addition to its voice recognition capability. It sells for about $600.

Once you have it set up—and that takes a certain amount of time—operating your Mac with *Voice Navigator* is straightforward. It is always on, and is always "listening." To activate a menu command, speak the command's name into your microphone. It is just like pulling the menu down and selecting the command with your mouse. *Voice Navigator* automatically loads the correct language file when you launch an application; you don't have to switch yourself.

Quite a number of reviewers like this product a lot. It has won a few awards as well. Although training can be tedious, *Voice Navigator* seems to be fairly reliable, although not perfect. At least it doesn't do anything disastrous when it doe not understand you. It seems to follow the physician's creed: "If you can do no good, at least do no harm," and that is about all you can ask. We expect to see continuing improvements in this area in the next few years; surely there will be competitor products before long. However, don't hold your breath waiting for a system that recognizes any voice without training: the world's top computer linguists have yet to crack that nut. Maybe in the next century...

There are lots of ways of getting sound into and out of a Macintosh. Sound, however, is only part of the picture. There is a special catagory of sound that we have not considered: melodic and harmonic sound, also known as music. The Macintosh has emerged as the premier music-making computer platform in the industry today. We look at the Macintosh and music in the final section of this chapter.

Soothing the Savage Mac: Macintosh Music

Years and years ago, at the very dawn of the Macintosh era, your gentle author expressed a fond wish to one of the editors of this very book. Musically inclined although not particularly talented, we wanted a computer system that would let us "program" music, to have it played back automatically over the appropriate electronic instruments. You might say we were thinking of a sort of network of electronic player pianos.

Evidently we were not alone in having this desire. In fact, some very prominent people had already gotten together to make this dream a reality. In the early 1980s, several manufacturers of electronic musical instruments hammered out the MIDI standard: a digital network to allow instruments of all kinds to be hooked together and controlled from a central computer. MIDI was not (and isn't now) a Macintosh-specific standard, but the Mac has become very prominent in the world of MIDI music. A number of prominent musicians, composers, and studios run Macintosh-based music systems. For a surprisingly modest investment, you can, too.

In this section we are going to look at MIDI on the Macintosh. After explaining more about the MIDI standard, we will look at the different kinds of MIDI hardware you can buy: interfaces, keyboards, synthesizer modules, tape recorders, and the like. We will then turn our attention to Macintosh-specific MIDI software, including MIDI sequencers, voice libraries, voice editors, and musical notation software.

About MIDI

The acronym "MIDI" stands for Musical Instrument Digital Interface. Fundamentally, it is a network protocol. In this sense, it is not all that different from the SCSI protocol used to connect peripheral devices (disk drives, plotters, voice recognition modules, etc.) to a Macintosh. Like SCSI, MIDI allows a number of devices to be "daisy-chained" together with cables. MIDI, however, allows a practically unlimited number of devices to be hooked up in one such chain, as compared with the eight (including the Mac itself and an internal hard disk, as we mentioned above) that SCSI supports. (There are only sixteen separate data channels in MIDI, but unlike SCSI, MIDI devices can share channels.) Like SCSI, MIDI defines how devices on the network communicate with each other. And also like SCSI, MIDI is capable of transferring large amounts of data at a fairly rapid pace.

There are some differences, of course. Although MIDI is now supported in Apple's System software (through the *MIDI Manager*), the Mac as it ships from the factory is not equipped to handle MIDI input and output. All Macs have a SCSI port, but to add MIDI you must buy a special box that plugs into one of your serial ports, transferring MIDI data into Macintosh serial format.

What's more, MIDI is considerably more complex than SCSI, with a greater number of possible commands to its component devices. Finally, SCSI has not been terribly successful outside the Macintosh world, whereas MIDI is supported by numerous computer and software manufacturers, including Atari, Commodore and IBM. In fact, MIDI is just about the only game in town.

MIDI is not really a set of pieces of hardware, or even of software. It's a formal set of rules. The rules are maintained and published by the MIDI Manufacturers Association (MMA), and are under constant review and periodic revision. Together, these rules constitute a communcations *protocol*.

The MIDI Protocol

A protocol is a set of rules for determing how something behaves, like a diplomat or a computer. In the case of the MIDI, the formal protocol has two parts. There is the hardware specification, which dictates how MIDI devices are connected. Then there is the language specification, which dictates how MIDI devices communicate with each other over this connection: what they say, how they say it, and what their sayings signify.

There are three kinds of MIDI connections. These are called "ports," like the serial ports or the SCSI port on a Macintosh. The three ports are "In," "Out," and "Thru." The *In* port accepts information from the MIDI network. The *Out* port transmits information to the network. The *Thru* port is a little tricker. It lets network information pass along to other devices on the network. In effect, it repeats the information received at the MIDI In port. Using the Thru port on each device, information from a single "master" controlling device can be sent to many other devices. (On a Macintosh network such as LocalTalk, In and Out are handled by a single port; transmitting information "Thru" requires a connector with two ports.)

MIDI ports use a circular connector with five pins, and are connected with a fairly fat coaxial cable. (In a coaxial cable, all the wires run along the same axis.) In, Out, and Thru all have the same shape connector. Typically, a cable will run from the Out port of a master device to the In port of a slave device. Interestingly enough, two of the five pins in a MIDI connector are not currently used. Some writers are itching to have the MMA issue a new, more intelligent MIDI specification that assigns meanings to these pins. To connect another slave device, you would run an additional cable from the Thru port of the first slave to the In port of the second.

What kind of messages are being sent? Each MIDI message consists of one to three bytes of information. That is *information,* not sound. From what we know about sound and how much information it takes to represent it, you can see that attempting to transmit sound would swamp the network. Actual sounds are generated by MIDI devices according to the information (instructions) they receive over the network.

The first byte in a MIDI message is called the status byte. It is, in effect, a command. There can be one or two bytes following the status byte; these are data bytes. For example, the status byte might say "Note on," telling a connected device to begin playing. The two data bytes would specify which note to play and how loudly to play it. You can see that there would be 128 different notes that might be played (a piano keyboard has only 88, so this is plenty) at any one of 128 different volumes. There are 128 different possible status byte messages, each corresponding to a separate MIDI command.

Beyond that, MIDI messages fall into two broad classes. There are *channel specific* messages and *system* messages. MIDI supports sixteen different channels. A channel specific message applies to only one of these channels. This is an important capability. You can, for example, assign each MIDI device in a chain to a separate channel or channels. In this way, one master device can send separate notes to each slave device. What you end up with is a mini-ensemble.

One of the editors of this book has three synthesizers (devices that can imitate, or *synthesize*, many different instruments) that can support all sixteen different MIDI channels, each playing a different synthesized voice. Several voices can play the rhythm part, another few voices can play the bass, a third set plays the melody, and a fourth the harmony (and on and on... the number of combination possible is incredible). We will talk a little bit more about how this is done when we discuss synthesizers under the heading MIDI Hardware, and when we look at sequencing software under the heading MIDI Software. There are, in turn, two kinds of Channel specific messages. They are as follows:

Channel Voice messages: These messages control how a device plays. They include Note On and Note Off, Pressure, Control Change (think of these as digital "knobs" and buttons; sending a control change message is like fiddling with a specific control on a device.), Program Change (if a device can store different setups—one imitating perhaps a violin, another imitating a flute—this command selects among them), and Pitch Bend (like the whammy bar on a guitar).

Channel Mode messages: Messages that dictate how a given device responds to any other message. For example, a device can be instructed to play only one voice at a time, or to play multiple voices. A device that can play more than one voice at once is said to be *multitimbral*. A device may be further restricted to a single note within each voice, or it may be allowed to attempt chords. The latter function is called *polyphony*, and it's a handy capability to have.

In addition to channel specific messages, there are system messages. These messages are sent to every device on the MIDI network. System messages fall into three classes:

System Real Time messages: These messages are used to synchronize all devices on the network. This is especially important when you have devices that are programmed to play set sequences of notes, such as MIDI drum machines.

System Common messages: These are miscellaneous functions. One such message, Song Position Pointer, specifies the current position in a sequence. (A sequence is a set of MIDI commands, the net effect of which is to store a musical composition. More on sequencing when we get to software.) This keeps everybody at the same place. Think of it as saying to all connected devices: "OK everyone, we're on page three, bar two, measure one of the score."

System Exclusive messages: These messages are intended for specific devices on the network. Using such a message, your Macintosh can send information to a connected device to make it sound like another instrument. (The information a synthesizer requires to sound a certain way is called a *patch*.) Only the target device receives the patch, other devices do not pay any attention to the message. As a rule, each MIDI manufacturer has a separate type of System Exclusive message for their equipment.

An important point to keep in mind about all MIDI messages is that MIDI is a large standard, with many commands. Not every device understands every command. In a computer network, this can cause trouble. But in a MIDI network, each device only pays attention to the subset of messages that it can handle, and ignores the rest. This keeps things humming along.

Sounds complicated? It is, in a way. Let's consider a very simple example, and see if we can't get our bearings that way. Suppose you have a MIDI-capable Macintosh, connected to one, multitimbral, polyphonic keyboard synthesizer. Your Mac has a MIDI box connected to one of its serial ports. This box gives it at least one MIDI Out and one MIDI In. A cable runs from the MIDI Out on this box to the MIDI In on your synthesizer. Another cable runs back from the MIDI Out on your synth to the MIDI In hooked to your Mac.

To play chords in four different voices, your Mac sends a Channel Mode message to your synth, telling it to switch modes. To play one note in each voice, your Mac sends four separate Note On messages, one on each channel. The result is a sustained chord in four parts. Your Mac sends additional Note On and Note Off messages on each channel, to create an ensemble performance.

Exactly what kind of hardware and software do you need to create such a performance? There are just gobs and gobs of it out there. We've waded through some of the best of it. The following two subsections will give you a taste of the kinds of MIDI hardware/software you can buy.

MIDI Hardware

Your Macintosh itself is among the most important pieces of MIDI hardware you can buy. Indeed, with the right software, a Mac can be made to imitate just about any other MIDI device except a keyboard. You will, however, need to buy other hardware if you mean to do serious work or have serious fun. MIDI hardware falls into a number of catagories, many of which are outlined below, with examples.

MIDI Interfaces

Before your Mac can talk MIDI with other devices, you need to connect a MIDI interface to it. Such an interface translate MIDI messages into serial data that your Mac can understand. It also translate Mac serial data into MIDI messages. There are several of these devices available. Apple sells one that they call the *Apple MIDI Interface*, but it is relatively expensive and has only one In and one Out. The *MacNexus Interface* from J.L. Cooper Electronics, The *MIDIFace LC* from Altech, and the *MIDI Translator* from Opcode Systems are better values. The last-named interface from Opcode is widely available through catalog merchants.

At the opposite end of the price spectrum, Mark of the Unicorn sells the *MIDI Time Piece II*. This interface has 16—count 'em, 16—MIDI ports; 8 IN and 8 Out. In this way it can support 128 different channels of MIDI information, although each "network" of 16 channels must be maintained separate from every other to avoid channel conflicts. In practice this is not hard to do. The device is fully programmable and sits in a rack. It is also expensive.

Keyboards

After an interface, a keyboard should likely be your next investment.. After all, you need something you can play, something that will make noise. Keyboards fall into two catagories (doesn't everything?): synthesizers and samplers.

A synthesizer uses electronics to imitate sounds. The idea is to use fancy electronic tricks to recreate the waveform of a particular musical instrument, or, indeed, other sounds like rain, applause, or footsteps. (The waveform is really just the graph of the instrument's actual sound.) Synthesizers can only get so close to the "real" sound of musical instrument. You will always be able to tell the difference, even when synthesizing something simple. On the other hand, synthesizers can be pretty inexpensive, and for making high-tech sounds they can't be beat.

Casio makes a full line of synthesizers; the CZ and VZ series were notable (this author has a CZ-1000 that we like alot. The model has been discontinued, though.) Yamaha also makes synthesizers. Roland Corporation produces perhaps the best-known line of synthesizers, and they have more models than you can shake a stick at.

A sampling keyboard uses snippets of real live sound to recreate other instruments. Frequently, the relevant samples are stored on CD, although some are included directly within the keyboard. Such a keyboard can be made to sound exactly like a saxophone (only without so much soul) because it has the actual saxophone sound within it. Examples include the Korg M1, the Yamaha SY77, the Kurzweil 1000, and the new E-mu MPS Plus. They sound great and are more expensive.

Whatever keyboard you buy, make certain it has *velocity-sensitive* keys. Put simply, this makes it a *pianoforte*: striking a key softly makes the instrument play soft (piano); striking it hard makes it play loudly (forte). Otherwise, all sounds will play at the same intensity, which gives a flat and uninteresting result. You also should make sure that your keyboard is both polyphonic and multitimbral. Just about every new synthesizer is.

Synthesizer and Sampler modules

These devices are like keyboards without the keys. If you have a simple keyboard, but want to add extra sounds and extra capabilities, you can connect one of these modules to your system. Roland sells the Sound Canvas SC-155, which is an extremely economic, powerful multitimbral, polyphonic sound module. Other well known and much-respected modules come from E-mu (the Proteus series) and Korg, which produces a sophisticated module version of many of its keyboards.

Drum Machines

There are specialized MIDI devices to produce percussion. Because they are optimized for this one kind of sound, they sound better than synthesizers attempting percussion. What's more, a typical drum machine is programmable; you set it up to play a particular percussion sequence which it remembers. The device will play the whole sequence upon receiving one MIDI command, rather than a command for each beat. This cuts down on the number of messages passing through the network. Network overload—which results in erratic play and slowed tempos—can be a problem if you have many devices attempting complicated rhythms and melodies. Alesis sells an excellent line of drum machines, including their SR-16. Yamaha and Roland also offer units.

Sequencers

If you have a Macintosh, you do not need a sequencer unless you want to take your MIDI setup places where your Mac simply cannot go. With the correct software, your Mac will behave like a sequencer at a considerable savings. Still, we ought to explain what a sequencer does because it can be the most important part of your MIDI system.

A MIDI sequencer records and then plays back lists of MIDI commands. Such a list is called a *sequence*, because the commands are played in order. A sequence can recreate an entire musical performance, such as Chopin's E-flat Nocturne. The sequence can be for one instrument in one voice or for several instruments each playing chords. The only limits are the number of MIDI channels available, and the power and sophistication of the sequencer you are using.

A typical sequencer will "listen in" as you play your keyboard, recording the notes you play and how you play them. The result is a small sequence of MIDI events. You can then edit that sequence; changing the pitch and duration of notes, repeating certain sections (this is called "looping"), adding other notes. There are typically several tracks in a sequence. You might have a bass track, a continuo track, a melody track, and a harmony track, for example. Each track can be assigned to a different MIDI channel or channels.

In addition to managing the creation and editing of a sequence, a MIDI sequencer handles playback as well. In a concert setting, the sequencer is the "master" of MIDI instruments, telling all the other ("slave") devices on the network what to play and when to play it. Generally, this kind of MIDI ensemble is used to "back up" live musicians, to make the band sound larger and more sophisticated. In a studio setting, however, it is possible to rely on sequenced music for everything but human voices.

Like we say, there are hardware sequencers available. Generally, these devices will save and accept sequences on 3-1/2" diskettes. However, you do not need to buy such a machine. In a little while we will show you some software packages that will turn your Mac into a very sophisticated MIDI sequencer. (Again, all of this is true unless you simply cannot take your Mac where your MIDI gear needs to go).

Alternative MIDI Controllers

Not every musician plays keyboards. After all, there are guitar players. (Sometimes, after a long stint watching MTV, it seems to us that there's nothing *but* guitar players.) There are guitar synthesizers that will turn a guitar into a MIDI controller, like a keyboard. Yamaha used to make a MIDI wind controller; it was a strange little device that you played like a recorder. It made no sound of its own; it simply relayed note and velocity data to a synthesizer or sampler that you had to provide. Thus, the playback quality depended mainly on your synth/sampler. It was a quirky little affair and has since been discontinued, but newer, improved devices exist.

MIDI Special Effects

You can buy special effects modules to change the nature of existing sounds. In these, the output from an instrument is passed through the effects module before it goes to your speakers; echo, reverb, and classic effects. However, the kinds of things you can do with MIDI aren't limited to messing with sounds. There are several MIDI devices that will control additional aspects of a live performance. You can buy a MIDI lighting controller which will play fancy tricks with your lights in step with your music. There are also MIDI mixers which will adjust the relative contributions of your instruments, changing the mix at different points in a song, or between songs.

We also could not pass this area without mentioning the nothing-short-of-revolutionary *Vocalist VHM5* from Digitech. This incredible module will actually sing backup vocals for you. In effect, it process your own voice and reproduces it, singing the harmony to your melody. It will even correct your pitch if you are singing slightly off key. And you wondered why some singers sound better in the studio than they do live.

Multi-Channel Tape Recorders

Once you have gotten your music sequenced right, you have just got to get it on tape. How else are you going to get it over to Capitol Records? You can buy MIDI-controlled tape recorders to take your final product and transfer it to cassette tape. That is better than trying to lug all your gear over to someone's office.

The typical semi-professional tape recorder lets you mix up to four channels (audio channels, not MIDI channels) into the final, stereo cassette. These recorders have a simple mixing board on the deck itself; you select the level you want for each channel. The MIDI In port on one of these recorders lets you have your sequencer control the recording process during playback, supposing the sequencer and the tape deck undestand each other. Tascam sells four-channel tape decks; they start at about $350. As always, you can spend more money and acquire a unit with more capabilities.

That is a lot of hardware. What do you really need? In addition to your Mac, you can get by with just three other pieces of equipment. You will need an interface, a keyboard, and a tape recorder. Remember to get an interface that has more than one MIDI Out; three is the standard number. Also, you will want a keyboard that is multitimbral and has velocity-sensitive keys. Finally, you can get away with an inexpensive four-track tape recorder. You can forgo MIDI on this item if you really need to; that brings the cost down a lot.

You still, however, are going to need software, or you are not going to get very far with this simple setup (or even with a very complicated one). With this in mind, we turn our attention to MIDI software. This is where our discussion gets entirely Macintosh-specific.

MIDI Software

There is probably better—if not more—MIDI software written for the Macintosh than for any other personal computer. (Admittedly, the Commodore Amiga and the IBM PC clones are close competitors.) There are, in fact, so many different kinds of Mac MIDI software, in so many different catagories, that the whole may confuse you. The following is our attempt to sort this mess out for you, followed by suggestions on what to buy.

Sequencing Software

If you bought no other Macintosh MIDI software, we would say you ought to buy a sequencer. We explained what a sequencer does a while back while we were discussing hardware. A sequencer ties your MIDI system together, enabling your Macintosh to control the whole shooting match.

There are several very good sequencers on the market. As an example, we will look at Mark of the Unicorn's *Performer*. This software will support one or two MIDI interfaces, for a total of 32 channels. (The networks on the two interfaces must be kept separate, or confusion will result.) You can record a practically unlimited number of tracks, although again you have a maximum of 32 MIDI channels through which to play back. *Performer* will "listen" to you playing a particular MIDI instrument, and record your performance as a separate track which you can then edit.

Performer lets you edit track data in several ways. In one format, pitch, velocity, and duration data are shown as letters and number. In another, data are shown graphically, with durations represented as bars. Finally, you can see notes in conventional musical format.

As with most sequencing software, tracks can be mixed, looped, and combined to your heart's content to yield a final sequence. You can select and change which MIDI channels to use for each track in a sequence, and you can add global dynamic and tempo data as well, changing the overal loudness and the speed at which your sequence plays back. *Performer* will save files in a standard MIDI format that other software packages can read, including simple ones intended for playback only.

One quirky but interesting feature that *Performer* (and most sequencers) has is called quantization. This feature is used to clean up "live" performances that you've recorded with the sequencer. It works like this: you set up to record, you play a few bars, and then you stop and save. You then quantitize the newly-saved sequence. The beginnings and endings of notes are then adjusted so that they fall on the beats.

At best, this can make a performance sound more "in time;" at worst, it can take all the human touch out. It is those subtle little anomalies—coming in a fraction of a beat too late, sustaining a 64th note too long—that give a live performance its feel. Most sequencers let you adjust the quantization sensivity so that it doesn't obliterate your playing style. On the plus side, if you do not play well, quantizing can at least keep your sequence from sounding amateur.

Performer does have one drawback: it is expensive. You may not need all that power. There are less expensive alternatives to consider. Opcode sells *EZ Vision*, a relatively inexpensive sequencer that still supports 16 channels. A step up from here are Green Oak Software's *Rhapsody* and *Beyond* from Dr. T's Music Software. (Dr. T. makes lots of cool Mac MIDI software.)

We ought to mention that some of the Macintosh catalog companies sell an Opcode starter package that includes *EZ Vision*, the *MIDI Translator* interface, PG Software's *Band-in-a-Box* (it accompanies you like one of those Hammond organs they are always playing in the mall), a multitimbral four-octave keyboard, and all the right MIDI cables. This is everything you need to get started with MIDI on the Mac (except the Mac) at less than $400. If you've already got a keyboard, you can buy a version of the kit *sans* keyboard for less than $200. Other sequencers in the same price range as *Performer* include Opcodes's *Vision* (*EZ Vision* is a less complicated version of this software) and Passport Design's *MasterTracks Pro 5*.

Notation Editing Software

Sequencers are not necessarily the only game in town. Another major class of Mac MIDI software is the Notation Editors, several of which can take the place of a sequencer, if on a limited scale. More frequently, though, a particular notation editor is offered by the manufacturer of a sequencer package; the two are intended with work with and complement each other.

Mozart could surely have used one of these software packages. Basically, they let you write and edit music on a conventional staff, with notes, accidentals, tempo and dynamics notations, the works. In addition, you can play back what you have written over your Mac's internal speaker through separate speakers, or even over a MIDI network. You can also print out a score: Adobe Systems has a special font called *Sonata* that many of these packages use to produce high-quality musical output on a laser printer.

As you might expect, Mark of the Unicorn offers a notation editor to complement their Performer sequencing software. They call it *Professional Composer*. *Composer* lets you arrange, edit, and print out musical scores. What's more, you can save *Composer* documents in MIDI format, and then play them back using *Performer*. Technically speaking, you could compose and play music without every touching a keyboard. We have tried this procedure, though, and frankly such a composition sounds like music played by a computer. So what do you want for nothing?

We do feel obliged to mention that the dread quantization problem creeps in again when you try to move *Performer* files back the other way, turning them into *Composer* documents. If you do not quantize exactly right, you will see the most amazing combinations of quarter notes tied to eight notes tied to sixteenth notes tied to thirty-second notes... That is because *Perfomer*, in saving your sequence, preserves the exact length of each note. Since MIDI works with eight bit words, we are talking 128th notes here. Anyway, the result is an uneditable mess. You need to quantize thoroughly, with the filter set fairly coarse, before saving a *Performer* document in *Composer* form.

As with sequencers, there are other notation editors. PassPort Designs offers *Encore* to go with their *MasterTracks* sequencer. They have a less expensive editor called *MusicTime*. Finally, Coda sells *MusicProse* and *Finale*, the latter of which is very well regarded.

Sound Editing Software

We need to draw a distinction between the sound editor/recorders we spoke of earlier in this chapter, and the software discussed here. Basically, these packages are used to control synthesizers. You use them to create new "patches" to send to your synthesizer, to make it sound like some other instrument (or some other thing altogether: a synthesizer can imitate a human voice singing a pure tone, a bird call, a laser gun, etc.). As such, you will find a different sound editor for every line of synthesizers on the market; no two are compatible. To be sure, not every synthesizer has a Macintosh sound editor available; if you have not bought a synthesizer, you might want to make the availability of such software a purchasing criterion. Dr. T's sells a whole range of sound editors.

Some software manufacturers have begun producing universal sound editors, designed to work with dozens of different synthesizers. Opcode, for instance, offers their *Galaxy Plus Editor/Librarian*, with support for over 140 synthesizers, effects processors, and mixers. Pixel Publishing makes their *Super Librarian*, which stores patches for over 100 MIDI different MIDI devices.

Other Software

This is the catch-all catagory. There are three musical education software packages that caught our eye, for instance. There is *Listen*, a simple application that teaches you how to recognize musical elements, particularly intervals. (An interval is two notes a certain number of notes apart. E and G span an interval of one third. Middle C and C above middle span an interval of a full octave.) *Practica Musica* is similar, but offers additional exercises and ear training. Both will play back through your Mac's internal speaker or over a MIDI network.

Then ther is the *Miracle Piano Teaching System*. This software includes a 49-key, velocity sensitive MIDI keyboard. The system teaches keyboard playing sort of in the manner of a video game. It is even said to "monitor" your progress and to make invidualized suggestions. This set up has been around for over a year on other computers, and has garnered considerable praise and attention from the mainstream media.

Finally, Digidesign offers the *Deck* four track recording software. This software eliminates the need for a separate four track recorder, presuming you own one of Digidesign's high-end audio cards, the *Sound Tools* system or the *Audiomedia* card. *Deck* includes a MIDI sequencer, and can play sequences created with other MIDI software.

So what do you need? Admittedly this is a tougher call than our hardware recommendations. Actually, all you really need to begin is sequencing software package like *EZ Vision* or Mark of the Unicorn's *Performer*. The former is inexpensive, the latter is full-featured. You do not really need a notation editor like *Composer*, unless you want to publish scores. As for musical sound editors, it might be a good idea to acquire one to go with your keyboard, if such is available. They generally make it much easier to modify and play with sounds on your keyboard, as opposed to using the keyboard's own controls.

If you are not terribly, terribly talented, we can definitely recommend that you look into a musical training package, either *Listen* or *Practica Musica*. Both these are quite inexpensive and the payback should be considerable, especially in decreased frustration.

Looking at the total Macintosh sound picture, we can ask: "What set up offers the most for the least?" If your Mac has a built-in mike, you can save serious bucks. With the *Voice Navigator* software package, and with the *EZ Music Starter Kit* (with keyboard), you will have sound recording and editing capability through *Voice Record*. You will be able to issue verbal commands to your Mac with the *Voice Navigator*. You will have a MIDI keyboard, an interface, and *EZ Vision* sequencing software with which to create and play back musical compositions. Throw in the *Talking Moose* to enliven your dull and inactive moments, and you'll have just about covered the whole spectrum of sound on the Macintosh. You can acquire it all for less than a thousand dollars.

What kinds of applications can you put such a system to? Well, who knows, you might compose the next Grammy-winning song. But even if you are not that talented, you will be able to create sophisticated sounds and music to accompany multimedia presentations. Many multimedia packages have "hooks" in them that let them play MIDI sequences in conjunction with video and graphics. At the very least, you will have a lot of fun playing around with a fun and interesting medium.

Sound Advice

You can see that the world of sound on the Macintosh is indeed a large one. But wait, ther is more! There are a number of resources you can turn to for additional help and information.

As for periodical publicantions, both *MacUser* and *MacWorld* publish reviews and articles on Macintosh sound hardware and software. For the musically inclined, a better choice is *Electronic Musician* or *Keyboard* magazine. These are not Macintosh-specific, but they do offer information on using Macintoshes in music. They also offer information and reviews on MIDI hardware that you will not find in the other magazines. Some hardware manufacturers have magazines for their customers. These are generally specific to that manufacturer's line of gear, but can have a lot of information, as well as interviews with famous users. You'll need to check with your hardware maker to see if they have a magazine or newsletter of their own, or know of one they can turn you on to.

There are also some interesting books out there. IDG has just published the Macintosh *Music and Sound Bible* and Sybex has published *The Audible Macintosh*. It chock full of all kinds of information, and comes very highly recommended. There is also Hayden's *Cool Mac Sounds*, which we have mentioned before. This nifty little book includes a diskette with some cute shareware and interesting digital sounds.

Finally, as always, there are the online information services, such as Compuserve and America Online. With a modem and a subscription to one of these guys, you can communicate with other folks who are into Mac music, benefitting from their knowledge and experience. You can acquire sampled sounds to play on your Mac, although beware that such transfers are generally time-consuming and hence costsly. (You pay by the minute for your connection with such an information service. Long calls ring up big charges and often high phone bills. Be careful your first month. We know someone who ran up $700 in connect fees before he knew it.) And you can be the first on your block to acquire those nifty little sound shareware tools.

With sound and music on the Macintosh, you can invest as little as $50, or more than $50,000. It all depends on what you want to do. If you have the resources, and the desire, and the talent, however, the sky is almost literally the limit. From recording your own voice to creating an opera, from designing a new synthesizer sound to scoring the soundtrack to a film, your Macintosh—properly equipped—can give you the power to sculpt sound into almost any form imaginable. All you have got to do is do it. That, to be sure, is the really tricky part.

Multimedia Technologies

 ## Multimedia Nuts 'n' Bolts

Of what use is a newborn baby? This retort has been given before by proponents of a nascent technology, when confronted with the skepticism of an unconvinced and uneducated public. We think it applies well to Macintosh Multimedia. Few areas have generated as much excitement among the cognoscenti of late, and yet few have generated more cries of "Yes, but what is it good for?" from the uninitiated. In this chapter, we mean to show what the excitement is about and to hopefully show the use to which this exciting new technology can be put.

What is multimedia? The term refers to application software and operating environments which integrate different computer output media—still and motion graphics, sound effects and music—into a single experience. By this definition, television is a multimedia experience; it combines moving pictures with sound. On the Mac, a multimedia presentation can incorporate video footage from television, animated and still graphics, sound, and music. In addition, such a presentation can be made interactive. What happens on the screen can be made to depend on actions taken by the user.

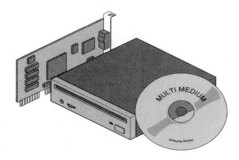

There are a number of different parts to creating multimedia presentations on the Macintosh. You need the appropriate hardware and software. Figuring out what is "appropriate" is the tricky part, but in this chapter we are going to give you information that should help you judge for yourself. We are going to talk about basic Mac hardware—your CPU, memory, and accessories—and how it contributes to good multimedia results. We will talk about the different kinds of multimedia software that you can buy, focusing on a particular example within each genre. And of course, we will talk about QuickTime, Apple's new system software extension designed to bring it all together under one roof.

Macintosh Hardware and Multimedia

One thing's certain: multimedia requires a powerful personal computer, one like the Macintosh. Now, all Macs are powerful, but not equally so. You can save time, bucks, and frustration by knowing the multimedia potential of the Mac you own or mean to buy. Each part of a Macintosh system has its own contribution to make; you need to know the potential of each. Of all the parts of a Mac system, none is more important than the central processing unit itself. We will start with it.

Macintosh CPUs

The central processing unit, or CPU for short, is the box containing the main computing circuitry of your Macintosh. All other parts of your system plug into the CPU. In a sense, the potential performance of the other parts of your system is limited by the power of the CPU. The CPU determines your Mac's speed, expandability, and compatibility with other hardware and software.

At this time, Mac CPUs fall into four broad categories. The *compact* Macintoshes include the original 128K Mac and the 512K Mac (long since discontinued, although some are still out there, chugging along), the Mac Plus, the Mac SE, the SE/30, and the Classic I and II models. All these Macs have built-in video. The modular Macintosh II line includes the original Macintosh II, the IIx, the IIcx (all discontinued), the IIci, the IIsi, the LC and the LC II, and the IIfx. The display for these Macs is housed separately, which gives you a certain amount of flexibility. It is difficult to add a larger display to the compact Macs, and your choices are also quite limited. With the modular Macs, it's just a matter of buying the new display and the appropriate display adapter hardware (see the chapter on Graphics Hardware-Output).

The newest Macintosh lines comprise the PowerBooks, which are laptop Macintoshes with built-in screens, and the Quadras, which are based on a more powerful microprocessor chip. As it turns out, the microprocessor—a computer on a chip that does all the real work—is really the important part of the Mac CPU as far as multimedia is concerned. Thus, the preceding categories aren't necessarily the best organization paradigm. A better organization scheme sorts out the various Macintoshes by the microprocessor they contain.

> **NOTE:** "Computer on a chip" is not a bad description of the latest microprocessors. The Motorola MC68040 chip contained in a Macintosh Quadra 700, 900, or 950 is in many ways more powerful than the CPU of an IBM 370 series mainframe computer, the dominant mainframe of the 1970s and early 1980s. If current trends continue, we may see the power of a Cray XMP-48 supercomputer on a desktop by the beginning of the next century, less than a decade away.

All Macs are based on the MC68000 series of microprocessors, manufactured by Motorola. (U.S. companies surpass foreign competition in developing and manufacturing microprocessors.) There are currently four members in this series which you will find inside Macs: the 68000 itself, the 68020, the 68030, and the most powerful of all, the 68040. The following chart shows which processor is contained in each Macintosh:

Mac Models and their Microprocessors

CPUs	Microprocessor
128K*, 512K*, Plus*, SE*, Classic I, PowerBook 100	68000
II*, LC*	68020
IIcx*, IIx*, LC II, IIsi, IIci, SE/30*, IIfx, Classic II, PowerBooks 140 and 170	68030
Quadras 700, 900*, 950	68040

*Models marked with an asterisk have been discontinued

Over the last few years, Apple has gradually been moving to replace earlier processors with the 68030 (at least). Recently, for example, the Macintosh LC—the Low Cost color Macintosh—received a breath of new life by getting (among other things) a 68030 processor to replace the 68020 it debuted with. You can see that, of the 11 models currently for sale, only two are based on the earlier chips.

Why is the 68030 so important? For one thing, the 68030 is an inherently faster design. Because it works with data in bigger chunks than did earlier processors (a full 32 bits instead of 16), it spends less time moving data around. That's good for multimedia applications, because they require more memory (places to hold data) and more data manipulation than any other kind of application. The amounts required are staggering, as we will see.

The newer processors also let you work with faster and larger amounts of memory. Actually, all Macs have built-in limitations on the amount of memory they can work with. No Mac, not even the newest, can work with the full amount of memory that its microprocessor can support. (The memory management chip in the Quadra 950 limits it to 256MB, for example. The MC68040 microprocessor in the Quadra could, in principle, handle more than 2 gigabytes.) Be that as it may, the newer Macs can handle much more memory, which makes them more suitable for multimedia work. A single, full-frame color graphics image can occupy more than a megabyte, for example.

In addition to the power of the microprocessor, there are other aspects of a Macintosh CPU that are important for multimedia work. For example, newer Mac CPUs can capture sound, a useful trick for multimedia applications. These Macs have a microphone port on the back of the CPU box. You can hook up the microphone that comes with the Mac, or you can connect an audio component, using an adapter jack that's also included with the Mac. The Sounds control panel lets you capture up to 10 seconds of sound using the microphone port. To capture more sound than that, you need special software.

Storage

You need someplace to store data, whether you are currently working on it or wish to retain it for future use. We've alluded to the first form of storage already; we called it "memory" in the last section. The technical term, of course, is RAM, for Random Access Memory. We call it random access memory because the computer can look at any point it chooses, just by giving the correct location.

As far as multimedia is concerned, the more RAM, the better. (Is there any application for this which isn't true? No. But for multimedia, it's especially critical.) You can work with black-and-white graphics on an older Macintosh that has only a megabyte (roughly one million characters) of RAM. To do color work, you need more. In fact, we've found that working with color video and sound on a Mac equipped with (some might say, "hampered by") System 7 uses up every bit of 8 megabytes at times. We find ourselves wishing for more. We would recommend a minimum of 4 megabytes for color work, especially if you are in System 7 land (more on Systems 6 and 7 shortly).

So much for short-term memory. For the longer term, data is stored on disks. The basic Mac floppy disk can store about 1.44MB on its magnetized surface. (Early Macs could only fit 800KB on a floppy; the very earliest, only 400KB.) These days, floppy disks alone just won't cut it, especially for multimedia work. Fortunately, almost every Mac you can currently buy comes with a high-capacity disk-based storage system, or *hard disk*. Most are built into the CPU; some are packaged in boxes of their own. Today's hard disks come in a range of sizes, from 20MB to over 1,500MB (also written 1.5GB, or gigabytes). (For more information on your storage options, see the Storage Technologies chapter of this book.)

Even more so than RAM, the more disk storage you have, the easier it is to work with multimedia. In fact, you will find that some manufacturers of multimedia software recommend a 200MB or larger hard disk for serious color work. That is not excessive. Macromind's Director 3.1, for example, can take up more than 10MB of disk space by itself, counting it's example and tutorial files. You can see that only a couple such applications would quickly swamp a 80MB drive. The files you create with these applications also tend to be huge: well into the multi-megabyte range isn't uncommon.

So if you are going to work with color multimedia, you can see that you ought to invest heavily in a large hard drive when you buy your Mac. For multimedia, drives in the 400MB range seem to be among the best choices. (Divide the size of a drive in megabytes by its price in dollars to get a measure of how cost-effective it is.)

If you already own a Mac, your hard disk (if you have one) probably isn't this large. There are, however, alternative storage systems that you can add on, expanding your capacity. Cartridge-based systems are among the least expensive options here. These drives are available in two sizes: 44 and 88MB. The latter can read data from the former, but cannot write to them.

These drives are pretty common. You may find these make it easier to exchange multimedia files with friends and colleagues. The principle advantage of these systems, though, is that you can buy additional cartridges upon which to store even more data. The storage cost is between one and two dollars a megabyte. Keep in mind, though, that an 88MB cartridge will only store a few minutes of color video. You may find yourself buying lots of cartridges. Don't despair: they are sold by the case at a substantial discount.

There are other options, of course (again, see the Storage Technologies chapter for more information) The more you can spend, the bigger system you can get. So what else is new? Buy as much storage as you can afford, but don't mortgage the kids or the dog. If you can't swing a big hard disk, stick to black-and-white work, or to still graphics. It's color—especially color video—that really eats up the storage. Of course, if you don't have a color display, you have nothing to worry about there. Speaking of displays, we ought to cover them at least briefly.

Displays

You can get the complete rundown on Macintosh display technology in "Graphics Hardware-Output" later in this book. Here is just a quick summary:

The displays on compact Macs are built right into the box. They measure 9" diagonally. They are monochrome, of course. You can add a bigger (still monochrome) display if you like. The process requires you to add a special board to the innards of your Mac, a task best left to a qualified technician. There are color display systems out there for the SE/30.

With the modular Macs, you must buy a separate monitor. You may also have to buy a piece of additional hardware to run the monitor, called a *display adapter*. The adapter fits into a special slot inside your CPU box; the monitor itself is then connected to the adapter with a cable.

Just as there are different sizes and types of monitors (sizes range from 12" to 21", types include monochrome, grayscale, and color), there are different kinds of display adapters. An important distinction involves how much data is needed to represent each picture element (pixel) on the screen. Using eight bits, you can represent 256 different colors at one time. (It is possible to generate more colors than that; at any given time, an eight-bit display adapter has a palette of 256 colors drawn out of the millions of colors that it can actually display.)

Eight-bit video is fine for color graphics and even animation. You need more for color video, though. With 24 bits per pixel, a Mac can display more than 16 million colors. This is more than enough for realistic color images. This display realism exacts a toll in dollars and in performance, though. The more bits per pixel, the more work the Mac microprocessor must do. Thus, working in 24-bit video is much slower than 8-bit. Need we mention that 24-bit display adapters are considerably more expensive than 8-bit ones? We thought not.

Many of the fanciest 24-bit display adapters are designed to avoid the speed problem (although they exacerbate the expense problem). Such adapters use a special chip—a graphics coprocessor (the Mac ought to have one; Apple should have given the microprocessor a break in this regard long ago)—to accelerate the speed with which the Mac draws the screen. Again, check out "Graphics Hardware-Output" for more information on display acceleration.

You may be able to get by without a display adapter. The LC II, the IIsi, and the IIci all have built-in 8 bit video. (On the IIsi and IIci, the built-in video uses up RAM and slows down the system. The LC II has separate RAM for the video, thus performance is not degraded compared with using a separate display adapter.) The built-in video on the Quadras can handle up to 24 bits. Their built-in video does not slow down the system compared with having a separate display adapter.

Recommendations here are trickier. You can easily get by with a smaller (13") monitor. If you don't intend to work with scanned color photographs or with color video, you probably only need an 8-bit display adapter. A larger screen is nice because you can work with more open windows at once. (Multimedia can involve a lot of switching from one application to another by cutting and pasting.) Screens in the 16" to 17" range are currently a good value. And to do color video work, you need a 24-bit display adapter. You probably need to buy one with display acceleration, unless you enjoy waiting for screen redraws.

System Accessories

Strictly speaking, you don't necessarily need any accessories to do basic multimedia work on the Macintosh. You can easily get by without a printer. For example, you may wish to expand your capability to work with captured video footage. There are add-ons to let you do just that. Accessories can be hooked up to the Mac in several ways. Some devices, such as modems, connect to the serial ports. (These are marked with one of two icons: a phone or a printer.) The drawback to serial ports is that they are pretty slow.

The Small Computer Systems Interface (SCSI port) is faster and a bit more flexible than the serial ports. It lets you connect devices like external hard disks and scanners. (A scanner is a useful tool; with it you can convert a photograph or drawing into a data file that your Mac software can work with. See Chapter 6 for more info on scanners.) SCSI compatible devices can be daisy-chained together. In fact, you can have up to seven connected to the same Macintosh at once. (There are a total of eight SCSI addresses: the Mac CPU itself takes up one. If you have an internal hard disk, it occupies another. That leaves six.) All Macs have had a SCSI port since the Mac Plus was introduced in 1986. However, the modular Macs offer an additional expansion option. They all have at least one slot inside the CPU box, to which you may connect any one of a number of goodies. We call these goodies cards.

The number and nature of slots vary depending on the Macintosh model. The LC II has a single processor direct slot (PDS) and the IIsi has a single processor direct slot (PDS) which can be converted with an adapter into a NuBus slot. The PDS connectors hook directly to the Mac's microprocessor. There are display adapters that fit these slots. There are also special cards to speed up these Macs (including instruction *cache cards*).

Other Macs also have processor direct slots, although each is slightly different (chalk up another one for Apple's engineers). The other modular Macs also have *NuBus* slots. NuBus is an Apple standard for all sorts of cards: display adapters, accelerators, video input devices, etc. The Quadra 700 has two NuBus slots. Unfortunately, you can't use both without blocking the PDS. The IIci has three NuBus slots in addition to its PDS slot. The IIfx and the Quadra 950 each have a total of five.

So much for the connections; what about the connectees? Multimedia output, for our purposes, is chiefly limited to the monitor. There are devices you can buy to let you transfer a multimedia production to videotape, but these are expensive and rather specialized. Besides, in moving a noninteractive multimedia production from the Mac to tape, you really move out of multimedia altogether and into the realm of video production. That's another topic altogether.

As for multimedia input, there are three broad categories: video capture boards, which take video from an external source and translate it for the Mac, still graphics capture devices (scanners), and audio capture devices (remember: newer Macs have the relevant hardware built in). You can read about scanners and about sound capture in other chapters of this book. For purposes of this chapter, we are going to concentrate on video capture; there have been exciting developments in this area of late.

Capturing Video

You can make some pretty interesting presentations using video footage, whether you shot it yourself with a camcorder or you rely on pre-taped material. (Don't violate someone else's copyright, though.) The question is, how do you get video information from your source into your Macintosh, where you can work with it?

You need a special piece of hardware, that can translate video footage into information that the Mac understands. The video output from a camcorder (or any television-related device) and the video output from your Mac rely on entirely different systems. Television in the United States is based on the NTSC standard. It uses an analog (continuously varying) signal, in which color and brightness information are combined and modulated by (carried on) a high-frequency wave. Mac video is digital (discretely varying), and separates colors into red, green, and blue components.

For several years, we have seen devices on the Mac market that can turn NTSC signals into digital video signals. The VideoLogic DVA-4000, the RadiusTV, the

RasterOps Colorboard 364, and the E-Machines QuickView come to mind immediately. There have been two problems with such boards. They tend to be very expensive—out of reach for the ordinary Mac user; they all haven't produced compatible data.

Recently, much less expensive video capture boards have been introduced. For example, SuperMac Technologies' Video Spigot, with its associated software program "ScreenPlay," can take a standard video signal from any NTSC video source—camcorder, VCR, etc.—and translate it into digital data that can be stored on a hard disk. This data can be "played back" on the Mac just as you would play a prerecorded tape in a VCR. Macs with built-in sound can also capture sound directly from a video source (or even from a separate audio source), storing it with the video data. Although there are several inexpensive video capture boards coming onto the market, we will focus on the Video-Spigot for this writing. It was among the first such boards of its generation and has been aggressively marketed and eagerly bought. So there are a lot of them out there. The principles involved in operating the Spigot can be generalized to other boards you might buy.

Opening the Spigot

The Spigot is relatively easy to install and operate. It comes in three versions: one each for the processor direct (PDS) slot on IIsi's and LC II's, and a NuBus version for all other Macs. The NuBus version is slightly more expensive. We found the manual to be one of the best and clearest we have seen for any piece of hardware in recent memory. Be sure to observe the precautions outlined in the installation procedure. You could damage your Macintosh or yourself if you don't. Power down your Mac before you start, but leave it plugged in; this grounds it, which can prevent certain electrical damage. When you open your Mac's case, ground yourself by touching the power supply cover. This will discharge any static electricity that's built up on your body. Static is absolutely deadly to computer chips. When inserting the VideoSpigot card into its slot, do not use excessive force. You could crack the card and ruin it. Save all your packaging in case you ever have to send the card back for repair.

After you install the hardware, you need to install the software to run it. Start your Mac and insert the Spigot diskette. Copy the "Video Spigot extension" file to your System folder. You have to install QuickTime too, if you haven't already. (Read all about QuickTime later in this chapter, when we talk about multimedia software.) Copy the ScreenPlay application (it's on a separate disk) to a convenient place on your hard disk. When you have copied everything, you have to restart your computer before it will all work properly.

227

There is a single RCA connector at the back of the VideoSpigot card. Standard audio/video patch cord hooks this connector to a video source. (Patch cord is the cable you use to hook your CD player to your amplifier, your VCR to your television set, etc.) If you are connecting a camcorder, you probably have the relevant connecting cable already. Likely, it came with the camera, and lets you record from your camera directly to your VCR. Frequently, the end that connects to the camcorder itself has a special, nonstandard connector.

You can also have an audio hook up, if your Mac is equipped for it. Plug your RCA adapter (it came with your Mac, if your Mac has a microphone) into the microphone slot and then plug the relevant audio patch cord (from your video/audio source) into the adapter. Most camcorders have RCA jacks for both audio and video, each clearly labeled. Remember: video plugs into the Spigot jack, audio plugs into your Mac's microphone jack (if any).

A tripod will prove very handy if you are connecting a camera for live video capture. In that case, you will probably also want to use your AC power adapter, to save your batteries. Some practitioners recommend that you buy a separate video playback unit (cheaper than a VCR; it doesn't record) to play your videos into the Spigot, rather than relying on your camera to play back. Do so if you like, but we are not sure it's worth the expense to save so little trouble. If you have only a single VCR in the house, you certainly won't want to lug it back and forth between the TV and your Mac.

About the Spigot

First, a few caveats. The amount of data you can capture is limited. Full-frame (640x480 pixels) video requires about 30MB of data capture per second. The Spigot can't handle that much data. At most, you can create video movies at quarter-frame size, which is 320x240. Actually, you will find yourself working with even smaller frames as a rule. The sixteenth-frame, 160x140 pixel video is most common. Such videos still can take up over 100K per second. Be prepared to chew up a lot of disk space.

Secondly, you should know that data in the Spigot only flows one way. Video information moves from a video source to your Mac, but not the other way. Thus, you can't use the spigot to record movies from your Mac onto video tape. Such a thing is possible, but you need additional (expensive) equipment to do it. Presuming we haven't scared you away, you are probably wondering how the Spigot operates. That, dear friends, is simplicity itself.

Working the Spigot

SuperMac's ScreenPlay application program controls the Spigot's every move. The ScreenPlay window is shown in figure 8.1.

Figure 8.1: The ScreenPlay application window, which controls the Video Spigot.

To see "live" video, turn on your video source and click the Live button (lower left). You may need to press the monitor button on your camcorder. This shows you what the camera's pointing at without recording anything. With "Live" clicked and your video source active, the center of the ScreenPlay window shows what's playing, but it isn't recording anything. To record, click the second button, which has a circle on it. A new window appears as video data is recorded to your hard disk. Click the third button, with the square, to stop recording. The recorded video footage appears in a playback window.

To play the movie, click the Play button (bottom left.) Click the button next to it (has a square on it) to stop. The other two buttons will advance or rewind by a single frame. By the way, note the legends at the top of the window. In the example shown in Figure 8.2, the nine-second movie we recorded takes up almost 2 megabytes of disk space. You can see that you are going to have to get a bigger hard disk. The sliding bar above the buttons lets you move to a given frame within the movie. The thumb tabs at either end let you control the starting and ending points of the clip prior to saving it. Then, you can edit unwanted footage before saving the final movie.

As for saving video clips, ScreenPlay has several options. In the File menu, you will find the Compression... command. It brings up a dialog box in which you control how much to compress images (see fig. 8.3). "Compression" saves disk space by eliminating unneeded data. With video, there is a tradeoff: compressed files may not look as good.

Figure 8.2: Captured video in a ScreenPlay playback window.

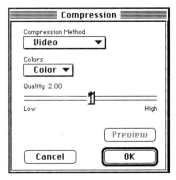

Figure 8.3: Controlling compression in ScreenPlay.

Choose the desired compression method from the pop-up menu. Drag the sliding bar to set the amount of compression. The bar says "quality." It means "compression." As a rule, lower quality=higher compression, and vice versa. Click OK when you've set everything the way you want it. Change hue and brightness settings on your movie using the Color... command in the Spigot menu. These controls are similar to the ones on your TV set. "Hue" controls how "green" or "red" the picture appears, "brightness" controls how vivid the color appears. (What you are actually setting are the overall chrominance and luminance values of the video signal, respectively.)

The VideoSpigot has one really neat feature for those who don't own a scanner: it will capture single frames as PICT files. To control this option, and others, use the Preferences command in the Spigot menu. The Preferences dialog box is shown in figure 8.4.

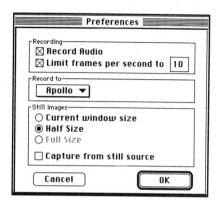

Figure 8.4: Controlling ScreenPlay preferences.

First, you can choose whether to record audio, and how many frames per second of video to take. (Standard television offers 30 frames per second; motion pictures use 24.) We think 15 is a good number. Motion will not be perfectly smooth, but you won't overwhelm your CPU and your disk drive as you might with a higher rate. (More frames=more data=more processor power and storage space needed.) Lucky Quadra owners, and those with monster hard disks, may wish to experiment with higher figures.

Next, set the disk to use as destination for recorded data. A Syquest cartridge drive (44MB) is attached to use as a capture place. Finally, set the size of the image to capture and specify whether the source you are using is "still." You get higher quality and larger images from a still source. A steady camcorder looking at a stationary object is a "still" source. Some laser disc players will display a single frame off some disks. This, too, would work as a still source.

This is the option that lets you use your camcorder/VideoSpigot combination as a scanner. We've done so, and have been quite pleased with the results. Text doesn't scan very well, but photographs come out fine. The process is also much faster than a conventional color scanner. (That's right, you get color scans to boot.) It takes a few seconds; the Spigot records a bit of live footage and then "averages" it into a single frame. This is why the video source must be completely still; otherwise, things come out all smeary. Once you've got a still source, capturing a single frame is easy. Just move the cursor over the live ScreenPlay window and drag (press and hold mouse button while moving the mouse) the picture off it.

We have had a lot of fun with the Spigot, and have found it handy if for nothing else than making color scans of photographs, etc. The nice thing is, objects you wish to scan don't have to be flat, they just have to sit still. This writer doesn't expect to win an Emmy award for his work, but what do you want for less than $500?

Other Video Solutions

There are other video capture cards out there, as we have said. Some of these do double duty as display adapters—even accelerated ones. One such product is the RasterOps 24XLTV. In addition to capturing video, it offers a 24-bit, accelerated display adapter for screens up to 21" in size. It is very expensive, however. A less expensive option from the same company is the Video Colorboard 364. It offers 24-bit color for 13" monitors. Finally, the TrueVision NuVista + will both capture and output video. This digital video wonder can be hooked up to the correct controlling hardware (specifically, Diaquest's DQ-Animag animation controller board for NuBus) to capture exactly the frame you specify, modify it automatically in either ColorStudio or Adobe Photoshop, and then output the results back to tape.

Summing Up the Hardware

There are a lot of ways you can put a Mac system together for multimedia work, and a lot of things you can hook up to your Mac once you get it together. Here's a stab at the bottom line: With a Classic I, SE, or Plus that has a 40MB hard disk, you can experiment with black and white animation and sound. To do multimedia work NOT involving video, try a Mac LC II with 4MB of RAM and an 80MB hard disk. You could use the built-in 8 bit video along with a standard 14" color monitor. To work with video or with color photographic images, you need more computer. Try a Mac IIci, and install a 24-bit, accelerated video display adapter. Install a video capture board to get video into your Mac to start with.

Software

Hardware is fun, but without software to tell it what to do, it is useless. We have talked a little bit about software already; specifically, the ScreenPlay application that runs the SuperMac video spigot. We also made passing mention of QuickTime, Apple's new multimedia system software. The Spigot is fully QuickTime-compatible, by the way. In this section, we want to talk about multimedia software in more depth; system software and how it relates to multimedia; dive into QuickTime; and we'll talk about the major classes of multimedia application software, considering an example of each.

System Software

All computers require special software that tells them what to do. On the Mac, the most important of these *system software* files are called the System and the Finder. The System tells the Mac how to draw the desktop, windows, and icons, and so on. It also tells the Mac how to run other software. The Finder is used to locate files and to launch (run) applications.

Not all that long ago. Apple released the newest version of its system software, System 7. The new System has certain advantages over its predecessor (System 6, which many Mac users are still working with), and disadvantages as well. It takes more RAM to run in, for one thing. You cannot run the single Finder any more; you are always running Multifinder. Some people find this annoying, especially those with limited RAM to burn. Still, you can't stop progress. (Especially if you own a Quadra: it will not run under System 6; you have to use System 7.)

System 7 has added certain features relevant to multimedia. One is *virtual memory*. This is a scheme for tricking your Mac into using hard disk space as RAM. Virtual memory takes over a large swath of your hard disk. The amount is equal to the total amount of memory you have, counting real RAM and virtual memory together. Thus, if you have 4MB of RAM, and you add 4MB of virtual memory, the System takes over 8MB of hard disk space for the virtual memory file.

This scheme lets you run certain memory-hoggish multimedia programs. In fact, you can keep more than one running at once, which is probably the chief reason for using it. As always, you must pay for this convenience and not just in wasted hard disk space. Virtual memory is considerably slower than conventional RAM. You may find yourself waiting for several seconds as you switch applications. You will hear your hard disk grind and grind again; it's "paging in" what it needs off the hard disk and into real RAM.

Another thing you need to know: do not try to add more virtual memory than you have physical RAM. If you have 4MB of RAM, do not install more than 4MB of virtual memory. If you try to install more virtual memory than you have RAM, the Mac will have to page data in more often, slowing you down to a crawl. To use any amounts of RAM in excess of 8MB, be it real or virtual, you need to enable another new capability, called "32-bit addressing." You can only use this option, and virtual memory too, on Macs with a 68030 chip, or with a 68020 and a paged memory management chip installed. This new scheme increases a Mac's RAM capacity 256-fold. Not all applications programs will work with 32-bit addressing yet; Apple says such applications aren't "32-bit clean." Software developers are rushing to address such problems; they've actually had a couple years to work on them already. You set these memory options via the Memory control panel. Changes to 32-bit addressing or to virtual memory only take effect when you restart your Macintosh.

In other news, System 7 offers balloon help (a feature we despise), which may make it easier to navigate in those labyrinthine multimedia presentation programs. The really big news in system software—at least from a multimedia perspective—has got to be QuickTime. Although not yet part of the System (it soon will be), the QuickTime extension considerably expands the multimedia capacity of any 68030 or 68040-equipped Macintosh.

QuickTime

Why QuickTime? The name is actually easy to explain. In so doing, we can tell you a little about what QuickTime is, and what it does.

QuickTime's name (at least) is modeled on an earlier Mac innovation called QuickDraw. You may have never heard of QuickDraw unless you have read the Graphics Technology Overview chapter of this book. It is almost invisible to the naïve Mac user. QuickDraw is part of the Macintosh's most fundamental operating software. It is so fundamental, that it is stored within the computer itself, rather than on disk as are the System and Finder.

QuickDraw is a set of programming instructions for producing graphics on the Macintosh screen. It is available to any application program that cares to use it, and provides the same tools to every Mac application out there. That is the important point. An application doesn't have to be concerned with how to draw a filled rectangle. It just tells QuickDraw it wants a rectangle with certain dimensions, located at a certain place on the screen, in a given color and pattern. In a twinkling, QuickDraw puts a rectangle on the screen, and handles much of the management details. The application can concentrate on manipulating the rectangle by leaving the dirty work to QuickDraw.

Because QuickDraw is available to all applications, it is easier for different applications to share files. For example, the objects in a PICT graphics file are really just sets of QuickDraw instructions. Any application can pass these instructions along to QuickDraw to render the file on your Mac display screen.

QuickDraw is at the heart of the Mac's success as a graphics computer. It even had a part to play in the desktop publishing revolution, though not as important as other system-level software (e.g., PostScript). In any case, QuickDraw served as the model for QuickTime (thus the name). QuickDraw is concerned with static data, whereas QuickTime is meant to handle changing data. In fact, it works with multiple channels of such time-based data, keeping each data channel synchronized with all the others. Hence the "time" part of the name "QuickTime."

One of QuickTime's most important tasks is to keep all the different time-based parts of a multimedia presentation running in harmony, while presenting them in an orderly fashion. QuickTime manages the complete flow of multi-media data from its home on your hard disk to its destination on your screen and your Mac's internal speaker. It is intended to do so without making you aware of its presence, just as QuickDraw hides in the background behind drawing and painting applications.

QuickTime is not an application; it provides tools for applications, just as QuickDraw does. You, as an application user access QuickTime's capability only indirectly. You do so when you work with applications that are aware of QuickTime and use QuickTime tools to accomplish their work. We can divide QuickTime's tools into four categories: system software, user interface guidelines, standard file formats, and compression technology.

System Software

QuickTime is a System Extension. You are probably familiar with other Macintosh System Extensions. Like other Extensions, the QuickTime extension file must be inside the System folder of your startup disk (in the Extensions Folder inside your System Folder, if you are running System 7) for the tools and capabilities of QuickTime to be made available on your computer.

The QuickTime extension has three parts. The "Movie Toolbox" provides tools to applications. These tools let applications create, edit, and play back QuickTime movies. Most important, they do so in a standard fashion by using a standard file format. The Movie Toolbox also synchronizes playback of the various parts of a movie—chiefly the video and the soundtrack. In addition, the Movie Toolbox makes certain that movies play back at the same speed, no matter what Macintosh they were created on and what Mac they are being played on. A movie created on a Mac LC II plays back at the same speed on a Quadra 950, even though the Quadra is inherently about ten times faster than the LC II.

The Image Compression Manager part of QuickTime helps saves disk space, it lets QuickTime-friendly applications reduce the size of their data files. Compression involves throwing out redundant data in a file, so that the same file can be stored in less space. The Compression Manager compresses and decompresses images in the background. You have control over the type and degree of compression used. Manufacturers can plug their own compression software routines into the Compression Manager; such routines are called *codecs* (for "compression devices").

QuickTime has a feature that lets software developers add other new functions of their own, in addition to codecs. This part of QuickTime is called the "Component Manager." The Component Manager can handle all sorts of software routines: converting video data into computer form, running hardware, etc.. Hardware manufacturers can use the Component Manager to plug their products directly into QuickTime, as SuperMac does with the VideoSpigot.

User Interface Guidelines

Apple has published *user interface guidelines* for QuickTime applications. An application's user interface comprises its controls and the way they respond to the user. Thus, the interface defines how you interact with the application. Apple wants applications to accomplish similar tasks in similar ways so that you don't have to learn a different way of doing things for each application you buy. Apple not only provides software developers with the tools to create and manage movies, it also tells them how this capability should be presented to the end user. If there is any place where you will be aware of QuickTime, this is it.

Standard File Formats

As they did with the PICT file format, Apple is introducing a QuickTime movie file format, so different movie-making applications can share data. This MooV (get it?) format offers a standard way for applications to store separate tracks of time-dependent data, including motion video and sound.

Compression Routines

Apple is providing video, still, and animation compressors as part of the first wave of QuickTime software. Compression is an important point. Without it, QuickTime movies would be too large and would take too much CPU power to process. Compression saves processing power and disk space. With compression, you can store about ten times as much data in the same amount of disk space, although the quality of the image may be affected.

Summing Up

QuickTime is a set of tools, standards, and guidelines for creating, managing, and playing back dynamic data on the Macintosh. Dynamic data includes animation, video footage, still photographs, and sound. QuickTime ensures that all data plays back at the same time and at a constant rate, no matter how fast (or slow, within limits) a Macintosh it's working on. QuickTime comprises system-software, user-interface guidelines for software developers, a standard file format for movies, and a set of compression routines for saving disk space.

Now that we have laid the hardware and the system-software groundwork, we can turn our attention to multimedia application software. These are the real stars of the show, the ones that get all the glory (or the boos and hisses). We find that multimedia applications fall into three categories: presentation software, animation software, and video editing/playback software. We will look at an example of each.

Presentation Software

Currently, this is probably the most important category of multimedia software, if for no other reason than that it appeals to users with money to spend: *businesses*. Presentation programs are used to create simple or elaborate multimedia "shows," or presentations. These presentations are meant to inform, educate, persuade, or sell. The presentation appears on the Mac screen, perhaps with sound played back through the speaker. A presentation can be made interactive. In such a case, the program responds to input from the viewer. The simplest form of interactivity is the request, "Press any key to continue the presentation." Here, the computer pauses until the viewer presses a key.

Presentations can incorporate video footage, sound, still graphics, and animation. Programs generally provide tools to create and modify certain parts of a presentation (especially still and animated graphics), to add titles and other forms of text, and to organize the whole. Be warned: presentation programs tend to be large, complicated, and expensive.

Our paradigm presentation application is just that: Director 3.1 from Macromedia (formerly Macromind/Paracomp) is a huge, hulking beast of a program. With its auxiliary files, it chews up over 15MB of disk space. It costs several hundred dollars (closer to a thousand than not). It comes with three separate users manuals, one for each major part of the program. However, it is the most popular such program out there, the one most people use. It has been around for a while, so we have picked it for a closer look.

Macromedia's Director 3.1

Director has, as we say, three major parts, each more complex than the last. First is the Overview. Overview is based on the notion of a *storyboard*. A storyboard is a visual aid used in video and motion-picture production. Frequently drawn on a poster-sized sheet of heavy paper stock, the storyboard shows each scene of a production. Scenes are represented by a sketch of the action. Each scene is described, and a rough idea of duration is given. Director's Overview is used to create relatively simple presentations. An Overview presentation resembles an animated slide show. Launch Director into its Overview mode, and you will see the window shown in figure 8.5.

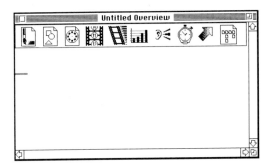

Figure 8.5: Macromedia Director Overview Window.

The icons across the top correspond to elements in a presentation: paint files, PICT files (graphics with objects and bit maps), Glue documents (Glue is a file format), other Macromind movies, and so on. To add an element, you drag an icon into the Overview work area. For example, to use a paint file as a background, drag down the paint icon which is the one furthest left along the icon bar. Then you are asked, via a directory dialog box, to locate the paint file. To place a PICT, you would pull down the second icon, locate the PICT file you want and select it.

Here is the rub: you have to create the various parts of your presentation elsewhere. You have to create your PICT files in a graphics program, your Sounds in an application that supports them, and so on. From this, you get the impression that Overview merely provides you a (relatively) easy way to link together canned artwork and sounds. Overview does let you create titles and transitions, however. By the way, the stopwatch icon represents a timer: You associate a time with an object; that's how long it stays on the screen during a presentation.

If you want to create objects within Director itself—especially animated ones—you have to work in the Studio. The Studio users manual is considerably thicker than the Overview manual; that should be a hint right there. The Studio part of Director works with a cast of actors. Actor is a single frame or cel of a drawn character or object. To achieve animation and motion, you first have to link all the actors together. Then, you define a path for the resulting animation by dragging. To keep animation and such in synch, you use the Score, (see fig. 8.6).

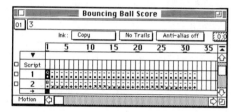

Figure 8.6: Score in Director.

Select the kind of score information to show from the pop-up menu at the bottom. The score gives a frame-by-frame summary of all the action for each actor in a presentation. Music and other sounds and other associated items are also shown. The Score is important: it's the way you control and modify much of the action.

Studio also has various tools for creating objects from scratch. The Paint window is shown in figure 8.7.

Figure 8.7: Creating a paint object in Macromind Director.

This window has all the typical paint tools—selection tools, the text tool, fill bucket, airbrush, paintbrush, pencil, shape tools, etc.—that you've come to expect to find in such applications. At the top of the palette, you can see which actor you are working on; in this case, number A11. The running boy is made of several actors, each showing a set position of the boys as he runs.

Now then, we have said that Director can create interactive presentations, where action depends on input from the viewer. To create such presentations you must use a truly wonderful and horrifying feature. Director has a built-in programming language called Lingo. It's somewhat similar to Hypertalk, the Hypercard programming language. Lingo requires the thickest users manual of all to explain.

Figure 8.8 shows part of an interactive presentation. This one was included with Director 3.0 (in 15MB of files, you should expect a few goodies). The picture changes; sometimes you see monkeys, cattle, or men felling trees. You click the buttons below the picture to hear various sounds. To return to the menu, you click "First Set." (This "Rain Forest" demo is called "Feature Examples"; it's in the Feature Examples folder.)

Figure 8.8: An interactive presentation from Macromedia Director.

All of this interactivity is controlled by a list of actions associated with objects on the screen. A button, for example, has an action list that tells the program what to do when the button is clicked. Lists of actions are called scripts. You can write a script to go along with just about any Director object: an animation, a whole movie, or a still picture. Scripts are composed of Lingo commands. One thing about Lingo that we found interesting is that all commands are presented in hierarchical menus. You don't type commands into a script, you select them from a menu. The menus group Lingo commands into alphabetical order and into logical categories (see fig. 8.9).

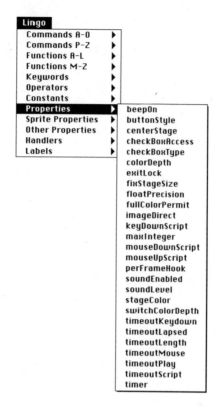

Figure 8.9: One of the many Lingo submenus in Director.

If you ever mastered all the intricacies of Director, you could create some nifty presentations, like the Rain Forest demo. Expect to invest a lot of time in learning Director that well, though. We should mention that Macromedia has added QuickTime support to Version 3.1 of Director. Director also has built-in interfaces to let you capture presentations on video tape.

There are other presentation packages on the market. Not all of them necessarily qualify as "multimedia" packages, however. In that regard, Aldus Persuasion comes to mind, as well as Microsoft PowerPoint. Macromedia has a smaller, tamer multimedia presentation package called "Magic." It's much easier to use than Director, but isn't nearly as powerful.

Animation Software

There is another category of multimedia software that has been approaching the area from another direction. We refer to animation software. Makers of these products have been adding so many features that they've started to resemble Director. However, they can still be viewed as a separate category, since many lack the interactivity that characterizes complex presentation software; some makes of animation products have been adding simple interactivity. Animation applications usually aren't nearly as expensive.

Interestingly enough, Macromedia Director got its start in life as an animation toy. It used to be called "VideoWorks." As we say, there are other animation applications that seem bent on following the same road.

One thing we believe distinguishes animation applications from their presentation brethren is their limited use of video. Animation still qualifies as multimedia, because it combines motion graphics with sound. It is true that the advent of QuickTime is breaking down these barriers. To be sure, makers of animation software have been hopping onto the QuickTime bandwagon as fast as anybody. However, the organizational paradigm of animation software still favors graphics over video as a rule.

One example that comes quickly to mind is PROmotion, by Motion Works. Motion Works got its start in animation with a program called "ADDmotion," which lets you animate Hypercard stacks. Responding to the call of users who wanted to animate outside of Hypercard, they came up with PROmotion. We found that it has a good balance of power to ease-of-use. Products easier to use than PROmotion tended to be not powerful enough, whereas products more powerful tended to be significantly more complex.

Motion Works' PROmotion

To begin with, you launch PROmotion past the startup screen and choose New Animation... from the File menu. The screen shown in figure 8.10 appears.

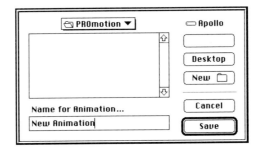

Figure 8.10: Starting PROmotion.

You can see that you are in a typical directory dialog box. PROmotion asks you to save a file before it has anything in it. It's best to humor it. When you have type in a name and click "Save," the actual program window appears.

You place graphics where you want them in this window. You also create paths for them here. A path tells a specific graphic element where and how to move. Using paths, you can make a still graphic slide across the screen.

The tool palette gives you access to most of PROmotion's features (see fig. 8.11). You can create paths for objects, move them, insert characters, use backgrounds, and so on. Access these features using the button on the right of the tool palette. To the left, there is a frame counter. It shows the current frame position in the animation. There are also buttons to play animations, rewind them, and advance by single frames. You can see that these buttons are labeled like those on a tape recorder or VCR. This is fast becoming a Mac standard for motion graphic and video applications.

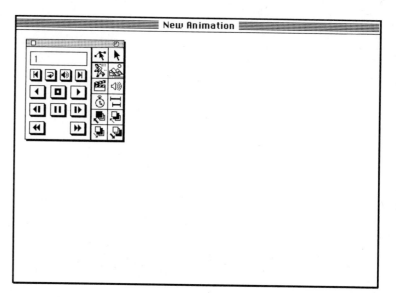

Figure 8.11: PROmotion's main window, with the animation tool palette.

PROmotion, like a Hollywood director, works with actors (see fig. 8.12). We talked briefly about actors (the computer kind) a while back when we were touring Macromedia Director. Again, an actor is an animated character. It has at least one frame or "cel." An actor made of many cels can give the illusion of movement, in the sense of changing shape. Translational motion, on the other hand, involves paths. Even a single-cel actor can move across the screen using a path. If you want the character's legs to move as the character slides across the screen, you must add cels to change the appearance of the legs. You then define a path to smoothly slide the character across the screen. PROmotion also works with background files called "props." Although props don't change shape, they can move. You could creating "rolling" credits from a text prop, sliding the static text up or down the screen with a path.

PROmotion has an important ability, that appears in or has been added to most animation software of late. You can add an "onion skin" layer to the current cel. It works like a light table. You see a dimmed version of the previous (or next) cel just behind the cel you are drawing. You can line up and "trace over" parts that don't change. This makes animated characters much smoother.

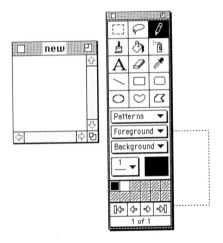

Figure 8.12: Cel window, and tool palette, from PROmotion. These are used to create and modify actors.

When you have created an actor and have moved it to the desired position on the screen (you just drag it), you then create a path for it if you intend for it to move. To do so, you select the actor and click the path tool button; it is at the upper left of the tool palette. The tools in the palette all change to path editing tools (see fig. 8.13).

Figure 8.13: PROmotion path editing tools.

These tools let you add points to a path, scale the number of points up or down, and so on. You can also associate a specific cel of your actor with each point in the path. This tool is called the Cel Sequencer. Select it (fourth one down on the left) to see the window in figure 8.14.

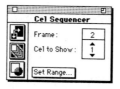

Figure 8.14: Associated each cel in an actor with each point on its path.

You see the current path point ("frame"), and the cel associated with it. To change the cel number, click on either the up or down arrows. To change frames, click the single frame advance/rewind buttons on the tool palette. There is also a timeline tool, somewhat similar to the Score window in Director. You control your actors and props entrances and exits, and how long they stay on-screen.

PROmotion lets you import graphics and sound from outside files. You can save animations in several formats, including QuickTime (MooV) format. The latter is about the only way you can get sound and animation together.

This is just a brief glance at how PROmotion works. The important thing is that many of its features have close analogues in other animation software. You will find actors, props, and paths in just about everything, although they may go by different names. For example, we saw them in Director.

As for other animation software, Cinemation from Vivedus has been getting a lot of attention. It is very powerful and has better QuickTime support, but it is much more expensive. There is a high-end application called "Animation

Stand," but it is intended for professional animators. On the low end, you might check out Animation Works from Gold Disk. It is inexpensive and easy, but has no QuickTime support. It won the 1991 MacUser Editor's Choice (Eddy) award, however.

We defined animation software as programs that are focused more on graphics than on video. There are now applications at the opposite end of this spectrum. QuickTime has made video editing and playback much easier. We will conclude our tour of multimedia applications by examining some video applications.

Uideo Editing & Playback Software

Of all the multimedia applications tested, we have had the most fun with QuickTime video. These applications are much easier to use and you don't have to know how to draw. All you need is a video source and a way to get video into your Mac. A camcorder and a Video Spigot will do nicely.

There aren't many QuickTime video applications available yet. Adobe Systems has published Premier. For a while, the SuperMac Video Spigot came with a free copy of Premier. This got the press's (e.g. our) attention pretty quick. We found Premier a neat toy for cutting together QuickTime movies, and adding soundtracks to them. As for playing back movies, there are really only two games in town. There is POPcorn, which is distributed on-line (through a dial-in information service like America Online or CompuServe) by Aladdin Systems, and the Simple Player which comes from Apple. You will find the Simple Player in the QuickTime sampler disk that Apple sells. We will look at both these applications briefly.

About Adobe Premier

You use Adobe Premier to cut together QuickTime movie clips into a smooth whole. The clips themselves must be produced someplace else, like with a Video Spigot or other QuickTime video capture device. You can add a soundtrack to your presentation, even if your clips already have sound. There are special effects for scene transitions. You can choose dissolves of all kinds (one clip fades another), you can fade the whole presentation to black, and so on. When you have assembled a complete movie, you save it in QuickTime format. An application like the Simple Player can then show it. The main movie construction window in Adobe Premier is shown in figure 8.15.

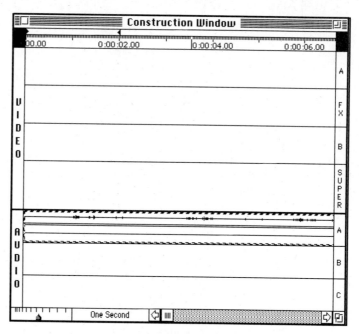

Figure 8.15: Adobe Premier construction window.

This window shows a timeline of your current movie project. You have two video tracks, a special effects track, and a Superimposed video track. You also have three audio tracks. Before you can use a clip, you have to import it. The clip then appears in a separate "Clips" window, represented by a thumbnail. A thumbnail is just a smaller, single frame of the clip's video. To put a clip into a movie, you drag its thumbnail into the appropriate place on the construction window. You have control over the beginning and ending points of a clip; the so-called "in" and "out" points. To edit a clip in this way, you double-click its thumbnail.

You have access to special effects that smooth transitions from one clip to another. To add an effect, drag it from the special effects window to the FX track. You can also superimpose one clip over another by dragging it to the Super track. In this way, you can put moving credits onto your movie, or you can make an animated character appear in a video scene.

You can edit the soundtrack as well. (The soundtrack for a QuickTime clip is imported automatically with the clip.) You can set the volume at any point by clicking in the area just below each audio track. You drag a point up or down to change its dynamics at that point. Thus, you can slowly fade music in and out.

You can preview a portion of your work with the band at the top of the construction window which shows what will be previewed. Drag the center of the band to change the part of the movie to preview; drag the ends to change the preview's beginning or ending , or to make the preview longer. Press the Enter key (on your keyboard) to play the preview. When you have finished, you compile a stand-alone QuickTime movie. Choose Make Movie... from the Project menu. You select the amount of compression and the number of colors to use, and whether to output the whole movie or just the preview area. It can take several minutes to compile a movie.

An important thing to remember while working on a movie project is that Adobe Premier does not actually import the data from your movie clips. It uses the original QuickTime files; until you compile a complete movie, you must leave the original files on your disk in their original locations. Otherwise, you will mess up your project.

The end result of all your labor is a QuickTime movie that the Simple Player can handle. The Simple Player comes from Apple; it's their QuickTime movie demonstration application. There aren't many others out there, so it is worth a look.

Apple's Simple Player

Double-click the Simple Player's icon to launch it, and then select Open... from the file menu, (see fig. 8.16).

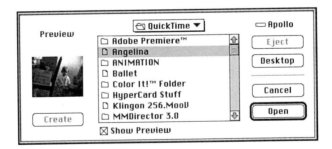

Figure 8.16: Opening a QuickTime movie with the Simple Player.

A small preview of the selected movie appears to the left (see fig. 8.17) . This single frame is called a "poster." Click Open to proceed.

Figure 8.17: A movie in the Simple Player.

Click the right arrow button, to play the movie; click again to stop. Drag the sliding bar to move to a particular frame; drag the bar all the way to the left to rewind. Click the arrow and bar buttons to rewind/advance by a single frame. You will find that QuickTime lets you play movies in the background. If you play a movie, and then click on another window to move the application, the QuickTime movie continues to play. You can also play more than one movie at once. Obviously, performance begins to suffer if you try to do too much at once. It's an interesting curiosity, though. Other Simple Player commands are contained in the Movie menu (see fig. 8.18).

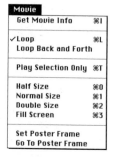

Figure 8.18: Simple Player Movie menu.

The first menu command, Get Movie Info, displays facts about the current movie, such as size and whether it needs any other files to play right. The next two options let you play a movie continuously; if you chose to Loop, once the movie gets to the end it will return to the first frame and keep playing. You can also choose to just play the current selection, if any. You can set the size of the movie window and choose which frame of the movie to use as the little thumbnail sketch that appears in the Open... dialog box.

That's it for our tour of multimedia applications. We are not quite finished with software yet. We now want to look at the sources for multimedia data, and at the results of an application's labors. We refer to data files: files used to construct multimedia presentations, and files produced by multimedia software.

Data File Formats

The purpose of multimedia is to merge several different kinds of data—still and motion graphics, video, and sound—into a single presentation. Your application software needs to be able to recognize the data with which it is being asked to work. This is where standard data file formats come in.

There are many ways to store data. Fortunately software manufacturers have settled on just a few file types for potential multimedia data. This means that data created with one application can be used in many others. Thus, you can use a still picture created with a paint program in a multimedia presentation. There still tends to be more than one standard file format for each type of data. Most are known by acronyms; it can get a bit confusing. We worked through it, and have summarized our knowledge of file formats below:

Picture Data

On the Macintosh, picture data can take two forms. One type is called bit maps. The bits in the file (remember: eight bits to the byte) correspond to pixels on the screen. Images can also consist of the actual instructions to draw objects. We call this "object data." Object data is more flexible, although it cannot be used to represent complicated images like faces or mountain vistas.

PICT   Old Reliable. PICT files may contain a combination of object and bit-mapped data; although such combinations may confuse some applications. The latest version of PICT, PICT2 supports 24-bit color. Thus, PICT files can store photographic images. We have noted a problem: PICT files, especially ones with lots of complicated bit-map graphics, can be very slow to print.

TIFF   "Tag Image File Format." A preferred format for black and white photographs. TIFF files can only contain bit-map data, no objects. Thus, the translation from PICT to TIFF isn't always smooth. They print faster than PICT files.

JPEG   "Joint Photographic Experts Group." Not really a file format, more of a compression standard. JPEG makes huge graphics files smaller. However, the more you compress a file, the lower its image quality will be.

EPS   "Encapsulated PostScript." Postscript is a programming language used to create text and graphics on laser printers and the like. EPS files contain Postscript instructions to create graphics. Postscript graphics can be modified easily, while retaining their quality.

These aren't the only picture formats, but they are the most common on the Macintosh. There are fewer file formats for sound and animation data files.

SND   Sound resources. They usually don't exist as separate files, but as resources within other files. Your System file contains sound resources; that's where the "beep" sound comes from. Some programs can peek into other files for their SNDs. The built-in microphone on new Macs records in sounds in SND format, storing them in the System. There are applications, such as MacRecorder, that can also make SNDs.

PICS   Animation files. A PICS file is really just a series of PICT files that are played in order. Each PICT in the file corresponds to one frame of animation.

MooV   QuickTime movie files. A new file format promulgated by Apple. It is already recognized by many applications that support QuickTime, as we have noted elsewhere in this chapter. Macromedia Director 3.1, PROmotion, Cinemation, and Adobe Premier are just a few of the applications that can import and create MooV files.

Putting Multimedia To Work

Now that you've got it—hardware, system software, applications, and file formats—what are you going to do with it? In the final section of this chapter we look at some of the applications of multimedia, how to handle the storage problem, and where you can turn for more information.

Uses of Multimedia

Multimedia may be a fun toy at times, but there is no way it would get as much attention as it has if it couldn't be harnessed for productive, business purposes. It also is being promoted heavily for use in education. Some typical applications of multimedia work are as follows:

Business Presentations

Business presentations are often (disparagingly) called "dog-and-pony" shows. The idea is to sell your idea, product, or services to a business client. You have seen numerous commercials for these. The idea is still used to sell desktop publishing to the masses. You know the company that does the *color* brochure gets to build the bridge. Formerly, presentations were given by a live person using visual aids. Now, through multimedia, the visual aids become the entire presentation. The trick is to make the show impressive without seeming flashy.

Point of Sale Demonstrations

You may have seen a few of these demonstrations; video forms are popular in department stores. They are used to hawk a product right at the place you buy it—the "point of sale." Flashier presentations ensure that consumers will stop and take a look.

Interactive Demonstrations

Similar to point-of-sale presentations, interactive demonstrations often are moved to a location other than a store. We have seen software manufacturers use them at trade shows. A demo like this relies on the interactivity tools found with its creator application. The idea is to let the viewer select what information he or she is interested in, and then give the viewer an idea of how the product works.

Educational Presentations

Educational presentations often appear in commercials for multimedia-capable computers. All kinds of information about a topic—Shakespeare, rain forests, etc.—can be drawn together into a single place. The student does not have to listen to, view, or read a set text. Instead, he or she is free to wander around the system, finding out about each part at will. It is said to be a perfect foil to the attention span now possessed by the MTV generation.

Amusing Applications

Some manufacturers are starting to sell multimedia presentations. Because of the size involved, they are almost always sold on CD-ROM. (See the Storage chapter for more information on this type of permanent storage technology.) For example, there are now interactive storybooks for kids. A voice reads the text and the illustrations are animated. The child can click on parts of the illustrations to see neat things happen. We can expect to see more of these.

These are just a few applications of multimedia, but they cover much of the work that is being done. The key idea is to inform the users more effectively and in greater depth than is possible with other media. The more channels of information that are open to the viewer, the more likely something will get through. (Anyway, that's the theory.)

Multimedia Problems: Storage Space/Compression

The number one problem in multimedia is storage space. Why do interactive storybooks come on CD-ROM? Because you can store hundreds of megabytes on it. Sound and motion picture data require prodigious amounts of storage space. Finding ways to store such data, and to do so in less space, has been the focus of considerable work.

There is at least a partial solution to the problem of storing many massive files. It is possible to compress a large file into smaller spaces, sometimes even without losing any information. The process of reducing a file is called *compression*. There are two basic types of file compression: lossless, which preserves all original information, and lossy, which discards the least important information in a file, while achieving greater compression.

There are several methods of compressing files (read more about it at the end of the Graphics Technologies Overview). JPEG, as we have said, is part of QuickTime. It is based on a technique called Discrete Cosine Transformations (DCT). *(DCTs are similar to the Fourier transform, but only the cosine part of the function is used.)* Using DCT, a 64 square (8x8) pixel region is assigned a color and light intensity. The DCT transform measures variance across the region and breaks it into a set of coefficients. Only the middle range coefficients are used. Outer range coefficients are tossed out, leading to the data reduction.

DCT converts color to the YUV (luminance, brightness, and chrominance) perceptual color model, the same used on color TV transmissions. The DCT process also achieves data reduction by throwing away every other pixel's *chrominance* value (a measure of color intensity). This works because the human eye does not differentiate chrominance well.

A separate group, the Motion Picture Experts Group (MPEG), is working on a similar standard for motion data. With QuickTime movies running off the end of data cartridges all the time, it can't come too soon for us.

Multimedia Resources

The following information lists additional places to investigate.

Magazines: *MacWorld* and *MacUser* magazines frequently run articles on multimedia applications. You can read reviews of new and revised products. Even the ads can be helpful: you can check out the prices on the latest software.

Clubs and Newsletters: Check out the *Call Sheet* from the Macintosh Movie Makers' Guild. There is also the *QuickTime Forum* from Way with Words. The former is at P.O. Box 893, El Dorado, CA 95623. The latter hangs out at 1455 Cedar Oak Rd., Placerville, CA 95667

On-line Information Services: If you have a modem, you can connect to all kinds of information and fun. You can also acquire multimedia files, graphics, and even QuickTime movies over the phone lines—heaven help your phone bill. The two main Macintosh services are America On-line and CompuServe. You can acquire sign-up kits for either at your local software dealer.

Books: New titles in multimedia are appearing all the time. Check out the computer book sections of your local bookstore. Frequently, you can find a specific book that covers the particular software you are interested in learning. We would be remiss if we didn't mention *Cool Mac Animation* from Hayden Books, written by the author of this very chapter. In addition to neat facts, the book includes a diskette featuring much of the software mentioned in this chapter.

An Overview of Communications Technologies

As you work with your Macintosh, information constantly moves among the parts of the computer: the motherboard, keyboard, mouse, monitor, printer, and so on. But your Mac can be much more than a self-contained system. Through an I/O port, you can connect to other computers. In this part of the book we will examine the world of Mac communications: connections to both Macs and to other types of computers.

There are two basic ways to connect your computer. First, you can use a modem to connect to another computer over a phone line. Later, we'll take a look at modems, what they are and how to choose one; and then we'll look at fax modems, special devices that combine a fax facility with regular Mac communications.

Using modems, two Macs can communicate at any distance. At first, this might not seem like much. However, there are an enormous number of modem-equipped computers in the world—by one estimate, about 10,000,000 such

personal computers just in the United States. With the right kind of software and a little bit of know-how, you can connect your Mac to any one of these computers. And, as you will see, there are many marvelous ways to make use of such an association.

The second way for your system to communicate with other computers is to connect them directly as part of a network, and this topic is covered in the Networking chapter, elsewhere in this book.

Mac communications is a large subject; whole books are written on specific aspects of the technology. In this chapter, we'll take a look at the most important ways that you can use your Mac as a communications device. In other words, once you have a modem, what is available to help you communicate and what kinds of communication can you do with the Macintosh?

In our overview, we'll discuss communications programs, electronic mail, bulletin board systems, and online services. Along the way we'll concentrate on practical information. To start, let's take a look at the basic communications terms that we need to know.

Communication Terminology

There are a great deal of communication terms but, fortunately, only a few that are essential. Think about your Mac being connected to another computer. In most cases, the remote computer will be in control. For example, say that you want to call another computer to check your electronic mail. Using a communications program and a modem, you connect to the other computer over the phone line.

Your monitor and keyboard now act as a window into the operations of the other computer. As you enter commands, the other computer carries them out and sends back the output to be displayed on your screen. In such a situation, the remote computer is called a *host*. Since the host does all of the processing, you do not need much more than a keyboard and a monitor. A device that provides these functions is called a *terminal*. Thus, to access a host computer, all you need is a terminal. The host/terminal connection is like a master/slave relationship, with the host being the master.

Your computer is much more powerful than a terminal. After all, a Mac has its own disks and memory, and its own processor. However, when you connect to a host computer your Mac must act in the way that the host expects. To do this, you run a program that causes your Mac to behave just like a terminal. We say that your Mac *emulates* a terminal. We will have more to say about terminal emulation later.

One of the most common uses of computer connections is to send files from one computer to another. When you do this, there are standard terms to describe the process. When your Mac sends a file to another computer we say that you are *uploading* the file. When another computer sends a file to your Mac we say that you are *downloading*. Although this may seem confusing, just imagine that the host computer is above you in the sky. Or better yet, don't imagine this. In any case, sending a file is "up," receiving a file is "down."

Finally, when a communications program is running and you are connected to another computer we say that your Mac is *online*. When there is no connection, you are *offline*.

Communication Protocols

In order for your Mac to connect properly to another computer you must make sure that both systems send and receive data in the same way. There are four basic communication parameters that describe how the data is sent. They are:

- speed

- parity

- number of data bits

- number of stop bits

Each host computer expects these parameters to be set in certain ways. You must tell your communications program which settings to use, before you can connect to a remote system.

Normally, your communications program will help you maintain a list of all the computers to which you connect. For each list entry, you can store the name of the system and the phone number. In addition, you can also put a reminder of which communication settings must be used when connecting to that host. So, whenever you tell your program to call a particular system, it knows how to set the communication parameters.

The first setting, speed, describes how fast data is sent between the modems that connect the two computers. This value, of course, depends on your modem and the host's modem. The most common low speed is 2400 bps, or bits per second. The most common high speed is 9600 bps, although some very fast modems work at 14,400 bps. As you might imagine, both modems must be set at the same speed. For example, say that you have a high-speed modem capable of 9600 bits per second, but the host can support only 2400 bps. You must connect at 2400 bps. It is possible that you may set your modem at 9600, but as it connects it will adjust itself down to 2400. Modems and modem speeds are discussed in detail in the next chapter.

The next setting, parity, describes a primitive type of error correction. Although there are several possible parity values, the only ones that you will probably run into are "no parity" and "even parity." All you have to do is make sure that the setting you use is the one that the host computer is expecting.

What Is Parity?

Regular serial communication sends each character in a package consisting of 10 bits: a start bit, followed by 8 bits, followed by a stop bit. The start and stop bits are always set to 0 and 1, respectively. They are used to synchronize the data transmission and, for our purposes, they can be ignored.

When serial communications was first developed, the standard 7-bit ASCII code was used. This means that, of the 8 bits, only 7 were actually needed. A system, called parity checking, was devised in which the 8th bit was used to detect transmission errors.

The parity of a bit pattern refers to the number of 0s and 1s that are transmitted. If the number of 1s is even, we say that the set of bits has even parity. If the number of 1s is odd, the parity is odd. For example, in the 7-bit ASCII code, the letter "H" is represented by 1001000. Since there are 2 bits with the value 1, the pattern has even parity. The code for the lowercase letter "h" is 1101000. In this case there are 3 bits with the value 1 and the parity is odd.

Parity checking is a scheme that uses the 8th bit—the extra bit—to help detect errors. As data is being transmitted, the 8th bit is set in such a way as to maintain a particular parity, either even or odd. If, after transmission, that parity is changed, we know an error has occurred. At first, this can be a bit confusing so let's take a look at an example.

Say that we decide that, as a whole, the 8 bits should always maintain even parity. Both the sending and receiving computers are aware of this convention. As each character is sent, its 7 data bits are examined. If there are an odd number of bits, the 8th bit is set to 1. This ensures that, overall, the parity will be even. If the 7 data bits already have even parity, the 8th bit is set to 0, maintaining the parity. For instance, suppose we send the character "h", represented by 1101000. As the data is being sent, the transmitting system sets the 8th bit to 1, to maintain even parity. Conversely, when we send the character "H," or 1001000, the 8th bit is set to 0, again to maintain even parity.

Now, at the receiving end, the system examines each set of 8 bits as it arrives. Normally, all is well and the 8 bits have even parity; that is, there are always an even number of bits that have a value of 1. However, say that a transmission error occurs and one of the bits has been changed. When the 8-bit package is examined it will have odd, not even, parity. The receiving system knows that something is wrong and can request that the data be sent over again. In other words, when only 7 bits are needed to encode a character, the 8th bit can be used to enforce an overall parity that may help indicate transmission errors. In our example we enforced even parity, but we could just as easily have used odd parity. As long as the sender and receiver both agree on the same parity, the system will work. In fact, serial communication with mainframe computers was long ago standardized as using 7 data bits with even parity.

Unfortunately, this system does not provide an adequate method of error control, and modern systems do not depend on parity. (In fact, many modems have sophisticated forms of built-in error control.) Thus, in practice, using the 8th bit for a parity check is not necessary; we might as well use it for data. This is why, most of the time, you will be using 8 data bits and no parity. However, when you connect to some computers—especially mainframes—you may need to use 7 data bits with even parity. To complete the discussion we should mention that, technically, the parity specification can be set in five ways:

(1) NONE: do not use parity (8 data bits)

(2) EVEN: maintain even parity (7 data bits)

(3) ODD: maintain odd parity (7 data bits)

(4) MARK: always set the parity bit to 1 (7 data bits)

(5) SPACE: always set the parity bit to 0 (7 data bits)

The only use for MARK and SPACE is to make a 7-bit character look like an 8-bit character in which the 8th bit is always 1 or 0, respectively. However, you will probably never need to use anything other than NONE or EVEN.

Electronic Mail

Electronic mail is the sending and receiving of computerized messages. When electronic mail was new, it was often referred to as e-mail; however, computer messaging is so commonplace nowadays that we usually just refer to it as mail.

Mail consists of messages, usually just text. On some systems, messages can be accompanied by a binary file, which might be anything from an application to a screen shot to a spreadsheet file.

Sending mail involves invoking some type of mail program. You can either compose a message within the program, or use a message that you have already prepared. According to the working of your program, you specify the address to which the mail should be sent. Most systems allow options, as follows:

- Send a copy of the message to another person. This is usually referred to as "cc" (carbon copy). Normally, all recipients know who else received a copy.

- Send a secret copy of a message to another person. This is usually referred to as "bcc" (blind carbon copy). In this case, no one else knows that this person received a copy.

- Send the message to a predefined list of recipients.

Some systems allow you to request a return receipt to let you know that the message has been delivered. The other half of a mail program helps you read the messages that you receive. As you are reading your mail, there are usually a number of ways for you to process each message, as follows:

- Delete the message.

- Save the message to a file.

- Print the message.

- Forward the message to someone else.

- Reply to the message.

When you reply to a message, you do not have to put in the address. The program automatically uses the address of the person who sent you the mail.

When you start using a mail system it is a good idea to remember two basic rules. First, do not assume that mail is private—be careful with your love letters and criticisms of the boss. Second, remember that anyone to whom you send a message can send a copy to someone else or even make it public. Most mail programs make it easy to forward mail and some people are habitual forwarders.

The World of Electronic Mail

A connection between two dissimilar networks is called a *gateway*. The world of electronic mail has many gateways, allowing you to send mail from one system to another. If you are working on a local area network or a host computer, you can mail to other users directly. Whenever you send a message to someone on the same system it is delivered immediately. However, when you send mail outside your local system, it is stored in a holding area. Eventually, your system connects to another computer—say, by establishing a phone connection at a predetermined time—and your message is passed on. This type of delivery method is called a "store and forward" system, and is at the heart of the global mail network. Of course, most networks are connected to only a few, or sometimes just one, other networks. Your mail may have to be passed on from one network to another for it to reach its final destination.

A great many of the world's networks are connected together in a large super-network, sometimes referred to as the Internet. In particular, the Internet connects the international academic and research community. The Internet has its own addressing system which makes it possible to send mail between any two computers. The Internet itself is connected to the major commercial mail services (which we will discuss in the next section), which are connected to one another. The Internet is also connected to the worldwide Unix-based UUCP network. In addition, many local area network mail facilities are connected to one of these other systems.

Bulletin Board Systems (or *BBS*es, another topic that we will discuss later in the chapter) also have their own interconnected networks, some of which are international in scope. Again, these systems usually have some sort of connection to the Internet. What all this means is that, with today's modern interconnected networks, it is easy to send a message anywhere in the world. All you need is access to the right network and the recipient's address. In fact, many business people have their electronic address printed on their business cards.

One of the more interesting problems in the mail community is figuring out exactly what type of addressing to use to send mail from one network to another. O'Reilly and Associates publishes a book, *The Directory of Electronic Mail, Addressing & Networks,* that contains information on all the world's major networks. For each network, the book explains what form of addressing you need to access the network via its principal gateways.

As a Mac user there are several ways you can send and receive mail. First, you can subscribe to a commercial mail service. Second, if you are on a network, you can use the network's mail facilities. If the network has a gateway to the outside world, you can probably send mail anywhere. Similarly, if you have an account on a well-connected computer, say the Unix system at a local university, you can use its mail facilities. If you are looking for such an account, you can subscribe to a so-called public access Unix system. For a set fee, you will be able to dial into the computer in order to send and receive mail.

Finally, you can connect to one of the many bulletin board systems. At the very least, you will be able to mail to other people in the same system. In addition, many BBSes have gateways to BBS networks; some even have gateways to the Internet.

Mail-Sending Standards

As you might imagine, sending mail between networks requires a multitude of communication standards. Although you don't need to understand the technical details, it is useful to be able to recognize the names that you are most likely to encounter.

Most Unix networks are based on a system called TCP/IP. From one TCP/IP computer to another, the mail is handled by a protocol known as SMTP. Much of the Internet uses SMTP. Between Unix computers that connect via the phone system, the UUCP protocol is used. On personal computer-based local area networks, the most common mail protocol is MHS. The full names for these protocols are as follows:

SMTP = Simple Network Transport Protocol

UUCP = Unix to Unix Copy Program

MHS = Message Handling System

Within the BBS community, there are a number of mail protocols that support wide area mail systems. The most common is Fido, which is used to connect many thousands of BBSes into the FidoNet. You may also encounter RBBSNet, I-Link, RelayNet, SmartNet, Ryme, MetroNet, EggNet, and AlterNet: all BBS-based networks.

Once you start sending mail around the world you will notice that each major system has its own type of address. An Internet address is different from a UUCP address, which is different from an MCI Mail address, which is different from a CompuServe address, and so on.

In 1984, two international organizations, the CCITT and the ISO, published a set of standards that describes a universal addressing system. Their goal is to foster the connection of the various types of different mail systems worldwide. These standards are referred to as X.400. Since its introduction, X.400 has gathered substantial support. It is likely that, one day, X.400 will form the basis for a truly global mail system. As a companion to X.400, the CCITT and ISO are developing X.500, a universal directory system. The goal of X.500 is to make it possible to find the electronic address of anyone in the world.

Commercial Mail Services

Perhaps the easiest way to access the worldwide mail system is to subscribe to a commercial mail service. Using your modem and a communications program, you dial into the system to send and receive your messages. With commercial mail services you pay only for the messages you send—receiving is free. Unlike regular mail, the price does not depend on how far the message has to travel or how long it takes to be delivered. The costs for each system are slightly different so you might want to check to see which service best meets your needs.

As we will see later in the chapter, there are many providers of online services, all of whom offer some form of mail. However, in most cases these services have no gateways and you cannot mail outside the system. For example, if you use Prodigy you can send messages only to other Prodigy users.

In the United States there are three major mail services: AT&T Mail, CompuServe, and MCI Mail. Throughout the country, these services are easy to reach, using either a local or toll-free phone number. This means that, wherever you go, it is easy to dial in and check your mail. For international travelers, there are numbers that you can call while abroad that offer the same access.

AT&T Mail, CompuServe and MCI Mail all have gateways to the Internet; and from the Internet you can mail to just about anywhere. Thus, if you plan to use mail as one of your primary tools you are better off with one of these major services.

For users of local area networks that use MHS (Mail Handling System), CompuServe can act as a mail hub. Any MHS network can connect to CompuServe and exchange messages. This connection can provide mail service, not only between LAN users and CompuServe users, but between any two LANs in the country.

The commercial mail systems offer more than just text messages—you can attach a binary file to a message. You can have your messages faxed, telexed, or printed and delivered. Printed messages can be delivered either by regular mail or by courier. You can specify that messages should be sent to just one person, or to everyone on a predefined list.

Some companies use these services extensively to stay in touch with clients or customers. For example, you can send a message and specify that it be faxed automatically to a particular group of people; or you can produce and distribute an electronic newsletter. Doing this with a commercial mail service is a lot easier than standing by the fax machine, feeding in the same paper over and over.

You can also create customized scripts to automate any task you want. For example, you might have a script that allows a customer to call a toll-free phone number and place an order electronically. Each order might generate a message that is sent automatically to your mailbox.

Mail services also offer a number of ancillary facilities, such as discussion groups and gateways to online databases. However, as we will see later, there are usually better ways to access these facilities. Finally, there are special pieces of software available to make the entire "electronic mail experience" far more palatable and—indeed—functional. For more information on these, check with the individual mail-service provider.

Network-Based Mail Systems

Network-based mail systems are available for virtually all types of local area networks (LANs). As we mentioned in the last section, there are a number of such systems, the most important being cc: Mail from Lotus and Microsoft Mail from Microsoft. LAN-based mail systems generally require an administrator.

The basis of a network mail system is a designated Mac called the mail server. The mail server acts as a hub, storing all the messages. In the language of LAN systems, this facility is sometimes called a post office. The mail system is coordinated by a master program that runs on the server. This program maintains the post office and coordinates mail throughout the LAN. There is also a local program that runs on each workstation and provides the user interface. In addition to the standard mail facilities, LAN-based mail systems offer a variety of sophisticated services:

- mailing list maintenance: you can define and modify lists of users to whom messages can be sent

- automatic notification when mail arrives for you

- compound messages: you can attach all types of data to a simple text message, including multimedia data

- discussion groups: similar to those found on bulletin board systems

The mail system works on its own to maintain the post office and to ensure the safekeeping and delivery of messages. If your network is connected to other LANs, the mail system can coordinate a wide area mail network. The system can also connect to external systems, such as commercial mail services and mainframe or midrange host computers.

Using a Communication Program

You will definitely want a general communication program for your Mac. This program will see to many of your communication needs: you can use it to connect to a commercial mail service, an online database, a bulletin board system, or even another Mac. In addition, you can also use the program when you need to send commands to your modem.

A communication program provides all the facilities necessary to connect your Mac to a remote computer. The program takes care of the multitude of technical details that arise when two computers communicate—all you have to do is tell it what you want. In the next two sections we'll examine the features that you will find in a general purpose communication program. Before we do, let's take a moment and look at a typical communication session. Your goal is to connect to a remote computer to do some work. You begin by starting the communication program. The program automatically initializes the modem. Once the modem is ready, the program waits for your commands. You are now ready to call the remote computer.

To keep track of the remote systems that you might want to call, your communication program helps you to maintain a dialing directory. Each entry in the directory specifies the name of a computer, the phone number to call, and the settings of the standard communication parameters (speed, parity, data bits, and stop bits). To call a remote system all you have to do is indicate the appropriate entry in the directory. Your program sets the parameters, dials the number, and connects to the modem at the other end.

Once a connection is established, your program begins to emulate a terminal. The program then checks to see if you have specified a predefined list of instructions—called a script—that should be executed. If so, the program follows the script. A script might be used to log you into the remote system by entering your name and password automatically. If it suits you, you can specify a different script for each remote system that you call. At this point, the communication program fades into the background and turns control over to you. You are now at the keyboard of an (emulated) terminal, connected to a remote computer, ready to work.

You can put the communication session on hold, at any time, by making a menu selection, or by clicking a special icon on the screen. This allows you to suspend your work on the remote computer in order to issue commands to your own computer. We say that you are "escaping" from the remote system to the local system. For instance, in order to upload (send) or download (receive) a file, you issue the appropriate command to the remote system. You then press the key combination or click on the icon and tell your communication program to start a file transfer. Another reason to "escape" temporarily would be so that you could put your external communication on "hold" while you are doing something else locally on your own Mac.

When you are finished using the remote computer, you terminate the session. Control now returns to the communication program which waits for your next command.

Communication Program Features

Communication programs have existed for some years now and offer a wealth of features. The basic capabilities are maintaining a dialing directory, emulating a terminal, and transferring files.

As we explained in the previous section, the dialing directory contains an entry for each remote system that you want to call. Your communication program will help you create and edit these entries. Terminal emulation refers to the communication program making your Mac act like a terminal so you can work with a remote host computer. The most commonly used emulations are VT-100, ANSI, and TTY. We will discuss these in more detail later in the chapter. File transfer allows you to upload and download files. When you transfer a file there are various protocols that you can use. All you have to do is make sure that both computers are using the same protocol—your communication program will take care of all the details.

We will discuss file transfer protocols in detail later. For now, we will just mention that the absolute minimum set of protocols that your program should support are Xmodem, Zmodem, and Kermit. If you plan to use CompuServe and are not interested in using the CompuServe Information Manager software that CompuServe sells, your program should also support the CompuServe B+ protocol.

In addition to the basics—a dialing directory, terminal emulation, and file transfer—almost all communication programs offer other features to look for when you choose your program. First, check if the program offers online help, preferably context sensitive. It is handy to be able to get help whenever you want it without having to fetch your manual. Next, make sure that the program can answer the phone and act as a host. This is useful when you want someone else to be able to call you in order to transfer files. You can set user names, passwords, and various security features. Some programs have elaborate host facilities that allow other people to call your computer and transfer files without your intervention. If you plan on making a lot of calls or using your Mac as a host, check to see if the communication program will maintain a log file for you. This file will record the salient information about both incoming and outgoing calls, including their duration.

If you will be working with someone by connecting your Mac to their computer, there are two other features that come in handy. First, chat mode allows you and the other person to type messages to one another. Whatever you type is echoed on the screens of both Macs. To invoke chat mode, you and your friend will probably have to be using the same communication program. Second, some programs allow you to switch back and forth between voice and data communications. For instance, after establishing contact with the other Mac, you can switch to voice mode. You can now pick up the phone and talk to the other person. When you have finished speaking, you can replace the handset and switch back to data mode.

The next two features to look for are capture files and a scroll-back buffer. Capture files allow you to make a copy of data that is being displayed on your screen. You should be able to start, pause and stop capturing. For example, say that you are logged into a database and you have searched for some informa-tion. You are just about to enter the command that will display the results of the search. As soon as you do, the data will be displayed on your screen. However, you wish to capture the data into a file on your Mac. You press a command-key combination or select "Capture" from a menu. Your communi-cation program opens a file on your disk and returns to the background. Now, you enter the command to display the results of the database search. As each line is displayed, your communication program captures it. When you are finished, you select "Stop Capture" and tell your program to close the capture file. The information you need is now stored in a file on your Mac.

A scroll-back buffer is a storage area of limited size that is maintained automati-cally by the communication program. At all times, the program maintains a copy of the most recent data that was displayed on the screen. For example, your program may keep the last 5000 characters that have been displayed. Whenever you want, you can examine the scroll-back buffer to look at information that has scrolled off the screen. For reference, Figure 9.1 summa-rizes the fundamental features of a communication program:

- Dialing Directory

- Terminal Emulation

- Online Help

- Dial-in Host Facility

- Chat Mode

- Switch Between Voice/Data

- Capture Files

- Scroll-back Buffer

Figure 9.1: Communication Programs: Fundamental Features.

Communication Program Features for Advanced Users

If you are a power user or a programmer, there are extra features that you should look for in a communication program. First, most programs have a way for you to put the communication session on hold and return to the finder. When you are finished, you can select the communication program from the Application Menu (System 7) or the Apple Menu (System 6) and return to what you were doing. This should all be possible without dropping the phone connection.

If you like programming, you will want your communication program to offer a built-in scripting language. This feature allows you to write communication-oriented programs (scripts). The usual use of such scripts is to automate the login procedure to a remote host computer. A complementary feature is a script generator. After you start a script generator, it watches you go through the motions of logging in to a remote system. It then generates a script that will do the whole thing automatically.

The final advanced feature is the ability to program keyboard macros. You can specify that pressing a certain key combination should send a sequence of characters. For example, say that there is a long command that you often use with a remote system. You might program an icon on the screen or a special menu selection to send that command. Of course, you can also use a dedicated macro program, like QuickKeys 2, to provide this feature. For reference, Figure 9.2 summarizes the advanced features of a communication program:

- Switch to Finder without dropping the phone connection

- Built-in Scripting Language

- Script Generator

- Keyboard Macros

Figure 9.2: Communication Programs: Advanced Features.

Terminal Emulators

As we explained earlier, when you connect to a host computer you must use a terminal to serve as your keyboard and monitor. Of course, you won't be using a real terminal; your communication program will emulate one for you. In other words, your Mac will act like a terminal.

As you can imagine, there are many different brands and styles of terminals. Your communication program will be able to emulate a variety of terminals; you can choose the one that is most appropriate for the work you are doing. Just make sure that the remote computer knows what type of terminal you are using. Although you may have many choices, there are really only three common emulators that you absolutely must have: TTY, VT-100, and ANSI.

The most basic terminal emulator is usually referred to as TTY (an abbreviation for Teletype). Just like the old Teletype machines, this terminal does nothing more than send keystrokes to the host and display lines of output. All a TTY can handle are simple ASCII characters. As each new line is displayed at the bottom of the screen, the other lines scroll up. Although other terminals have more features, a TTY emulation is useful to have around. It is the lowest common denominator and will provide basic terminal functionality with just about all host computers.

Perhaps the most widely used terminal emulator is the VT-100. The VT-100 is an old terminal manufactured by DEC, the Digital Equipment Corporation. Although DEC hasn't actually made a VT-100 in years, it has become a *de facto* standard for terminal emulation. In most cases, if you are not sure what terminal to choose, use VT-100—virtually every type of host computer will work with these terminals.

The only other terminal emulator you may encounter—particularly if you use BBSes—is known by a variety of names, all of which are some variation on "ANSI." The name comes from the American National Standards Institute.

Through the years, this organization has created various sets of standards for terminals. In fact, the VT-100 was the first commercial terminal to meet the 1977 standard, named X3.64. Many IBM-based bulletin board systems use ANSI so they can draw images using graphics characters and colors.

To summarize, here is a general rule: If you are not sure which terminal emulation to use, choose VT-100. If you're calling an IBM-based BBS, and your communications program provides ANSI emulation, select it. For other computers, if nothing else works—and until you can get in touch with whoever is running the system and find out from *them* what to use—try TTY.

Choosing a Communication Program

There are several ways to acquire a communication program:

(1) buying a commercial program

(2) downloading a program from a bulletin board

(3) receiving a program free with your modem or your computer

(4) buying an integrated package that includes communications

(5) buying a starter kit for an online service

Before you choose a communication program, take note of the following considerations. First, make sure that the program works with your modem. This is especially important with high-speed modems. Second, review the features of communication programs that we discussed earlier in the chapter. Make sure that the program you buy has all the features that will be important to you.

An alternative to buying a program is to download one from a bulletin board system. Such programs are usually shareware, which means that you can try them out for free. (We will talk about shareware later in the chapter.)

An alternative to a general communication program is an integrated package. This is a set of programs, usually offering word processing, databases, spreadsheets, and communications. Since the programs are integrated, they work well together. However, you probably won't find all of the features that are offered by a stand-alone communications program. A good example of such an integrated package is GreatWorks, from Symantec.

Finally, if you buy a starter kit for an online service, a communication program will probably be included. (We discuss online services later in the chapter.) Such programs are fine if all you want to do is use that particular service; however, they are not adequate for general work. In fact, some programs—like the one that works with the Prodigy online service—are customized and will only work with one service.

File Transfers Basics

Consider the simplest way to copy a file from one computer to another: over a communication link. At one end, a file transfer program sends lines of text, one after the other, just as if you had typed them at your keyboard. At the other end, another program receives the lines of characters and puts them together, one by one, to re-create the original file. This method, called a text- or ASCII-transfer, does work but it has some serious limitations. The most obvious shortcoming is that only text files can be sent. There is no easy way to send and receive binary programs.

However, there is another, more serious problem. Communication lines can be noisy, and noise causes errors. With a simple text file transfer there is no way to ensure that the file that was received is the same as the file that was transmitted. To overcome these limitations, we use file transfer protocols to control the flow of data. There are a number of such protocols that you will encounter. The most important ones are the Xmodem family, the Ymodem family, Kermit, Zmodem, and CompuServe B+. We will discuss each of these protocols in turn. But first, let's go over a few of the basic terms.

As we discussed earlier, sending a file to a remote computer is called *uploading*; receiving a file is called *downloading*. The file protocols do not upload or download an entire file as one big chunk. Rather, they divide the file into packages called blocks. Each block is the same size. Older protocols use 128-byte blocks. (Remember, one byte holds one text character.) More modern protocols use larger 1024-byte (1 KB) blocks.

As each block is being prepared for sending, the file transfer program performs a mathematical calculation on the data. The result of this calculation, a number, is sent as part of the block. At the other end, the remote program performs the same calculation using the data that has just arrived. If the numeric result is the same, the remote program signals that all is well—this is called an acknowledgment—and the next block is sent. Otherwise, an error has occurred and the previous block must be retransmitted. In this way, a file protocol can guarantee that the received file is free of errors.

The first file protocols used a relatively simple error checking method called a checksum. Nowadays, a more sophisticated system is used. It is called a Cyclic Redundancy Check, or CRC, and is more suitable for telecommunications. Error checking is important because it guarantees the integrity of our data. Unfortunately, it slows down the file transfer process. Most of the time this is necessary, but there are two situations that we know of where there will be no transmission errors and we can dispense with the extra overhead. First, many modern modems have built-in error correction. The modems themselves check for data errors and retransmit bad blocks automatically. Thus, the software does not need to be concerned about mistakes. Second, it is possible to connect two

Macs directly using what is known as a null modem cable. Such a connection is much more reliable than a phone line and is almost always error free. Again, the software can assume that all data will be sent and received correctly and can dispense with the overhead of periodic error checking.

A file transfer protocol that uses an error-free link can transmit data continuously, sending blocks one after another without having to wait for an acknowledgment. This process is called streaming. The file is not checked for correctness until the entire transfer has been completed. Usually, all will be okay. However, if there is any error at all, the whole file must be sent again.

The final term you may run into is a "sliding window" protocol. This describes a system which is faster than the one-block-at-a-time protocols, but still retains intermittent error checking. With fast modems, waiting for an acknowledgment after each block greatly slows down the file transfer process. A sliding window protocol uses the capabilities of modern high-speed modems to send and receive data simultaneously. Like the regular protocols, the receiving program sends an acknowledgment after each block. But the other system does not wait for the acknowledgment before sending the next block. In other words, the sending of the data overlaps the sending of the acknowledgments. The maximum amount of data that is allowed to be sent before receiving an acknowledgment is called the window. The size of the window can be modified to adjust for transmission delays so as to not overwhelm the system; hence the name "sliding window." Sliding window protocols are especially efficient for systems in which delays are inevitable, such as packet switching networks (discussed later in this chapter) or satellite links.

File Transfer Protocols

In the last section, we explained how a simple text file transfer has two important deficiencies:

- You can send only text.
- There is no error control.

The first file transfer protocol that came to be used with personal computers was invented in 1978 by Ward Christensen, in order to overcome the limitations of ASCII file transfer. Although this system is sometimes called the Christensen protocol, it is usually known by the less euphonious but simpler name of Xmodem. (Think of "X" as in "Xmas.") Ward Christensen, by the way, is also the inventor of the online bulletin board system.

The original Xmodem, the grandfather of modern file transfer protocols, uses 128-byte blocks and checksum error control. A later version of Xmodem uses the more sophisticated CRC error control. This protocol is often referred as

Xmodem CRC. The Xmodem protocol was designed to transmit all types of data and not just text. For this reason, Xmodem requires 8 data bits per character and no parity. (Data bits and parity are discussed earlier in the chapter.) There are two variations of Xmodem that you should understand: Xmodem-1K and Xmodem-1K-G. Xmodem-1K is similar to Xmodem except that it uses 1KB (1024-byte) blocks. This means that, during a file transfer, Xmodem-1K requires only 1/8 the acknowledgments of Xmodem (128 x 8 = 1024). This lower overhead makes Xmodem-1K faster, especially over a high-speed connection. Xmodem-1K-G is a streaming variation of Xmodem-1K designed for error-free connections. As we discussed in the previous section, you would not use such a protocol unless the two computers were connected by error correcting modems or by a null modem cable.

The next protocol, Ymodem, is a derivative of Xmodem. Ymodem allows more than one file to be sent as part of a single transfer. As each file is transferred, Ymodem keeps track of its name, size, and date. Ymodem can use either 128- or 1024-byte blocks. Ymodem-G is the streaming version of Ymodem. As with Xmodem-1K-G, Ymodem-G can be used only with error free connections.

Although the Xmodem and Ymodem families are effective file transfer protocols, they work only with 8 data bits per character and no parity. However, as we explained earlier, many host computers and packet switching networks use 7 data bits and even parity. To solve this problem, two programmers at Columbia University— Bill Catchings and Frank da Cruz—developed a file transfer protocol named Kermit (named after the frog from Sesame Street).

Kermit restricts itself to the standard 7-bit ASCII character set. As you remember, 7-bit ASCII encodes only 128 bit patterns. In order to transmit all the 256 possible 8-bit patterns, Kermit uses a coding scheme in which some patterns are represented by more than one ASCII character. Using this scheme, Kermit can transfer files between almost any two types of computers. To encourage its acceptance, Columbia University placed Kermit in the public domain. Today, there are few computers that do not have their own version of this protocol. However, because of its dependence on 7-bit encoding, it is usually the slowest of the protocols. Kermit does have some built-in data compression but, still, it is slow.

The most useful of the file transfer protocols is Zmodem, developed in 1987 by Chuck Forsberg. This protocol incorporates the benefits of all the other protocols and can also use streaming or a sliding window. Zmodem is very fast and is the most popular protocol in use today. The nice thing about Zmodem is that it is so easy to use. Your communication program has to issue only a single command to initiate a file transfer—the Zmodem program at the other end knows what to do automatically. Moreover, you do not have to tell it what file transfer method to use; Zmodem will figure it out. Even more impressive, Zmodem can recover from a file transfer that was interrupted, say by a dropped phone connection. You can restart the file transfer and Zmodem will continue where it left off.

The last protocol you may run into is CompuServe B+. This protocol was developed especially for file transfer to and from the CompuServe online service (described later in the chapter). CompuServe B+ uses a sliding window for speed and reliability over the packet switching networks that CompuServe uses. Like Zmodem, B+ can restart when a file transfer is interrupted accidentally If you are a CompuServe user there are two older versions of the protocol that you may see. The original CompuServe B used a smaller block size. It was slower and had no restart capability. The later CompuServe Quick B used a sliding window but could not recover from an interrupted file transfer.

So, how do you know which protocol to use? As a general rule, use Zmodem whenever you can. If you are connecting to a system that cannot support Zmodem—such as a mainframe computer—you will almost always be able to use Kermit. If you are using CompuServe, choose CompuServe B+. For reference, a summary of the various file transfer protocols are as follows:

> **NOTE:** You should be aware that some programs erroneously refer to Xmodem-1K as Ymodem, and to Xmodem-1K-G as Ymodem-G.

General Purpose Protocols

Xmodem

- the original personal-computer file transfer protocol
- old version uses checksum for error control, revised version uses CRC
- block size = 128 bytes
- requires 8 data bits per character, no parity

Xmodem-1K

- more efficient variation of Xmodem-CRC
- block size = 1024 bytes (1 KB)
- uses CRC error control

Ymodem

- replaces both Xmodem and Xmodem-1K
- can send batches of files

- keeps track of file name, size, and date
- block size = either 128 or 1024 bytes

Zmodem

- replaces all previous members of the Xmodem family
- does everything that Xmodem, Xmodem-1K, and Ymodem do
- automatically chooses which method to use
- can use streaming or a sliding window
- can restart an interrupted file transfer
- the best all-around file transfer protocol

Protocols for Error-Free Connections

Xmodem-1K-G

- fast variation of Xmodem-1K
- uses streaming

Ymodem-G

- fast variation of Ymodem
- uses streaming

Zmodem

- best overall file transfer protocol
- uses streaming or a sliding window

Other File Transfer Protocols

Kermit

- available on virtually every type of computer
- can use 7 data bits/character connections
- slow

CompuServe B+

- for CompuServe users only
- uses a sliding window
- fast and reliable over packet switching networks
- older versions are CompuServe B and Quick B

File Compression and Libraries/Archives

File compression refers to storing a file in a coded format that takes up less space than the original file. For example, a file may be compressed to, say, 30 percent of its original size. The benefits of compressing a file are straightforward:

(1) It takes less room to store a compressed file on a disk.

(2) It takes less time to transfer a compressed file from one computer to another.

Of course, the compressed file is encoded and must be expanded to its original form before it can be read. If you have files on your hard disk that you use infrequently, you can compress them to save space. Whenever you need a file, it takes only a moment to restore it. Similarly, you can compress sets of files and then archive them onto diskettes for long-term storage. This is an excellent way to clean up a large, cluttered hard disk. Modern file compression programs offer a second service: They can combine a group of files into a single compressed file called a library or an archive.

What Are Bulletin Board Systems?

A bulletin board system—or BBS—implements a simple idea. One computer, equipped with a modem, acts as a repository for messages and files. Using your Mac and a communication program, you can connect to the BBS and access the data. The BBS computer runs a program that answers the phone, logs in the users, and maintains the database. Once a BBS is set up, it can run unattended (although it does require intermittent administration). Most BBSes are available 24 hours a day. The person who administers a bulletin board is called a sysop—system operator.

Here is a typical scenario showing how BBSes are used. You call a BBS, log in, and leave a message. Ten minutes later, someone else calls the BBS and reads what you have written. He decides to respond to your message. He then submits a file that contains an interesting program that he wants to share. The two messages and the file are stored on the bulletin board for anyone who wants to access them. Now a third person calls the BBS. After reading your message and the second person's reply, this new person leaves a reply of his own. He then requests a copy of the program left by the second person. The program is sent to his computer as he waits. Once the file transfer is complete, he disconnects from the BBS, leaving the line free for someone else to call in.

The first personal computer-based bulletin board was created by Ward Christensen in 1978. Since then, BBS systems have been established in large numbers all over the world. As an example, the December 1991 issue of *Boardwatch Magazine* (a publication for BBS users) lists the phone numbers of 609 bulletin boards in the Netherlands. The software to run a BBS is readily available and just about anyone with a Mac, a modem, and a phone line can start their own bulletin board. Nobody knows how many BBSes there are but it is safe to assume that there are tens of thousands in the United States alone. In fact, many BBSes—perhaps most of them—are private systems set up by companies and organizations for their own purposes.

Using a Bulletin Board System

Using a bulletin board system is simple. From within your communication program, create a new entry in the dialing directory. Put in the name and phone number of the system you want to call. Specify parameters of 8N1 (8 data bits, no parity, 1 stop bit). Now have your program call the BBS. Once the two modems connect, press the [Return] key once or twice. You will see a prompt inviting you to log in. Typically, the prompt asks you to enter your first and last names. The BBS will then check its list of registered users. If you are on the list, you will prompted for your password. If not, you will be asked to answer a series of questions for new users.

Most public bulletin boards allow at least limited use for free. Some BBSes are completely free while others ask you to pay a fee. Many systems allow you to register online by specifying a credit card number. The cost is usually a flat fee: so much money per month or per year. The only other cost is any long distance phone charges you may have to pay to reach the BBS. Some BBSes can be used for free by anybody, but offer extra privileges to registered users. For example, it is common for a sysop to set a time limit as to how long you are allowed to use the BBS. Registered users may receive more time.

As part of the login process, you may be asked if you want to use graphics. If you are using an ANSI terminal emulator, say yes. This will allow the BBS to draw boxes and use colors on your display. Otherwise say no. The BBS will confine itself to plain text. Some experienced users decline graphics, simply because plain text is faster. Once you log in, the BBS will display the main menu. For the most part, BBS commands are straightforward and you should have no trouble. If you need assistance, there is always a help command for you to use. You will find that there are only so many variations of BBS programs. Once you have learned how to use one bulletin board, you will be able to use all the BBSes that run the same software.

Services Offered by Bulletin Board Systems

There are three main services offered by bulletin boards: mail, conferences, and file transfer. As a BBS user you can leave mail messages for anyone who uses the same BBS. Whenever you log in, you can check to see if there are any messages for you. If so, you can read them and, at your option, send a new message in response. Some systems are connected to a wide area BBS network. On these systems you can send mail to anyone who uses a BBS that is part of the network. Each BBS cooperates by storing messages as they are submitted. Late at night, a special program calls the nearest BBS neighbors and exchanges mail. The whole thing is cleverly designed to minimize long distance charges while propagating messages around the world.

The oldest and most well known BBS network is called FidoNet. FidoNet was started in 1984 by Tom Jennings. (The name of his computer was Fido—go figure.) By 1991, FidoNet had grown to encompass over 10,000 systems and serve an estimated half a million people worldwide. Other BBS networks that you may encounter are RBBSNet, TBBS, I-Link, RelayNet, SmartNet, Ryme, MetroNet, EggNet, and AlterNet.

The second basic service offered by bulletin board systems is a conference facility. Most public BBSes support a series of ongoing discussions. Various topics—sometimes called *special interest groups* or *SIGs*—are set by the sysop and maintained as separate conferences. Each conference consists of messages sent in by callers. To participate, all you have to do is log in and choose a conference. You can read the messages that have been left by others and submit new messages of your own. Conferences provide a wonderful means for meeting people, offering advice, and just plain talking.

It is no exaggeration to say that just about every interesting aspect of human endeavor is being discussed somewhere in a conference. From programming, to hobbies, to classified ads, to sex—you will find it all if you look hard enough. It is the conferences that a system supports, more than anything else, that define the personality of a BBS. Many entrepreneurs and hobbyists have started bulletin boards devoted to one particular interest. They are supported by people who have the same interest. With BBS networks, discussion groups can be connected with one another. Many BBSes carry conferences that are joined by people all over the world. When the computers connect to swap mail, they also share conference messages. Such discussion groups are called echo conferences or message echos.

The third main service offered by BBSes is file transfer. Receiving a file from a remote computer is called downloading; sending a file is called uploading. Some BBSes maintain large software libraries and ask you to pay for access. Other BBSes are free while some are free with limited access. Some sysops set up their systems to encourage people to upload new programs. The amount of time you are allowed to download will vary depending on how much you have uploaded. The more you contribute, the more you get to download. Many programs are shared via bulletin boards. Some BBSes have, literally, thousands of programs online. You should have no problem finding any type of software: communication programs, word processors, spreadsheets, and graphics programs; even software to start your own BBS.

As we discussed earlier, virtually all BBSes store files as compressed archives. You can download a whole software package as a single file but you need a decompression utility to restore the program to its original form. Thus, the first thing you should do is download a compression/decompression utility, if you don't already own one of the Mac standards, such as StuffIt.

File compression utilities are offered as self-extracting archives so you can restore them easily. Once you have the utility installed on your Mac, you can decompress anything that you may download from a BBS. Just as important, you can compress any programs or files that you want to upload. Some BBSes accept uploads only in compressed format. Once you have a compression program, the next thing you should do is look for a list of all the programs that the BBS carries. Download this list and peruse it at your leisure.

Shareware, Freeware, and Public Domain Software

Soon after BBSes became popular, programmers found that they had an instant audience for their software. They could upload a new program to a few bulletin boards and, not long afterward, it would be available all over the country. Anybody with a modem could take advantage of this free distribution system to show off his software.

The proliferation of bulletin board systems has spawned a new type of software distribution called shareware. Shareware works as follows. A programmer or a company uploads a piece of software into the BBS community, often as a compressed file. As a BBS user, you can download the file, decompress it, and try out the program.

All shareware comes with a license agreement, usually stored in a file called "READ ME FIRST." The agreement suggests that, if you like the program, you should become a registered user by paying a fee. These fees are usually low; certainly far less than what you would pay for a comparable commercial product. You are allowed to make as many copies of the software as you want to give to other people. However, you must make sure to include all the files, especially the one that contains the license. If you want to sell disks containing the program, you must first obtain the programmer's permission. There are several variations to this theme:

- You may use the software for a certain amount of time for free, say 30 days, after which you must register.

- You may use the program as long as you want, but a small donation would be appreciated.

- The program you have is a limited version; if you register you will get the more powerful program.

Some shareware programs display a special screen each time you start the program. This screen reminds you of the licensing terms and encourages you to register. The version of the program that is sent to registered users does not display this screen. (Some programs go even further. At various times, a window pops up with a message asking you to send in money. Such programs are known as *nagware*.)

There are two ways to register. You can always send money to the address specified in the license agreement. Alternatively, some shareware companies have their own bulletin boards. You can call their BBS and enter a credit card number. You will instantly get a registration number which you can type into the program. The program now knows that you are registered and treats you as such. Some people never register for the shareware they use. However, there are several reasons why registering is a good idea.

First, complex shareware programs come with a manual stored as a text file. If you want a printed copy, you will have to make one for yourself. When you register, you will be sent a printed manual that is easy to read. Second, registering entitles you to call the company, or their BBS, and ask questions. Third, when you register you will be sent the latest version of the software. You will also be kept informed of any new updates.

There are now so many shareware programs that mainstream business and government types have joined in. There are distribution companies that do nothing but collect shareware. They publish large catalogs and sell software by the diskette. Be aware that these companies act only as distributors, not salesmen. If you want to use the software permanently you still need to register. In addition, the U.S. Copyright Office has started a service called Computer Shareware Registry for shareware authors to register their products.

The first cousin to shareware is freeware. Freeware is software that is given away for free and requires no registration fee. There are many programmers who send freeware into the world out of the goodness of their heart, as a public service, or because they honestly believe that software should be free. Do not confuse freeware with public domain software. Freeware, like shareware and commercial software, is copyrighted. You cannot, for example, sell it without the consent of the author. Public domain software belongs to everybody (or nobody, depending on your outlook). Should you use shareware and freeware? It depends. It's nice to be able to use or test out software for free. It's also rewarding to know that your money is going directly to a deserving programmer. Then again, shareware is convenient. There are many worthwhile programs that are only a phone call away. On the other hand, regular commercial software is usually of higher quality with better manuals, better support, and more frequent updates. *Usually...*

 # What about Viruses?

Once you become part of the worldwide electronic community you may start to feel concerned about viruses. Are you placing your computer in jeopardy every time you download a program from a bulletin board or an online service?

Let's start by asking the question, what is a virus? Although it may seem obvious, it is important to realize that viruses are programs developed by people. They do not live on their own, they do not grow, they do not mutate, and they do not willfully infect innocent Macs.

When you read about viruses and antivirus programs you will see a lot of medical terminology. For instance, you may read about how viruses "infect" computers and "spread" from one system to another. Such hyperbole is inaccurate and misleading. The viruses that trouble Macs no more infect those systems than the ancient Greeks inside the wooden horse "infected" the city of Troy.

There is only one way to get a virus, just as there is only one way to get any program. You must copy it—or allow it to be copied—to your computer. How is this done? You know that when you install software the installation program copies files from a diskette to your hard disk. Similarly, a virus program is written to copy itself from one disk to another. However, a virus program will not usually copy itself to a new file. Instead, it inserts its instructions within another application. When you use that application, the virus instructions get control and run amuck.

Here is a typical example. A child brings home a diskette from school that has a virus program on it. He puts the diskette into your Macintosh and uses the application that contains the virus. The virus, which was designed by a very clever person, notices that it is being run from a diskette and copies itself into one of the applications on your hard disk. The child, who has no idea of what he did, removes the diskette and turns off the Macintosh.

Now, let's imagine a worst-case scenario. Like all viruses, this one cannot do anything until it is executed. As it happens, the person who programmed the virus was particularly evil. He designed the program to wait for two hours and then format your hard disk. By chance, the virus copied itself to a shareware program that you have been working on for the last six months. Later that evening, you turn on your computer and upload the program to a BBS. The program is so useful that many people copy it to their own Macs and to other bulletin boards. Within a week, hard disks all over the world are being formatted mysteriously.

Although this may seem farfetched it is certainly possible. The worldwide distribution of software is far more fluid than most people imagine. What keeps these great disasters from happening is that there are special programs written to detect viruses. After all, viruses are just programs and they all have telltale byte patterns within them. A virus detection program searches for these patterns, called signatures. The case that we just described will probably never happen because responsible BBS sysops run a virus detection program on all new files before they make them available for downloading.

How widespread are viruses? It is possible that you will never encounter one at all. On the other hand, a study released in November of 1991 by Dataquest (a market analysis organization) and the National Computer Security Organization described a survey that covered over 60,000 personal computers. The survey showed that there were more than 600 known virus programs and that 63 percent of the PCs had been affected in some way. Fortunately, protecting your system against viruses is easy. Remember, a virus must be executed on your Mac to cause you any harm. All you have to do is obtain a virus detection program and use it to scan all new programs before you run them. There are excellent commercial programs available, like the *SAM-Symantec Anti-Virus for Macintosh* program, from Symantec.

Regular shrink-wrapped software is usually safe—the manufacturers make sure that the master diskettes are checked for viruses before the diskettes are duplicated. (Although, there are odd cases in which a software company has accidentally shipped diskettes that contain a virus.) Most often, though, commercial software is completely safe. There are, however, three situations in which you should be especially careful. They are as follows:

(1) When you download software from another system.

(2) When you copy files from a diskette that someone gives you

(3) Most important: After you get your computer back from the repair shop. It is all too common for a repairman to test a personal computer with a diagnostic diskette that has a virus. Although it seems hard to believe, people have had their computers acquire viruses in just this way.

Here is a simple system to follow to avoid a virus from infecting your computer. Start by obtaining an anti-virus program. The first thing you should do is scan all your disk space for viruses. Once you are satisfied that all your programs are okay, create a special folder called NEW to hold any new programs. Make a rule that you download and copy programs only to the NEW folder. Before you execute a new program for the first time, use your antivirus software to scan the program. Once a program has passed the test, you can move it from NEW to wherever you want. If you download a program from a BBS it will probably be in compressed format. Be sure to restore (expand) the original files *before* you scan for viruses. If the program is a self-extracting archive, you must check for viruses before *and* after you expand it.

The only other consideration is keeping your virus program up to date. An anti-virus program only knows about the signatures of the viruses that were recognized at the time the program was released. However, new types of viruses are always appearing. (Of course, they don't appear out of nowhere. Unscrupulous programmers create them and upload them to bulletin boards.) When you install your antivirus software, be sure to check how to get updates. Some companies charge a fee for this service, others provide it for free. As an example, Symantec runs a BBS that users of the SAM Program can use to download the latest antivirus updates for their program.

Finding Bulletin Boards

There are several ways to find bulletin boards to call. First, some computer magazines have listings. Each issue of Boardwatch Magazine publishes a national list of BBSes. Local computer publications are an especially good source for BBSes in your own area.

Second, many bulletin boards contain files of BBS listings. In particular, you can look for a file named USABBSxx.ZIP that contains a list of BBSes in the United States. "xx" is the number of the current month. For example, USABBS07.SIT is for July. This file is updated monthly. Be forewarned: many of these BBSes go out of business faster than the list can be updated.

Finally, computer publications often have ads taken out by BBS operators. Like the personal ads found in regular newspapers and magazines, these announcements have a language all their own. Figure 9.3 shows a typical BBS advertisement for a fictitious system.

```
Mac Connector  (313)-555-1234

Los Angeles, CA  since 06/86.

Sysop: John Q. Smith.

10 lines available

Quadra 950 with 3500 MB storage.

Operating from 1200 to 14400 bps.

$35/6M $50/Year fee.

A BBS with one of

the best collections of

Mac-Compatible Shareware.

Many areas have free download access

including an extensive library of

Legal Software & Case files.

Access to hundreds of Gateways.

The most litigious BBS around
```

Figure 9.3: A Typical BBS Advertisement.

A translation of the advertisement is as follows:

The BBS is named "Mac Connector." Its phone number is (310) 555-1234. It is located in Los Angeles, California. The BBS has been in operation since June of 1986.

The system operator is John Q. Smith. He has 10 lines available, and his computer is a Macintosh Quadra 950. The computer has 3500MB of online storage.

The BBS can operate at speed from 1200 to 14000 BPS.

Becoming a registered user costs $35 for six months and $50 for a year.

There is a large collection of programs for Macintosh. The programs are organized into categories. Many of these categories can be accessed for free, including a large number of programs and files devoted to astronomy.

There are hundreds of BBS-network discussion groups.

This BBS is especially good for lawyers.

Starting Your Own Bulletin Board

Once you are a veteran bulletin board user, you may begin to think about starting your own BBS. Be forewarned that running a BBS takes a fair amount of effort, at least in the beginning. However, once you have set up and customized your BBS, it will run unattended, 24 hours a day. You will need to perform only intermittent maintenance and troubleshooting.

There are two ways in which you might start a BBS: as a personal project or for an organization.

Perhaps the main reason to start your own personal BBS is that it can be a lot of fun. Most bulletin board programs have a great deal of flexibility, and there is a lot of room for individuality. You will be able to design your BBS the way you want with customized screens, menus, conferences, and file transfer areas. Controlling your own system will give you a sense of satisfaction. Moreover, you may be able to turn your BBS into a business. If you can attract enough people that share a particular interest, you may be able to serve them with a specialized BBS and make money at the same time. To be realistic, it is difficult to make a lot of money with a personal bulletin board. However, you may be able to do well enough to support the board (hardware, phone lines, and so on).

The second way you might start a bulletin board is as a service provided by an organization. For example, a BBS can act as an internal mail system. Aside from handling individual messages, the BBS can distribute newsletters, company-wide memos and so on. This is a useful resource for employees that travel. With a portable computer and a phone line, they can stay in touch with the office wherever they are. Some companies find that a BBS is a good alternative to a wide area network. The commercial BBS programs are designed to provide good security. In addition, a BBS is much easier to implement and administer than a network and often has more flexibility. If a company already has a local area network, the BBS can be integrated into the system. This allows users to log in directly from their workstation.

Aside from providing internal services, a corporate BBS is useful for helping customers. Many companies use a bulletin board to provide technical support. A user with a problem can dial the BBS, leave a question, and call back later for the response. In addition, the BBS can manage technically-oriented conferences and store a database of questions and answers. A bulletin board can also serve customers in other ways: You can use it to offer product information, to take surveys, to accept orders, and to allow users to register their purchases without having to mail in a card.

Planning Your Own Bulletin Board

Running your own BBS can be enjoyable and rewarding, but doing a good job requires careful planning. In this section we will discuss the basic issues that you should consider. But first, let's take a moment to discuss how you should approach the creation of your own BBS. Before you make any final decisions—what computer to use, what software to buy, how many phone lines to support—take some time and gather information.

There is a lot of hype in the BBS world and it pays to be knowledgable. It is a good idea to read some Mac communication books before you start. However, don't depend on a book for current information. Call the various BBS-oriented companies and request literature about their current products. Compare carefully before you buy. Look for practical features. For example, if you want to run a BBS business it will help to have software that makes it easy for users to register with a credit card.

There are many different BBS programs available. If you want to run a business system, you should probably buy a commercial product. It will offer the features and technical support that you need. If you want a personal system for your own amusement, you can save some money by using a shareware or freeware BBS. However, check prices before you make a decision. Some commercial products are not at all expensive for a single-user system. To test out the various types of software, call a variety of bulletin boards and evaluate them. Ask different sysops how they like their software and what they recommend. Always ask, if you had it to do over again, what would you do differently? At the same time, read Boardwatch and the many similar magazines—they offer valuable articles along with BBS phone number lists. Now, let's move on to the practical issues.

Single-User and Multiuser BBs

In the BBS world, there is a great dividing line between single-user and multiuser systems. To support one caller at a time requires only one computer, one copy of a BBS program, one modem, one serial port and one phone line. If you decide to have your BBS support more than one person at the same time you have to make some fundamental decisions. Of course, each phone line requires its own modem and serial port. However, there are several possible ways to organize the system. For example:

(1) You can have a separate Mac for each phone line. Each Mac runs its own copy of a BBS program. The Mac's are networked together so as to share a common file server.

(2) You use a single computer to support multiple phone lines. This requires a multiuser BBS program that is built to handle more than one user at a time.

Each approach has advantages and disadvantages. A network of dedicated Mac's provides excellent response time. Moreover, it is safe to let a user pause the BBS to do something else while remaining online. However, the setup is extremely expensive and there is no way to allow users to interact with one another in real time. A single computer with a multiuser BBS program costs less, but limits your choice of BBS software. Multiuser software is more complex and creates the fewest headaches if you have some programming experience. Moreover, software to support many users can be expensive (not as expensive as separate Macs though). One big advantage is the capability of letting your users interact, which can be an attractive feature.

The Hardware You Need To Run a BBS

To run a BBS on a Mac you will need at least 4MB (megabtyes) of memory. More memory is valuable, especially if you plan on supporting more than one user on the same Mac. However, you will probably not need more than 8 megabytes. If you have a slow single-user system, you will probably be alright with any modern Mac. However, if you plan on having a fast modem or a multiuser system you will need to focus on one of the faster Macs.

For each phone line you will need one modem and one modem port. If you are planning a large system you should look into special multi-port adaptors. You can also buy a special product that has many modems packaged together in a single box. This device can be attached to a single modem port or expansion slot on your Mac.

Since the main product you will be offering is information, you will need a large amount of online storage. This may be one or more hard disks, or a hard disk in combination with an optical disk of some type. It's hard to predict how much storage you will need. The only thing you can say for sure is that it would be difficult to have too much. What you must realize is that a fast disk and a disk cache is essential. A BBS spends much of its time waiting for I/O. Anything you can do to speed access to your files will prove to be important.

Finally, give some thought as to which modem will be best for you. Almost every modem manufacturer will offer you a substantial discount if you tell them you run a bulletin board. The idea is that you should buy one of their modems so that your customers will buy the same modem (This is why, in the

United States, so many BBSes use HST Courier modems from U.S. Robotics.) In the past, the best way to get a fast connection was to use two modems that supported the same proprietary communication protocol (like HST). Nowdays, there are well established international standards for high-speed transmission. If you're going to be interested in high-speed transmission, your modem should support high-speed connections (V.32 and V.32bis) and error control (V.42bis and MNP 5). If your BBS is to be a business, you would be making a mistake to use a slow 2400 bits/second modem just to save a few dollars.

Online Services

The commercial online services are probably the most attractive segment of the Mac communications market. These services allow anyone with a modem, a Mac, or any other personal computer, (and a credit card) to participate in the world of computerized information.

There are many online services, each offering its own variety of products. All of them have mail, file transfer and discussion groups (conferences). One of the most popular items is the online chat facility. This enables people from all over the country to "talk" to one another using their keyboards. It is like a huge CB radio with different channels. You can find a conversation that appeals to you and jump right in.

> **NOTE:** Not all services have mail gateways to external networks. Some services allow you to send messages only to people in the same system.

Figure 9.4 shows the major online services in the U.S. All of these are oriented towards the general public and are available to anyone. In fact, they are often marketed as family and entertainment services. Other commercial online services are public, but oriented towards specific groups.

Online Service	Company
America Online	America Online
CompuServe	CompuServe
Delphi	General Videotex
Genie	General Electric
Prodigy	Prodigy Services

Figure 9.4: The Major Consumer Online Services in the U.S.

The cost for some online services depends on the time that you call. During the day—called prime time—the charges are the highest and you pay by the hour. In the evenings and on weekends, the cost goes down. Some services offer a flat rate. For a fixed cost per month, you can connect for as long as you like (sometimes only during non-prime time). Flat fees usually allow you to send a limited amount of mail; extra mail costs more. Receiving mail is always free.

Before you sign up, compare all the programs that are offered for the service you are considering. The costs can mount up faster than you might anticipate. While some services offer everything for a fixed price, others let you access only selected parts of the system.

An interesting example is Prodigy. It was designed to be a family-oriented service and, from the beginning, has offered everything (except unlimited mail) for one monthly charge. This is possible because Prodigy carries a lot of advertising. Almost all of the time, the bottom part of your screen (18%) is displaying an ad. The ad changes every time the screen is updated. This can be annoying. But it does keep your costs down.

(Between us, you can cut out a piece of cardboard the size of the advertising and tape it to the bottom part of your screen. Covering the ads makes Prodigy a lot more pleasant to use. One good idea is to use the cardboard for a quick reference of frequently needed information, such as what various command-keys do.)

To access an online service, call a local or toll-free phone number so there are no long distance charges. However, you might have to pay a surcharge to connect to a high-speed (9600 bits/second) modem. If you will be transferring a lot of files, the extra cost may be worth it. Of course, you will need a program for your Mac to handle the communications. There are two ways to do this. You can use a regular communication program to emulate a terminal. After you log in, you will enter commands and make selections from menus.

Alternatively, you can use a special program that is designed to act as an interface into your particular online service. Such a program simplifies common tasks and takes advantage of the power of your Mac to make your interaction more sophisticated. For example, you may see color and graphics. In addition, some programs allow you to use function keys or a mouse to make your work easier.

All the popular online services offer an interface program that you can buy—either by itself or as part of a starter kit. Some services, like Prodigy and America Online, can be used only with a special program. Other services have shareware or freeware interface programs that are readily available. (CompuServe has one of each.)

What Do Online Services Offer?

It would be difficult to exaggerate the variety of features you will find on a public online service. To help you appreciate the vastness of this medium, we have compiled a list showing many of the ways in which you can use an online service. We can divide the list into two areas: using the computer by yourself, and communicating with other people in real time. You access the following by yourself:

- mail

- discussion areas on specific topics

- technical support for all kinds of products

- classified advertisements

- encyclopedias

- news, weather, sports

- travel information and reservations

- business and financial information

- shopping (much more than you would imagine)

- libraries of computer programs

- bill paying

- online banking

In addition, you can also interact with other people:

- chat with others using your keyboard and display

- interactive games, competing against other people

- for children: tutoring and help with homework

- broadcast events: quiz shows, seminars, lectures, discussions

Some online services publish a schedule of online broadcasts. There are regularly scheduled programs and one-time specials, just like television. A typical special event might be a discussion with a celebrity.

In the next section, we will discuss online databases: large repositories of information. From an online service it is possible to access many of these databases via a gateway. All it takes is one command. You do not have to subscribe to each separate database, nor are there minimum charges that you must meet. And no matter how many databases you access, you only need to pay one bill. However, be aware that accessing a commercial database service costs extra and is usually expensive.

Commercial Online Databases

There are literally thousands of computerized databases that you can search for a fee. The amount of information is staggering and often exhaustive: newspapers, wire services, magazines, journals, research reports, statistics, financial reports, and on and on.

There are hundreds of information providers who sell access to databases. The major services offer sophisticated tools for searching and reporting as well as special Mac programs to access the system. The larger online databases are so complex that it takes a long time to fully master the system. In fact, there are professional researchers who work full time finding data. The database companies themselves offer training seminars on an ongoing basis. Figure 9.5 shows the major commercial database providers in the U.S.

Database System	Company
Dialog	Dialog Information
Dow Jones News/Retrieval	Dow Jones and Co.
Easy Link Services	AT&T
Newsnet	Newsnet
Nexis/Lexis	Mead Data Central

Figure 9.5: The Major Commercial Database Providers in the U.S.

Access to so much data is marvellous but, as you can imagine, it does not come cheap. Generally speaking, commercial database services are used by businesses; they are just too expensive for individuals. The heaviest users are professional researchers, attorneys, corporate librarians, journalists, public relations professionals, analysts, speech writers, and politicians.

The exact cost depends on several factors. The most important considerations are what data you want to access and how long the search takes. All databases do not cost the same to search. Some services have special rates for non-prime time searches (evenings and weekends).

Each company has a catalog showing its databases and the costs. Here are a few examples taken from the 1991 Dialog catalog. To search the Los Angeles Times database (say, to find all the articles in which your name was mentioned) costs $1.60/minute; that is, $96/hour. In addition, it costs 50 cents for each full text article you display or print.

Searching the Agrochemicals Handbook, by comparison, is not for the faint of heart. An hour of search time costs $265. On the other hand, examining the U.S. Government Printing Office Monthly Catalog costs only $36/hour.

Packet Switching Networks

When you use your modem to call a bulletin board system or a friend's Mac, you are making exclusive use of a single communication link—from your wall outlet to the local phone company, through a number of switching systems, to the remote computer. While your call is in progress, the phone system reserves certain circuits that nobody else can use until you are finished. When you speak over the telephone you are using these circuits continuously. But when you connect two computers, the circuits lay idle much of the time, waiting for data. A packet switching network implements a system in which high-speed communication links are shared by many computers at the same time.

Use a packet switching network to connect to a remote computer. To start, you connect your Mac to the network by dialing a particular phone number. The system then creates a path for you, through the network, to the point at which the remote computer is connected. Whenever your computer sends data, the network automatically breaks it into pieces, called packets. Each packet is sent over the network independently. At the same time, many other packets are being transmitted over the network. At various points along the way, the packets are examined and directed along the proper path.

Eventually, all your packets end up at the place in the network to which the remote computer is connected. At this point, the packets are reassembled into their original form and delivered. Of course, all the packets are numbered so they can be put together correctly.

The device that converts a stream of data to and from packets is called a packet assembler/disassembler or PAD. As your data enters the network a PAD divides it into packets. At the other end, another PAD converts the packets back into regular data. In between, many users can share the communication lines, lowering the overall cost.

There are numerous packet switching networks around the world, both public and private. In North America there are three very large public networks: Sprintnet, Tymnet, and DataPac. Both Sprintnet (which used to be called Telenet) and Tymnet are worldwide networks. DataPac is a Canadian network.

There are two ways in which you might use a packet switching network. First, you can register as a user with the network company itself. To connect to the network, your computer dials a special access phone number. In most cases, the call is local or toll-free. Once the link is established, you enter a command to connect to the remote system that you want. You can connect to online services, commercial databases, and even bulletin board systems. With some networks, you can connect to any remote computer that can be reached by phone. Like a long distance company, the network will bill you directly: either a flat monthly rate or a per-minute fee. The alternative is to pay for a regular long distance call.

The second way to use a packet switching network is to dial the access number for a large online service or database. All of these companies use packet switching networks although you may not know it. Some companies lease time on commercial networks, others maintain their own networks. Some companies do both. For example, when you call the local CompuServe access number from most places, you are dialing into CompuServe's own packet switching network. In other locations, where CompuServe does not have a local number for their own network, you must call a public network, like Tymnet or Sprintnet.

Before you sign up for a packet switching service, compare carefully. First, check the costs. When you call long distance with a regular phone company, you pay by the minute and only for the time you use. Packet switching networks may require you pay for a certain amount of time, whether you need it or not. If you end up using all the time, it is cheaper than dialing on your own; otherwise, you may be paying more than necessary. Second, packet switching networks generally follow an international standard called X.25. Unfortunately, X.25 is an old technology, developed in the days of 1200 bits per second (bps) modems. Nowadays, 2400 bps is considered slow while fast modems connect at 9600 or 14400 bps. You may well find that a packet switching connection is slower than a regular long distance call.

Finally, many parts of the country have no local number to call for 9600 bps access. If you have to call long distance to connect at 9600 bps over a network, you might as well call the remote computer directly. And in places where you do have 9600 bps access, you will have to pay a surcharge to use it. Access at 14400 bps, at this time, is not even available. On the other hand, using a global packet switching network means that you can log in to a remote system no matter where you are. Both Sprintnet and Tymnet have local access numbers around the world.

10

Modems

When we need information from someone across town or across the country, we just pick up the phone. These same phone lines are also capable of exchanging computer data, for example, text files, formatted word processing, desktop publishing, database and spreadsheet files, and complete computer programs. The hardware device that makes this possible is called a modem.

In your Macintosh (or any other computer, for that matter), data is stored in digital form as strings of zeros and ones. Unfortunately, telephone lines are designed to carry analog data (represented by tones), not digital data. To move data over the phone lines, the digital information must be converted by the modem into analog data (this process is called modulation) and then translated by the receiving modem, changing it back into its original digital form (demodulation) so it can be interpreted by the receiving computer. This two-step conversion process, MOdulate and DEModulate. is responsible for the name of the device—the "modem."

Selecting a modem is potentially one of the most confusing purchase decisions that can confront a computer user. Modem manuals tend to be extremely technical, reading as though they were designed for individuals who want to build a modem rather than use one. It's easy to get bogged down in the terminology. (Scan through a couple of modem ads and you will quickly see what I mean.)

In addition to a multitude of esoteric features and supported standards, you must decide between internal and external models and determine the speed you'll need. This chapter will explain the different available features and options, and help you make an informed purchase decision.

Internal and External Modems

After you have decided to purchase a modem, one of the first choices you will have to make is whether to get an internal or an external modem. If your Mac has an empty NuBus slot, a Processor Direct Slot (PDS), or a modem slot, you can install an internal modem. Internal modems draw their power from the Mac's power supply. Since they reside inside the Mac, internal models don't require desk space and are as portable as the Mac itself. (For this reason, internal modems are very popular with PowerBook owners.) The disadvantages of having an internal modem include the difficulty of resetting following a failure or lock-up—since internal modems are turned on automatically when you boot the Mac, it may be necessary to shut down the Mac and reboot to reset the modem; the lack of status lights, and a slightly higher price than a comparable external modem.

You should note that internal modems for Macs and PCs are very different; one system's modems cannot be swapped for the other's. When buying an internal modem, be sure to specify the model of Mac in which it will be installed, particularly if your Mac does not have NuBus slots. Figure 10.1, for example, shows an internal modem for the PowerBook.

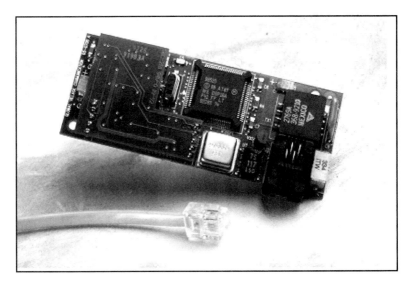

Figure 10.1: The PowerPort/Gold internal modem. (Photo Courtesy of Global Village Communication.)

Since most external modems are connected by cable to the modem port on the Mac's back panel, an external modem can be hooked to any Mac. The availability of a PDS or NuBus slot is irrelevant. External modems usually have their own power supply and on/off switch. One big advantage, particularly for users with multiple systems, is that as far as external models are concerned, a modem is a modem is a modem. Not only can an external modem be used with any Mac, external PC and Mac modems are generally functionally identical and interchangeable. Figure 10.2 shows a Hayes Ultra 96—an example of an external modem.

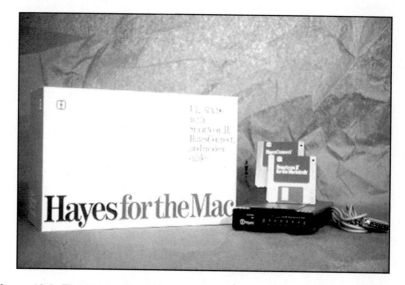

Figure 10.2: The Hayes Ultra 96. (Photo Courtesy of Hayes Microcomputer Products, Inc.)

Although manufacturers normally market their modems specifically to Mac or PC users, the only thing that differentiates most external modems is whether they include a Mac cable and telecommunications program or a PC-specific cable and software. Regardless of which external modem you purchase, the internal components are frequently identical for the Mac and PC models.

Making the Connection

If your Mac has easily accessible slots, such as the NuBus slots in a Mac II series computer, installing an internal modem couldn't be easier ... find a free slot, push the card into place, and then connect the card to a telephone wall jack with standard telephone cable (normally this is supplied with the modem). Optionally, a telephone can be connected to the card as well, allowing you to use the phone when you aren't working with the modem.

The insides of many Mac's, however, aren't readily accessible. If you have a normally sealed Mac, such as the SE or a PowerBook, opening the case by anyone other than an Apple-authorized dealer can void the Mac's warranty. If your Mac is still under warranty or you are not comfortable with "cracking" its case, the relatively small fee to have the card professionally installed will be worthwhile.

Most external modems have a standard RS-232C 25-pin connector on the back panel. All that is needed to hook a "PC" modem to a Mac is the appropriate modem cable and a Mac communications program. Macs starting with the Mac Plus require a DIN-8 to DB-25 modem cable. Earlier Macs (the 128 and 512K models) use a DB-9 to DB-25 cable. The only real advantage of buying an external modem that's advertised as a "Macintosh" modem is that it will usually include the correct serial cable and a rudimentary communications program.

> **NOTE:** When installing a modem that was originally purchased for use with a PC, you will need to buy a Macintosh modem cable. Be sure to tell the dealer or mail-order house that the cable will be used to connect a modem to your Mac, the model of Macintosh you'll be using, and the connectors needed (normally DB-25 and DIN-8).

Connecting an external modem (as shown in Figure 10.3) takes only a couple of minutes. The DB-25 end of the modem cable connects to the back of the modem, while the DIN-8 (or DB-9) end plugs into the Mac's external modem port. A supplied RJ-11 telephone cable plugs into your phone outlet on the wall and to one of the connectors on the back of the modem. (This connector is often labeled "Wall" or "Line.") Optionally, a telephone handset can be connected to the remaining RJ-11 jack on the back of the modem (labeled "Phone"), using the phone's RJ-11 cord (before you purchased the modem, this cord was used to plug the phone into the wall). Finally, the modem's power cord—usually an A/C adapter—is connected to the modem and then plugged into a wall outlet. External modems really are external in every respect. To connect one, there's no need to open the Mac's case.

High-speed modems (9600 bps and up) normally require a special cable—one that implements RTS/CTS hardware handshaking between the modem and the computer. This ensures that incoming data (sometimes as fast as 57,600 bps) will not be lost as it attempts to enter the computer. The flow control established by this type of cable (hardware handshaking) is the appropriate option to specify in your communications software, rather than XON/XOFF, for example. And if you are using XMODEM, YMODEM, or ZMODEM for protocol file transfers, you must use hardware handshaking.

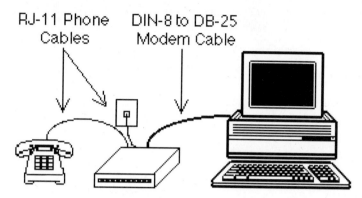

Figure 10.3: Connecting an external modem.

 # Modulation, Error Control/Correction, and Data Compression Standards

When reading advertisements for modems, you will see many strange-looking sets of letters (MNP, V.xx, and V.xxbis) that are included as part of the modem's name or are mentioned in the technical specifications. These cryptic text strings are the error control and data compression protocols and the modulation standards to which the modem adheres.

These standards and protocols are all implemented as code inside the modem's chips (firmware). Some of the protocols are in the public domain (MNP-2 through MNP-4) and are supported by virtually all modems. Others must be licensed by the modem manufacturer. Others are proprietary and are found on only a particular brand and model of modem. Still others are standards that have been proposed by CCITT (Comité Consultatif Internationale de Télégraphie et Téléphonie), an international communications standards committee. The following discussion will help you weed through and decipher the numerous standards that you will encounter.

Modulation Standards

Modulation standards are concerned with the speed at which a modem normally operates. The existence of and adherence to these standards assures that one modem can communicate with another, regardless of the manufacturers involved. From lowest to highest, the following standards are currently in use.

Standard	Speed
Bell 103	300 bps
Bell 212A	1200 bps
V.22	1200 bps
V.22bis	2400 bps
V.32	4800 and 9600 bps
V.32bis	14,400 bps

These speeds, however, are hardly cast in stone. Coupled with an appropriate compression protocol, throughput (the actual rate of data transmission) can effectively be doubled, tripled, or quadrupled. Most modems can communicate at lower speeds, too.

Error Control and Error Correction Standards

Standards also help assure error-free communication sessions, including the transmission of large text files, as well as the formatted documents and programs that are normally transmitted using an error-control protocol that is part of your communications package. Error-control protocols are used to determine whether a byte or block of data has been sent and received correctly. If not, a request for retransmission of the erroneous data is made. Error-correction routines, on the other hand, send a sufficient amount of redundant data to enable the receiving modem to determine the nature of the error and, in most cases, correct it without requiring a retransmission of the data. You should note that several of the error-control and correction standards below also incorporate some elements of data compression.

Standard	Description
MNP-2	Confirms each byte of data as it is received by echoing it back to the sending modem.
MNP-3	This is an improved version of MNP-2 that effects a 25% reduction in the amount of data that needs to be transmitted.
MNP-4	Error-control protocol that also incorporates data compression by allowing data to be transmitted and checked in larger blocks.
MNP-9	Acknowledgments of data packets are trans-mitted with the next packet rather than as a

Standard	Description
	separate confirmation byte. When an error is detected, only the erroneous data is retransmitted instead of the entire packet.
MNP-10	An advanced set of error-control procedures designed for less than optimal phone conditions, such as cellular communications.
LAP-B	Link Access Procedure, Balanced is an error-control protocol that was designed for packet-switched services such as Tymnet and was in use before the V.42 standard was introduced.
V.42	Worldwide error-correction standard for high-speed modem connections (between 4800 and 14,400 bps). LAP-M (Link Access Procedure for Modems) is the error-control method used by V.42. This standard incorporates MNP-4 as an alternate, so it can also communicate with modems that only support MNP.

If the modem's error-control/correcting protocol is in effect for a given session, it is best to restrict file transfers to protocols that don't also introduce their own error-control scheme—effectively duplicating the error-control and adding unnecessary time to the transfer. YMODEM-G is an example of a file transfer protocol that does not introduce its own error-control scheme. It also offers the bonus of allowing files to be transferred as a group, rather than one at a time. ZMODEM can also be used and has the advantage of not aborting the transmission following a single error as YMODEM-G does.

 # Data Compression Standards

Like error control and correction, data compression occurs in the modem's firmware. As long as both the sending and receiving modems support the same compression standards, the originating modem compresses data as it is transmitted. The receiving modem then uncompresses the data as it arrives. As with the compression methods used by popular programs such as StuffIt, Compact Pro, and DiskDoubler, the actual amount of compression you will receive will vary with the particular file or files you are attempting to transmit.

Protocol	Description
MNP-5	Microcom compression protocol that can double throughput with some types of data.
MNP-7	Microcom compression protocol that can triple throughput with some types of data.
V.42bis	Worldwide compression protocol that can quadruple throughput with some types of data.

NOTE: All versions of MNP (Microcom Networking Protocol) were developed by Microcom, a U.S. telecommunications company. MNP-2 through MNP-4 are in the public domain and are widely supported by modems in this country. To offer higher versions of MNP, manufacturers must license the protocols from Microcom (thus, there is a slightly higher cost for including MNP-5 or higher). Modems equipped with MNP-6 (not discussed above) can begin communicating at one speed and, if line conditions warrant it, can switch to a higher speed. There is no MNP-8.

Standards Summary

If you are looking for a modem that is as compatible as possible with current standards, MNP-2 through MNP-4 are routinely supported as error-control protocols, and MNP-5 is widely used for compression. V.42 and V.42bis are fast on their way to becoming the new standards for error control and compression. In many cases, to ensure compatibility, current modems will support all of these standards and perhaps several others. When connecting with another computer, during the negotiation phase at the start of the session, your modem will offer these standards to the other modem in a predetermined order and the most powerful ones that the two units have in common will be selected.

In general, it is best to steer clear of units that offer only proprietary standards unless they also support the standards listed above. Who wants a 9600 bps modem that can only operate at 2400 bps with most other modems, for example, because its 9600 bps protocols are not in favor with the rest of the computing world? Unless there is an overwhelming increase in throughput with the proprietary standards or the modem will be dedicated to working in conjunction only with similar modems, there is little sense in being out of step.

NOTE: Even though many modems offer similar sets of features, not all modems are created equal. This is especially true when it comes to error control/correction and compression. The way one manufacturer decides to implement the same data compression or error-control protocol can differ substantially from the way another vendor does it. The result can mean major differences in how modems perform. Tolerance for adverse conditions—noise on the line, for instance—can also affect throughput. The less tolerance for noise, the quicker the modem will drop to a slower speed.

Advanced error control/correction and data compression typically increase the purchase price of a modem. These features, however, are also available as standard parts of most communications programs. Error control is handled by the XMODEM, YMODEM, and ZMODEM file transfer protocols. And there are several excellent commercial and shareware data compression programs. Are these features worth paying for in firmware? According to my good friends at Metriplex, Inc. in Cambridge, Massachusetts: "You should buy the fastest modem that you can afford. Let your communications software and utility programs take care of error control and data compression. Modems that depend on firmware features are only useful if you can find other similarly-equipped modems with which to communicate."

If, on the other hand, you are charged with outfitting several company sites with modems that will be used primarily for between-office communications, it may pay to buy modems that offer high-level MNP or V.42 error control/correction, along with V.42bis data compression. Similarly, it is a good idea to contact your colleagues and the information services with which you intend to connect to find out what standards their modems support. Having the communication industry's version of "bells and whistles" only makes sense if you will be communicating with other modems that support the same features.

More Modem Features

Now that the standards have been dealt with, let's move on to the other features that you will find in today's modems. As with the error control and data compression standards, the fact that a modem has a particular feature does not necessarily imply that the feature's implementation is well thought out, convenient, or easy to use. Hands-on testing, word-of-mouth, and reviews in the computer magazines are your best sources of this information.

Power Switch

External modems normally have a separate power switch that allows them to be turned off and on independently from the Mac. Having a separate power switch provides a convenient means of resetting the modem when things go badly.

Speaker

An on-board speaker or the ability to use the Mac's speaker should be considered essential. Having a speaker enables you to hear the phone being dialed; to determine when you have reached a busy or disconnected number; when you have connected with a human rather than another modem; or when the connection has been broken. Psychologically, the speaker can also be reassuring. It enables you to hear what is happening, rather than simply trusting that all is going well and according to plan.

Included Cable

Although cables are inexpensive, having an appropriate modem cable in the package means that you will be up and running that much sooner, and you won't have to worry about locating a compatible cable. This is especially important for high-speed modems (9600 bps and faster), since you may require a specially wired modem cable that implements hardware handshaking for proper flow control.

Indicator Lights

Most modems include a row of mode lights on the front panel. Although not essential, indicator lights are helpful for troubleshooting. If on-screen messages from the modems are not plentiful or clearly worded, the modem's indicator lights will tell you what's happening from one moment to the next—whether the modem is sending or receiving, as well as the special features that are currently in use (MNP, for example).

Display panels vary considerably from one modem to another. If possible, look for a panel with labels that are understandable and large enough to read. (Some modems, such as the SupraFAXModem V.32bis, have foregone the normal row of half a dozen or more lights in favor of a large LED block. Two-character messages, such as "DI" for dialing and "M4" for MNP-4, are flashed on the display.)

Additional Serial Ports

The Mac only provides two serial ports: one designated for a printer (or an AppleTalk/LocalTalk connector) and the other for a modem. Most external modems contain a single serial port that is used to make the connection with the Mac's modem port. Some modems—internal models, in most cases—

provide additional serial ports that you can use to control other serial devices, such as a video capture unit. A useful feature to look for is if the extra port or ports can be used simultaneously. If the ports must be used one at a time, you can obtain the same capabilities by purchasing an inexpensive 2- or 4-position serial switch box.

Intelligent Dialing

Many modems support auto-dial and auto-answer. Auto-dial enables you to dial phone numbers from your keyboard (usually within a communications program) without having to use your telephone handset. Auto-answer allows the modem to answer incoming calls without requiring your presence. These are normal features on most modems.

Because many modems now include a small amount of RAM on board, they can often be programmed to store one or several frequently called phone numbers. If your modem doesn't have this feature, though, don't worry. Communications programs for the Mac usually provide the capability to store and dial an extensive directory of phone numbers.

Hayes Compatibility

Whether typed from the keyboard or sent from your communications software, instructions are sent to the modem using AT commands. AT commands can be used to put the modem into a specific mode (such as auto-reliable or a particular MNP level), set on-screen feedback options (text versus code numbers), and hang up the phone, for instance. The standard set of AT commands were developed by Hayes Microcomputer Products. Compatibility with this basic command set is commonly called Hayes compatibility.

Virtually all modems boast Hayes compatibility. The advantage of having a Hayes compatible modem is that of software support. Since all Mac telecommunications programs support Hayes-compatible modems, buying one assures you of finding software that works with the modem.

> **NOTE:** Don't be surprised if your modem supports additional, non-standard AT commands or provides separate commands for managing MNP support, for example. Because the commands are for controlling your modem rather than the one on the other end of the phone line, the additional commands offer you greater flexibility in setting and resetting your modem's features.

Issuing AT Commands

In most cases, your communications software will handle the task of controlling your modem. Instructing the program to dial a particular number, for example, will frequently be accompanied by the appropriate AT command appearing on-screen automatically—typed for you by the communications program.

Although there is seldom a reason to issue an AT command manually, knowing how to do so can be a big help when trouble-shooting (various modem tests are part of the AT command set) or when you need to put the modem in a state that is not supported by your communications program.

Once your communications program is running—but before you've made a connection with another computer—is when most user-initiated AT commands are often issued. (To issue a command during a session, type +++ first to switch from communications to AT command mode. Once the modem responds on-screen with an "OK" message, it is ready to receive your commands.)

To issue an AT command, you type **AT** (Attention) followed immediately by the AT code and a <Return>. Commands can be typed in upper or lower-case, but must not contain spaces. Multiple commands can be entered on the same line. To make the modem dial a particular phone number, for example, you might enter:

```
ATDT555-1234<Return>
```

The **D** instructs the modem to dial, the **T** indicates that it is a touch-tone rather than a pulse call, and the string of digits is the phone number.

Many of the AT commands enable you to configure the modem in a particular way. **L** commands, for example, set the modem's speaker volume. Either L0 or L1 can be used to set the speaker for low volume, L2 sets it for medium volume, and L3 sets it for maximum volume. Many AT command codes work in the same fashion—a code followed by a modifier digit (in this case, the numbers 0 through 3).

If the modem contains nonvolatile RAM, it is capable of storing the settings of frequently-issued commands as a profile. Typically, two active profiles can be stored by issuing the AT&W0 or AT&W1 commands. By typing **AT&V**, you can see the profiles and phone numbers that have been stored in the modem's RAM. The AT&Y0 or AT&Y1 codes are used to select which of the two profiles will be active on start-up.

The commands supported by each modem are normally documented in the manual that accompanies the modem. If you want to take greater control of the modem than that afforded by your communications program, this section of the manual is where you should turn. (It's also an excellent way to get a better understanding of your modem's capabilities.) Figure 10.4 displays a summary of the AT command set for an Abaton InterFax 24/96, generated by typing **AT&H0**.

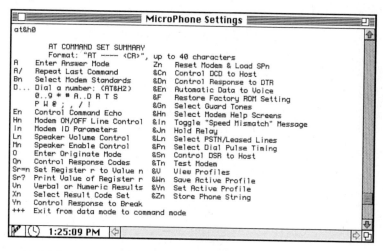

Figure 10.4: The AT command set summary.

NOTE: Before you change and store any modem settings by sending AT strings to the modem, be sure that the modem also supports a reset code that will restore the modem to its original factory settings. Not all modems do. Without a reset code, it is possible for you (or a system error) to leave the modem in an unusable state.

Automatic Fall-Back

At the start of a communications session, the two modems automatically negotiate a transmission speed for the session that is based on a combination of the highest common speed supported and the current line conditions. The ability to fall back to a slower speed assures that your 9600 bps modem can still communicate with a 2400 or 1200 bps modem, for example. A few advanced modems continually monitor line conditions throughout the session and can also adjust the transmission rate upward if conditions warrant it.

Although many modems offer automatic fall-back, it is not safe to assume that all do. For most users, this feature is critical. For example, no one wants a 9600 bps modem that cannot talk to a 2400 bps modem or can only communicate with optimal line conditions. Lack of fall-back support in either of these cases would normally result in your modem failing to make the connection.

Voice/Data Switching

A number of modems allow you to freely switch between voice and data modes without breaking the connection. This feature can be particularly helpful for managing initial communications sessions—assuring that speed, data bits, and other parameters are correctly matched.

Security Features

The threat of an unauthorized user gaining access to your data via a modem is a possibility that—for many companies—should not be taken lightly. Some modems provide built-in security features that can restrict the individuals who will be allowed to connect with your system. The most popular options are passwords and dial-back. With the former feature, incoming calls must be accompanied by the correct password or they will be disconnected. With dial-back, the modem immediately disconnects each incoming call and then dials the phone number that has been assigned to the modem for the particular user.

Bundled Software

If the modem that you select is being marketed as a "Mac" modem, it's not unusual for the package to also include a communications program. The bundled programs tend to be stripped-down versions of popular communications software or simple public domain programs. Obvious features, such as auto log-on and the more advanced file transfer protocols such as YMODEM and ZMODEM, are frequently absent. While they are certainly good enough to get you up and running, it's best to treat the software as a learning tool. If you telecommunicate with any frequency, don't be surprised if you quickly outgrow the package.

Different Modems for Different Needs

Now that you are familiar with the common modem features, which modem should you buy? Here are a few extra considerations that may point you in the right direction.

What Will the Primary Use of the Modem Be (How Fast is Fast Enough)?

If you intend to use the modem mainly for connecting to information services (CompuServe or America Online, for example) and bulletin board systems (BBSs), and occasionally transmitting and receiving files, a standard 2400 bps modem may be the best choice. Currently, 2400 bps is the fastest data exchange rate supported by most information services without requiring a special surcharge. Reading messages and interacting on an information service at faster than 2400 bps is pointless. Incoming text will scroll quickly at this speed—often faster than you can read it.

At the low end, a 1200 or 300 bps modem (unless it's free) is probably a bad investment. Most manufacturers have phased out the 1200 bps modems in their line in favor of the currently popular 2400 bps models. Although you can certainly use a 1200 or 300 bps modem with any information service, as well as for exchanging data files with colleagues, the slower the modem, the higher your phone bills and information service charges will be. (If you intend to restrict your communications activities to local communications and information services that charge a flat monthly fee for unlimited on-line time, however, one of these slower modems may suffice.)

If your main use will be transmitting and receiving data files (from one company site to another, for example), the faster the modem, the better. A 9600 or 14,400 bps model is highly recommended, particularly if the files you will be transmitting are large. For error-free, non-protocol transmissions, you may want a modem that includes appropriate MNP or CCITT V.42 error-control protocols, too.

If a 9600 bps or faster modem is within your budget, you can still use it for slower speed transmissions. You might log-on to an information service at 2400 bps, capture the list of new program and data file uploads, and then log off. After examining the list off-line and deciding which files you want to download, you can log back on at 9600 bps and quickly download the files. In general, when using a 9600 bps modem with an information service, whether you will save money is highly dependent on how efficiently you spend your time on-line. Browsing through text messages at 9600 bps is expensive and pointless. Downloading files at that speed, however, can be a great money saver.

Do You Have a Network?

If you work out of your home or are employed by a business that has only stand-alone computers, adding a modem to your setup doesn't require much forethought. If the company's computers are networked, however, it may make little sense to purchase separate modems for each potential user. Since most people only require communication capabilities sporadically, a better solution may be to share a modem among the network users.

309

Shiva Corporation currently manufactures a line of modems called NetModems. A normal modem has an RS-232 port on the back. Instead, the NetModems provide a LocalTalk or EtherNet connector that is used to link the modem to your network. At a minimum, the NetModems allow outgoing modem access to every individual on the network—one person at a time. Once they get past the modem's built-in security measures, incoming callers are treated like any other network node. The advanced NetModems also provide remote routing— two geographically separated LANs, each with a NetModem, can be linked over the phone lines to form a single, larger network. See Figure 10.5 for an example of a NetModem.

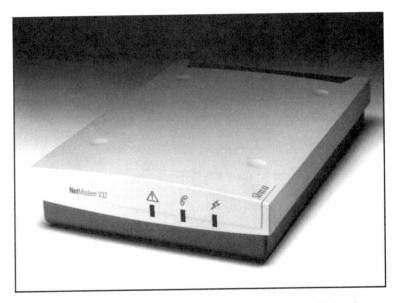

Figure 10.5: The Shiva NetModem V.32. (Photo courtesy of Shiva Corporation.)

Do You Need Fax Capabilities?

When selecting a modem, you might want to consider fax modems—modems that also have fax transmission capabilities. As discussed in the next chapter, without incurring a huge increase in price, your modem can also function as a Group 3-compatible fax unit.

What Can You Afford?

Price isn't much of a problem with modems, regardless of the speed and features you require. Depending on the manufacturer, the difference in price between a rock-bottom 2400 bps modem and one capable of speeds up to 14,400 bps (and up to four times higher with data compression) may only be a couple hundred dollars. Unless you insist on a particular model of modem from a specific manufacturer, the normal price range for most models will be between $100 and $600—hardly a budget-busting affair.

What about the Warranty?

At a minimum, most manufacturers offer at least a one-year warranty on modems. If you read the magazine ads, however, you'll note several manufacturers who offer 5-year, 7-year, and even lifetime warranties. Don't let the length of the warranty alone be the deciding factor, however. The manufacturer's reputation for honoring the warranty, the quality and availability of technical support, and the likelihood that the manufacturer will still be in business when or if the modem fails should also be considered.

A Typical Communications Session

The easiest way to get a taste of telecommunications is to begin by logging onto an information service (GEnie, CompuServe, Prodigy, or America Online, for instance). Many modems are bundled with one or more introductory accounts and a free period of time that you can use. Some, such as Prodigy and America Online, even provide special software that you'll use to connect with the service.

Using a service is easy. Even if software is not provided by the service, simple instructions are available concerning the appropriate set-up parameters to use with your regular communications program. The more difficult task is hooking up with an associate—getting the two modems on speaking terms and successfully exchanging data. To give you a better idea of what is involved, this section presents a brief example of a communications session between two Macs running MicroPhone II, a popular communications program.

Setting Up

Here's the scenario. You have promised to send out the annual report to Jim, your supervisor in the district office. He needs it as soon as possible. An overnight delivery service could get it there by tomorrow, but your modem can deliver it the moment the report is finished! Rather than sit at his desk breathlessly awaiting your call, Jim turns on his modem, launches MicroPhone II, and selects Wait for Call from the Phone menu (see Figure 10.6). Because receiving the data does not require Jim's presence, he heads down the hall to a meeting.

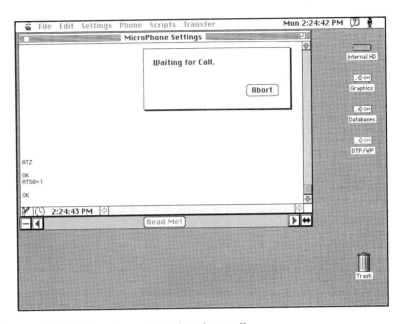

Figure 10.6: Waiting for an incoming data call.

Before transmitting the report, you must create a settings file that you can use to connect with Jim's modem. The settings file contains your modem configuration settings. First, launch MicroPhone II by double-clicking its icon. A blank screen labeled MicroPhone Settings appears.

To check your current settings, select Communications... from the Settings menu. The dialog box in Figure 10.7 is presented. From a previous discussion with Jim, you know that his modem is configured similarly to yours. Start by making sure that the number of bits per character (data bits), stop bits, and parity match his settings; in this case, 8, auto, and none. The agreed-upon speed is 2400 bps. (Although you can set Baud Rate for the fastest speed handled by your modem—regardless of what the other modem is capable of—setting the speed to match the other modem eliminates any concern that the two modems will be unable to successfully negotiate a common speed.) The options at the bottom of the dialog box for Modem Driver, Connection Port, and Hardware Handshake are specific to your modem. These should be set once to match your particular modem configuration and then left alone.

Next, there are some minor modifications that need to be made to the terminal settings. (The terminal settings determine how and when text will appear on your screen, and whether your terminal will be configured to operate like a dumb terminal, a TTY or teletype, or act like another standard terminal, such as DEC VT-52.) Select Terminal... from the Settings menu. The dialog in Figure 10.8 appears. Click in the check boxes for Local Echo and Auto Wraparound to switch them on. Local Echo assures that anything you type at your keyboard will also appear on your own screen, not just on Jim's. Auto Wraparound takes long lines of text and wraps them to the next line—just like your word processing program. (If Jim isn't at his Mac when your call comes in, these features won't be used. Still, they'll be useful in future attended sessions with Jim.)

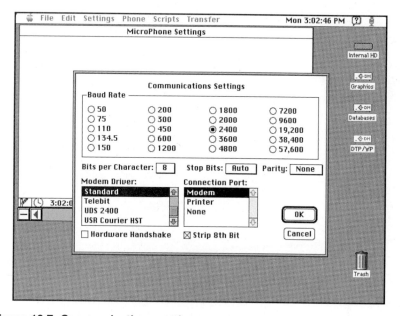

Figure 10.7: Communications settings.

Next, because we will be transferring a nontext file (a formatted word processing report), select Protocol Transfer... from the settings menu. The Protocol Transfer Settings dialog appears. Click the XMODEM/YMODEM... button. In the XMODEM/YMODEM Settings dialog that appears, click the YMODEM-G radio button to set it as the Default Type. Click OK in the two dialog boxes to record the changes and return to the blank session screen.

The final step in preparing for the session is to define the service that you want to call—Jim, in this case. Select Create Service... from the Phone menu. In the dialog box that appears, fill in a name for the service and a phone number (see Figure 10.9). Click the Pulse or Tone radio button—depending on the type of phone service you have. Although we can also specify a startup action that will occur automatically after connecting, there's no reason to do so for a simple communications session. (This feature is extremely handy for automating the process of logging onto a BBS or information service, on the other hand.) Click OK to close the Create Service dialog. The new service "Jim (supervisor)" is added as an option to the Phone menu.

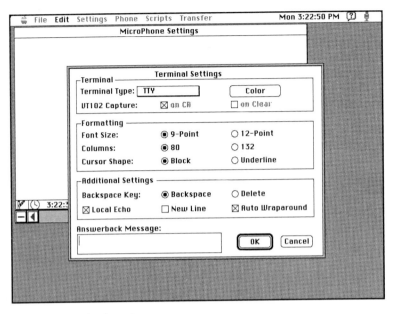

Figure 10.8: Terminal settings.

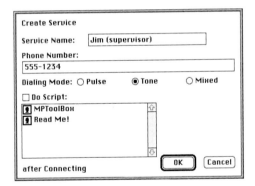

Figure 10.9: At a minimum, creating a new service requires specifying a service name and a phone number.

Dialing and Connecting

Now we are ready to go. Turn on your modem and dial Jim's computer by selecting the option for it in the Phone menu. In this example, the service is named "Jim (supervisor)." Assuming all goes well, the two modems will take a moment or two to negotiate a speed and optional error-control/correction and data compression standards to use for the session. After the negotiation has been completed, you will see a CONNECT message in the session window. (The specific message you receive will depend on your modem's configuration. You may also see the bps rate, for example).

From now until you disconnect, anything typed on either computer's keyboard will be transmitted to the other modem and appear on-screen. Since Jim may or may not be at his system, you might type a message to him, such as "Jim, are you there?<Return>," before beginning the file transfer. If you receive a response to your message, you can carry on an on-line conversation, if you wish. Unfortunately, there is nothing to stop you both from typing at the same time. If you don't take turns, your initial message may look like: "JiBobm, aires thyoau tthyoereu?" A common way to avoid this problem is to take turns and to signify the end of your turn by pressing the <Return> key once or twice.

Transferring the File and Wrapping Up

Since Jim isn't there, we'll proceed with the file transfer without him. From the Transfer menu, select either Send YMODEM (MacBinary)... or Send ZMODEM (MacBinary).

> **NOTE:** If you do not have a modem-generated, error-control protocol in effect, you can use the XMODEM option instead. To make XMODEM appear in Transfer menu (if it isn't there already), select Protocol Transfer... again from the Settings menu and configure MicroPhone II to use XMODEM instead of YMODEM.

After specifying YMODEM or ZMODEM, the Mode of Transfer dialog appears. Click the buttons to send "a file" and "MacBinary" as the file type. Then click OK to proceed. A standard file dialog appears and allows you to pick a file (or files) to transmit. Once selected, the file transfer begins immediately as shown in Figure 10.10.

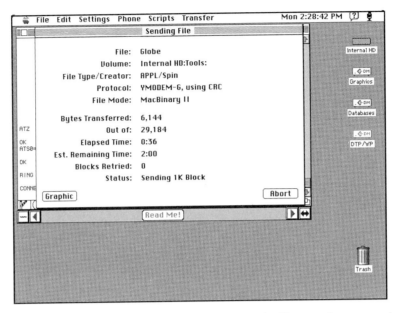

Figure 10.10: MicroPhone keeps you abreast as the file transfer proceeds. A similar screen appears on the receiving computer.

Assuming that the file transfer was successful, a copy of your file is now on Jim's hard disk in the folder Jim designated with the Select Receive Folder option in the Transfer menu. To end the session, type a message for Jim and then select Hang Up from the Phone menu. If the session went well, you may want to save the settings file so that you can reuse it the next time you call Jim. Select Save Settings As ... from the File menu and specify a new file name. The next time you need to communicate with Jim, you can open and use his settings file by double-clicking it. You can now quit from MicroPhone and turn off your modem. If Jim had been at his Mac, little would have changed. The file exchange, however, could have gone in either or both directions—regardless of who initiated the session.

But back to reality... The preceding example shows a simple communications session that went perfectly. In real life, particularly in initial sessions with a new user, things don't always go so smoothly. It can take one or several tries to even make the connection. Other than XMODEM, the file transfer protocols that your communications package offers may bear little resemblance to those provided in your colleague's program. When the connection is broken—frequently in the middle of transferring a huge file—the only error message that you will see is NO CARRIER or something equally informative. The cause of the problem will usually be unknown. Was there something wrong with the modem settings or a mismatched parameter in one of the communications programs? Did someone pick up an extension in one of the offices or was the line interrupted by a tone from call waiting? Or, maybe this just isn't your lucky day!

As marvelous and useful as modems can be, perhaps some suggestions for safe communicating practices are in order:

(1) If it works, don't fix it. Depending on the status messages that your modem presents on-screen and on its display panel, you may suspect that the modem's error-control and compression protocols are never being used. So what? If file transfers are generally successful, your only problem may be that they are not happening as fast as they might. Tinker at your own risk.

(2) Before changing the modem's stored profiles, use the AT&V command to display the current profiles and print them using your communication program's Print function. Store them in a safe place, such as in your modem manual. With the printout in hand, you will always be able to restore the individual settings to their factory defaults—even if the AT command set doesn't provide a command to do so. Similarly, if you have created and stored a new profile that seems to work for you, print that as well so you can get back to it if needed.

(3) If it works correctly, be sure to save the communication settings file (or whatever your communications program calls it). First, you never know when you will need to communicate with the same individual again. Second, if the settings were appropriate for working with a colleague, they will probably make a good starting point for a new settings file to be used with someone else.

Fax Modems

In the last several years, fax machines have launched a convincing invasion on corporate America. Not surprisingly, they have made important in-roads into small businesses and homes, too. Sending a fax is one of the most straightforward means of getting a message to someone without playing "telephone tag" or worrying about the message being tossed into the trash along with the junk mail. Unlike a brief phone message, a fax can say everything that's on your mind, and faxes are still considered important by most recipients.

Recently, Macintosh owners have been able to inexpensively add a *fax modem* to their systems. This enables them to exchange faxes with any CCITT (Comité Consultatif Internationale de Télégraphie et Téléphonie, an international standards committee) Group 3-compatible fax machine or another fax modem. Group 3 transmissions can occur at speeds of up to 9600 bps (bits per second).

Fax modems are available for only a fraction of the price of a standard fax machine, yet offer similar features. As a bonus, most current fax modems now provide fax *and* data capabilities in the same unit. (The most common data component of a fax modem is a 2400 bps modem. See the "Modems" chapter for additional information on modem capabilities and features.) This chapter contains discussions of the following topics:

- The advantages of fax machines and fax modems.

- Internal versus external fax modems.

- How a fax modem works.

- Hardware and software features to consider when choosing a fax modem.

- Selecting appropriate fonts for use in faxes.

- Handling phone traffic with a phone line manager.

Fax Machines versus Fax Modems

Fax machines and fax modems work by converting documents into graphics—lines of dots that make up the particular images and text on the page. Fax machines process a document by scanning each page in almost the same way as a photocopier or a computer scanner processes an image. Fax modems accomplish the conversion process through software. Both fax machines and fax modems have advantages, as shown in the following table (Figure 11.1):

Features and benefits	Fax Machine	Fax Modem
Send paper documents	√	some (with scanner)
Eliminate paper		√
Print on plain paper	some	√
Large address books	some	√
Automatic cover sheets		√
Transmission logs	√	√
Group transmissions	√	√
Polling	√	√
Delayed transmissions	some	√
Notifies user of received faxes		√
Can be shared by multiple users	√	some
Phone handset can be attached	√	√
Data modem capabilities		√
Inexpensive		√

Figure 11.1: Features and benefits of fax machines and fax modems.

Although more expensive, a fax machine is the best choice when the majority of your documents are printed material—documents that are not present in the Macintosh as files. Fax machines also are easily shared, making them very useful when faxing will be done by several people in a company rather than just one. Only a handful of fax modems can be shared, and only by purchasing the appropriate network software (see the discussion of "Faxing Over a Network" at the end of this chapter).

Perhaps the biggest drawback of fax machines is cost. A bottom-of-the-line fax machine with a built-in paper cutter will normally cost at least $500 and often considerably more. For the same money, you can purchase a top-of-the-line fax modem. Most fax machines require expensive paper. Faxes received by a fax modem, on the other hand, can be printed by your laser or dot-matrix printer using ordinary paper. Plain-paper printing is an expensive option offered by few fax machines. Most fax modems can even eliminate paper costs. Because fax modem software normally allows you to view received faxes onscreen, most faxes do not need to be printed at all! And since the faxes can be saved on disk, they can be viewed any time you like.

Fax modems have several other important advantages. Fax machines are normally located in a remote corner of the office. Although you may be able to hear when a fax is received, you have to leave your desk to see if the fax is for you. Fax modems can display a message or a flashing icon on the screen to let you know that a fax has arrived. And on a personal fax modem, there's no need to guess who the fax is for—it's for you!

Hand writing a cover sheet to be used by your fax machine takes time. All the information for a fax modem cover sheet can be stored in a fax directory. Adding a cover sheet to a fax seldom takes more than a button click or two.

The ability to send the same fax to several individuals is built into most fax programs and each fax can be accompanied by a personalized cover page. Trying to accomplish this on a standard fax machine would require that you create a cover page for each recipient and—unless the machine has a memory feature—you will have to feed each set of documents through again for every recipient.

For individuals who spend much of their day in front of a computer, a fax modem makes good sense. Since your documents are, for the most part, already in your Mac as data files, you can send them without leaving your desk and without having to make a printed copy first.

Dealing with external documents (signed contracts, for instance) can be difficult, however. To get them into the Mac for faxing, you must have a scanner as part of your system. If you already have a scanner, you're in business. If not and you need to regularly fax external documents, you'll find that adding a full-page scanner to your set-up is considerably more expensive than just buying a standard fax machine.

Internal versus External

Like hard disk drives, fax modems come in two basic varieties: internal and external. If you own a Macintosh with one or more NuBus card slots or Processor Direct Slots–the SE/30, II series, LC, or Quadra—you can purchase an internal fax modem on a card. PowerBooks also provide a connector for an internal fax modem. All Macintoshes, on the other hand, support external fax modems (normally connected to the modem port).

> **NOTE:** Unlike data modems, there is less interchangeability between PC and Mac fax modems. Internal models designed to work in a PC slot cannot be used in a Macintosh and vice versa. External fax modems, however, can be used with either a Mac or a PC—assuming that the modem manufacturer can provide the required fax software and cable for both systems. Since there is no universal Macintosh fax software that will work with *all* fax modems, the modem manufacturer is the best (and, perhaps, only) source of compatible fax software for a fax modem.

Which should you select: an internal or an external fax modem? If you have an early Macintosh (a Mac Plus, for example), the decision has been made for you. If the Mac does not contain one or more NuBus slots or a receptacle for an internal modem (the Mac Plus has neither), you will only be able to use an external fax modem. Otherwise, you can use either an external or internal model. The following table (Figure 11.2) lists the advantages of each type of fax modem:

Advantages	Internal Fax Modem	External Fax Modem
Does not require its own power supply	√	
Requires no extra desk space	√	
Less expensive		√
Separate power switch		√
Mode LEDs or display panel		√
Can be used with either Macs or PCs		√

Figure 11.2: Advantages of internal and external fax modems.

Installation can be problematic for internal fax modems. Unless your Macintosh has easily accessible NuBus slots (as in a Mac II, for instance), self-installing an internal fax modem may void the Mac's warranty. To preserve the warranty, it may be necessary to pay an Apple-authorized dealer to perform the installation. As an example of an internal fax modem, Figure 11.3 shows a unit that plugs into the Macintosh LC's Processor Direct Slot (PDS).

Figure 11.3: The DataLink LC send/receive fax modem. Photo courtesy of Applied Engineering.

External fax modems, on the other hand, are easily installed by any user and have no impact on the Mac's warranty. Most external fax modems are connected with a 25-pin to DIN-8 serial cable, as shown in Figure 11.4.

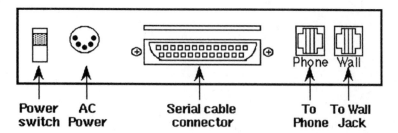

Figure 11.4: The back panel of a typical external fax modem.

It only takes a couple of minutes to hook up an external fax modem. The AC power outlet is connected to a provided AC adapter. The serial cable connector hooks to the 25-pin end of the serial cable, while the DIN-8 end of the cable plugs into the Mac's modem port. An RJ-11 phone jack is used to connect the unit to the telephone wall jack. A second jack is normally provided so that you can connect a telephone handset to the fax modem, if you want to. Internal units normally provide only the RJ-11 jacks. Some may also include one or more additional serial ports.

> **NOTE:** One new type of fax modem connects to the Mac's Apple Desktop Bus (ADB) port—the same port you normally use to connect your keyboard and mouse. Like an internal modem, it draws its power directly from the Mac.

When deciding between an internal and external fax modem, *where* you expect to use the fax modem can also make a difference. Although you can certainly carry along an external fax modem to use with your PowerBook, for instance, the convenience of an internal fax modem—particularly since it does not require a separate power supply—is undeniable. If your fax activity will generally be restricted to the office, on the other hand, either an internal or external model will do.

How a Fax Modem Works

Fax modem software generally includes several components: an INIT, a Chooser fax driver, and a fax program. The INIT or INIT/CDEV (Control Panel device) is responsible for the modem's ability to send and receive faxes in the background without interrupting your work. You use the program to view and print faxes, examine the fax log, and change the transmission times for scheduled faxes. Once selected, the Chooser fax driver reroutes all document Print... commands to the fax modem, sending documents over your phone line instead of to your printer. The following procedure is normally used to send a fax with a fax modem:

(1) Create or load the document you wish to fax into your word processing, database, spreadsheet, desktop publishing, or other program.

(2) Select the Chooser desk accessory from the Apple menu and select the fax driver that was included with the fax modem software (see Figure 11.5).

(3) Select the Page Setup... command to set the page dimensions for the fax.

(4) Select the Print... command. A fax file is created from the current document.

The Print... command is responsible for converting the current document to fax format. Depending on the fax software, you may also be able to specify a recipient for the fax, a transmission time, and transmit it in the same step. Once a document has been converted to fax format, the fax modem then takes over changing the digital data to analog so that it can be transmitted over the phone line.

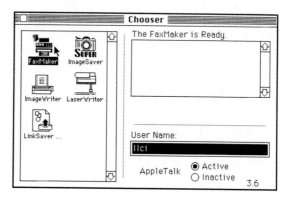

Figure 11.5: The FaxMaker Chooser driver is part of the Abaton 24/96 InterFax software. Selecting it reroutes the output from all Print... commands to the fax modem.

Receiving a fax is usually done without user intervention. If the fax modem is on when the call comes in, it will pick up the line after a predetermined number of rings. If it hears a CNG fax tone, the fax modem will negotiate a data transmission speed, receive the fax and store it on disk, and then hang up the phone line—all without interrupting your work. Most fax software also provides one or more ways that you can be notified of a received fax, such as flashing the Apple menu icon or displaying an alert box.

 # Choosing a Fax Modem

As with data modems, selecting a fax modem can be confusing. Once you have decided whether you want an internal or external fax modem, there are an array of features to consider—some essential and some that you can probably ignore. Depending upon the manufacturer, some fax modem features are provided in software, some in hardware (as well as some available as add-ons), and some not at all. The features you should be willing to pay for will depend on their usefulness to you, the additional cost, and your needs.

Hardware Features

Power Switch

The quickest and surest way to reset a fax modem that refuses to hang up or is having some other problem is to turn it off and back on again. Similarly, if you find that you are mistakenly blasting someone in the ear, you can use the power switch to turn off the fax modem and have a normal conversation. Obviously, having a power switch is a definite plus. Fax modems that draw power directly from the Mac (internal and ADB models) will not have a separate power switch. To completely reset them, it may be necessary to shut down the Mac and cut *its* power. The following is a list of hardware features and options you should know about.

Speaker

Most fax modems—both internal and external, either have a built-in speaker or can use the Mac's speaker. Regardless of how efficient and informative the fax software may be, the speaker will immediately let you know about trouble on the line. For instance, when trying to transmit a fax and a person answers the line, you'll be able to hear the problem. By listening to the transmission, you will also learn to identify when the fax was not properly received or when one of the faxes abruptly hung up.

A fax data stream is not the most pleasant sound you'll ever hear. (It sounds a lot like radio or television static.) In a business office, a speaker—particularly a loud one—can be a liability. The best units provide a way to adjust the speaker's volume, usually through the fax software. Although not essential, a built-in speaker or the capability to use the Mac's speaker to monitor transmissions is extremely helpful.

Indicator Lights and LEDs

One advantage that external fax modems generally have over internal models is the presence of a lighted display panel that shows the modem's current state. The lights are very useful for trouble-shooting. Depending on the lights or indicators provided, you may be able to determine whether the modem is in data or fax mode, the speed of the current transmission, when a connection has been lost, and when the modem is in "off-hook" mode.

As with data modems, the lights and indicators have varying degrees of usefulness, depending on their number and visibility. Some fax modems have just one or two lights, showing only whether the unit is in fax or data mode. Other fax modems—because they combine fax and data indicators on the same display panel—may present a row of tiny indicator labels that you will not be able to read unless your face is within six inches of the modem. Some of the newest units provide an LED display that spells out the current mode and transmission speed in the same way that numerals are displayed on digital watches. It's worth a bit more to have a fax modem with visible, clearly labeled, informative indicators.

Pass-through Port and Extra Serial Ports

Early fax modems often had no data communications capabilities. Since they were normally connected to the Mac's modem or printer port, the user had to buy a serial T-switch if he or she also had a data modem. Smart manufacturers sometimes added a pass-through port on the fax modem that allowed users to connect a second serial device to the unit. Since virtually all fax modems now provide data communications functions, few fax modems now include pass-through ports. However, if you have additional serial devices, you may find it more convenient to look for a fax modem with this feature.

Internal fax modems are normally treated by software as though they are connected to the external modem port, although they are actually inserted into a NuBus or another internal slot. So that you don't lose access to the external modem port, some internal fax modems contain one or more extra serial ports. They provide software that allows you to switch between the ports, to switch between the fax modem card and the external serial port, or to use the different ports simultaneously. The technique of pretending that the card is actually connected to the external port (so that your communications program, for example, is able to recognize the existence of the modem) is commonly referred to as *shadowing*.

If your serial devices will be limited to a printer and the fax modem, the presence of a pass-through port or extra serial ports may not be worth the premium that is charged for them. If you have an extra serial device or two that you use only occasionally, a 2- or 4-position switch box can be purchased inexpensively.

Fax/Modem Switching

In the better fax modems, switching between fax and data mode is done transparently; that is, without user intervention. Whether sending or receiving, an intelligent fax modem should be able to tell whether it is handling normal data or a fax transmission and adjust itself accordingly. Less intelligent fax modems require the user to specify the type of transmission that is occurring by pressing a button or flipping a switch on the fax modem, or by selecting an option in the fax software. Anything less than automatic data/fax switching is, at best, annoying. At worst, it can lead to lost data and botched communications sessions.

Voice/Fax Switching for Incoming Calls

Unlike fax/data switching, automatic switching between voice and fax modes is currently handled by only a small number of fax modems. Those units that provide voice/fax switching typically have firmware that can identify an incoming fax tone at the start of a call. If the tone is detected, an answering tone is sent to the other unit and the fax transmission proceeds normally. If a fax tone is not detected within a certain period of time, the fax modem assumes that it is a voice call and routes it to an attached telephone handset. If you don't want to dedicate a separate phone line to the fax modem, voice/fax switching is an excellent feature to have.

If the fax modem does not provide fax/voice switching (only a few currently do), an external phone line manager can provide the same function for an extra $100-$200. For additional information, see the discussion of "Phone Line Managers" at the end of this chapter.

Auto Wake-Up

Since there is no way to predict when incoming faxes will arrive, fax machines are frequently left on 24 hours a day. Unless you always leave your Mac and its fax modem on, you can miss faxes. Some fax modems now include an auto wake-up feature. Auto wake-up allows the Mac to be booted automatically on detecting an incoming fax. After receiving the fax, the fax software turns off the Mac after a specific number of minutes or after so many minutes have passed without modem port activity.

Auto wake-up can only turn on your Mac, not external peripherals. For example, if you have an external hard disk, it must be left on at all times if you want the newly awoken Mac to use it. Also, if your system has many INITs, the wake-up period may be too long to catch the fax on the first try. Luckily, most fax machines and fax modems are programmed to retry a number several times, so auto wake-up will almost always receive the fax on subsequent attempts.

Voice Mail

A few of the newest fax modems can take on the role of an office message center by combining voice/fax switching with answering machine capabilities. If no fax is detected and the intended recipient is unavailable, the caller is given the option of leaving a brief message that is recorded on the Mac's hard disk. For many users, this combination of features will be the all-in-one solution for which they have been waiting. An external voice/fax switching device coupled with an answering machine can provide similar capabilities for individual users.

Send-Only versus Send/Receive

Not all fax modems can send and receive faxes. Some are "send-only"—they can send faxes but are not equipped to receive them. Send-only fax modems have a couple of small advantages for some users. First, they are often slightly less expensive than units that can both send and receive. Second, if you do not need the capability to receive faxes, a send-only unit eliminates the necessity of having a dedicated fax line. Since only out-going faxes will be transmitted, you do not have to worry about switching between voice and fax modes when receiving incoming calls.

Most users, however, will be better off paying a little more for a send/receive unit. Unless you also have a dedicated fax machine, the added convenience of being able to receive faxes—even if only occasionally, and view them onscreen will quickly make up the relatively small difference in price.

Data Transfer Rates

Although Group 3 fax machines are designed to send and receive at a maximum speed of 9600 bps, fax modems are offered in a number of configurations. You may be able to save some money by buying a fax modem that sends at the normal 9600 bps but receives at a slower speed, such as 4800 bps. (The difference in receive speed will be reflected on the phone bills of the people that send you the faxes, rather than on your bill.)

Some fax modems can send at a maximum speed of only 4800 bps. If you intend to send faxes infrequently, you can save money by purchasing this type of fax modem. If your long-distance fax activities increase, however, the additional money spent on a 9600 bps fax modem will quickly be offset by reduced phone charges.

Fall-Back Rates

When a fax session is initiated, most fax modems are able to negotiate a common fax transfer rate based on the highest common shared speed of the two units. Suppose, for instance, that you are attempting to send a fax to a fax modem that can only receive at a maximum of 4800 bps. After the machines connect, they send tones to each other that indicate their supported speeds. Data transfer rates that are less than the fastest speeds supported by each unit are known as *fall-back rates*.

If telephone line conditions are less than optimal, fall-back rates also come into play. Fax modems can communicate at slower speeds to assure both compatibility and relatively error-free transmissions. It is not uncommon for fax modems to support fall-back rates in 2400 bps increments. Starting at 9600 bps, the two units will continue to drop their rates in 2400 bps increments until a common rate is found and the line conditions are taken into account.

Although it would be unusual for a modem to not offer fall-back support, it's worth checking rather than assuming that your unit provides this feature. If it doesn't, any connection at less than the highest supported speed will be aborted.

Software Features

After you have determined which hardware features are essential, you'll find that the biggest difference in fax modems is in the software: in the features list, ease of use, and quality. At present, there is no such thing as universal fax software for the Macintosh—a fax program that is capable of controlling all or even most fax modems. For better or worse, you may be stuck with the fax software that comes with the fax modem. If features are missing or are poorly programmed, you'll have to make do with the software until—or if—the manufacturer offers a new version.

Your best source of information about fax software is the reviews you will find in magazines such as Macworld and MacUser; also users comments on the major information services, such as CompuServe, GEnie, and America Online. Advertisements will often list software features. Unfortunately, they will not tell you how easy or convenient the features are to use. The following is a list of some of the most important features for good fax software.

Background Send and Receive

Many of the early fax programs sent faxes entirely in the foreground. Any work that was being done was interrupted until the transmission ended. Now, most fax programs operate in the foreground only while converting the document into fax format—usually a brief process. Sending and receiving is normally done in the background. Note, however, that the speed of the fax conversion is dependent on the algorithm used in the software. Some programs are extremely fast and efficient, and some aren't.

Phone Directories

Good fax programs should allow you to create one or several directories of frequently-called fax numbers. The amount of information that can be entered for each fax number and the way in which the directory information is displayed can vary considerably. For example, some fax programs do not alphabetize their directories making it extremely difficult to find particular numbers. Others allow you to enter a recipient's name or company, but not both. For easier use, the manner in which the directory feature is implemented can make using the fax software a pleasure or a constant annoyance.

Distribution Lists and Group Transmissions

A distribution list feature allows you to categorize fax recipients by something they have in common. If you occasionally need to fax the same material to each one of your company's sales representatives, for example, this feature is invaluable. To be useful, however, the fax software must also support an automatic cover page feature so that each fax can be personally addressed. Sending one document to several people is referred to as a group transmission.

Cover Page

Good fax programs will either provide graphic cover pages or allow you to design your own. Once a recipient for the fax has been selected from the fax directory, the cover page details (date, recipient's name and fax number, number of pages, and so on) are automatically filled in for you.

If your fax modem software omits this feature, you will have to create your own cover page in a word processing or graphics program). Type in the recipient information manually for each fax, and then attach it to the other documents that make up the body of the fax.

"Quick" Fax

Some people consider cover pages (for anything other than a group transmission) a waste of paper and transmission time. A "quick fax" option lets you combine the cover page and a brief fax message on the same page. Since many faxes are short, the quick fax option can readily be used for the majority of faxes. To make it even quicker, the quick fax option is often implemented as a desk accessory or some other type of pop-up program, so you don't have to interrupt work in progress.

Page Setup Options

In addition to standard paper size options (letter, legal, and A4), better programs will allow you to specify an exact page length or they provide a feature that automatically trims pages to length. This avoids paper waste on the receiving fax machine and also shortens transmission time by not sending white space at the end of the page. Being able to specify a custom page length is often useful. A wide spreadsheet, for example, is easier to handle when printed continuously, rather than having it broken into letter-sized sections.

At a minimum, most fax programs provide two Page Setup... quality settings: standard (200 x 100 dots per inch) and fine (200 x 200 dots per inch). Other options may also be provided, such as an exact size setting (useful for engineering drawings).

One particularly helpful option is to have the program automatically delete the fax document after it has been successfully transmitted. Although you can keep faxes on disk indefinitely, since they are graphics they can take up large chunks of disk space. A single-page text-only fax can require between 40 and 60K of space, for example.

Auto-Redial

Like most fax machines, fax modems are usually able to retry a connection several times (in case of a busy signal or an error in transmission). The best software will let you specify the number of retries, as well as the interval between retries. In the case of an aborted transmission, most fax programs will re-send the entire fax. Better programs will keep track of the pages that have been successfully sent and will pick up from that point on successive retries.

Delayed Transmissions

One advantage of fax modems over fax machines is that you can specify a particular time to send the fax rather than immediately. Since most companies leave their fax machines on 24 hours a day, you can use the delayed transmission feature to send faxes after 11 PM when long-distance rates are reduced.

Polling

At the end of a transmission, polling allows your fax modem to check the other fax machine or modem for faxes that are waiting for you. If there are any, they can be transmitted in the same call. This feature is most useful for communicating between branch offices of a company—where there is a greater likelihood of having faxes that need to move in both directions. The polled machine may require you to transmit a security code to identify yourself; if the program supports polling it should also provide a means for you to enter a security code. For most users polling is seldom used or needed.

Fax Log

Like a good fax machine, fax software normally maintains a log of all outgoing faxes (see Figure 11.6). The amount of detail in the log varies considerably from one program to the next. Ideally, the log should show the date, time, duration of each call, the recipient's name and/or company, and the names of the documents that were faxed. Better programs will keep a log of received faxes as well.

Fax Viewer

To save paper, most fax programs provide a fax viewer option that allows you to examine incoming and outgoing faxes on your Macintosh's screen. Better programs will let you examine the fax pages at a number of magnifications and rotations (useful for viewing fax pages that are transmitted upside down). Although a full-size viewer should be considered mandatory for viewing incoming faxes and checking outgoing ones for conversion problems, some programs only show faxes in "thumbnail" view; a tiny representation of each page that is too small to enable you to examine the actual text of the document.

Date	Time	Fax Machine	p.	Elaps.	Document
2/1/92	2:57 PM	Crosby!	1	0'25"	FAX Untitled
2/1/92	11:08 AM	Crosby!	1	0'42"	FAX Untitled
1/30/92	6:17 PM	Apple Computer	1	0'26"	FAX Untitled
1/30/92	6:15 PM	Goldstein & Blair	1	0'33"	FAX Goldstein
1/29/92	8:43 AM	Synex	1	0'31"	FAX Untitled2
1/29/92	8:32 AM	JVC Musical Industries	1	0'25"	FAX Untitled
1/26/92	2:35 PM	Prudential (Claims)	1	0'34"	FAX Untitled
1/26/92	2:18 PM	Macworld	1	0'25"	FAX Untitled2-QL Fax temp...
1/23/92	8:43 PM	Crosby!	3	2'06"	FAX Comparison for sales f...
1/23/92	8:13 PM	Funk Software-General	1	0'22"	FAX Untitled2-QL Fax temp...
1/22/92	9:11 PM	Crosby!	1	0'39"	FAX Fax Template
1/22/92	8:31 PM	Crosby!	1	0'39"	FAX Untitled
1/21/92	5:05 PM	Microcom	1	0'26"	FAX Untitled2
1/21/92	3:11 PM	Triffix Entertainment Inc.	1	0'58"	FAX Untitled

Table title: Delivered Mail

Figure 11.6: The Abaton InterFax Delivered Mail log shows the date, time, recipient, pages, connect time, and the document name for each transmitted fax.

Scanner Support

Using a scanner is the only way to get external documents into the Mac without retyping them. A few fax programs can directly control a scanner and then convert the resulting scan into a fax document. Although not a critical feature for most users, it eliminates the need to run two programs to create a fax based on a scanned image.

Document Conversion Options

For convenience, some fax programs provide conversion options that enable you to take existing documents and convert them to fax format without using the originating program's Print... routine. Perhaps more important, however, is the capability to convert received faxes into one or more graphic formats. After changing the fax to a graphic, you can open and edit the fax in your graphics program.

Special Triple-Sized Fonts

When fax modems were first introduced, it was commonplace for manufacturers to include a copy of the ImageWriter LQ screen fonts. Restricting text to the LQ fonts assured highly legible faxes. Few manufacturers currently provide special fonts with their fax modems. Other solutions are discussed below (see "Fonts Make the Fax").

Fonts Make the Fax

A fax is just a graphic composed of tiny dots. There are no fonts. Letters, numbers, and other characters are simply collections of dots. When a standard fax machine creates a fax, it does so by scanning the document and converting each page into a graphic image. The legibility of the fonts in the fax depend on the fax machine's scanning capabilities, how smoothly the document fed through the fax machine, and the clarity of the text in the original document.

Fax modems, on the other hand, do not scan documents before converting them to graphics. Faxes sent through a fax modem are based on the screen resolution of the document rather than on a scanned image of the document. The standard screen resolution of a Macintosh is 72 dpi (dots per inch). The resolution of Group 3 fax machines is 200 dpi—slightly less than three times the resolution of the Macintosh screen. To achieve fax resolution, the fax modem software—using Apple's QuickDraw routines in the system software—triples the resolution of the image onscreen and then compresses it to achieve fax resolution.

Fonts also are handled in this process. As with graphics, font reproduction is based on what appears onscreen. When converting screen fonts to fax material, the system software looks for a screen font that is precisely three times the size of the original font. The triple-sized font image is then compressed to one-third its original size, sent to the receiving fax station, and printed at three times its original screen density.

There are three ways that you can assure yourself of having attractive text in your faxes. You must restrict your font choices to fonts for which you either have:

- triple-sized screen fonts.
- TrueType fonts (included with System 7).
- PostScript printer outline fonts and Adobe Type Manager (ATM).

For example, to accurately reproduce Times 12 pt. text in a fax, you must either format the text by selecting the Times TrueType font, be running ATM, and have the Times printer outline font installed in your System folder, or have a Times 36 pt. screen font installed in the System file. Because they are based on outlines, ATM PostScript fonts and TrueType fonts are infinitely scalable. As such, all sizes of these fonts will look excellent in fax output.

Fonts that do not meet one of these criteria will be created by taking the existing screen font for the text, scaling it up by tripling it, and then compressing it (see

Figure 11.7). Those fonts will appear jagged and may exhibit problems with between-letter and between-word spacing. The worst problems typically result from mixing different fonts or a variety of styles (normal, bold, and italic, for instance) in the same line of text.

Sample
Sample

Figure 11.7: Faxed versions of two similar 72-pt. serif fonts: Times and Adobe Garamond. The clean Times on top is a TrueType font. The Adobe Garamond rendition is based on scaling a bit-mapped font without an installed triple-sized System font and without Adobe Type Manager.

For new faxes that you create, this should pose little problem. Just restrict the text of your documents to fonts that meet one of the three criteria. Faxing an older document will require you to change the fonts or to "make do." If you want to see how the output will look on the receiving fax, most fax programs have a fax viewer that enables you to examine faxes onscreen. Select the fax Chooser device and create the fax as usual, but do not send it. Then run the fax program and look at the fax.

When Macintosh fax modems were first introduced, most included a set of triple-sized letter-quality fonts for Times and Helvetica. Now, however, most fax modems ship without special screen fonts. These fonts are not normally available for purchase through independent font vendors. To get the best text reproduction, you should either plan to upgrade your Mac to System 7 (so TrueType fonts can be used) or buy a copy of ATM and the PostScript outline fonts that you will need.

Other Considerations

Just like other devices you can buy for the office or home, fax modems—even those with identical feature lists—are not equal. They may differ in several important ways:

- Quality of fax output: Depending on the complexity of the document, line thicknesses, and the accuracy of the algorithm used to convert documents to faxes, some faxes may contain graphics with missing lines. Sentences can occasionally overprint each other. Even with these potential problems, the quality of faxes generated by a fax modem is often superior to that of faxes generated by a fax machine.

- Throughput/transmission speed: When is 9600 bps not 9600 bps? Some fax software and hardware is more efficient in compressing the fax data and assuring error-free transmissions. Depending on the software/hardware combination, it can take as little as 30 seconds or as long as several minutes to fax the same document from different fax modems.

- Tolerance for line noise: When line noise increases above a particular level, a fax modem will fall back to a lower transmission speed. The amount of line noise required for this fall-back to occur can differ from one fax modem to the next.

New and Innovative

The standard 9600 bps fax modem/2400 bps data modem and provided software isn't for everyone. Some situations call for creative solutions, such as the following.

Faxing Over a Network

Network administrators face a unique problem. Although sending and receiving faxes and data may involve many people in the company, it can be expensive and inconvenient to provide everyone with fax modems and separate phone lines. A better solution is to share a fax modem among network users—in the same way that other network resources, such as laser printers, are shared.

Software makes this possible. Fax Gate is a software package that allows network users to send and receive faxes over a single fax modem and phone line. The Fax Gate software is integrated with Microsoft Mail. Users can send faxes from their desk which will then be transmitted by Fax Gate through the shared fax modem. Incoming faxes are routed by the mail system back to the recipient's Mac.

As mentioned earlier, because of differences in fax modem chips, there is no universal Macintosh fax program. Fax Gate only works with BackFax-compatible modems, such as the now defunct AppleFax; fax modems from Orchid, Circuit Research, Relisys, and selected units from Prometheus. For other supported models, contact Delrina (the publisher of BackFax) and Microsoft (publisher of Fax Gate for Microsoft Mail).

ADB Fax Modems

Not all fax modems connect to the modem port or slip into an internal slot or connector. One of the newest types of fax modems connects to the ADB port. Like an internal fax modem, an ADB fax modem can draw its current from the Macintosh. With appropriate software and a wake up cable, the ADB fax modem can also be set to start up a Mac II series computer when a fax is received. The TelePort/FullFax from Global Village is an example of this type of fax modem.

High-Speed Fax Modems

Group 3 (9600 bps) is the current standard for fax machines and fax modems. As with data modems, computers, and hard disks, the trend is towards ever-faster fax modems. While maintaining downward compatibility with the slower Group 3 fax devices, some of the newest fax modems now offer speeds as high as 14,400 bps (CCITT v.17)—50 percent faster than current fax machines or modems!

One of the first high-speed fax modems for the Mac is the SupraFAXModem V.32bis, a combination 14,400 bps fax/14,400 bps data modem (see Figure 11.8). With the 4-to-1 data compression possible with CCITT V.42bis, the unit has a maximum potential data throughput (the effective transfer rate) of 57,600 bps.

Figure 11.8: The SupraFAXModem V.32bis. (Photo courtesy of Supra Corporation.)

The "down side" of these modems is that only "like" modems currently support speeds over 9600 bps. Fax transmissions to or from a normal fax machine will still occur at 9600 bps. If you equip your company's offices and branches with the same model of high-speed fax modem, you can produce significant savings in transmission times and telephone charges.

Since continual improvements in transmission speed has always been the trend, 14,400 bps is the likely trend of the future. However, you should be aware that transmissions faster than 9600 bps are pushing the limits of current analog phone lines. Faster, error-free transmissions require special cables and relatively clean phone lines.

Phone Line Managers

After purchasing a fax modem, many users will immediately encounter a significant practical problem—how can the fax modem be used on a phone line that also receives voice calls without causing enormous headaches? If you simply leave the fax modem on at all times, voice callers will be blasted with a fax tone whenever they call. If you normally leave it off (in deference to voice callers), you'll have to scramble to avoid missing incoming faxes. If the fax modem does not have voice/fax switching capabilities (few do), some possible solutions include:

- Adding a separate phone line for the fax modem.

- Using the fax modem for sending only.

- Instructing all potential callers to call ahead to arrange for a fax transmission.

- Answering each call manually and attempting to switch to fax mode before losing the call.

- Purchasing an external phone line manager device.

In general, most of us want incoming faxes and voice calls to be handled automatically. Unless you anticipate few incoming faxes, the need to manually arrange for each one quickly becomes a bother to both you and the people who wish to send faxes to you. A phone line manager, either built into the fax modem or as a separate external unit may be the best solution.

Prices for most phone line managers range between $100 and $200. Like fax modems, phone line managers vary widely in capabilities and the manner in which they work. Some units only support fax and voice switching; others add data modem support. A few Mac-specific units can also start-up your Mac, route the call to the fax modem, and then shut down again after detecting a fax tone. Virtually all phone line managers can include an answering machine in the configuration, either as a separately supported device or hooked in series with the telephone.

Ideally, a phone line manager should operate like an efficient receptionist. It should answer each call for you; determine whether it is a fax, data, or voice call; then transfer the call to the appropriate device. All this occurs without requiring you to fumble for switches, quickly open desk accessories or Control Panel devices, and without unduly inconveniencing or confusing the caller. Upon receiving a call, the two most popular approaches taken by phone line managers are as follows:

- Install a "dummy" ring that the caller hears. This gives the phone line manager time to listen for a fax tone. If the fax tone is not heard, the device rings your telephone so the call can be answered normally. (Very few callers will be fooled by the ring. It often sounds like a phone on a rural party line.)

- Insist that you or an answering machine answer every call. The phone line manager then listens in on the conversation. If a fax tone is heard, the device reroutes the call to the fax modem.

Some units also provide a special option for handling data and manual fax calls. They listen for an additional touch tone that results from pressing a particular number on a telephone handset (for example, 3 for a manual fax; 4 for data). If the tone is heard, the call is routed to the fax or data component of the fax modem. The disadvantage is that you must either tell all potential callers about the tone routine or have your answering machine respond to all calls and instruct callers at that time.

When shopping for a phone line manager, pay attention to the company's return policy. In the quest for a unit that meets your needs, one or more of the following stumbling blocks may be encountered:

- The device may have to be connected to the first line coming into the office or home. This would require some rewiring.

- The device may insist on being the only equipment on the line (no extensions allowed).

- Although virtually all phone line managers support a connected answering machine, not all answering machines may be supported. Ask for an exception list before ordering the device.

After examining several phone line managers, you may well decide that the best solution is the one that involves the least technology. Get a separate phone line and limit it to fax, data, and—optionally—outgoing voice calls. If you do not give out the number for incoming voice calls, you never have to worry about losing faxes or inconveniencing your customers, clients, or yourself.

Networking Technology

 ## Local Area Networks

Interest in Local Area Networks (LANs) is increasing rapidly. Many small to medium size businesses are using LANs in their daily operations because they are economical. Also, LANs help these organizations to become more competitive and productive. There are even environmental reasons for using LANs; just think of all the excessive amounts of paper that many companies waste by

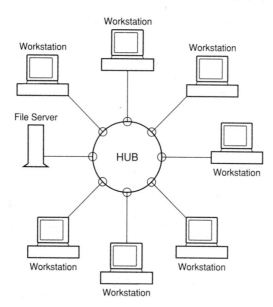

producing reports and memos. These companies range in size from small law firms, accounting and real estate offices, to major oil companies, giant telecommunications organizations, and multinational banks.

Advantages of Local Area Networks

- Reduction in excessive use of paper and paperwork.

- Easy Access to Shared Data.

- Elimination of duplication of data entry efforts.

- Lower Costs of Software products, i.e., word processors, spreadsheets, and database managers.

- Lower Costs of hardware products, i.e., less need for expensive individual work stations with expensive high capacity disk drives and printers.

- Increased user productivity through use of multi-user application software. This is especially true in word processing, project management, order entry, and accounting applications.

- Shared Resources. This refers to sharing expensive peripheral devices such as Faxes, modems, CD-ROMS, and laser printers.

- Better communications throughout the office through the use of Electronic Mail.

- Ease of Training. Applications could be developed with standard menus.

Typical Local Area Network Users

Basically, there are two very distinct classes of users who are interested in LANs. The most common category of Macintosh user is the small business user or departmental users. Some examples are businesses such as realtors, CPAs, law offices, wholesalers, distributors, drafting and engineering offices, or departments within small to very large corporations and government agencies. They are interested in linking their personal computers together because they can share software resources such as word processing, graphics, database, and spreadsheet packages. Additionally, they can share their data files and expensive resources, thereby reducing costs and improving productivity.

The other group of users are larger organizations that have suddenly discovered the benefits of the personal computers and networking over the traditional mainframe solutions. These users are trying to move their applications from expensive and cumbersome mainframes to the user friendly and inexpensive LAN environments. This type of activity is generally referred to as downsizing.

In this chapter we will address Local Area Networks in general, so that both classes of users could benefit from reading this chapter. I will use the terms Local Area Networks or LANs or Networks interchangeably throughout the rest of this chapter since all these terms are used by users to generally mean the same thing.

What Is a Local Area Network?

Basically a Local Area Network is a combination of two or more computers or workstations that are physically[1] and logically connected to each other. A network may contain as many as one thousand or more workstations or nodes. However, the average number of nodes on a small LAN is approximately six. The average number of workstations on most medium to larger networks is probably closer to 25 to 50. A node is basically a point on the network through which a device such as a workstation or a printer or fax or a file server is linked to the network. Networks can be interconnected to other networks in other parts of a building or other parts of the country. This is known as Wide Area Networking or WAN (see Figure 12.2). This is usually accomplished through public telecommunication lines such as telephone company lines, satellites, microwave, and fiber optics transmissions. Bulletin Board Systems (BBS) or information-services providers such as CompuServe or America Online could be considered as operating under wide area networks. Finally, networks can be connected to mainframe computers through a Gateway (see Figure 12.1). A Gateway is basically another computer or any processor that allows access for data and programs between mainframe computers and workstations or between different networks with different operating systems.

NOTE: An Apple Macintosh network is somewhat different from other (i.e., IBM PC) networks. As a general rule, you will have wider selection of software and hardware vendors to chose from when you use IBM compatible PCs for networking. However, a basic Macintosh network is much easier to install and use.

[1] *Obviously, in case of a wireless LAN, the computers are not physically connected to each other.*

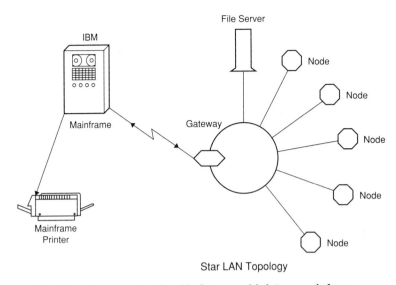

Star LAN Topology

Figure 12.1: Local area network with Gateway Link to a mainframe.

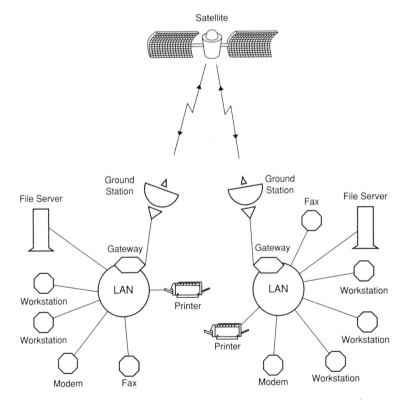

Figure 12.2: Wide area network connecting two local area networks.

The Lay of the LAN

There are several types of LAN cabling systems. The physical layout of a LAN is called its topology. Topology refers to the way nodes, i.e., workstations, printers, file servers, and other devices are connected to each other. There are really two types of topologies. One is the actual physical connection between the various workstations and the file server. The other is the way data flows between workstations, which is really the Protocol. This will become clearer as we go along. It is not really necessary to know the details of LAN topologies to be able to use them or even function as a LAN administrator. However, it could be helpful to understand the differences to be able to make meaningful business decisions about acquiring a network. Also, it will help you converse on an equal footing with your LAN vendors and consultants. The three main Macintosh topologies are as follows.

The Daisy Chain Connection

This is the simplest Macintosh networking method. All you need is a cable (LocalTalk cable) with eight pin connector plugs at both ends (The connector is called a DIN-8). One end of the cable is attached to the printer port on one Macintosh while the other end may be attached to another Macintosh or a LaserWriter printer. In fact, most LaserWriter printers have a Macintosh processor inside. The new Apple LaserWriter NTR does not use one of the Motorola 68000 series processors; it uses the AMD 29005 processor.

You can extend the network by hooking up additional Macs or printers to the end of the LocalTalk cable connection. This system is very cheap and extremely easy to set up. There are several drawbacks to this kind of connection. One is that the data transfer rate between the units on the network is limited to 230,400 bits per second (230 Kilo Bits per second or 230 Kbps) which roughly translates to about 28,000 characters per second. While this may sound like a huge amount of data, in reality as networks go, it is very slow.

The other reason is that 230 Kilo Bits per second is the rated speed of the network under optimum conditions. There are always overheads associated with transfer of data. A good analogy is the advertised horse power of a car. It is almost impossible to achieve the factory-stated horsepower of a car under normal driving conditions. If there is other traffic on the network, any given station may have to wait its turn before sending a packet of data to its destination, see later discussion on CSMA/CD. The other disadvantage of this network is the limitation to the number of nodes that you could attach to a network.

Finally, there is a limit to the distance of nodes from each other. As a signal travels along the Apple LocalTalk cable, it will get weaker the further it gets from its source. After a few hundred feet, the data may become unintelligible to the receiving node. Farallon's standard PhoneNET is advertised with a maximum capacity of 24 nodes per daisy chain network. The fact that the AppleTalk is in reality a Peer-to-Peer network and LocalTalk hardware/software connecting the Macs has an optimum speed of 28,000 characters per second, should weigh your decision in limiting the number of active users in an office to around ten to twelve. Other topologies and protocols allow you to link many more, in fact hundreds, of Macs together, at a price. While daisy chain is an effective and very inexpensive mode of establishing a working network, it should not be considered for large offices or where there is a lot of CAD/CAM or desktop publishing activity. The final drawback has to do with network integrity. In a daisy chain topology, if one node or workstation is disconnected, the rest of the network may also go down until that node is reconnected.

The Daisy Chain network can be enhanced by using third party add-on products. For example, Farallon Company Inc. markets a connector that allows the users to link Macs and other peripherals with standard telephone wires (also known as unshielded twisted pair cable or UTP) instead of the LocalTalk cable.

Back Bone Topology

This is also known as the bus topology (see Figure 12.3). Under this topology all workstations and other devices such as printers are connected to a central bus (i.e., a data Cable). Data is sent from station to station, and if one station goes down, the rest of the nodes on the network are not affected.

The bus topology is one of the most common forms of LAN connection. It is also used extensively to connect various networks in large or multi story buildings together. Basically, a long coaxial cable acts as a data passageway or a bus. The file server, workstations and other devices such as printers, communications servers, modems and faxes are attached to it at different locations. Data travels to and from the workstations through the cable. The travel rate of data, over regular coax copper wire cables, can range from less than a million bits of data per second (MBPS) to sixteen million bits of data per second. You could achieve 100 MBPS over fiber optics lines. Currently network hardware manufacturers are trying to establish standards for 100 MBPS data transfer over copper wire.

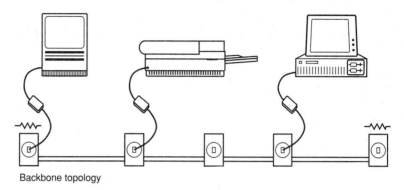

Backbone topology

Figure 12.3: A simple backbone topology.

The Star Topology

This, in concept, is the oldest topology in existence. It is patterned after the telephone company's wiring closet concept. All telephone lines in a typical office building are usually routed to a central wiring closet through which all internal and external connections are made. This concept offers the greatest flexibility in networking. The Star topology has several advantages. One is that since all workstations or nodes are connected to a central hub, there is no danger of the whole network going down if one line is broken (see Figure 12.4). The other advantage is that nodes can be added, deleted, or moved around without the necessity of bringing the system down.

Another advantage is that trouble shooting of the network is simplified since all lines end in the closet. Also, adding new phone lines is much easier. You can add lines without disconnecting any other phone connection. Finally, you can connect your network to the outside world or other floors through this central closet. So instead of hundreds of telephone lines going outside, you will have only a few lines between various networks and the outside world. The standard telephone wire used for most voice communication is a twisted pair copper cable. There are usually four actual lines in a twisted pair cable. Only two of these lines are used. The other two could be used to carry data between various nodes of the network. Alternatively, you may use brand new dedicated twisted pair cables for networking. Some newer buildings are, in fact, prewired for networking using the star topology concept. The star topology comes in two flavors: Passive Star and Active Star.

Passive Star

In this type of topology, all nodes are connected to a central hub or a punchdown block (see Figure 12.5). Traffic flows from the networks to the central hub and then is routed to other computers or a printer. The central hub is usually a punchdown block which acts as a rerouting center for the network traffic. This topology has more integrity than the daisy chain topology. Loss of a node will not render the network useless. Also, you can use either twisted pair or coaxial cables to connect the nodes to the central hub. There are two disadvantages in this type of network. You are limited to a relatively few nodes on each hub and there is a limit to the distance that signals can travel to other nodes. In a typical passive star network you can have up to four network branches (see figure 12.6). Each branch can have one or more devices attached to it.

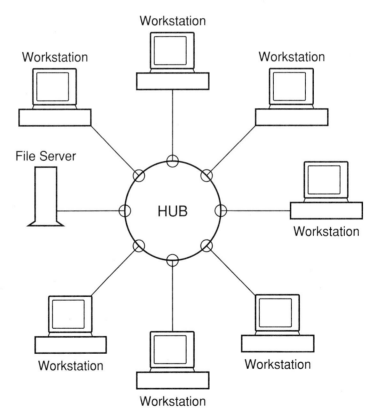

Figure 12.4: Basic Star Topology.

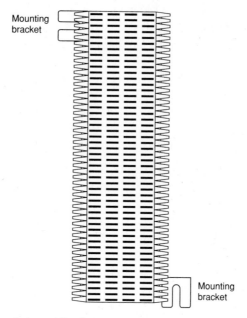

Mounting bracket

Mounting bracket

Figure 12.5: A Punchdown Block.

Active Star

This is similar to the passive star topology except that an electrical active hub or controller is placed at the center of the hub (see Figure 12.8). All the nodes terminate at this unit which can then amplify the signals and send them over to their destination. With an active hub you can increase the distance of nodes from each other as well as increase the number of nodes on the network. A typical Macintosh active star controller costs about $1,400. A typical active star controller can support up to 3,000 feet of cabling and four network branches (see Figure 12.7).

Token Ring

This is a relatively new concept. It is needed if a Mac has to be connected to an IBM mainframe. Token ring is the combination of the ring topology, where data is passed from node to node until it gets to its final destination, and the token passing method of data transfer. Token ring can handle either 4 or 16 million bits of data per second. Again that is the optimum speed. In this case your Macs and printers may not be able to cope with that kind of speed anyway.

In any case, Token Ring is a very expensive combination of hardware and software. With some planning you can achieve the same through-put with a star network and EtherNet network interface cards.

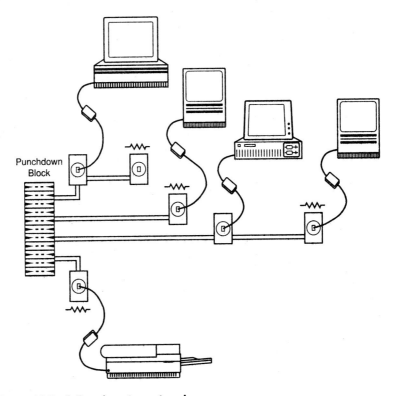

Figure 12.6: A Passive star network.

Hybrid Topologies

This is a combination of several topologies as part of a network. For example, in a large multi-story building, you could have a central bus running the length of the building. At each floor different types of networks with different topologies and/or operating systems could be attached to this main bus or backbone (see Figure 12.9).

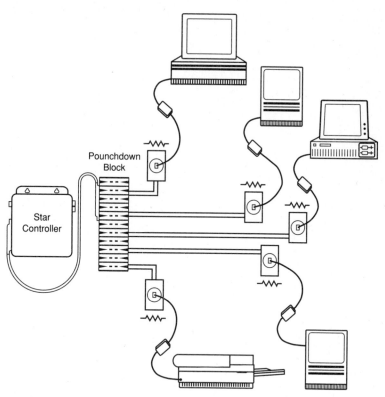

Pounchdown
Block

Star
Controller

Figure 12.7: An Active Star Network.

PhoneNET
StarController

Figure 12.8: A Star Controller.

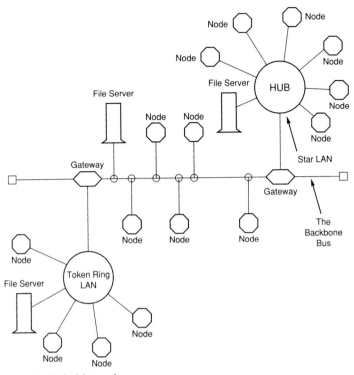

Figure 12.9: Hybrid topology.

 A Few Words about the Software

So far, we have discussed the hardware. The LAN operating system or system software plays a major role also. The LAN operating system is responsible for redirecting commands and accessing files in volumes and folders.

There are two basic types of LAN software: Client/Server operating system and Peer-To-Peer or distributed LAN. The client server consists of two logical parts: a file server, and workstations (clients). In a Peer-to-Peer network, each workstation can be a file server as well as a client.

 Hardware and Software Consideration and Selection

Before you attempt to decide on computer equipment such as network cards, cabling, the processor type, and the network operating system, you should define your business requirements first. In other words, review your needs or requirements and ask the following questions.

Making the Right Selection

(1) What am I trying to accomplish? For example, are we working in an office where everybody is trying to access a single laser printer? Are we trying to share information via electronic mail? Do we have to send a great number of faxes every day and want to avoid time consuming trips to the fax room? A yes answer to any one of these questions may justify the investment of funds for setting up a local area network.

(2) What other solutions are available to me? For example, if people only need to use the laser printer occasionally during the day, an alternative approach to a local area network would be to store the document that needs to be printed on a diskette, take the diskette to a Macintosh that is attached to the laser printer, and print the document through that computer. This approach which is also known as "Sneaker Net" or "Walk Net" is less expensive if the volume is low. However, it does not always work. For example, if people in an office use different types of word processors, you would have to convert your files to a common format before attempting to print it at a machine that uses a different word processor than yours. In many corporate offices, people are given the choice of ordering their favorite brands of word processors, database management systems, graphics packages, and other business applications software. Unfortunately most of these packages are incompatible with each other. In these cases a LAN would be the best answer for sharing printers and plotters because the conversion is handled by the LAN operating system.

(3) Another solution worth considering may be the purchase of a multi-user operating system. This will be less expensive than purchasing the LAN equipment and software but small multi-user computers are very limited in their growth capabilities. Also, you may need expert assistance with your applications at some point and there is little expertise in multi-user systems in the market place.

(4) Other options to consider are linking to an existing minicomputer or joining a time sharing service.

Components of a LAN

A LAN basically consists of the following parts:

(1) A dedicated File Server or a workstation which is also a File Server.

(2) The Network Interface hardware. This is usually the LocalTalk hardware that is built into each Macintosh. This interface is responsible for directing the flow of communication between the workstations and other devices such as a LaserWriter printer and the file server. You can increase the data transfer speed on a network by attaching other network interface cards such as EtherNet boards to your Macs.

(3) The cabling system linking the nodes to each other.

(4) The Workstations.

(5) The Network Operating System.

(6) The network shell programs. These are usually NetWare for Macintosh by Novell or AppleTalk by Apple. These programs are responsible for redirecting the network related commands and requests to the network operating system.

What Type of LAN Do You Need?

Unfortunately, there is no single LAN standard that we could adopt. There are many different types of LAN hardware and software around and they each have their particular market niche. The real power behind the LAN is in the network operating system. The main players in this field are Apple Computer with AppleTalk, Novell with NetWare for Macintosh, and Sitka's TOPS.

When choosing a LAN, you or your networking consultant are really choosing a particular operating system that you feel will match your requirements. Having made that selection you will need to make a choice about the cabling system or, as is commonly called, the topology of the network. Topology refers to the physical layout and connection of cables between workstations and file servers. The next step is choosing the actual type of cable that you will use in your system. Finally, if you decide against using Apple's LocalTalk hardware, you will need to buy special add-on EtherNet boards. You can attach these boards to your SCSI interface port at the back of your Mac. There may also be a need for intermediate interconnecting devices to boost the signal or route the traffic. These devices are known as bridges, routers, and repeaters.

The Two Basic Network Concepts

Every Macintosh comes equipped with the LocalTalk networking hardware. This allows AppleTalk to run on the network. LocalTalk can transfer data between workstations and the file server at 230.4 Kbps (230,400 bits per second is equal to approximately to 28,000 characters per second). This speed is quite adequate if there are only a few Macintoshes networked to each other. Sitka offers *Flash Card* which has a speed of 780 Kilo Bits per second. This is better, but not really fast enough if you use software packages with lots of graphics and special characters, such as desktop publishing with PostScript printers. In these cases you should consider migrating to EtherNet. EtherNet provides transfer speeds of 10 megabits per second. To take advantage of EtherNet, you will need to add a special network interface card to your workstations and file server.

If you decide to link your Macintoshes to a dedicated file server, say running under the Novell NetWare operating system, you will need to purchase additional equipment and software. You, therefore have a choice of two entirely different concepts for implementing your LAN. These two concepts are called the Client/Server network and the Peer-to-Peer and the Client/Server networks.

Peer-to-Peer Networks

This type of LAN is used by smaller organizations. In a typical Peer-to-Peer network, any workstation can be a file server as well as a client looking for data or programs on other computers. A Peer-to-Peer network consists of a series of workstations that are usually linked together in a daisy chain fashion (see Figure 12.10).

Each workstation can be either a client or a combination of client and server. Therefore, a workstation may end up serving several other workstations as well as being used as a personal computer by a user. Only two main requirements must be met for a user at any workstation to use the data on another workstation. One is that the user must have been authorized to share folders and files on the network. Otherwise, he or she cannot manipulate any program outside his or her own Mac. Under the Macintosh operating system, you can make a folder shareable to other users. The other requirement is that if more than one user is likely to use an application program on another workstation simultaneously, that application program must have been designed as a multiple user package. In a multiuser application program if more than one person tries to update a record, his or her request will be rejected until the first user has released the record. This concept is known as record locking and is an essential part or multiple user business applications. As a network user or designer, you do not have to be concerned about developing multiple user applications. Just make sure that the application that you plan to use is network certified.

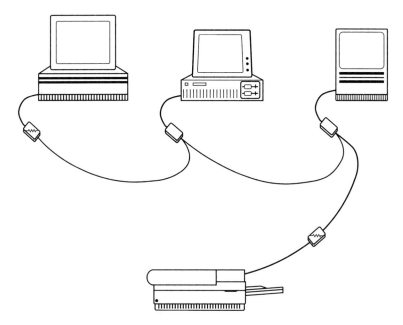

Figure 12.10: Macintoshes linked to each other in daisy chain fashion.

Peer-to-Peer (LocalTalk) networks have all the basic functionality of the Client/Server networks. However, they are slower than most Client/Server networks and there are practical limits to the number of workstations that can be daisy chained together. This number varies depending on the manufacturer of the product. However, according to independent tests, most Peer-to-Peer networks tend to max out at around 12 to 25 users.

Advantages of Peer-to-Peer LANs

(1) They are usually very inexpensive to acquire. A typical Peer-to-Peer network could consist of two Macintoshes plus an Apple personal LaserWriter II. To connect these units together, you will also need LocalTalk cables and boxes. A better choice would be three PhoneNET LocalTalk connectors. These units come completely ready for networking and have ample installation instructions. Each connector unit contains a DIN-8 attachment which connects to the Mac's printer port's socket. The other end of the connector has two female RJ11 sockets. The RJ11 sockets are identical to the modular telephone jack in most homes and offices. All you need to do is plug the connector

to the printer ports of the Mac and the printer, and connect them together with telephone wires. The remaining two ends of the units that are attached to your Macintosh systems should be plugged with a resistor which is included in the package. These connectors cost around $30 to $40 each and are available in most computer stores.

(2) They are very easy to install. You could install a starter pack in approximately two hours. What's more, you may not need an outside consultant or network administrator to set up the operating system and to designate file servers and client machines.

(3) They are easy to use for non-computer literate people. Almost anybody who can use a word processor or a spreadsheet can become familiar with a Peer-to-Peer LAN in a very short period of time. It is all a matter of clicking on an icon to link to an application on another system.

(4) They are very cost effective for small businesses or offices that just need file sharing, printer sharing, electronic mail, and word processing.

Disadvantages of Peer-to-Peer LANs

(1) They are rather limited in their growth potential. They are very good for offices with 2 to 12 users. The original AppleTalk Phase 1 protocol had a theoretical limitation of 256 nodes on one cable. Some manufacturers of Peer-to-Peer networks claim that up to 100 users or more could simultaneously use their systems. That may be true under certain controlled environments. The standard speed of LocalTalk under AppleTalk is 230 Kilo Bits per second. You could imagine the tremendous degradation in throughput if most of workstations in a medium to large Peer-To-Peer network became active and tried to access and use resources from each other.

(2) The workstations designated as file servers as well as clients can become almost too slow to be used by their users; if too many workstations try to access their files and/or send document for printing to their printers.

(3) There is very limited upward compatibility from Peer-to-Peer to larger, sophisticated Client/Server networks.

The Client/Server Network Concept

This is the type of LAN that is preferred by the corporate world. In this type of LAN, a central computer, usually a high speed Macintosh IIci or above or even an IBM compatible PC with an 80486 processor is designated as the central processor and message handler of the system. This is the server of the network. The workstations are the client machines and are all linked to the Server.

A typical and very popular client/server network is the Novell for Macintosh which allows Macintoshes to be connected to IBM file servers, and through the servers to other computers and devices such as printers and faxes. There are several ways that a client/server system could work as indicated below:

(1) The server could hold all the data. Under this scenario, all the files are stored on the hard disk at the file server. User needed application software programs such as Word Perfect, Excell, FoxBase or a graphics package are stored on the user (client) computers. The user invokes his or her application program on his or her own Mac. The user then accesses his or her files which are stored on the file server's hard disk. If other users have been given authorization, they can also access these files and either read them and/or manipulate them. With this kind of arrangement the users are really using the network to extend their hard disks and share files and resources.

(2) The Server could hold all the data and programs. In this case, the users do not even need a hard disk to store the application software programs. All these programs are stored on the file server. Each user will link to the server. The next step is to access and invoke the application software programs such as Word or Excell or FoxBase. The user is then free to create or manipulate documents and files. The files are, of course, available to other users who have been granted access to them. This type of network usage is more efficient than the first one because there is really no need for a user to have a hard disk at his or her workstation. In fact, the user could be at a remote location with a portable Macintosh and a modem, and can access the network and use all the resources just like local users. In any case, the output generated by the user could either be routed back to the user at his or her own workstation for filing or printing, or could be printed at one of the network's dedicated printers. A variation to this approach would allow the user to actually download a copy of the software programs such as a word processor to his or her own personal computer for execution. The copy is, of course, erased when the user shuts down his or her machine.

(3) The database server machine. This is a relatively new approach. An additional high speed computer with its own high capacity hard disk

(i.e., 400 megabytes or more) is assigned as a dedicated database server and is attached to the file server. The LAN version of a database management system (DBMS) package is loaded into this database machine.

(4) Several departmental servers could be linked together.Under this scenario, each application would have its own LAN. For example, the accounting department would have all its general ledger, accounts payable and accounts receivable on one LAN. The engineering department could have its production information on another LAN. The human resources department would have its own LAN for payroll and personnel. The LANs are connected to each other through devices such as bridges and routers. This is truly distributed data processing. Each department has a dedicated LAN, yet they can share their data as needed. Most LAN operating systems have excellent built-in security features. Some LAN security systems are as good as their mainframe based counterparts costing tens of thousands of dollars. If set up properly, the network security programs would protect against unauthorized access or inadvertent corruption of data by the users.

Many Client/Server networks do not allow the users to access other user's disks and other devices such as local printers, modems, and faxes attached to individual workstations. You can overcome this limitation through a number of approaches. One solution would be to upload the data from a client workstation to the file server and then download the data from the file sever to the workstation that needs the data. The data can then be accessed at the local level by the second workstation. You could also purchase software that will perform the upload and download for you. Another, more efficient, way is to separately link up one or more workstations to each other with Peer-to-Peer hardware and software.

Cabling Systems

So far we have discussed the topology of LANs and various operating system protocols. The actual type of cables that connect all the nodes in a network is our next subject.

LocalTalk Cable

This is a round cable, similar in thickness to a cable television cable at home. At each end, the cable terminates into a plug which fits in a LocalTalk connector. This cable is used to connect Macs and printers to each other. The LocalTalk connector will fit into an eight pin interface port at the back of a Mac or LaserWriter printer. There are no industry standards (i.e., IEEE designation) for this kind of cable. It is rated at 230,400 bits per second. It is probably the easiest cable, in any networking environment, to install.

The Twisted Pair Cable (10BASE-T)

This kind of cable is essentially the same as the standard telephone company wires used in residential homes and business offices. The use of twisted pair is a new concept in LANs although it has been around for over 50 years in homes and offices. You can use this cable instead of the Apple's LocalTalk cable or either the regular EtherNet or thin EtherNet cables to connect your Macintoshes and other network devices together. You will need an adapter between the twisted pair cable and the network port (i.e., the LocalTalk port on Macintosh) or interface card. Also, twisted pair cable is usually used with a Hub. Each four or eight cable is routed to a Hub. The Hub is either connected to another Hub or to the file server. Twisted pair comes in two types. The most common one is the unshielded twisted pair (UTP) or voice grade twisted pair. There is also a data grade UTP which is more reliable and can carry data over longer distances. Finally there is shielded twisted pair.

Thick EtherNet Cable (10BASE-5)

Years ago, there was only one type of cable that was used to connect terminals to computers. This was the shielded coaxial cable—a half inch thick cable that was braided with copper shielding. Each end of the cable terminates in a "D" type connector. This kind of cabling was heavy, bulky and very difficult to route around corners. This kind of cable is still around but is hardly ever used on networks. The original network cable was the EtherNet cable which conformed to IEEE 802.3 standard. It is also known as 10Base-5. This kind of cable is capable of carrying signals over 500 meters (2500 feet). The range can be extended by adding repeaters along the cable's length.

The Thin EtherNet Cable (10BASE-2)

Several years ago the thin EtherNet cable was developed. This cable was 0.2 inch thick and conformed to EtherNet standards except that it was much more flexible and lighter. The thin EtherNet is also called CheaperNet. Each end of the cable terminates at a BNC connector which is a bayonet type connector similar to what is used in home cable television to connect the cable to the television set. The IEEE standard for this kind of cable is 802.3. This cable type is also known as RG58.

Fiber Optics Cable (10BASE-F)

This is the fastest and most expensive type of cabling used in local area networks. It can carry data at 100 megabits per second, and unlike other cables is immune to electrical and magnetic interferences. Unfortunately, it is not very easy to splice, it is expensive, and you may not need that kind of speed on your network.

Wireless Link

This is another new concept. Wireless technology allows you to by-pass the mess and the problem of cables. There are several methods of wireless transmission. One is infrared transmission, which is good for short distances as long as there are no obstructions between the transmitters. The other method is Spread Spectrum long distance radio transmission which can actually transmit through solid objects (walls), but its range diminishes in relation to the thickness of the object. Finally, there is the High Frequency radio method of transmission. This method has a shorter range than the Spread Spectrum long distance radio technology. It can, however, penetrate thin walls. If you want to select a wireless link, make sure that you have considered the distance between your workstations and the file server (range) and the obstructions in your office. Wireless transmission cards are more expensive than regular cable cards and they may be subject to electromagnetic interference.

Protocols and Access Method Standards (Physical versus Logical Topologies)

AppleTalk

AppleTalk serves as the base on which cabling systems such as LocalTalk, EtherNet, and Token Ring can reside. AppleTalk is not a cabling system. Apple changed the name of standard Macintosh network cabling from AppleTalk to LocalTalk several years ago. AppleTalk is actually a suite of protocols that define the networking capabilities of the Macintosh. These protocols are loosely based on the International Standards Organization's Open Systems Interconnection (OSI) reference model. This connection is discussed later in the chapter.

AppleTalk supports more than just LocalTalk. It also supports EtherNet, Token Ring, Fiber Distributed Data Interface (FDDI) and other cabling systems.

There are actually two AppleTalks—Phase I was developed for small networks, while Phase II, released in 1989, is the revised protocol able to handle larger networks.

AppleTalk Phase I did not work on Token Ring networks and only worked with Xerox EtherNet, not the IEEE 802.3 standard. Phase II supports IEEE standard 802.3 EtherNet and 802.5 Token Ring. Most significantly, AppleTalk Phase II extends the capacity of AppleTalk from 256 users to 16 million users.

EtherNet

The Bus topology is very simple and cost-effective for smaller networks. However, there is need for certain rules or a protocol. What happens if two workstations try to transmit data at the same time. This is just like two or more cars travelling at high speed, on single lane highway, in opposite directions. The result is, of course, utter chaos and disaster. In networking, this phenomenon is known as data collision. The more nodes that you have on the network, the more likelihood of the collision occurring.

For a solution, let us go back to the cars and the single lane highway example. To avoid collisions and disruption on the highway we could instruct each driver to stop at the on ramp and look for traffic on the highway. If any traffic at all is sensed, the driver should back off and wait a few seconds before trying to enter the highway again. If all drivers obey these rules, there will never be a collision and all drivers will get to their destinations safely.

The same technique is used under the EtherNet protocol in the bus topology. The network interface hardware in the workstation or the file server senses the change in voltage of the cable (bus) before attempting to send a packet of data to its destination. If no voltage disruption is detected, the packet of data is transmitted down the cable towards its destination. However, if the network interface card senses the presence of data it will wait a random amount of time before trying to send its packet of information to its destination. This technique is known as Carrier Sense Multiple Access/Collision Detection (CSMA/CD). Naturally, if you had many workstations on the network, the response time on the network would deteriorate rapidly as more and more workstations would have to wait their turns before transmitting their data. The standard data transfer rate on EtherNet networks is 10 megabits per second, much higher than 230.4 Kilo Bits on the LocalTalk.

Token Passing

The Token Ring network topology from IBM employs the ring topology and the token passing concept. This means that all nodes are connected to each other through a circular cable. The Protocol or the set of rules for sending data from node to node is based on Token Ring which means that data is sent, from workstation to workstation, in packets of information called tokens. The data transfer rate on the IBM Token Ring network is either 4 or 16 megabits per second.

LAN Installation and Use

Installing a basic LocalTalk Mac network has always been very easy. In this chapter we will go over the installation procedures for a Peer-to-Peer daisy chain network. We have selected the Farallon's PhoneNET hardware as an example for its simplicity and ease of use.

Peer-to-Peer Network Installation— Hardware and Software Requirements

Let us assume that we have a three node network. This will include two Macs and a LaserWriter printer. You will need the following devices and software:

(1) Two Macintosh computers.

(2) A printer. This could be any type of a printer. We have, however, assumed that it is an Apple LaserWriter II printer.

(3) Three PhoneNET LocalTalk connectors. You can use other boxes to connect your network. However, PhoneNET is a very inexpensive and easy system to install and maintain.

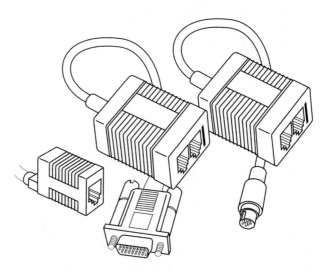

Figure 12.11: Three models of the PhoneNET connector.

Installation

Hardware Installation

(1)   Each PhoneNET connector box (see Figure 12.11) includes the following:

    (a)   A LocalTalk to RJ11 connector. One end of the connector ends in a Macintosh 8 pin connector (Mini PIN-8). This end can be inserted into the printer port on the back of newer Macintoshes. This includes Macintosh Plus, SE, II series and all newer Macs. Older Macintoshes such the Mac 128K, 512K, and the IBM PC use the DB9 plug. The other end of the connector contains two female RJ11 jacks. These jacks are identical to the modular wall jacks on your home telephone system.

    (b)   A resistor for closing the open end of the connector.

    (c)   A 7 foot length of modular cable. This is similar to the regular extension phone lines used in offices and homes. Both ends of the cable terminate with modular male jacks, just like the modular jacks on your home telephones. These jacks are known as the RJ11 jacks (see Figure 12.12).

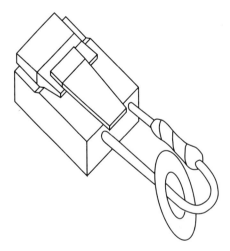

Figure 12.12: The RJ11 mounted terminating resistor.

(2) Arrange your Macs and printers within 7 feet of each other. Note that you are not really required to space the Macs within 7 feet of each other. The PhoneNET network can be up to 3,000 feet wide. The extension cord that is enclosed with the packet is 7 feet long and is really there to allow you to connect your Mac to an RJ11 Wall socket. You can, of course, use a much longer cable.

(3) Take a PhoneNET connector and insert it into the first Mac's printer port socket.

(4) Connect the other two connectors to the other Mac and your printer.

(5) Insert one end of the modular extension cable into one of the two RJ11 jacks on the connector attached to the first Mac.

(6) Insert the other end of the same modular extension cable into one of the modular jacks on the connector that is attached to the printer.

(7) Take another modular extension cable. Insert one end into the remaining open jack on the connector that is attached to the printer. The other end of the cable should be attached to one of the open jacks on the connector that is attached to the second Macintosh.

(8) By now, you should have the two Macintoshes connected to the printer, and to each other through the connector attached to the printer.

(9) The final action needed is to close the two open RJ11 openings on the two PhoneNET connectors connected to the two Macs. If you do not plug those openings, data will basically flow through them like water running through an unplugged plumbing system. To close these ports insert one RJ11 resistor into each open port. The RJ11 resistors are basically male plugs with an attached resistor.

(10) A very important item to remember is that this is a daisy chain connection and not a ring structure. Therefore you do not connect the two ends of the network to each other. The two ends are terminated with resistors, as stated above.

At the end of hardware installation, you should have one piece of 7 foot cable and one terminating resistor left over. You could use these for future additions and as spares.

To add new Macs to the network, all you need to do is to remove the RJ11 resistor plug from one of the Macs connectors and daisy chain another computer to it. The first and the last computer in a network should always be plugged with an RJ11 resistor.

Software Installation Under System 7

As mentioned previously, the Macintosh system software diskettes contain all the required AppleTalk networking programs. To activate networking, you must make sure that the AppleTalk software is installed on the System Folder. Next, you must activate AppleTalk from the Chooser menu. The following gives a general overview for activating an AppleTalk network. However, you should always follow the user manual's guidelines.

(1) Select the Chooser menu from the Apple menu.

(2) On the Chooser menu, activate AppleTalk if it is not already activated.

(3) Open the "Sharing Setup" Control Panel.

(4) On the Control Panel select the "Sharing Setup" icon.

(5) The "Sharing Setup" control panel menu contains three separate sections. The top part is the "Network Identity" section. In this section, you should enter the network owner's name. For example, if it was a network developed by Richard, he might call it Richard Taha.

(6) Enter the "Owner's" password as requested in the menu.

(7) In the "Macintosh name" box enter the public name of this network. This is the name that other users will see this Macintosh as when they go to the Chooser menu. As an example, if this application belonged to the Accounting department, you could call it the "Accounting Mac." Always try to use descriptive names.

(8) Next, while still on the "Sharing Options" control panel, activate the "File Sharing" function by clicking on the "Start" button. This will allow the files to be shared by several users. At this time, you do not need to worry about the "Program Linking" section.

(9) Your next step is the process of identifying your users to the system and allowing them to access your system and its folders. There are several steps involved here as listed below:

  (a) Go to the Control Panels again.

  (b) Double click on the "Users and Groups" Control Panel.

  (c) Select the "File menu" and choose the "New User" option.

  (d) Next, add a new user, i.e., James Barker or July Adamson.

  (e) Next, double click on each new user to open the new "User Information" menu.

(f)   For each user, use the "User Information" menu to either allow or restrict user access to your files. Also, it is a good practice to require every user to enter a password. However, passwords are not mandatory.

(g)   After creating a few users and filling in the user information, you can create a group. You can do that while you are still in the "Users & Group" menu. You use the File menu to create a new group—you could call it, say, "Our Group"—and to attach your authorized users to that group. You can add users to the group by dragging their icons to the group icon. It is also very easy to restrict users from accessing the network by dragging their icons to Trash in the group menu.

(10) Sharing Folders and Files.

(a)   Create a new shareable Folder. You could call this something like SYSHARE.

(b)   Open the file menu and select "Sharing" option.

(c)   In the "Sharing" menu box, select "Share this item and its contents" option. This should open up the rest of the box and allow you to make changes to the levels of user access that your group of users are entitled to.

(d)   Save the changes.

Now, any authorized user can access the network by going to the Chooser menu and clicking on the network name, i.e., "Accounting Mac." Next, follow the system's instructions for accessing the network.

You can now install and share multi-user application programs such as databases, word processors and groupware products.

Network Operating Systems

While System 7's built-in file sharing capabilities are fine for low-end file sharing under System 7, a variety of other options are available for the Macintosh. These include Novell NetWare, Sitka TOPS and other peer-to-peer LANs, Banyan VINES, AppleShare, and Microsoft LAN Manager for Macintosh. These operating systems provide *interoperability*, allowing you to connect your Macintosh to a wide variety of computers besides Macs, including computers using UNIX or MS-DOS.

Three networking systems in particular—NetWare, VINES and LAN Manager—are particularly useful if you are networking Macs in an environment where PCs are already networked. VINES is particularly well suited to the world of wide area networks, or WANs, which are multiple local area networks connected over a wide geographic area. AppleShare is your best bet for Macintosh-only or Mac-dominant networks where a dedicated server is required. Peer-to-peer LANs are nice for small networks where a dedicated server is not required.

A network operating system is primarily a set of file and print services. It essentially replaces the single user operating system on your desktop, letting you share files and peripherals with other computers on a network. In order to be used effectively, it must work much like the operating systems people are used to. In other words, an MS-DOS network should look like DOS or Windows and a UNIX network should look like UNIX. Since Mac users are used to AppleShare and the Macintosh desktop, the network operating systems here build on the Macintosh desktop and AppleShare's features as a base. They work and look like AppleShare to Macintosh users.

With network operating systems, you can share files and printers, send electronic mail, and make Macintoshes equal with computers from other environments. Macs and PCs use the same file server, so network managers can back up all data on a network in one step.

Apple includes built-in networking capabilities to make sharing hard disks and printers easy. Once selected via the AppleShare option on the Chooser, any hard disk on the network looks and works like a local drive on your Macintosh desktop. You can save, delete or drag files just as you would with a local hard disk. Using the Chooser, you select network printers just as if the printer were connected to the back of your Mac. These network services are available to you no matter what type of network operating system you choose.

AppleShare File Server

AppleShare File Server is the networking option of choice for large Macintosh networks that do not have to interact with computers using other operating systems. AppleShare also supports Apple II and MS-DOS computers on the network, so it's a good solution for networks with limited numbers of DOS and Apple II machines.

The latest version of AppleShare, AppleShare File Server 3.0, requires System 7 to run. As mentioned earlier in this chapter, System 7 includes excellent peer-to-peer networking capabilities, allowing you to share files without a dedicated file server. All you need is cabling connecting the computers. AppleShare also supports file sharing without a dedicated file server. However, it is best to use a dedicated file server over a network as performance will be better.

The latest version of AppleShare, version 3.0, supports up to 120 concurrent users (and 8,192 connected users) and five network printers. Formerly a separate option, the print server provides print queuing, error tracking, and spooling. It also includes centralized administrative and security features, such as password control, administrator controlled log-off, application launch count, and the ability to send messages from the administrator to any user.

AppleShare is also the only networking option that uses a Macintosh as a centralized file server. Most networking software vendors require an Intel-based PC instead of a Macintosh as a server, largely because there wasn't a Mac powerful enough to be a server on a large network and the simplicity built into AppleTalk makes it difficult to get peak performance out of the Mac.

The Quadra series of Macintoshes has changed the perception of the Macintosh. The Quadra is a tower-configured Macintosh with a powerful Motorola 68040 processor, an enhanced small computer systems interface (SCSI), two SCSI inputs, the ability to handle massive hard disks, and much more. While network software vendors are not flocking to develop a server-based Mac version of their software, the Quadra makes AppleShare a viable choice for users of Macintosh-only networks.

Unfortunately, AppleShare 3.0 does not have a variety of high-end features such as fault-tolerant disks, automatic reconnection after crashes, and disk-space quotas for users. AppleShare 3.0 also doesn't provide multiple printers per queue (something found in VINES) and doesn't limit the number of pages one can print at a time. While not as extensive as NetWare, AppleShare does include some password control, including the ability to control the minimum length of passwords and forcing users to change their passwords at specific times.

The companion to AppleShare FileServer is AppleShare Workstation, Apple's built-in networking capability that comes with each Macintosh. AppleShare Workstation includes such features as the Chooser and built-in AppleTalk to allow the Macintosh to be networkable right out of the box. AppleShare uses AppleTalk Filing Protocol (AFP) to provide file services over the network and AppleTalk Print Services (ATPS) for printer services. The other network operating systems discussed here also use these protocols to allow Macs to work on their networks.

AppleShare 3.0 is available for $1,199 per server. It works with EtherNet and Token Ring cabling in addition to LocalTalk. To use AppleShare or any of the other network operating systems discussed here, with anything other than LocalTalk cabling, you must purchase an appropriate network adapter card and connect your Macintosh.

Novell NetWare

Novell NetWare is far and away the most popular network operating system, dominating the market for MS-DOS machines. NetWare for Macintosh lets Mac users share files and network resources with DOS, OS/2, UNIX, and Windows users, in addition to other Macintosh users. It supports LocalTalk, ARCnet, EtherNet, and Token Ring networks.

NetWare for Macintosh supports internetworking, multiple remote connections, system fault tolerance, resource accounting, and security. It also includes network management features, including backup, troubleshooting and system maintenance.

NetWare for Macintosh is much better than it used to be when it was first introduced in 1989. Version 1.0 installed as a value-added process (VAP) on a NetWare file server running version 2.15 of NetWare. Version 3.01 runs as a NetWare Loadable Module (NLM) on version 3.11 of NetWare, which makes it run much faster. NetWare 3.11 actually uses a set of NLMs to support the Macintosh. These NLMs essentially add AppleTalk functionality to NetWare's own network protocol, Internetwork Packet Exchange/Sequenced Packet Exchange (IPX/SPX). Mac users use their own built-in AppleTalk services, such as Apple Filing Protocol (AFP) and Printer Access Protocol (PAP), to communicate with NetWare. NetWare runs AppleTalk and IPX/SPX concurrently.

Other NLMs offer database and printer server functionality and connections to other environments such as UNIX. NetWare for Macintosh is included with NetWare 2.2 servers. It is available at an extra cost with NetWare 3.11, which is a much more powerful version of NetWare.

NetWare for Macintosh is available in three configurations—20, 100, and 200 users. It is licensed on a per server basis. It requires at least 5 MB of RAM in the server (6 MB in the 200 user version).

NetWare for Macintosh includes two utility programs—the NetWare Desk Accessory (NDA) and the NetWare Control Center (NCC). NDA helps view and set file privileges, send messages using NetWare's built-in messaging facility, and monitor and control print jobs. NCC helps network administrators create, delete, and manage user accounts and groups.

File Sharing

The NetWare file server appears on the Macintosh desktop as a local drive. Macs can share files with other computers by copying them to the file server. Other Mac users can access the data freely. MS-DOS, OS/2 and UNIX users can access the data if it is compatible with their own applications.

For example, text or ASCII files can be shared with anyone on the network. However, ASCII files lose all formatting information, including bold, italics and special characters. Graphics files cannot be converted to ASCII. Also, the last 128 ASCII characters usually cannot be converted from Mac to PC. This is because the Macintosh operating system defines all 256 ASCII characters, while DOS defines 128 characters and leaves the rest to DOS applications.

You don't have to worry about ASCII if you use the same applications in each environment. For example, files created in Microsoft Word for the Mac can generally be shared with anyone using Microsoft Word in other environments. But unless files are shared in a common file format, they cannot be shared with others on the network.

Macintosh files appear to Macintosh users as graphical icons, such as to indicate a Microsoft Word file (actually, using the View option on the desktop, you can make files appear as icons or names). Users of other environments see Macintosh files and folders in the format of their operating system. So, for example, a Macintosh folder appears as a directory to an MS-DOS user. Unfortunately, NetWare lacks an extension mapping facility to identify DOS files as their Macintosh counterparts. This feature is found on other networking software, such as LAN Manager for Macintosh and VINES option for Macintosh.

Some graphics files can be shared between Mac and PC, especially if they are saved in Encapsulated PostScript (EPS) or tagged image file format (TIFF). Most Macintosh graphics files use EPS and many DOS programs also use it. Some Macintosh programs also support CompuServe's graphic image format (GIF). Spreadsheet files are usually fairly easy to translate, since the most popular spreadsheets, Lotus 1-2-3 and Excel are available in both environments and support each others file formats.

Printing

NetWare lets Macintosh users access any PostScript compatible printers, no matter where they are connected. As with any other printer, select the printer to use via the Chooser. Users of other computing platforms can also use Macintosh printers via NetWare. While DOS and OS/2 NetWare clients have to log onto the network before they can use network printers, Macintosh users do not.

In general, print jobs go into a print queue at the file server. The server then generally holds the incoming print jobs in the queue and sends them to the printer on a first-in, first-out basis. Users can go about their work while the server waits for the printer. NetWare for Macintosh supports several types of cabling media, including LocalTalk, ARCnet, EtherNet and Token Ring. It complies with AppleTalk Phase I and AppleTalk Phase II.

Network Management

To aid managers in troubleshooting their networks, NetWare for Macintosh includes the AppleTalk Console, a diagnostic tool that works in conjunction with NetWare's ECHO utility to graphically monitor network traffic and configuration information. AppleTalk Console displays the name and address of every AppleTalk device on the network, including servers, clients, and printers.

Network management is available from any Macintosh on the network. System administrators can assign rights and privileges to files and folders, set up users and groups, manage printing, and set file and folder attributes. Users can assign rights to files and manage their own print jobs by either stopping them, restarting them, or deleting them.

Security

NetWare supports Apple's security features, which allow you to set three options for data. You can set files to let other users see folders, see files, and/or make changes. As the creator of a file or folder, you automatically have all three security rights to the file or folder. You can then grant those privileges to others on the network, either individually or as a group.

NetWare offers a variety of security features that are much more sophisticated than those found on standard Macintosh networks. For example, Apple's standard passwords can be a maximum of eight characters. However, NetWare supports passwords of up to 128 characters. The longer the password, the greater the security; however, it is hard to imagine anyone using a password as long as 128 characters. NetWare also stores and sends passwords in a much more sophisticated manner than AppleShare. Both AppleShare and NetWare encrypt passwords over the network to deter hackers who can use network protocol analyzers to capture login packets and learn passwords.

AppleShare servers generally store passwords in an encrypted format, decrypting the passwords for password checking during login. NetWare file servers store passwords in a one-way encrypted form. The server never keeps the password in memory or on disk in unencrypted form, and no one, not even the system administrator, can look at passwords stored on the file server.

NetWare also includes a security feature that restricts user accounts to using the network during certain time periods during the week and to certain stations by physical address. For the Macintosh, the time restrictions apply, but the station restrictions do not. Due to AppleTalk's method of assigning node numbers, it is very difficult to determine the physical network address of a Macintosh workstation.

NetWare 3.1 for Macintosh sells for $895 for 20 users; $1,995 for 100 users; and $2,995 for 200 users. It requires NetWare 3.11, which costs $3,495 for 20 users, $6,995 for 100 users and $12,695 for 250 users. The lower-end version of NetWare, version 2.2, is also available. NetWare 2.2 is slower and includes less services, but it is also much less expensive. NetWare 2.2 costs $895 for five users or $5,495 for 100, and includes the Macintosh VAP.

NetWare 3.2

A new version of NetWare is expected by the end of the year. It is expected to have a variety of new features, including one that provides users access to any NetWare server on the network, rather than just the one they have logged onto. This technology is a partial result of Novell's recent purchase of International Business Software, vendors of DataClub Classic and DataClub elite, Macintosh networking products that combine disk space from multiple Macs into a "virtual server"—a single logical AppleShare server volume. Network administrators can manage all of the network services as though they all resided on a single server. NetWare 3.2 will also include global directory services, a distributed computing feature that helps track distributed applications across the network. The Macintosh part of this technology could come from DataClub's distributed file server features.

Third-Party Software

There are a number of third-party products available that let Macintosh users connect to NetWare without purchasing it. Two in particular are NetMounter, from Dayna Communications and MacLAN Connect, from Miramar Systems.

NetMounter is a good choice for those with only a few Macintosh users to connect to a NetWare LAN. Priced at only $99 per user, $395 for five users or $595 for 10 users, it works with NetWare versions 2.15, 2.2 and 3.11. NetMounter is easier to install than NetWare and less expensive for small networks. Its installer program installs NetMounter in the Mac's System folder, then restarts the system. There is nothing to load on the NetWare server. A NetMounter icon appears in the Chooser that lets users log on to a Novell network. All available NetWare file servers are displayed in the Chooser. Users can log on to any server to which they have access rights. NetMounter also includes one feature that NetWare lacks—extension mapping, which lets users link DOS file extensions with Macintosh applications. More about extension mapping later in this chapter.

MacLAN Connect for NetWare is a software gateway that lets up to 40 Mac users connect to a NetWare server. It retails for $695. While NetWare for Macintosh connects each user to the server, MacLAN Connect appears to the server as a single user. Like NetMounter, it also includes extension mapping. MacLAN Connect for NetWare requires a DOS PC as a server. It provides file- and printer sharing of anything connected to it. It also makes any shared resource, such as a CD-ROM drive, on the NetWare LAN appear to Mac users as well. Since it uses Novell application programming interfaces (APIs), it automatically works with users and groups defined in NetWare also.

LAN Manager Services for Macintosh

Microsoft's LAN Manager version 2.1 is the first version of the software that provides Macintosh connectivity. Called LAN Manager Services for Macintosh, version 1.0, the product is an attempt to gain more market share in the LAN market. LAN Manager for Mac offers one major advantage over NetWare for Macintosh — extension mapping. MS-DOS files always have a three-character extension following the filename, which indicates the application in which the file was created. Macintosh files have invisible four character creator names and four character format names along with the filename. Extension mapping essentially assigns the MS-DOS extension to the Macintosh creator and format.

As a result, DOS files on the network look like Macintosh files to Mac users. Mac users can click on an icon to open the file. For example, WordPerfect PC files look like WordPerfect Macintosh files. The extension mapping facility includes several predefined file types, and users can assign more.

In its basic form, LAN Manager provides file, print and network services for DOS and OS/2 computers. Like NetWare, LAN Manager for Macintosh takes advantage of Apple's built-in networking capabilities to facilitate file and printer sharing. Macintosh users can access any PostScript printer on the network through the Chooser. Macintoshes can share DOS and OS/2 file and print services, but cannot use network services, such as messaging, alerts, administrative programs and mailboxes.

Like NetWare and VINES, LAN Manager for Macintosh requires a DOS or OS/2 machine as a file server. Its MACADMIN program, which runs on the file server, performs all Macintosh volume and printer management. Macintosh files are kept in an area called shared directories on the network. These directories can be available to both DOS and Mac users, but they must be set up as Macintosh files as well as DOS files.

LAN Manager supports LocalTalk, EtherNet, and Token Ring cabling. It is available for $995 for 50 users. It requires an MS-DOS or OS/2 server with 8MB of RAM and LAN Manager 2.1. LAN Manager 2.1 is available for $1,995 for up to ten users; $995 for each additional ten users and $5,995 for unlimited users. Since it requires a DOS or OS/2 file server, it is a good choice for users in mixed networks, but not for Macintosh-only networks.

VINES Option for Macintosh

Like LAN Manager, VINES for Macintosh requires an MS-DOS server on the network. Also like LAN Manager, VINES for Macintosh includes an extension mapping facility to make it easier to use DOS files on the Mac. VINES stands for VIrtual NEtworking System, a wide area network (WAN) software package. It is intended for multi-platform, multi-site networks. It works with Macintosh, DOS, OS/2, and UNIX machines.

The key to VINES is StreetTalk, Banyan's distributed naming feature for VINES. StreetTalk discovers and maintains resource information distributed between servers on the network. StreetTalk details the name, location and attributes of all users and devices on the network. This information is held at every server on the network. Servers update this information to each other regularly. StreetTalk works with all of VINES services, including security, electronic mail, and network management.

The VINES extension mapping features include limits on the number of mappings allowed; only 21 mappings are available under normal conditions, although you can increase this to 44 if you limit Macintosh filenames to eight characters or less. Like NetWare and LAN Manager, VINES is compliant with AFP, so printer sharing and volume selection is controlled through the Chooser. VINES WAN orientation means VINES thinks of a file server as just one server on a network of LANs. Therefore, VINES distinguishes between attaching to a server and connecting to the network. However, once connected to the network, you can use any Macintosh-compatible printers, hard disks, or other peripherals on the network.

Because it is WAN-oriented, VINES offers an AppleTalk tunneling feature that lets Mac users internetwork a collection of dispersed AppleTalk networks. This actually wraps AppleTalk data packets inside VINES packets to pass them through the VINES network of servers, gateways, and routers. Macintosh users on a VINES network can set file rights for shared files. However, user and resource management has to be performed from a DOS or OS/2 machine. Its network messaging capabilities let users send one-line messages to each other.

VINES lets Mac users access any PostScript printers. It lets users reprint, hold, or redirect their documents to other printers. As with files, however, printer management must be performed from a DOS or OS/2 computer.

Security is controlled by the VINES Security Service, called VANGuard. This offers security above and beyond that of AppleTalk. For example, VINES lets users set expiration dates for accounts and passwords, and provides temporary disabling of accounts. It also provides password encryption with no replay, *ala* NetWare.

VINES Mail for Macintosh is an optional ($895) electronic mail package that lets Mac users directly connect to VINES Mail Service. Mac users can exchange mail each other and with any DOS, Windows, or OS/2 VINES client. They can also send and receive mail through a variety of gateway services such as fax and MCI Mail. Messages have a limit of only 6,000 characters (about 1,000 words, or four pages of text), however.

VINES Mail includes the StreetTalk Directory Assistant (STDA), which lets users search through a directory of names to find a potential addressee. Users can also have their own address book. VINES users can use LocalTalk, EtherNet, or Token Ring cabling. VINES is available for $7,495 plus $1,995 for Macintosh support of an unlimited number of users.

Peer-to-Peer Solutions

A variety of peer-to-peer networking solutions are available for the Macintosh, from System 7's aforementioned file sharing capabilities to the networking products discussed here. Peer-to-peer networking is a good solution for small networks that do not require the security and reliability that centralized servers provide. This method essentially eliminates the need for a dedicated file server by utilizing the disk space of all Macs on the network. This is a good option for small networks that don't require the security and reliability that a centralized server provides.

Peer-to-peer networks for the Mac were pioneered by TOPS, now owned by Sitka, a subsidiary of Sun Microsystems Computer Corp. TOPS provides cross-platform, peer-to-peer network services that connect Macs, DOS computers and UNIX workstations over a single network.

MacTOPS sells for $299 to $995 for up to ten users, while DOSTOPS is $249 to $995 for up to ten users. SunTOPS, which lets TOPS users use a Sun workstation as a server sells for $1,295 for SPARCstations and $1,395 for other Sun workstations. One of the biggest advantages of TOPS is its easy connectivity and data sharing between DOS machines and Macs. To facilitate this, TOPS includes Dataviz's MacLinkPlus Translators to make it easier to transfer files between DOS and Mac. TOPS works with LocalTalk, EtherNet and Token Ring. SunTOPS costs $1,295 to $1,395. PenTOPS is bundled with pen-based computers such as GO Corp.'s PenPoint and PenCentral.

One of the problems with peer-to-peer networks is a lack of a centralized server. Without one, any Mac that crashes makes the data on that Mac inaccessible to anyone else until the Mac is back on-line. Also, data can sometimes be very difficult to find if you do not know which workstation has it. And, if someone uses the computer on which the data you are retrieving is located, you'll experience a significant degradation in performance.

DataClub Elite from IBS, now owned by Novell, offers a solution to the data recoverability problem—it distributes files all over the network, but shows them as one file server to the other users on the network. It doesn't require a dedicated server, but it does include some safeguards to improve performance. Its LockScreen application locks the computer you are accessing so no one will use it. DataClub also includes load statistics showing disk usage on participating Macs. DataClub Classic is available for $395 while DataClub Elite sells for $1,395.

 # Interconnectivity

Repeaters, Bridges, Routers, Gateways, and Zones

We should also discuss the concept of zones, repeaters, bridges, routers, and gateways. Due to recent advances in technology, the distinction between gateways, routers and bridges has become very blurred. Many bridges are now capable of handling router's functions. Also, some network vendors are trying to incorporate the bridging and routing functions as part of the network operating system.

Repeaters

A repeater is basically at the lowest level of LAN interconnectivity intelligence. Its sole purpose is to receive network messages (electrical signals), amplify them and send them on. By using repeaters you can extend the range of your network considerably.

Bridges

A bridge performs additional functions. It has some intelligence built in. It only works on local area networks with the same protocol. Therefore, you can insert a bridge between two or more EtherNet networks. When a bridge encounters a message routed from a workstation on the network, it will check the receiving address. If the receiving user's address belongs to the same network, the bridge will just let it go on on its way. If it belongs to another network, it is forwarded to that network. Bridges work on the bottom two layers of the OSI model.

Routers

A router has more intelligence. It can route messages across different networks with different topologies. So, user Richard on an EtherNet network can send a document or message to user Maureen on another EtherNet network with a different topology. Basically, a router connects separate networks with different topologies but the same protocol, although this may change soon as routers are getting more sophisticated. A router can also look for different paths to forward the data to another network. If another path is available, the router will try to use it to send its messages on to their destinations. Routers work at the network layer of the OSI model and do not provide protocol translation.

Gateways

A gateway goes much further. It can provide a link to a completely different LAN or even a mainframe. It is usually a PC with enough sophistication built in to translate one protocol to another. So, a user on an AppleTalk network or a Novell NetWare could download files from an IBM mainframe and execute applications on the mainframe. Gateways allow terminal emulation on the workstation so a PC or Macintosh on a network can act like an IBM 3270 mainframe terminal. A gateway is usually also capable of allowing simultaneous mainframe access sessions to several network users in addition to providing protocol exchange and file transfer capabilities. When accessing an IBM mainframe computer, a computer attached to a gateway can emulate IBM's 3174 or 3274 controllers. With gateways, you can also use the mainframe as a file server. Gateways operate on the top three layers of the OSI model.

Zones

Zones are basically a method of dividing a network into several smaller or sub networks (see Figure 12.13). You will need gateways or bridges to define one or more zones or subnetworks within a larger network. Groups of users and devices, such as special printers with similar activities and requirements could be divided into different zones. However, users can still access other network services and devices by selecting other zones from the Chooser menu (see Figure 12.14).

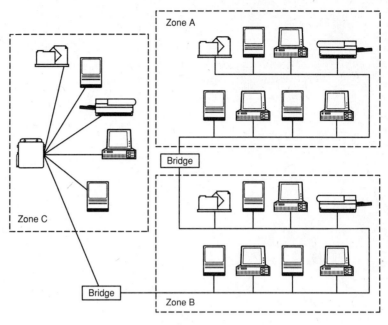

Figure 12.13: Three zones on an AppleTalk network.

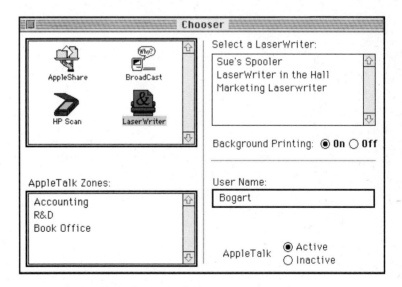

Figure 12.14: The Chooser menu showing several AppleTalk zones.

The Future

Well, this is the end of my discussion about local area networks. The future is extremely bright for networks. Elsewhere in this book, you have read discussions about memory, hard disks, modems, graphics and other interesting subjects. Nothing is really more exciting and challenging than local area networks. It has been the real sleeper of the Eighties. In the Nineties, there will be fiber optics, wireless LANS, distributed Client/Server processing, and downsizing.

Good Luck and happy networking!

Don't forget the detailed glossary of LAN terms which is at the end of this chapter. The glossary will explain many terms that we have not had time to discuss in this short chapter.

The OSI Model as Related to the Macintosh

The OSI (Open Systems Interconnection) model is a series of telecommunications standards and rules that has been developed by the International Standard Organization (ISO). There are seven layers to the OSI model. The purpose of ISO in developing the OSI model is to set a standard that will allow incompatible terminals and computers to communicate with each other. While there are seven layers of the OSI, the only physical link between the computers is at the first level, the physical level. Data really flows from physical layer to physical layer over the communication lines and then traverses the layers up to level seven which is the application layer.

Eventually all hardware and software manufacturers and distributors will have to abide by the OSI rules. The U.S. Government has already adopted the OSI standards in the form of GOSIP (Government OSI Profile). Not to be confused with LocalTalk, which is the cabling that most Macs use for networking, Apple-Talk is the suite of protocols that define Macintosh communications. AppleTalk protocols work with all seven layers of the OSI model (see Figure 12.15).

Application Layer	Layer 7
Presentation Layer	Layer 6
Session Layer	Layer 5
Transport Layer	Layer 4
Network Layer	Layer 3
Data Link Layer	Layer 2
Physical Layer	Layer 1

Figure 12.15: The OSI 7 Layer Model.

(1) **Physical Layer.** This layer is responsible for transmission of data between two points on a circuit such as a host (file server) and a terminal (workstation). At this level, the fluctuation of the electrical voltage on a circuit creates a series of 0s and 1s to represent data that is flowing between the two ends of the circuit. Some of the characteristics controlled by the physical layer are: the speed data on the line, i.e., 2400 bits per second over public networks or 10 megabits per second over coax lines; rules for connecting and disconnecting the lines; and rules for full duplex and half duplex transmission and types of cable connectors such as the RS232 "D" type plug. From a practical standpoint, the physical layer of a Macintosh network is the cabling, in most cases, LocalTalk, although EtherNet (EtherTalk), Token Ring (TokenTalk), and other options, such as Fiber Distributed Data Interface (FDDI). This is also the method by which information gets transported at the next layer. The LocalTalk protocol at this level is Apple's LocalTalk Link Access Protocol (LLAP), which uses telephone-style modular plugs and unshielded twisted-pair wiring to link Macs and printers on a network.

(2) **Data Link Layer.** This layer is responsible for putting the bits of data into manageable blocks of data or frames. It is also responsible for sending these frames, in sequence, to their destination and expecting an acknowledgement of safe arrival of data. If data is not received correctly at the other end, this layer is responsible for retransmitting the corrupted or bad frames of data. This layer can be software driven, i.e., through programs or hardware driven, i.e., through integrated circuit chips on a network interface card. The X.25 protocol is an example of this layer. It creates packets with the receiving addresses, control information, and the message and routes them to their destination. A long string of data may have to be chopped up into several packets. However, X.25 in reality performs functions across the first three layers.

(3) **Network Layer.** This layer decides where data should go and what route it should take through a network. This layer is responsible for taking a message and reformatting it into packets and directing them to their proper destination. AppleTalk includes the Datagram Delivery Protocol (DDP) at the network layer, which transmits data over an internetwork connection. Datagrams are actually packets of data. Datagram delivery is the base on which other AppleTalk services, such as electronic mail, can be built.

(4) **Transport Layer.** This layer provides a logical connection for the transfer of data (messages) between nodes on a network. This layer allows us to control the flow of packets of data. For example, dupli-

cate packets are dropped at this stage. Addressing, routing, and alternative routings, if possible, take place at this layer. For example, IPX (Internetwork Packet eXchange) is a program that handles the functions of the transport layer for the Novell's NetWare operating systems. This layer is filled with AppleTalk protocols. The AppleTalk Transaction Protocol (ATP) serves as a conduit between communications processes, letting one process have another handle an action and respond with a result. The AppleTalk Echo Protocol (AEP) lets one node transmit data to another while receiving a copy for itself. This is useful when troubleshooting a network, as it confirms that a node exists, and helps to identify transmission delays. The Name Binding Protocol (NBP) creates tables containing the names and addresses for network devices. The Routing Table Maintenance Protocol (RTMP) routes datagrams through router ports to other networks; ensuring the correct path is used for data delivery between two points.

(5) **Session Layer.** The software programs in this layer manage the entire communication session by synchronizing data flow between the nodes. This layer is also responsible for establishing and terminating a session. Logging in, and logging out, access security features such as password processing, and transferring of files between nodes are part of the session layer's responsibilities. This layer is also a hotbed for AppleTalk protocols. The AppleTalk Session Protocol (ATSP) provides the communication connection between server and workstation. The Printer Access Protocol (PAP) manages printer traffic on the network. The AppleTalk Data Stream Protocol (ADSP) is used by some applications for peer-to-peer communications. The Zone Information Protocol (ZIP) gives the NBP location information about network groups.

(6) **Presentation Layer.** It is in this layer that the AppleTalk Filing Protocol (AFP) is found. AFP allows workstations on an AppleTalk Network to access files on an AFP file server.

(7) **Application Layer.** This is the end user's real interface or window into a network. A user who is working on a spreadsheet is working at the application layer. Basically, all application programs are part of the application layer. All network operating systems, such as AppleShare File Server, Novell NetWare and LAN Manager, also exist at this level. There is no Application Layer built into the AppleTalk protocol, however.

- *PhoneNET is a registered trade mark of Farallon Computing, Inc., which we thank sincerely for their permission to include certain illustrations in this chapter.*

Glossary of Useful Networking Terms

10Base-2   Thin EthernNet coaxial Cable. Also known as Thin Net or CheaperNet. 10Base-2 means that the cable is Baseband and can carry data at up to ten megabits per second for 200 Meters. 10Base-2 conforms to IEEE 802.3. This type of cable is 0.2 inch thick and has a resistance of 50-ohms. It is also known as the RG-58 coax cable.

10Base-5   Thick EtherNet coaxial cable. This is the shielded cable and can carry data at up to ten megabits per second for 500 meters. You can extend the range by adding Repeaters along the cable. 10Base-5 conforms to IEEE 802.3. This kind of cable is 0.4 inch thick and has a resistance of 50-ohms.

10Base-T   This is a relatively new standard. It refers to Unshielded Twisted Pair (also known as UTP) which is rated to carry data at ten megabits per second. UTP is the standard telephone wire used at homes or offices. This kind of cabling can replace the 10Base-2 or 10Base-5 coaxial cables. The maximum distance that data could be carried over UTP cables without a repeater or bridge is approximately 100 meters. However, under test conditions, data has been carried over UTP cables for up to 180 meters without the loss of data or excessive error.

10Base-F   Fiber Cable for EtherNet cabling. Fiber Optics cables are capable of carrying data at 100 millions of bits per second (100MBPS).

Abend   Abnormal End. A Novell NetWare term borrowed from the IBM mainframe environment. Certain hardware problems and/or program logic errors could cause the user program or even the network itself to stop working completely. This condition is known as Abending. Usually, the only solution is in re booting the system. Normally, whenever the system is halted due to an Abend condition, the network operating system will display an error message before coming to a complete halt.

AppleTalk   The Apple's networking protocol. Appletalk is the software that is responsible for transfer of data between a Macintosh and other Macintoshes or printers on the network. Every Macintosh comes with the AppleTalk software.

AppleShare   The file server network developed by Apple for the Macintosh family.

ARCnet Attached Resource Computing Network. An older but quite popular networking technology initially developed by the DATAPOINT corporation. ARCnet is basically a token passing bus network architecture. ARCnet could be implemented over coaxial or unshielded twisted pair cables. In a typical ARCnet setup, the file server is connected, through a network interface card, to a hub with several ports which in turn is connected to the network's workstations or other hubs. ARCnet is rated at 2.5 Megabits per seconds (2,500,000 bits per second). This is roughly equivalent to about 300,000 characters per second which is quite sufficient for many low volume office applications. ARCnet LAN is very easy to install and hardly requires any maintenance.

BNC Short for Bayonet Neill Concelman. This is the bayonet type connection at the ends of thin EtherNet cables and "T" connectors and network interface cards (NICs).

BALUN Short for Balanced/Unbalanced. A small converter that converts a coaxial cable Thin Net signal to a twisted pair signal and vice versa. One end of a BALUN is a bayonet type BNC connecter for connecting to the Thin EtherNet Network Interface Card in the workstation. The other end is shaped like a regular telephone line's modular wall plug. The UTP cable is plugged into this end. With a BALUN, a user can link Ethernet cards over regular UTP (i.e., regular telphone lines) lines in the office.

Bridge A device for connecting two Local Area Networks together. The bridge allows messaging and passing of information between LANs with the same operating system.

Bus A channel or an electronic pathway or a signal route or a cable with two or more devices attached to it.

CDDI Copper Distributed Data Interface. The new standard specifying FDDI speed (i.e., 100 Megabits Per Second) over Unshielded Twisted Pair cables. This is a new technology without an official standard. It may not be practical to transmit data at 100 Megabits Per Second over standard voice grade telephone lines without excessive error. However, it is possible to do so successfully on data grade twisted pair telephone lines.

CheaperNet The same as Thin EtherNet. A thin EtherNet cable is more flexible than the thick EtherNet cable. The thin EthernNet cable is connected to the Network interface card with a bayonet type connector. The maximum range of a thin EthernNet cable is 200 meters.

Chooser   Macintosh's Desk Accessory that allows the users to activate AppleTalk. Additionally, users can select networks and zones from the Chooser menu.

Cladding   In fiber optics, a sheathing of reflective glass covering the inner optical cable. The cladding prevents the loss of data by reflecting the light rays back into the core fiber cable instead of allowing them to escape and dissipate.

Client/Server   This refers to a network structure where a central computer acts as a central hub to serve the workstations connected to it. The only traffic allowed on the network is through the central server. The server acts as a repository where application software such as word processors or database management program, user data, and the network operating system are stored. The users can access and invoke the application software programs. Depending on the type of application software programs, they can be executed on the server computer, the user's workstation or on a different computer on the network, which is dedicated as a database server. User data can also be stored on any of these three mediums. Reports are usually either printed at the workstation's dedicated printer or through the server at one or more common network printers. A Client/Server network can serve many numbers of users simultaneously. There are already some LANs in the market with 1000 or more users.

Coaxial Cable   Also known as coax cable. A cable used in networking. In a coax cable the central core wire carries the data. It is surrounded by two outer coatings. The first coating is an insulating material and the second one is a metal shield. There are two kinds of coaxial cables. Thick EtherNet is 0.4 inches in diameter and is bulky. Thin EtherNet is only 0.2 inches in diameter and is more flexible and can therefore be used in tight spots and around corners.

CSMA/CD   Carrier Sense Multiple Access with Collision Detection. A system used with EtherNet and AppleTalk networks. The Network Interface Card (NIC) in the workstation or the tranceiver listens and tries to detect a carrier before attempting to send data. It monitors for collision, i.e., data from other workstations by sensing for the distortion in the electrical pulse, which is caused by the transmission of data from another workstation on the network. If another signal is detected, the system will back off and try to send its data again.

DB-25   The RS232C wiring jack and plug standard. There are twelve connector pins in the bottom row and thirteen connector pins in the top row of a DB-25 jack or plug.

DIN-8   The printer port connector for the LocalTalk hardware. DIN-8 is the connector in later Macintosh models. Older Macinthoshes had a DB-9 port at the back of the system.

FDDI   Fiber Distributed Data Interface. This is the standard for Fiber Optics cabling in Local Area Networks. The FDDI data speed is set at 100 Megabits Per Second (MBPS).

Fiber Optics   The new technology that allows transmission of data and/or voice over very thin glass or plastic strands of wire. Fiber Optics cables are capable of carrying much higher data load than the traditional copper wire cables.

Gateway   A control unit or a personal computer that usually connects a Local Area Network to a mainframe or minicomputer system. The Gateway is also the unit that connects several AppleTalk networks together. The Gateway system has enough intelligence built-in to allow translation of one protocol or message format to another protocol.

HUB   A network device used to connect several workstations in a network via a centralized box. Hubs allow bus and ring topologies to use the best features of the Star topology by linking all the nodes to the central hub or hubs and using the Token Ring or EtherNet Bus protocol within the hub(s). Hubs can be passive, active or intelligent. A passive hub is usually employed on smaller networks. It allows the user to expand one physical network node to 2 or 4 nodes. An active Hub allows linking of eight or more workstations. An active hub improves data integrity by regenerating the electronic signals. Signals can be regenerated for up to 600 meters or more. An intelligent hub usually provides some sort of network fault tolerance capability and some form of network traffic and management information.

IEEE   Institute of Electrical and Electronics Engineers. This is a professional organization of engineers. Various committees within the IEEE are chartered with setting up data communications standards. IEEE is affiliated with the International Organization for Standards (ISO) and American National Standard Institute (ANSI).

LocalTalk   The Apple networking hardware. LocalTalk refers to the networking hardware, i.e., cable and interface cards on Macintoshes or printers.

LU 6.2   An IBM System Network Architecture (SNA) term. This is a protocol that allows peer-to-peer communications for computer applications.

MAU   Short for Multistation Access Unit or Multiple Access Unit or Media Access Unit. MAU is a device used on Token Ring networks to allow multiple connections to the network. This unit in effect allows a Token Ring network to act as a star network. The workstations are individually connected to the central MAU. Within the MAU, data is transferred from workstation to workstation in the Token Ring fashion. As a result, if a cable to a workstation is disconnected, the network does not stop functioning.

NETBIOS Network Basic Input Output System program. In local area networks, this usually refers to an emulation of the IBM's network input output programs. Some network programs such as certain database managers will require NETBIOS or a NETBIOS emulator program to be loaded into the workstation. When NETBIOS is loaded, it allows the workstation to establish communications on a Peer-To-Peer basis with another workstation or a database server through the network.

Node A point at network where devices such as workstations, file servers and printers are attached. A network with ten attachments is a called a ten node network.

OSI Model Open Systems Interconnection. A series of Telecommunications standards and rules developed by the International Standards Institute (ISO). OSI has 7 layers.

Packet A group of characters grouped together as a message. This grouping includes the receiving address, the control characters and the data. The packet is transmitted as a block.

Peer-To-Peer A networking system where a workstation can act both as an independent workstation (Client) and a file server (Server) station for other workstations. Under this configuration, each workstation can access the files and programs resident on the local disk drives of other workstations and execute or print them. A Peer-To-Peer local area network is very cost effective for smaller offices and businesses. However, its performance usually degrades as more users are added to the network. A practical limit for a Peer-To-Peer network is probably between 6 to 12 users.

Repeater A device to increase or amplify the strength of electronic signals in a local area network.

RJ-11 Standard US modular telephone plug. This is the plug found in most homes and offices. It is usually a 2 wire circuit, but it can be 4 wires. Under certain networking hardware, such as the Farrallon's PhoneNet, the two unused wires of an RJ11 cable could be used to transmit data from the computer to a central hub.

RJ-45   Similar to RJ-11. RJ-45 is fatter and is used on four wire circuits. There can however be six or eight wires on a cable.

Router   A device on the network that allows connection between two different local area networks. Routers are similar to bridges but have more intelligence. They are usually capable of forwarding data to remote networks and can connect networks that user different types of transmission on their cabling systems. For example, a router can connect an EtherNet network to an ARCnet network. Some routers can also route traffic around network breaks, if at all possible.

SNMP   Simple Network Management Protocol.

TCP/IP   Transmission Control Protocol/Internet Protocol. A seasoned networking standard. TCP/IP is used extensively by universities and government agencies to allow transfer of data and large files over networks across US and other countries. TCP/IP is a very reliable protocol. It is known for working even over unreliable lines.

Thin EtherNet   Same as 10Base-2. This is also known as Cheapernet. This kind of cabling conforms to IEEE 802.3 and allows transmission of data at up to 10 megabits per second for up to 200 meters without loss of data or needs for re-transmission.

Token   An electronic carrier of data being transmitted from workstation to workstation.

Token Passing   A method of passing information between two points on a network. A Workstation or terminal first acquires a token (an electronic carrier) and then uses it to pass messages (data) to its required destination. Tokens are passed from workstation to workstation until they reach their destination.

Token Ring   IBM's main local area network topology and protocol. This system uses the token passing concept. A token (an electronic carrier of data) goes in circles around the network ring. It stops at every workstation. If a workstation has a message (i.e., traffic or data), it is appended to the token which then continues to the next station and is passed on until it finds its destination and the token is then released.

Topology   The physical layout of a local area network. This refers to the layout of workstations, cables and the fileserver.

Transceiver   Short for transmitter receiver. An electronic device that is used to receive, amplify and re-transmit electronic signals (data) on a network. The transceiver is similar to a repeater and contains circuitry and logic to monitor data packet collision and re-transmit data when a collision is imminent. The transceiver could be externally attached to the network interace card. on the cable or internally mounted on the network interface card (NIC).

Twisted Pair Standard telephone wiring. In the twisted pair wiring standard two copper wires are twisted around each other to reduce electromagnetic interference from each other and from other external sources such as photocopy machines, printers and fax machines. There are two types of twisted pairs in use. The Unshielded Twisted Pair (UTP) and Shielded Twisted Pair (STP). The theoretical maximum length of cable between workstations is 100 meters.

WAN Wide Area Network. A network consisting of several LANs which are separated physically from each other. A WAN can span several buildings, cities, states or even countries. The interconnection between LANs is usually provided by common carriers over micro-wave, T1 or satellite circuits.

Workstation A personal computer or terminal that is connected to a network. In general, a workstation could be any simple or very sophisticated desk top computer that can perform data processing functions independently. A workstation could be connected to a Local Area Network, a mainframe computer or to a time sharing service over public access networks.

X.25 This is a protocol for data transfer. Under X.25, packets of data are generated which include the actual data (i.e., the message) as well as addressing information and control information needed for data integrity.

X.400 The Open Systems Interconnection Standard (OSI) for message handling services. The X.400 protocol or rule sets standards for creating electronic mail messages that could be transmitted between different types of networks.

X.500 The OSI standard for network directory services. This is rather like creating a universal white pages directory for networks. With X.500, users at any network could interrogate the list of users and resources available at other networks.

Zone The logical method of dividing AppleTalk networks into several smaller networks or sub networks. To create zones, you will need gateways and/or bridges to define one or more zones or subnetworks within a larger network. Groups of users and devices could be divided into different zones. For example, you could put users who use a special PostScript printer and that printer on a separate zone. Users can still access other network services and zones by selecting these zones from the Chooser menu.

CHAPTER

13

Computer Security

In this chapter we are going to talk about computer security. We are not concerned with "acts of god"—fire, storm, earthquake, etc. (These threats can be countered by adequate data backups, discussed elsewhere in this book.) Rather, we will discuss ways that you can protect yourself from acts of *man*, from acts intended to damage your data or computer system, from attempts to steal information, and from forgery and data tampering.

If your Macintosh is at home, you may feel that security is not really your concern. After all, you trust your family, and the chance of a burglar breaking in and sitting down at the monitor is pretty slim. Until around 1987 you might have been correct. But no computer is an island. Even if you are the only person who ever touches your keyboard, your computer is linked to the outside world in a number of ways. Each time you install a new computer program, load a data disk, or use a modem to dial an information service or bulletin board, you are bringing your system into contact with other computers. The introduction of *viruses* into the computer world made security a problem for everyone. The first known computer virus was created in 1983, and by 1987 computer viruses were

so widespread that they threatened virtually *all* computer users. A recent *Byte* magazine poll found that 28 percent of their readers said their companies had lost program and data files to viruses.

So as you read this chapter you may want to evaluate the threats that are a problem for you. Some serious problems for network managers won't concern the user with a computer at home, for example. But some problems threaten everyone. Let's start by looking at the type of threats to your computer.

Industrial Espionage

Your company's computers may contain information that would help a competitor, from financial statements to product development reports. The information may be stolen by an employee or by a knowledgeable outsider. While you can't imagine any of *your* co-workers selling information to the "enemy," it *does* happen. All it takes is one disgruntled employee—one person passed over for a promotion or an employee with financial problems.

Intentional Damage

When the results of a person's work is stored in a computer, it is easy for someone to inflict enormous damage in a few seconds. An angry co-worker can select the *Erase Disk…* command, for example, and in two seconds wipe out months of work. Or a virus can enter the computer invisibly, and destroy data or take over system resources. Also, there will always be some forms of intentional damage that cannot be protected against by using computer technology.

Material Theft

Computers manage so many systems, that a knowledgeable person can use the computer to direct the theft of money or other tangible goods. Computer theft is thought to cost U.S. industry as much as $5 billion each year. The most common example, of course, is bank theft. Much of this is unreported, and in a number of cases banks have even bribed computer thieves to keep quiet about system penetrations. In one case a London bank let a programmer keep £1 million of the £8 million he stole—as long as he didn't tell anyone! (What a deal!)

Theft of Confidential Information

Computers contain a lot of information that you wouldn't want other people to have, for a variety of reasons. Names and addresses, financial records, confidential memos, phone logs—such information can be used to embarrass, threaten, or rob you.

Theft of National Security Secrets

If you work for a company or agency involved in classified projects, you already know a little about security. It's a big concern for most government agencies, but one they haven't been able to eradicate. In 1989 a 14-year-old boy penetrated the Air Force's satellite positioning system. A West German group broke into 30 computers—including one owned by the Lawrence Berkeley Laboratory—and sold stolen information to the KGB. A group called the West German Chaos Computer Club broke into a Strategic Defense Initiative (SDI) computer. New stories of hackers entering government computers seem to appear in the press monthly.

The Areas of Weakness

Now that you know the types of threats—the reasons that someone would want to get to you or the type of damage they might want to inflict—let's look at the way the threats could be carried out.

Media Theft

Probably the simplest way to steal your information is to walk away with your disks, tapes, or printed information. While it is important to make regular backups, it is also important to make sure that the disks or tapes are stored somewhere safe.

Unattended Computers

If your computer is left unattended in an area where other people have access, it's easy for someone to wait until you've left the area and then meddle with your machine. A fellow employee could come to the office at the weekend, or wait until you've gone for lunch or gone home. Or an intruder could break in at night and use your computer. Either way, the information on your computer could be damaged or stolen.

Inserting Disks

You can unknowingly damage your own system by placing a disk into a disk drive. Perhaps you are installing new software or loading a data file from another computer. If the disk contains a virus, the virus may enter your system and do damage immediately—or months later.

Modem Communications

Computers permanently connected to auto-answer modems can be attacked from the outside. In his book, *The Cuckoo's Egg*, Cliff Stoll explains how hackers in West Germany were able to use international phone lines to enter computer systems in the United States and steal information related to various military projects. You may also be vulnerable during communications that you initiate. Although most online systems now go to great lenghts to prevent it from happening, each time you download files from a bulletin board you *could* be downloading a computer virus.

Network Communications

If your Macintosh is connected to a network, it may be possible for someone at another computer to access your hard drive to steal or damage files. Also, computer viruses can spread across networks very quickly.

Intercepting Emanations

A really determined data thief could intercept and decipher the electromagnetic radiation emanating from your computer or network. This is very rare, though it could be quite easy for someone with the knowledge and resources. Although it's not a threat to the average computer user, it is of some concern to the U.S. government.

Tapping Communications

The determined data thief could tap into your data communications. In fact, it's relatively easy to intercept data transmitted by a modem connected to a cellular phone. If you transmit data across ordinary telephone cable it's more difficult, of course, though still possible to tap directly into the line.

When do you need to implement a security system? Everyone needs some form of data security. The question is not "should I or shouldn't I?," it's "what type do I need?" The most basic data security action you *must* take is to back up your data. Backing up data each day limits your loss to one day's work. If someone intentionally deletes your entire hard disk, or if a virus destroys all your data files, you can restore your backed-up data.

The next thing you should do is to protect your system from viruses. Let's start with a discussion of what viruses are and how you can deal with them.

Viruses, Bombs, Salamis, and Other Threats

A *biological* virus is a "simple organism, multiplying in living cells and often able to cause diseases." A *computer* virus closely fits this description. It's usually a relatively simple program; it may be cleverly designed, but it is generally small and unobtrusive, often less than 4K bytes. Computer viruses multiply in computers that are running, and they may cause damage. The term *virus*, incidentally, was originally used in a science fiction story written by David Gerrold in the early 1970s.

How can a computer program act like a living organism, reproducing itself and traveling from computer to computer? Anything you can do with computer commands—such as copying files—a program can do, so it is a relatively simple process to create a program that will copy itself at certain times. For example, a virus on a startup diskette will "come to life" when the Mac is started-up. A virus hidden inside an application will start operating when the application is run. Once active, the virus can copy itself onto any diskette loaded into the computer, or onto any other computer system connected by modem, or into other applications. Some viruses even search for previous versions of themselves and update those versions!

Many viruses are little more than irritating. They may cause a message to pop up on your monitor unexpectedly, or display a small picture. One virus displays a Christmas "card" on a particular date, for example, while another displays a bouncing ball. But viruses can also do great damage, wiping out months of work or destroying application files.

Viruses work in many different ways. *Boot sector* viruses insert themselves into the boot sector on floppy or hard drives. The boot sector is the first part of the disk read into memory when the computer is turned on, so the virus is loaded into memory before anything else. Boot sector viruses spread by copying themselves to the boot sectors on other disks—disks inserted into the floppy drive, for example, or the hard drives of computers into which an infected floppy has been placed. Another type of virus—*file viruses*—attach themselves to applications and extensions (INITs). When the file is executed, the virus is executed too. Viruses are even reported to have caused actual *physical* damage. By adjusting a video monitor's scan rate, one virus supposedly caused the monitor to overheat and eventually burn.

Strictly speaking, a virus is a fragment of code that inserts itself into a larger program, though these days the term is used rather loosely to cover just about any program that intentionally causes damage. Here are a few specific terms for other types of malicious "organisms," all of which fall under the "virus" umbrella these days:

Bacteria   Programs that simply reproduce themselves. They don't cause any other kind of damage, but eventually use up your system's memory and disk space, making it inoperable.

Bombs   An independent program or code fragment hidden inside an application by a system developer. A bomb carries out some kind of unauthorized action at a specific date or time, or when a particular condition occurs. A *time bomb* goes off after a particular time has elapsed, or on a particular date. For example, on Friday the 13th, 1988, a time bomb (now known as the Friday the 13th Virus) "exploded" and began damaging computer files. A *logic bomb* goes off when a particular event occurs, such as when the application user selects a particular menu item.

Crabs   Programs that damage the display of data on computer screens.

Rabbits   Programs which simply reproduce themselves rapidly.

Salamis   A program which slices away small pieces of data, altering information almost imperceptibly. Because the damage done by salamis is so slow, they are often not noticed for some time.

Trap Doors   Also known as *back doors*, these are left in programs by the designer. This allows the designer to enter the program at a later date, without going through the normal logon procedures. There is often an innocent reason for a programmer to create a trap door—so he can enter the program for testing without going through a slow logon, or in case there is a problem with the logon procedure. Such trap doors are normally removed before the program is released, but in some cases programmers may design a secret trap door to give them illicit access at a later date. A programmer working on a banking application may want to sneak into the system later to steal money, while the designer of a system for a government laboratory may want to steal secrets.

Trojan Horse   A program that hides inside another useful program and performs unauthorized actions while its host program is operating. A trojan horse may even trick a user into providing information. For example, it might prompt the user to provide his logon password, which it can use for its own purposes.

Trojan horses don't reproduce themselves, but travel around when users pass copies of the program to their friends.

Worms   A program that copies itself from one computer to another. Worms are independent—they are not inserted into other programs, unlike viruses, and usually doesn't destroy data. Worms "damage" systems by taking over system resources until the system comes to a standstill. In 1988 a worm infected over 6,000 computer systems connected to Internet, the world's largest computer network.

Basic Precautions

Most computer users have never seen a virus in action. But if the experts are correct, users are increasingly likely to find their computers infected. The number of viruses is increasing rapidly, and changing work habits—more computers on networks, more shareware, and more bulletin boards—are making them spread quickly. It's a good time to be a virus; literally hundreds have been identified. Even if your computer hasn't been infected yet, there is a chance it may be in the future. And as you have already seen, your computer could *already* be infected by a virus that is waiting for a particular date or event to trigger it.

How can you protect yourself against viruses and other dangerous organisms? Some basic precautions you can take are listed below:

- Before installing new software, set the write-protect tabs on the diskettes to "protect"; to stop viruses spreading from the Mac to the disks.

- Install only licensed software from reputable sources. Return software if the inner packaging has been opened.

- If you have to use public-domain or shareware programs, be careful. Buy these programs from companies that use a virus-prevention system to keep their disks clean; programs downloaded from bulletin boards may not have been checked for viruses (some bulletin boards *do* check all their downloadable software, though). Be especially careful with programs that don't identify the author.

- Check local bulletin boards for information about viruses found in shareware programs in which you are interested.

- Only install software that you need and will use.

- Buy and use anti-virus software. *Vaccinate* new software before using. (We will learn about virus-checking programs in a moment.)

- After your computer returns from a repair shop, use anti-virus software to check the hard disk.

- Use an anti-virus program to check shareware and bulletin board files.

If you are a system administrator,

- Don't allow users to install their own software; only allow software that you have checked first. Make sure visitors—salesmen, consultants, computer repair people—don't install software without your knowledge.

- Use one Mac as an isolated "demonstration" machine for testing software brought by employees, salesmen, and consultants.

- If you have a network, consider using diskless workstations so users cannot install their own software.

- Make sure users transfer files over the network, not by carrying disks between Macs.

- Carry out regular network backups, and ensure that users back up their hard disks regularly.

Remember that nothing is 100 percent reliable. Even software from "reputable sources" has occasionally been infected, and when you back up data you could also be copying a virus onto the backup tape or disk. Although if you do back up infected files, you may still be able to restore from backup and then use anti-virus software to clean the restored files before using them. Some backup programs even incorporate virus checking.

Anti-Virus Software

There are now several anti-virus programs on the market. They range in price, although most are in the $75 to $150 range. Remember that these are list prices—"street" prices may be as little as 50 percent or 60 percent of the list price.

Anti-virus software can protect your system in a variety of ways. It can load an extension (INIT) to continually watch for viruses, and warn you if one is found; it can scan your disks—both hard and floppy—looking for viruses and removing or neutralizing them before they can do any harm; and it may "immunize" files, making sure that they cannot be infected.

How can a program differentiate between useful files and harmful viruses? There are several commonly used methods. Anti-virus programs can literally recognize many types of viruses. Promotional materials will usually tell you that they "recognize more than 800 viruses," for example, or "detect over 450 viruses." By scanning the files on your disks bit by bit and comparing them with the library of known virus files, the program can recognize and destroy known viruses. The publishers of anti-virus programs are constantly upgrading their virus libraries, adding new ones as they are discovered. You can add the new ones to your software by getting the program upgrade every so often.

Upgrades are usually released once a month or once a quarter, and are often free. Symantec Corporation, which produces *SAM-Symantec Anti-Virus for Macintosh*, also provides a BBS from which SAM users can download the latest virus information and signatures.

Some programs do little more than scan for known viruses, so they can't catch new ones. More sophisticated programs, like *SAM*, are able to watch for virus-like activity. Programs may look at each file on the hard disk and then assign a checksum according to the file's contents. Later, the program scans the disk again and calculates new checksums, comparing them with its database of the original checksums. If they are different it warns you that a virus may have attacked the file. Anti-virus programs can also load extensions (INITs) that will constantly watch for viral activity and sound an alarm if any are found.

Another method for dealing with viruses is to immunize files by adding a special code to them—an *integrity statistic*. This acts like a checksum; when the file is run, the integrity statistic is checked to see if it has changed. If a virus has incorporated itself into the file, the program warns you that an infection has occurred. Unfortunately, this isn't a foolproof method; some applications do their own integrity checks which may set off false alarms.

If a virus does damage a file, some anti-virus programs are able to restore the file to its original form by removing the virus. Some programs also provide a way for you to get your Mac running even after a virus has damaged the hard drive's boot area or directory. Some products are also network compatible, allowing a system administrator to check for viruses on all the workstations in the network.

System-Access Controls

System-access controls are the ways in which you limit who may gain access to your computer equipment. How serious a problem is access control? That depends on where your Macintosh or workstation is, and the type of data that could be stolen or damaged. If you have a Mac at home, you are probably not too worried about access control. If you are the system administrator for a large network containing proprietary information, financial documents, and other sensitive information, then access control is very important. One vengeful—or incompetent—employee navigating through the network's directories could do an awful lot of damage in a very short time, so controlling who gets onto the network and to which areas they are allowed access is very important.

The first way to limit system access is to simply stop unauthorized people from getting near the computer. In the past, this was the preferred form of access control. Computers were large, expensive machines locked away in the basement or back room. These days things are more difficult, for two reasons. First, most large businesses have personal computers and computer workstations spread throughout the building. Second, data communications are much more common. Employees take their PowerBooks on business trips and dial up the company computer; branch offices transmit accounting information each night; and overseas offices replaced telex messages with electronic mail and computer fax. So these days access control has become more sophisticated. Rather than assuming that the "wrong" people can be kept away from the computer itself, each terminal and each phone line is seen as a potential point of entry for an intruder.

Of course, the locked room is still an important element in computer security. Large computer facilities are protected by closed-circuit television, infrared and laser detectors, security officers, fingerprint scanners, and a myriad of other expensive solutions, few of which are within the scope of this book. But remember that the key to your office door *is* an effective security tool that can keep intruders at bay (as long as the cleaning staff remember to relock the door when they leave!).

So how can you stop a person from using your Mac or from dialing into your network? There are a number of ways to do so, using software, hardware, or a combination of the two. First, there are some simple methods you can use to stop an intruder from getting to your data, even if he manages to boot your computer. For example, you could use a special utility program to make files invisible so the intruder can't find the files or can't delete them. There is software that has powerful password functionality that stops unauthorized users from launching applications. These methods are simple, and not always effective. They will only stop the mildly curious and intruders with little knowledge of computers. (They might keep your kids out, at least for a while.)

Many applications let you assign passwords to specific files. Although the application can be started, the specific file cannot be opened. Some programs actually encrypt their own data files, so even if you open it in TeachText or another text editor, or in a utility program such as the Disk Editor in Norton Utilities for Macintosh 2.0, you still won't be able to get to the data (you'll learn more about encryption later in this chapter). But again, if the user really wants the information, there may be ways to get to it. For example, what would you do if you forgot your password? You could call the software publisher and ask what to do. They may tell you how to "break in," or even lead you through the break-in procedure. If *you* can call the publisher and get this information, so can someone else! (Encrypted files generally *cannot* be broken into, though, and some publishers may not tell you how to break into nonencrypted files. In such cases, if you really forget your password, the file's gone for good!)

An excellent (and cheap) way to protect computer data that you don't want seen is to remove it from the computer when you leave. Don't put information you don't want people to find on your computer—copy it onto a diskette and take it with you, or lock it in a diskette storage box. This is especially important in businesses where small groups often share passwords so that critical files may be found when an employee is sick or out of town. (This is not good security, but it is reality; many business groups work like this.) Many programs have simple password functions that lock the screen; these are often sold with screen savers like AfterDark 2.0. When you go for lunch you can make your computer screen display flying toasters or fireworks, and nobody can get the system running without entering a password—or restarting the computer, of course.

Also remember that a deleted file is not a dead file. In the real world the word "deleted" may mean "gone forever," but in the arcane world of computers it just means "gone for the moment." Because deleting a file doesn't actually remove it from the disk—it just removes its identifying information from the directory—deleted files can be recovered, at least until the area of the hard drive on which the file was stored has been written over. There are many programs that help you clean the hard drive, though. So if you want to make sure a file will never come back to haunt you, use a file-utility program like Wipe Info (in the Norton Utilities for Macintosh 2.0) that will write garbage characters onto the area of the hard disk on which the file was stored. Or periodically use a hard-disk compression program that writes garbage over the unused portions of the disk.

If you are concerned about serious—really *serious*—threats to your data, there are a number of methods, both hardware and software, that can be used to protect your computer from intruders. They generally rely on two things:

(1) Something you know—such as a password

(2) Something you own—such as a card or key

Some of the more advanced systems depend on a third thing: something you *are*. So-called *biometric* systems analyze something about you to see if you are really the person you say you are—your fingerprints, voice print, retinal pattern, signature, or handprint. Biometric devices are generally quite expensive and relatively rare. While you might think that a biometric device should be sufficient to allow a user access—after all, how can you forge a retinal pattern—they are currently not 100 percent effective, so they are normally combined with one of the first two methods.

Access-Control Software

Security software can limit access to your computer, or to particular files, directories, floppy disk drives, and external ports. Some programs limit floppy drives to read-only, so an intruder may be able to view files but won't be able to steal them. Software security products are not as safe as hardware products. Their great advantage is low cost which may be especially important in very large installations. These programs vary in cost from around $60 to $300, list price. Many file-utility programs also include a number of access-control features such as data encryption, and file and directory locking.

Early programs could stop intruders from accessing a hard drive, but they were easy to circumvent by starting-up from the floppy drive. The latest products are much more advanced. The types of protection available are as follows:

- Stop access to the hard disk until a password has been entered.

- *Startup protection;* deny access to the hard disk if the computer is started from the floppy disk.

- *Data encryption* makes a data file unintelligible without a special key (password) and a decryption program. Some systems set up automatic file encryption.

- Deny access to certain files and folders.

- Deny access to certain applications.

- Deny use of the printer and modem ports.

- Deny the use floppy disk drives, or make them read-only so data cannot be copied onto a disk.

- Deny access to the Finder, forcing users to use a customized interface that limits areas that may be accessed.

- Prevent applications from performing standard Finder tasks, such as deleting or copying files.

- Prevent writing to the hard disk.

- Keep records of user logons and system use, to track unauthorized activity.

Access-control software is especially useful for networks. The administrator may set up different classes of user. Some users (for example, visitors) may be given very limited system use; read-only access to floppies, access to just one or two folders and applications, no access to modem ports, and so on. Other users may get far more rights, allowing them to use the floppies and modem ports, but still denying them access to certain folders. Keep in mind that the security and access control provided to networked Macs using the File Sharing in System 7 is of limited sophistication and complexity. If security threat is real, you will need to look beyond your system software. Additionally, most software access-control products are not foolproof, and some cannot protect against an intruder who wants to destroy rather than steal. For example, a knowledgeable user can still bypass the security program and select "Erase Disk..." from your hard drive. (That's when your regular backups come in handy.) They are probably more than enough protection for most users, though.

A common form of access control used for dial-up networks is called *Call-back*. Quite simply, a user dials the network, tells it that he wants to log on, and hangs up. The network then calls the user at a number already registered as that user's number. Of course, the major weakness with this system is that it limits users to preregistered telephone numbers, so it makes calling while "on the road" difficult. Call-back systems are rapidly being replaced by smart card technology, which we'll hear about a little later in this chapter.

Picking Passwords

Passwords are almost a joke these days. Many employees regard them as simply the way to start their computers in the same way a key starts a car. They don't think of passwords as a way to keep their data secure. Easy-to-crack passwords are common—children's names, first names, initials, hobby-related terms—and are even written down and taped to the computer screen so colleagues can boot the computer when necessary. In fact, the most common way to break into a network is by guessing weak passwords. Hackers may simply guess passwords using knowledge about a particular user (pet's names, car license plate numbers, etc.), or may search electronic mail for references to passwords. Some hackers use dictionaries of common password terms (you can bet they contain the words "Gandalf" and "TARDIS") and password-cracking programs that can apply these terms.

Using techniques such as these, hackers—often high-school kids, it seems—created over $2 million in damage on *Computer World*'s voice mail system; stole a $1 million artificial intelligence program from a lab in New Jersey; got into the U.S. Naval Coastal Systems Command computer; and sent a computer worm across the Internet computer network, infecting over 6,000 computers. If you are serious about keeping others away from your computer files, though, there are a few simple tricks to make your password a real barrier to entry. They are as follows:

- If you are on a network, don't keep the password originally given to you. Change it immediately.

- Don't give your password to anyone else. If you break this rule, change the password as soon as the other person has no need to be using your computer.

- Change your password regularly—weekly or monthly.

- Don't enter your password while someone is watching. If you do, change the password soon afterwards.

- Use passwords that don't make any sense. Especially don't select passwords that can be guessed by people who know you: your car's pet name, your birth date, your children's names, your favorite character from DuckTales, or your telephone number.

- Select a password that appears totally random—em96nlsa, for example. However, if you find it difficult to remember such a password, try using several short words mixed with numbers or special characters (and$or/so), or an acronym based on a phrase; timlyatj, from This Is My Last Year At This Job, for example—but not a common one such as tgif.

- Try creating a password by picking three or more short words at random from a dictionary. Combine them, then separate them with special characters.

- Don't record your password on paper, on disk, or on-line. Intruders have successfully scanned electronic mail for passwords. If you have to write the password down on paper, don't leave it anywhere near your computer, and don't write it down with the telephone number of your network's modem.

- Some systems let you decide how many characters your password will contain. Remember that the longer your password, the harder it is to crack.

- Don't use the same password for all the networks or systems you log onto.

- If you are a network manager, monitor passwords closely. Make sure passwords are changed immediately when employees are fired or quit, or when visitors leave. Also, make sure users don't create easy-to-break passwords.

Access-Control Hardware

Access-control hardware varies from the simple and cheap to complicated and expensive. One of the simplest forms of access-control hardware is the lock. You can get a lock that stops someone from walking away with the whole computer. Another form of lock you may want to add to your computer is a floppy-drive lock. These cost about $25 to $30. They stop anyone from inserting a disk into your drive or removing one from it, so an intruder can't load his own software, copy your data onto a disk, or even boot the computer from the floppy disk.

Another way to protect your computer is to take the hard drive with you. Many companies make removable hard drives. These are connected to the SCSI port, or—with the Quadra series of Macs—may be installed in the Mac's case. Either way, with the information on the hard drive gone, an intruder can't get at your data. A trespasser may be able to startup the computer using the floppy drive, but without the hard drive there's not much that can be done. Intruders probably won't even be able to get onto the network, though a determined person could find a way. Removable drives are extremely common and are increasingly efficient. They also have the added advantage of letting you expand your hard drive capacity by simply buying another cartridge.

Tokens

Many access-control systems use the computer equivalent of a key—*security tokens*. Tokens are small objects that must be inserted into some sort of reader before the user can log onto a computer or network. They are usually combined with passwords, making the system more secure by asking for both "something you have" and "something you know." For example, some Mac security systems use key-shaped or card tokens. Before users log on they must insert the token into a reader. Once the computer recognizes the token, the user can enter a logon ID and password. The computer then compares this information with the information encoded on the token to make sure they match. If they don't, the user has a few more chances to enter the correct information before being locked out. The cost for simple token systems like this start at around $200.

The security-card is often a magnetic-stripe card. In fact, some of these systems work with any magnetic-stripe card—credit cards or ATM cards, for example. These systems usually allow you to create a dedicated security card, but credit or ATM cards are more likely to be remembered and protected. This also means you have one less card to carry.

More sophisticated systems use *smartcards*, credit-card size pieces of plastic that contain computer chips with logon information; *time-based smartcards* make the technology interactive. The smartcard has an internal clock, which is synchronized with the clock in the computer. Every 60 seconds or so the smartcard and the computer pick a new passcode. When you want to log on you look at a small display on the card, read the passcode, and enter the code at a log on prompt. The computer checks the entered code against the computer's current code to see if it matches. If it does, the computer then prompts for the user's password.

Other token systems use calculator-type cards to take the principal a step further. The computer sends a *challenge number*, which the user enters into the keypad on the token. The token uses the challenge number to generate another encrypted number, which the user enters into the computer. The computer then compares the number with its own encrypted version of the challenge number. If they match, the logon continues.

Because they don't require readers, these interactive tokens are becoming the preferred way to keep remote hookups secure, replacing simple passwords and inconvenient call-back systems. Companies that regularly need modem hook-ups with traveling employees can use interactive tokens to be sure that the person at the other end of the phone line really is authorized to log on.

Security tokens can aid security in two ways. Not only do they restrict access to people owning a token, but they allow the system administrator to assign rights according to the user. Instructions stored in the token can tell the computer which system resources the user will be allowed to use: write to a floppy disk, access certain folders, or use the printer and modem ports.

Biometric and Behavioral Measurements

Biometric hardware measures unique human characteristics such as finger-prints, handprints, and retinal patterns. Other systems may one day be available that will measure lip prints (embarrassing), footprints (not too convenient), wrist vein patterns, brain waves, skin oil, and facial geometry. Behavioral systems test types of behavior such as keystroke patterns, voice patterns, and signatures. (Keystroke pattern systems prompt the user to type a block of text, and then examine the speed and rhythm of the typing.)

These systems are an attempt to make computers recognize people; you can recognize your colleagues, so you know they are authorized to be in your office. If computers could recognize people they could also determine if the person requesting access is authorized. At the moment, however, biometric and behavioral systems really use the human body as a form of security token, employing it along with a password to make doubly sure that users really are who they appear to be.

Two major problems exist with this type of equipment; it is expensive, and people find it threatening. For example, retinal pattern devices are some of the most accurate biometric devices, yet they are the least acceptable to most people who naturally fear having a machine shining lights into their eyes. Although keystroke pattern and signature devices are quite acceptable to most people, they are also some of the least accurate of the biometric systems.

It has some important advantages—there is no token to lose and it is very difficult to fake the biometric measurements. In addition, if the systems become accurate enough it may even be possible to do away with passwords, perhaps by combining two or three different biometric measurements. Biomet-ric systems may even be able to recognize when a user is being coerced into logging on to a system; the user could use a predetermined code, such as pressing the thumb down extra hard while having a fingerprint analysis. (Some fingerprint systems currently in use even check for a pulse—just in case an intruder has managed to obtain a user's finger without permission!)

Currently, biometric and behavioral systems are not too common in the Macintosh world—or even in the IBM-compatible or mainframe world, for that matter. As the technology improves in quality and drops in price, and as people become more familiar with the equipment—and less suspicious—it will probably begin to catch on.

Data Encryption

Data encryption is based on a simple idea that goes back thousands of years: whatever you do to protect your data, it may be intercepted—a messenger on the battlefield may be captured, a computer transmission may be tapped into, or an intruder may gain access to your hard drive. To protect against such events, sensitive data should be in a form that makes it totally useless to the enemy (the other army or the computer hacker). How? By *encrypting* or *enciphering* it. As children we all played with coded messages, replacing one letter with another to change a meaningful message into gibberish. Encryption programs do this in a more sophisticated manner. In fact, modern data-encryption techniques owe much—in spirit, at least—to the German military's "Enigma" machine, an encrypting typewriter that puzzled British, American, and Polish mathematicians for about 20 years. The Enigma was able to encrypt messages using a different character translation scheme for *each letter* in the message, making its coded messages extremely difficult to crack.

Encryption programs take your original data—known in the encryption world as *plaintext* or *cleartext*—and convert it into *codetext* or *cipher*. The new information appears to be nonsense, a hodgepodge of unintelligible characters. Anyone coming across such data is unable to make sense of it unless they have the same program and the encryption *key*, a sort of encryption password. Encryption programs use relatively simple mathematical algorithms, combined with a key provided by the user. The algorithms and key are applied to the data several times to convert the data to a form that cannot be decrypted without knowing the algorithms and the key. There are various types of encryption techniques; the two main forms are *substitution* and *transposition* ciphers.

The simplest form is the *substitution* cipher. These ciphers replace the original characters with new characters; the positions remain the same. The new characters might be letters, numbers, or even symbols. The simplest substitution ciphers replace a letter with another letter several places in front or behind in the alphabet. Julius Caesar supposedly wrote messages by replacing each character with the one three places ahead. A would be replaced by D, B by E, Z by C, and so on. Another, more complicated, form would be to assign a letter at random to each letter in the alphabet, and then substitute each character in the message with the assigned letter. For example:

```
Alphabet:       ABCDEFGHIJKLMNOPQRSTUVWXYZ

Substitutions:  CHMDBWEGJLVAKOXSRFPUYQZITN

Original word:  MICROPROCESSOR

Coded word:     KJMFXSFXMBPPXF
```

Here's another example, using more complicated substitutions:

```
Original word:  MICROPROCESSOR

Coded word:     %C4E7KE74E**7E
```

These are known as *monoalphabetic substitution ciphers*, ones in which characters are always replaced by the same character. *Polyalphabetic substitution ciphers* make cracking the code more difficult, by varying the character substitution. An example is the Vigeniere cipher, which encrypts messages using keys that consist of as many characters as the message contains. For example, a word is selected and repeated. Each letter in the word represents a number (A=0, B=1, and so on). Each line of the message has a corresponding letter in the key, and the number of the letter determines which letter should be used as a substitution. If the letter in the key is C (C=2), and the corresponding letter in the message is B, then the substitute will be D, two letters above B. For example:

```
Key:    THENTHENTHENTHENTHEN (T=19, H=7, E=4, N=13)

Original word:  MICROPROCESSOR

Coded word:     FPGEHWVBVLWFHY
```

This form of cipher disguises the character frequency of the plaintext, which would otherwise provide a strong clue to the code breaker. A single letter has a different substitution each time it appears.

Transposition or *permutation ciphers* literally rearrange the data by jumbling it up into what appears to be a random pattern (though, of course, it is not truly random as it is done according to a mathematical formula). The data becomes, in effect, a giant anagram; the original characters all remain, but they are in different positions. For example:

```
Original word:  MICROPROCESSOR

Transposition cipher:  RIOROCRPMESCSO
```

Transposition ciphers can be more complicated than simply mixing letters in each word. They could, for example, rearrange long strings of text into several columns, read the text *down* the columns, and place the result in a string again. For example:

```
Original word:MICROPROCESSOR
```

```
Step 1              MIC
               ROP
                  ROC
                  ESS
                  OR

Step 2              MRREOIOOSRCPCS
```

Another example is the *rail fence* cipher, which dates to the Civil War. Alternating letters from the plaintext are strung together to form the codetext. For example:

```
Original word: MICROPROCESSOR

Step 1          M C O R C S O

                I R P O E S R

Step 2          MCORCSOIRPOESR
```

The columnar and rail fence ciphers are *route transposition ciphers*. The message is put into a matrix (columns and alternate letters in these examples), read in a particular route through the matrix, and then rewritten as a string of data. The column could be read in other directions, of course. If the cipher read the columns backwards, the coded word would be

SCPCRSOOIOERRM.

Or the columns could be read from bottom to top.

Of course, encryption programs can mix both methods, use far more sophisticated formulae than the examples shown here, and also combine the user's key to further scramble the information. For instance, a key might determine the order in which the columns are read. In the columnar example, a three-digit key, 213, would tell the cipher to read column two first, making the codetext look like this:

IOOSRMRREOCPCS.

There are two types of encryption-key systems: *secret* or *private* key systems and *public* key systems. Secret-key systems, such as the Data Encryption Standard (DES), use a single key that is known to only the people who encrypt and decrypt the file. An encryption program will prompt the person encrypting the file to enter a key, and apply that key to the encryption algorithm. Then the key must be given to the person who will decrypt the file; again, the program will prompt for the key before it can decrypt the file. The security of the file, then, depends on the key. The key must not only be kept secret, but it must also be hard to guess—just like passwords.

Public-key systems (sometimes called *two-key* or *asymmetric-key* systems) use *two* keys—a private key and a public key. Private keys are kept secret, but public keys may be openly distributed and recorded—they are not protected in any way. In fact, the system requires that the public key be easily accessible to anyone. Each system user—on a computer network, for example—has a public key printed in directories and a private key. The two keys are mathematically related, so a message encrypted with one key can be decrypted with the other. Public-key systems commonly use *prime factorization algorithms*. This system uses mathematical equations based on multiplying the two key numbers together to get a third number which is then used to encrypt the code.

For example, if you wish to send a message to another person on the network, you don't need to know that person's private key. Simply look up the other person's public key and use that to encrypt the message. The recipient can then use his *private* key to decrypt the message. Anyone who intercepts the message is unable to decrypt it without the correct private key. You can also encrypt a message using your private key, and the recipient can decrypt it using your public key. The two keys only work together, not with other keys; if you use Joe's public key to encrypt a message, only *Joe's* private key will work to decrypt it—no other private key will do the job.

There are a couple of advantages to public-key systems. We will probably see more of them in the future, in every walk of life. First, a public key system is in some ways more secure than a private key system. Although anyone may use your public key to encode a message, you are the only one who may decode it. Your private key is known to only one person—you—limiting the chances of the key being learned by anyone else. Perhaps more importantly, public-key systems provide a way to create electronic "signatures," to solve the growing *authentication* problem, which you will learn more about in a moment.

The Data Encryption Standard—DES

In the 1960s the NBS (National Bureau of Standards, now called the National Institute of Standards and Technology, or NIST), in cooperation with the NSA (National Security Agency), began a cryptography program. Their intention was to create a standard form of encryption that could be used by the government for unclassified documents, as well as by the private sector. IBM eventually contributed something called the Lucifer algorithm, which it had been developing for use in automated funds transfers in the banking business. IBM had been looking for a product that would stop people from using on-line terminals to "empty the cash box," as one developer put it.

The Lucifer algorithm was modified—weakened—to become the Data Encryption Standard (DES) algorithm. Although the NSA was criticized, and claims were made that they had *intentionally* weakened the algorithm so they could read encrypted communications, a U.S. Senate investigation absolved them of any wrong doing, and found the new algorithm acceptable. IBM was persuaded by the National Bureau of Standards to release DES to the public domain, even though they originally developed the algorithm as a profit-making product.

DES has become a widely accepted algorithm that is used in many encryption products, both hardware and software. DES encrypts data by dividing the plaintext into 64-bit blocks, then dividing each block in half and encrypting each character, scrambling them 16 times. Both substitution and transformation is used alternately.

Of course, DES-encrypted documents can, in theory, be cracked. Research has shown that there are certain weak keys that can cause messages to be automatically deciphered if they are enciphered twice. Cracking DES would require the sort of special knowledge and equipment that make it a very remote threat. In fact, there are no known cases of DES being cracked, at least outside of laboratory experiments. As far as the average Macintosh user is concerned, DES is essentially uncrackable.

Many products that use DES are available; it is in wide use in government and industry. (The software versions are not officially DES-standard products, because it is possible to modify them. Only firmware and hardware products are *true* DES products; still, most Macintosh users are likely to work with DES in its "unofficial" software format.) When you use your cash card to get money from an ATM, DES is at work making sure that the transactions between the ATM and your bank are kept secret. DES is the cipher of choice in government for all but the most secret communications. It is also used for the Department of Treasury's electronic funds transfer program, and for communications between the Federal Reserve and the Depository Financial Institutions. DES is also used by Internet.

An inexpensive form of DES is available for Macintoshes in encryption programs that come with utility programs, such as the Norton Utilities for Macintosh 2.0. Some free-standing applications even use DES to encrypt data files that have been secured with a password. Many network products use DES to encrypt data communications. Of course, DES isn't the only system available. DES has been modified, for example, by using 128-bit blocks instead of 64-bit blocks, and by increasing the number of encryption cycles encrypting the data more than the standard 16 times. Still, DES is the most widespread data encryption method currently in use.

Data Authentication

When you receive a computer communication, how can you tell who it *really* comes from? When a bank receives an order to transfer money, how can it be sure that the message is from someone authorized to make such a transfer? When a business receives a large order on its computer network, how does it know it's not a forgery? These are all authentication problems, the sort of problems that computer criminals take advantage of. Because of these uncertainties, electronic documents are rarely accepted as proof; electronic contracts may not hold up in court as proof of an obligation, for example.

This is a weak link in the "paperless" office we used to hear so much about, but a weakness that will soon disappear. Both industry and government have been looking for a way to add electronic "signatures" to documents—signatures that would be harder to forge than those written with pen and ink. Public-key systems can provide this signature; proof that the document comes from the person it purports to come from—or at least, someone who knows that person's key. A moment ago we mentioned that one person could code a document using a private key, and another person could decode it using the corresponding public key. That's not very secure because the public key is public knowledge. But it does prove who the document came from. If John Doe's public key decodes a document, then John Doe's private key must have been used to encrypt it in the first place. If the message is encoded using the private key to provide the signature, and then encoded again using the public key, or by using DES, the document is both secure and obviously authentic.

Banks are often more concerned with authenticity than security. The danger is not so much that an intruder will be able to read a transaction, but that he will modify the transaction in order to defraud the bank. A public-key system provides the authentication that banks require. For example, if bank A wants to send a transaction to bank B, it can use its private key to encode the message. When bank B receives the message, it uses bank A's public key to decode it, so it knows the message must have come from bank A.

The RSA Algorithm

The most common public-key system is the RSA encryption algorithm. Named after its MIT developers (Ronald Rivest, Adi Shamir, and Len Adleman), RSA is a stronger encryption algorithm than DES. It's currently sold by RSA Data Security, and is used by a number of government departments (such as the U.S. Navy) and dozens of private companies, such as IBM, Lotus Development, Microsoft, and Novell. These companies intend to make RSA the standard for data communications encryption and digital signatures. They are also developing methods by which digitally-signed documents will be compatible between different operating systems and software.

RSA keys are created by combining large prime numbers. RSA is commonly combined with DES, with RSA being used to generate a random DES key, which is used to encrypt and decrypt the message. The DES key can then be discarded.

RSA is widely used outside the United States, and has been backed by several international standards bodies. RSA has become the *de facto* standard for private network communications in the U.S. However, NIST's attitude toward RSA is very controversial. NIST will not accept it as a national standard for digital signatures, even though it is so widely accepted that—as RSA Data Security, like to point out—the companies using RSA produce 75 percent of all U.S. computer-business revenue. RSA Data Security claim that NIST has been fighting RSA "every step of the way." In spite of a clear cut acceptance of RSA by the computer industry, NIST has proposed that RSA be replaced by an essentially untested algorithm, the DSS (Digital Signature Standard).

Companies using RSA claim that DSS is slower and more vulnerable than RSA. It also raises old suspicions that the NSA doesn't want RSA as the standard because it is unable to break it. As evidence, they note that DSS was originally presented as a NIST product though it later turned out to have been created by NSA. They also point at the "trapdoor" recently discovered in DSS. Researchers at Bellcore found that certain prime numbers used to create multiple DSS keys contain mathematical weak links—a code breaker who knows the prime number could reproduce the keys produced from that number.

NIST has proposed that a government agency should distribute prime numbers that could be used to create certified keys ensuring that all digital signatures are unique. In theory, the agency issuing prime numbers could intentionally issue weak numbers, prime numbers that contain the trapdoor, allowing them to break the coded communications of the companies using the numbers (most users will not be able to figure out if the number they have been issued is one of the trapdoor numbers). NIST originally denied that DSS had any problems, then reversed itself after one was found and admitted knowing of the trapdoor, but denied that the trapdoor represented a problem.

NIST now has little credibility within the computer business. Bellcore, for example, which originally intended to release a public domain implementation of DSS, has shelved its plans, believing the algorithm to be too weak. The National Security Agency's cryptographic research is highly secret and NSA generally refuses to comment on cryptographic matters such as the DSS trapdoor, preferring instead to use NIST as a mouthpiece. The NSA's involvement in the cryptographic standards process leads to suspicions that the government is attempting to control the standards to its own advantage. As Stanford University cryptographer Martin Hellman said, "They don't want too high a level of security because it then stymies their operation."

U.S. computer companies are also concerned about the commercial implications of government involvement in the standards procedure. Export restrictions stop U.S. companies from selling DES abroad. If continued NSA involvement in standards means restrictions on future algorithms, U.S. industry will find itself at a competitive disadvantage. Also, if foreign customers see U.S. algorithms as trojan horses that would allow the U.S. government to crack coded messages, U.S. encryption technology will certainly lose its luster. Further controversy has arisen from the announcement in late 1991 by RSA developer Adi Shamir that he and an Israeli colleague had succeeded in cracking DES. Although the announcement doesn't immediately threaten the security of DES (duplicating Shamir's would be very difficult), it may indicate that DES is reaching the end of its useful life.

Important changes may have occurred in cryptography by the time you read this book, as proponents of the various encryption algorithms prepare for battle. The Secretary of Commerce will soon decide whether to accept DSS as a new standard for digital signatures, and the Data Encryption Standard is up for renewal in 1992. The NSA has occasionally proposed that DES be superseded by an NSA algorithm. While DES will continue to be used in industry for some time, there will be growing pressure to find a new algorithm that can eventually take its place.

Using Encryption

How does data encryption affect the Macintosh? We have already seen that utilities, such as *Norton Utilities for Macintosh,* contain data encryption. They can be used to secure files on your hard drive; anyone trying to open the file will be unable to do so without the password. You could also encrypt files before transmitting them by modem. The computer user receiving the files would have to have the same data encryption program and would need to know the password. Or you could encrypt files you are transporting on floppy disks. If the disks are stolen the information stored on them is useless. Let's take a look at an example of coded text. Here's the original:

```
Code n., & v.t.  2. system of military etc. signals esp. used to
ensure secrecy; system of letter or figure or word groups or
symbols with arbitrary meanings for brevity or secrecy, or for
machine processing of information.
```

Here's what the text looks like after being encrypted by one popular encryption program (we've removed tabs and line breaks to save space):

```
PCT5___Ïp¨"º_ÇDGÈ_'_°—dP:ÒFcÂò_(b__"vA_/[ÀmJ1:_ESûY¬yY_—
_2vÛûtC,â§È2y1_"Ànó§Camôèõ"-8XxM·°<:á«·éÚ"»>_—g_Õh¦)¤3J_Â_Î2C¿Áx/
_B z`ÀW∂9—Æ 1X'ìV·&Ü·@ _?_E_ösÓ_áVê°ñ_Pè6Áj_Û"2x–ÄP_õ*°á_Zy__DIö8
__æA_:FÙAaj._Õ"_ÆÑx_)Ó «_)_áÜê1XÎ_%Zù µ4¢¯`Û8_    U—
9—ù@._«_¦ÏEqè 7µMe__[Ùø{4I__W«_À__.)OÉz'_¤IIé"KÃ-_#_ÿöa
H_M¢µ¥MÎX¶m#Ö_öEø[q,-J`b¤7Àqä7Ãì>^5V°__`>_°f0P_1£    --
_A75rLyìÄQ_ëy$¤_à·]^é;ÁÙ_HX£#9Ñ___ÚìQs"_n"øm.Q_Ú-Vq_B!/
`GN'6_82É__^Ôä"¦-·éêöaÄÖÁ,~—[©´,®{jó-@Ñ,·_C A_j__   É--
AdSfeW_ÏbÄ"_NY#_RG.W_NZz_N_ósyÄR_H«,ê%Mv±G]ò[â)BXYÑÂ_`ÄÍ Á"'d –ùE_-Îç"Ç_õGT_
_=;0–Ã_Î_R_£ç9ºrá_ç.k·©o_é_Ø¬ seÏ*3'WÃ` Aÿ_%,_÷¨¦¥,v/
_Ñ±6_ó£Ü_¶ÖÕõïDíÉÕú_ü–©"°3SZt¨ú_è¿Ù¢_W_5£ÈÄ4Úú_óí°8___Y>d&h—
Û«okTÎc_Z-ü;+_'ñÜo=ßÑ∂
Éf÷%'ºìîÑ¯n—Ê_-®÷BKËT_¿ó,]º3b_*»)M∂ö_@<._ÒÃ¶zVØ3/-GyI ÍXº3ûl
```

```
?ÁÂ¥±Í±W_-_xy}1Ó1ê·æsÍÂ ó è µ¶_Àir[}Õ¢ $q"¦_Bc-
!ÅîY*2__@®I6dk÷üú_Y___Qæ-
_ø_.:-9å_@¤2_œ!_håöñ¡¡Y¦¿2ßÛ3I¦ÍÓj@RÕKÇS,_¯[ÎQ___L_ÿ[-Ûx`tKîsuopÑRìé_Ïú`_«ªämÍY_·É_oZ"Ï-öîÍÚ/
t·RhXe_éä·,£"_GÓ[T:_˜é4ÆVóú\ "öë3_z0GNååÅÏ_KmñYâo`*ï¦ ñª(U*È-
7_«_ºm*4Ç_9K
```

This seems rather long. Actually, this is the encrypted version of a Microsoft Word 5 file, so it contains all the file header and formatting information. If we encrypt an ASCII copy of the same file, the result is much shorter:

```
PCT5___Ïp¨"_Å/_aÓî'°±Ú"m_x_-%2SxÒÛ $øÜ¤Øùóâ>±xY$_A__0Y_—
_2vÛûÔz-¯¥ ª[_yÖ3çwBÁ]'ë-»__¢>k_0'__ØZ_-JxÅy¥Ùïu"¦
H&åW_»L01)ço~ñp0 _5v´ªÙ^úlz@_ñ hQ"~â(.ò_Õ@—åÙà?íßå_ò?_k_&5ü?µ/
ôOr_[·41dçDÔF,Ñì3ä__Jàr_õ@_e_Ö 2A`2r{ß÷-d9º_va___-ò Ö~ö6qµÀ
```

You can see from these examples that encrypted files are useless to intruders. No code is uncrackable, of course, but the chance of this code being cracked is almost nil. The only practical way for the intruder to make sense of this would be for him to find the program and key used to create the encrypted file. If you are careful about the way you pick your key and don't leave it written down, breaking the code shouldn't be a problem.

A quick word about backup files. Many programs create backup files. You may not even be aware that the program is doing so, especially if the program's "File Open" command doesn't display the backup files. So if you are going to encrypt data files, either delete or encrypt the backup files also! A word of caution about data encryption programs: don't use them just for fun. If you are going to use a data encryption program, take it seriously. In particular, make sure you remember your key or password. If you don't, the program becomes, to quote one such program's documentation, "the electronic equivalent of a paper shredder." Your files become useless to *everyone*, including you. Only encrypt files that really need encrypting. From the organizational point of view, encrypting too many files holds another threat: If the person encrypting those files leaves the organization or is out of commission due to accident or sickness, he may leave behind important documents in a form that cannot be used. Also remember that if you pick an easy-to-guess key, your files are no longer safe. The intruder only has to find the encryption program—probably somewhere on your hard drive—and apply the key to decrypt your files.

Data encryption is often built into network and communications products, allowing users to send encrypted data, use public keys to authenticate the source, and encrypt information on hard drives. Encryption modems, for example, automatically encrypt data as it is transmitted; a corresponding modem is needed at the other end, of course.

Incidentally, some of the encryption products described here are not available overseas. Due to the government's fear of foreign governments with uncrackable communications, export restrictions have been implemented that stop U.S. companies selling DES overseas. For example, publishers of networking software that contains encryption facilities may produce two versions, one with DES encryption for sale in the U.S., and one with a nonrestricted form of encryption for sale elsewhere. Some file utility programs that allow you to encrypt files also have different domestic and export versions. This makes little sense. If a foreign nation really wants a copy of *Excel* or *Norton Utilities for Macintosh* it can send the embassy chauffeur to CompUSA or Egghead Software store. (Although some export restrictions even apply to foreign nationals inside the U.S., it's unlikely that many store clerks know—or care—about such regulations.)

These regulations are not only illogical but create real problems for international businesses which need to transmit encrypted messages and transactions to foreign branches. The regulations force companies to take special measures to find an encryption method that may be used in all its branches, perhaps using one method in the United States and another for international communications. It also forces them to use a form of encryption that may not be as secure as those available within the United States.

Dongles

There is another form of data security that we should touch on before leaving this subject: protecting against software theft. In the Mac's early years, software was often copy-protected, and some programs even came with *dongles*, small boxes that plugged into the computer's printer or modem port. Copy-protected commercial software is rare these days, and most users have probably never seen a dongle, but they are alive and well. Many companies that produce software for in-house use, or high-cost software for limited commercial sales, want to protect their investment. Dongles provide a way to make the theft of valuable software more difficult, though certainly not impossible.

The dongle is a security key that must be present in order to run the program. It has a small amount of read/write memory that is used to store important data needed by the application. This makes stealing the application more difficult, because if a thief copies the program code to a floppy disk, he loses the data stored on the dongle. The software can even be programmed to expire on a particular date or after a certain number of executions, just in case an entire computer, dongle and all, is stolen.

Of course, there are some problems with dongles. For every Mac on which you want to use the program, you must purchase a dongle, which, ideally, should be closely monitored to ensure that it isn't stolen. Also, dongles sometimes have system conflicts and compatibility problems with extensions (INITs) and applications running in the background.

Dongles are by no means a perfect solution. They have a number of problems, which probably accounts for their limited use. They provide a low level of security and can be defeated by a knowledgeable programmer with the right tools. Dongles accomplished their original purpose quite well—ensuring that a software purchaser could only use the number of copies purchased—but they provide limited protection against the theft of program code.

Security is a difficult problem. Like insurance, you never know how much you need until you need it. The greatest threat to your data is not from viruses, industrial spies, or angry employees, but from equipment failure and user error. A logical system of data backups and storage will protect you against these problems. As for malicious threat, it's possible to get overly paranoid by investing thousands in access-control software, smart cards, diskless LAN stations, and other esoteric hardware. It is important to carefully consider what needs to be protected, and from what or whom it needs protecting, before leaping into a security plan. Much electronic data is fairly worthless to people other than its owners. The great majority of internal memos are usually of little use to the competition; most financial documents—expense reports, requisitions for paper and office furniture—are pretty irrelevant to the "big picture." Even many technical documents are unlikely to interest anyone.

Certain basic procedures and some fairly inexpensive software can be used to avoid virus infection. Your regular data backups will protect against intentional damage to your information files. Some simple, inexpensive techniques can be used to limit users to only the files and directories they need. Most companies and individuals probably don't need to go beyond that.

Finally, remember that no system is perfect. Each system depends on the goodwill of human beings. There is always someone who knows how to break into a system—the system administrator or the application programmer, for example. On a network, the threat may not be from outside but from the users themselves. Passwords are worthless when the password owners or the system administrator—who has access to wherever on the system he wants to go—cannot be trusted. If someone is determined to damage your computer or data, there are many ways to do so. The best software in the world won't protect against someone heaving a computer out of the window. Computer security often depends not on hardware or software, but on human relationships. As Richard Baker states in the *Computer Security Handbook*, "You cannot just throw technology at a security problem. Security is a human problem."

Upgrading to System 7 and System 7 Technologies

This Appendix will give you an overview of Apple's System 7 by explaining the most important features of the operating system and giving you some guidance about whether, how, and when you should "make the switch." Beyond that, it examines some post-System 7 features Apple has presented and offers a strategy for maintaining currency with Macintosh software.

Moving from one operating system to another, even when the transition is as relatively simple as it is from System 6 to System 7, is not without trauma. But before we discuss System 7 and the transition in detail, we should make one solid statement: System 7 is one of the most stable, reliable, and worthy versions of the Mac operating system that Apple has yet released. Though there have been some incompatibilities with certain hardware and software, most of those incompatibilities have disappeared as developers have released new versions of their products. What your upgrade decision should turn on is not, therefore, necessarily compatibility with your existing software and hardware. Rather, you should consider such things as the benefits System 7 gives you, and whether your Macintoshes are capable of running it well.

)verview of System 7 Features

This section will give you an overview of the major features of System 7, showing how they can help you increase your productivity. We will also examine the benefits, as well as the costs of each feature.

One of the best features of System 7 is Personal File Sharing. In short, this means that any Macintosh connected to a network can become a *server,* making the hard disk—or a single folder on the hard disk—available to others on the network. Before System 7, sharing files on a network usually required the purchase of a separate Macintosh to act as a stand-alone file server. While you still want to use a stand-alone server if your network is larger than, say, half a dozen users, you can now share files when using as few as two Macintoshes.

Apple made System 7's File Sharing compatible with the AppleShare Networking software. This means that any machine that can work with networked volumes created by AppleShare (version 2.0 or 3.0) can work with Personal File Sharing. Thus, Macintoshes running System 6 can use hard disks shared by Macintoshes running System 7. This means you need not upgrade all of your Macs to take full advantage of File Sharing. However, you will need to install the AppleShare *client software*—the software that allows a Mac to use a networked disk—on your System 6 Macintoshes. You can do this using either the System 6 or System 7 Installer disks. Even IBM PCs and clones, when equipped with the appropriate hardware and software (such as Farallon's *PhoneNetTalk*), can use disks shared by System 7 file sharing.

Personal File Sharing does have its costs; you do pay a price for it. When File Sharing is enabled (through the "Sharing Setup" Control Panel), it uses about 256K of RAM. You will not want to enable it on Macintoshes with only 2MB of RAM (System 7's minimum, discussed in more detail below).

File Sharing can also exact a direct performance penalty. First, LocalTalk (Apple's standard system for cabling networks) and PhoneNet (the popular alternate solution from Farallon) are not very fast network mechanisms. Data moving over them is faster than data moving from or to a floppy disk, but not by a great deal. Generally, when using LocalTalk you want to work with small chunks of data—as in copying small files. Secondly, when another Macintosh is reading from or writing data to a hard disk, performance on the Macintosh that owns that hard disk degrades. Typing into a word processor, copying to a floppy disk, or virtually any other operation can be slowed down quite a bit.

Finally, although it is beyond the scope of this Appendix to discuss security in detail, you should be aware that when used carelessly, System 7 File Sharing can present a security risk to your data. If a machine contains a lot of sensitive data that you want kept private, you should take pains to restrict access to that data.

There are several ways to do this: by turning off File Sharing altogether on that machine, by disabling guest access, by not sharing one particular disk at all, or by not sharing folders that contain sensitive data.

Apple Events and AppleScript

This feature of System 7 is still, at the time of writing, largely more a "future" than a feature. Apple events is a protocol by which applications can send messages and data to other applications. For example, a database program can open a spreadsheet program, send it some data, and tell the spreadsheet to graph that data.

At present, several things are missing from this scenario. The first thing missing is universal support for Apple events: not enough programs support it to make it truly useful. However, this is changing quickly. Two leading applications in their categories—*Aldus PageMaker 4.2* and *Microsoft Excel 4.0*—include full support for Apple events; others are appearing.

The second missing component is a universal means of tying separate programs together. *UserLand Frontier* is one program that does this, however. It includes a scripting language that can send Apple events to other applications. However, partly because it is not from Apple Computer itself, Frontier has not reached the status of "standard" that some believe it deserves.

Apple's entry into this category, *AppleScript*, is due early in 1993. *AppleScript* will do several things that may make system-wide user scripting more ubiquitous. First, it will provide a *recording* mechanism, somewhat like that of QuicKeys or Apple's own MacroMaker program. Using the recorder, you will be able to record a series of actions and then save those actions, which you will be able to edit in a language that is something like HyperCard's HyperTalk. Apple is also making AppleScript *open*. This means that other applications will be able to edit scripts produced by the recorder. Thus, UserLand Frontier will be able to edit those scripts and will let you integrate them into scripts produced in Frontier's own language. Other developers are adding support for AppleScript to their products, and you can expect utilities such as QuicKeys to support it in one way or another.

AppleScript will also probably solve a big problem with current Apple event-aware programs: lack of documentation. Since there is no standard environment from which to use Apple events, developers are uncertain about how to document them for users; the standard AppleScript environment will assist developers in explaining events to their users. Developers are also uncertain about which Apple events to support and how to do so; AppleScript will probably solve this problem as well.

Improved Finder

The primary Macintosh program—the Finder—has been improved in many ways in System 7. This section takes a look at the changes.

MultiFinder Always On

With System 6 and earlier versions of the Finder, you had the ability to enable *MultiFinder*, a program that allowed you to open several applications at one time. With System 7, the term MultiFinder has disappeared; in effect, it is always enabled. This means that whenever you start a new application, the Finder remains open "behind" the application you started. You can switch back to the Finder by clicking on the desktop, or by using the Application menu (see Figure A.1).

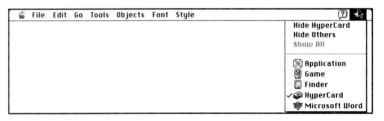

Figure A.1: The Application menu, which is available in every application, lets you switch between programs.

As with most of the new features of System 7, this has its pluses and minuses. On the plus side, the integration of MultiFinder can eliminate confusion on the part of users: many never enabled MultiFinder with older versions of the System and were not even aware of it. Since it is a standard part of System 7, a lot of confusion should disappear. It is also very useful to always have the Finder available, and for those who have enough RAM, it is very handy not to have to close one application just to start another.

On the down side, this does mean you pay a RAM price. More of your system's RAM is devoted to maintaining the Finder than was previously, and you do not have as many choices of how to best use the RAM in your system. Some applications that worked fine when *not* running MultiFinder under System 6 may be cramped in the new situation, and you may need to add RAM.

Find Command

Another useful new feature of the Finder is the *Find* command. Versions of the Finder prior to System 7 gave you no help in locating files that might be buried deep within its folders. Finder 7's Find command allows you to search by file name, type, date created or modified, comments, and more. You can also specify where the Find command should look for files—to a specific disk or folder.

As a side note, while the Find command allows you to search for text you have entered into the Comments field of a file's *Get Info* window, you should still not rely on these comments. As with previous versions of the Finder, these comments are lost when the desktop files are rebuilt. Retaining Finder comments across desktop rebuilds was slated to be part of Finder 7, but was abandoned due to lack of time; perhaps in a future reference release, we will see it. If you need this feature now, preserving Finder comments is possible through FileSaver, part of the *Norton Utilities for Macintosh, version 2*, from Symantec.

Outline Views and Labels

The System 7 Finder also improves file management in several other ways. First, there is the ability to assign labels to your files, using a new Labels menu in the Finder. This menu replaces the Colors menu that was available on color Macintoshes in System 6. The Labels menu allows you to not only assign colors to files in the Finder, but to assign text labels to those files. You can use the Labels control panel to customize your own text labels. When those files are viewed on a Macintosh with color, the file icons have the specified color; when they are viewed on a Macintosh without color, you can still see their labels in all list (or outline) views.

Outline views in the Finder are very handy. In previous versions of the Finder, you could see the contents of a folder only by double-clicking on it to open it. With the System 7 Finder, when you are using any of the list views (i.e., View by name, kind, size, or date), small triangles appear to the left of folders. Clicking on these triangles opens the folder in the same window, indenting the contents like an outline so you can tell which folder they belong to. Figure A.2 shows such a view of a System folder.

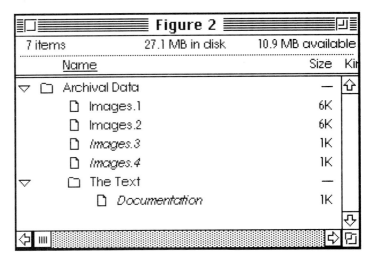

Figure A.2: The Finder's outlining capability lets you view the contents of a folder without opening a new window for it.

One useful aspect of Finder outlining is that it lets you select files from several different folders at the same time, by shift-clicking. Thus, if you want to copy a number of files in different locations to a floppy disk, or drag them to the trash, you can do so by using the outline views and the Shift key.

Aliases

One of System 7's greatest time-saving features is its ability to make *aliases* of particular files. An alias is a very small file that contains nothing but a pointer to another file. Double-clicking on an alias is the same as double-clicking on the original. This feature comes in very handy when you need to manage a lot of files.

For example, many users create a folder on their hard disk called Applications or Programs where they store, in separate folders, all the applications they use. Thus, to open an application you first need to open the Applications Folder, then the Folder containing the application itself. Now, you can make a separate folder into which you place aliases of all your applications. You can even place aliases of applications into the Apple Menu, which is discussed below.

Aliases come in handy when dealing with networks, too. Connecting to a network server can be a tedious process, involving opening the Chooser, selecting perhaps from different zones until you find the machine you want to connect to, selecting the proper disk on that server, and then entering a password. You can nearly eliminate this process by making an alias of a server. Double-clicking on an alias connects you to the server; all you need do is enter your password. Aliases are also very useful in maintaining the items you want to appear on the Apple Menu, as will be discussed in more detail later in this chapter.

Publish & Subscribe

The Macintosh has always featured a copy/cut and paste procedure that you use to move data between documents. The clipboard was one of the Mac's great innovations and is duplicated in most environments. However, the clipboard is *static*—if the data in the location from which you copied something changed, that data you pasted somewhere else did not change.

System 7 modifies this by giving you a new means of moving data between documents or between locations in the same document. This mechanism is called *Publish and Subscribe*; while using it is somewhat involved, it does update data you have moved between documents.

Publish and Subscribe works by using special files called *Editions* which contain the data you want to be updated. In the originating document, you select the data you want to share. You then use the *Create Publisher* command found on the Edit menu. This gives you a standard dialog for saving files. When you save the file, the portion of the document selected will have a gray border. This portion is now called the *Publisher*.

In the document where you want to use the data, use the *Subscribe To* command, also found on the Edit menu. The last edition you created is selected automatically. That edition is now placed into your document at the insertion point (just as data you paste is placed at the insertion point). It also gets a gray border and is called the *Subscriber*. From then on, changes that you make to the publisher are automatically reflected in the Subscriber. (Changes are updated automatically when you save the publishing document and when you open the subscribing document.)

Publish and Subscribe can be used in conjunction with File Sharing (or AppleShare) to make data available to others on a network simply by saving the Edition file to a disk or folder that is available to others. Thus a corporate accountant can publish summary figures without having to share an entire document. An artist can make interim versions of a new logo available to those laying out a newsletter, without worrying that these interim versions would be used in the final documents; when the artist saves the logo in its final form, this form will automatically be updated into the newsletter documents.

Publish and Subscribe is not a perfect mechanism. For one thing, it basically generates three copies of the data: the one in the Publisher, the one in the Edition file, and the one in the Subscriber. If you use it frequently, and for large selections, you will find that it uses a *lot* of disk space.

Balloon Help

System 7 supports a standard mechanism for providing help to users, adding a new menu—the Help menu shown below—to all applications. Figure A.3 shows the Help menu when the Finder is in front.

Figure A.3: The Help menu

Most applications have some sort of help system. Usually this system has been available as the first or second item under the Apple Menu, but there has been little consistency in this regard. System 7's Help menu provides a standard location to access help.

But the most innovative portion of System 7 help is Balloon Help. When you enable it using the Show Balloons command on the Help menu, the Macintosh displays small balloons, named after dialog balloons in comic books, next to your mouse cursor when you point at objects such as close boxes, window borders, menu commands, some files, and the like. It is important to note that the Mac has not entered a new *mode* when you enable Balloon Help; everything operates just as it did before, except that the balloons appear. You can still select menu items, open files, close windows, and so on.

There are few negative aspects to balloon help. It may not be able to perform quickly on slower Macs, such as the Classic or the PowerBook 100. The main complaint about the balloons is that it doesn't provide very deep help: there is still no standard Macintosh method for providing more detailed help on operations. This is particularly noticeable when compared to the generally excellent standard help mechanism in Microsoft's *Windows 3.1*. (We would like to put forth, however, the observation that you are much more likely to *need* help if you are trying to successfully use *Windows*.)

Smarter System Folder and Configurable Apple Menu

With previous versions of the Macintosh system software, it sometimes seemed you needed to be the proverbial rocket scientist to add a new font, desk accessory, or other utility to your Macintosh. System 7 makes adding new features much easier in several ways. Chief among these ways is the "smart system folder," although really it should be called the smart Finder. Previously, when you wanted to add a new control panel, you simply dragged it into the

System Folder and restarted the Macintosh. The same was true of "extensions" (previously called INITs). This is still the case. However, System 7 does not store these items in the top level of the System folder. Instead, there is a place for each of them, and each of them goes into its place.

For example, when you drag a control panel file and drop it onto the closed System Folder, the Finder asks if you want it to be placed into the Control Panels folder. The same is true of printer drivers and other extensions (such as fonts, discussed in more detail later). Here is a rundown of the special folders inside the System folder, and how you typically use them.

Apple Menu Items

At one time, only a special class of item could be added to the Apple menu: a desk accessory. Adding desk accessories required using one of the most confusing programs Apple ever released, the dreaded *Font/DA Mover*. System 7 vastly improves the utility of the Apple menu by allowing you to add virtually anything to it: by simply placing a file, or an alias of a file, into the special Apple Menu Items folder inside the System Folder. This makes for an especially useful means of opening common documents.

Here are some tips about things you might put into the Apple Menu Items folder (note: we are generally speaking of aliases of these items, not the items themselves):

The System Folder: Putting an alias of the System Folder into your Apple Menu Items folder makes it easy to get to the System Folder to change your configuration.

The Apple Menu Items Folder: If you change the configuration of your Apple menu often, put an alias of the Apple Menu Items folder into the Apple Menu Items folder. (Read that sentence carefully.)

Control Panels and Extensions: Although these items should remain in their own folders, aliases of control panels that you use often can be placed into the Apple Menu Items folder for easy access (see the next section). Good candidates for this are Sharing Setup, Monitors, and Extension managers.

Applications and Documents: You can place aliases for frequently-used applications and documents into the Apple Menu Items folder for quick access.

Control Panels

The Control Panel desk accessory of System 6 and prior systems has disappeared. Instead, control panels now reside in their own folder called, appropriately enough, *Control Panels*. System 7 automatically places an alias of this folder into your Apple Menu Items folder. Selecting this item opens the Control Panels folder, and you can open any individual control panel simply by double-clicking on it.

Extensions

Formerly, Extensions were called INITs, because they generally initialize or execute when your Macintosh starts. These items now have their own folder. Additionally, a number of items that do *not* execute when your Macintosh starts up are located in this folder. This includes such things as downloadable PostScript fonts (however, this is changing; fonts are discussed in more detail below), Chooser devices such as LaserWriter and other printer drivers, Apple's Tuner files, and much more.

Preferences

Preferences is a special folder in which applications should store the various files they use to hold their preferences. Normally, files are installed into this folder automatically when you install the software or when it first runs, and you will not need to deal with its contents directly. The only time you may need to take a look inside is when you *delete* an application from your hard disk (or if you are having difficulty with a piece of software and that software's technical support staff suggests that you delete that software's own Preferences file). Make sure you also delete related files, unless told to do otherwise.

Startup Items

Prior to System 7, you could specify that a certain application or document (or group of them) automatically open when your Macintosh started by using the Startup command on the Finder's Special menu. In System 7, all items (or, of course, aliases of items) you place in the Startup Items folder (which is in the System Folder) are opened automatically.

Of course, the prime use of this is to automatically launch certain applications every time you startup. You may put an alias of your word processor into the Startup Items folder, for example. Remember that this means it will take much longer to start your Macintosh. You can also place aliases to *folders* in the Startup Items folder, if you always want specific folders opened when you start your Mac.

TrueType Fonts (and Some Comments on Adobe PostScript)

TrueType is a new mechanism for encoding font designs that lets the Macintosh automatically scale fonts in that format to look good (meaning, their lines are smooth) at virtually any size. As such, it is similar in result, though not in design, to *Adobe Type Manager* which does the same thing for PostScript fonts.

Although it was one of the most heralded features of System 7 upon its announcement, the impact of TrueType has been somewhat underwhelming. To see part of the reason why, a brief history of TrueType is in order. Apple introduced System 7 in May of 1989 and discussed this technology, code-named Royal, at that time. In 1989, Adobe's Type 1 standard (at the time, Adobe's most sophisticated font technology) for describing characters in a font was proprietary—that is, Adobe did not make the specification available to other type developers. In August 1989, Adobe announced their Adobe Type Manager (*ATM*) program: software for the Macintosh that could automatically scale fonts so they looked good on the screen and when printed to non-PostScript printers. Later in 1989, Apple announced that it had cross-licensed TrueType to Microsoft for inclusion in Windows, in exchange for a license to the TrueImage software Microsoft was developing as an alternative to PostScript in printers.

Seeing that these announcements amounted to an attack on PostScript, Adobe countered with a version of Adobe Type Manager for Windows. It also opened up the Type 1 font standard for PostScript fonts to allow others to work with this high-quality standard.

Finally, in May 1991, Apple released System 7, incorporating TrueType. In the spring of 1992, Microsoft released Windows 3.1, also incorporating TrueType. Between these two events, Apple and Adobe reached a rapprochement that means that in future versions of the system software, Adobe Type Manager will be built-in. It is not clear at the time of this writing precisely how this will be implemented.

NOTE: In the meantime, Apple and Adobe jointly announced, on October 28, 1991, that Apple will include a coupon for a free copy of ATM with every new Apple printer and with Macintoshes configured with 4MB (or more) of memory. Further, if you have already gotten your printer and Macintosh, the October, 1991 joint press release states that you can order the English-language version of ATM directly

continues

continued

from Adobe (within the United States) by telephoning (800) 521-1976, extension 4400, or (303) 799-4000, extension 4600 from outside the United States. A small shipping fee is charged. As of this writing, the offer is still valid. The press release promised that the offer will remain valid, in fact, until Apple finally *does* incorporate Adobe Type 1 font technology in a future version of the System.

It turns out that TrueType in System 7 can be a mixed blessing. For example, TrueType is slower to print to PostScript printers than are downloadable PostScript fonts; font substitution can also be a problem. For example, Apple includes a TrueType version of the Times font with System 7. However, when printing to a PostScript printer, the printer's version of Times is always used (all PostScript printers have Times built into them); since there are subtle differences between the TrueType and PostScript versions of fonts, this can lead to documents that have different line breaks on the printed page than they did on the screen. The same is true of Helvetica.

Given this, what is the Mac user to do? There are a couple of answers. First, if you are not using a PostScript-capable printer, then you do not need to worry; both TrueType and PostScript (if you are using Adobe Type Manager) print well to non-PostScript (also sometimes called QuickDraw) printers. If you are using a PostScript printer, the main thing to do is not to mix the two types of font definitions: remove the TrueType versions of printer fonts from your System file, and use PostScript versions instead (Adobe Type Manager comes with PostScript versions of these fonts). Similarly, it is not a good idea to mix TrueType and PostScript fonts in the same document: this can slow printing quite a bit, as the printing software for both font technologies must be sent to the printer.

Font Handling

On a related topic, System 7 makes it much easier to deal with installation of fonts than previously. And, as you will see, System 7.1 will make it even easier. In System 7, the System file has a new look, as shown in Figure A.4.

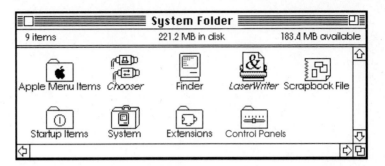

Figure A.4: The System Folder, showing icons for the System file and special folders.

Under System 7, you can *Open* the System file just as if it were a folder on your hard disk (or, to use the metaphor of the icon, just as if it were a suitcase... which it actually is). To do so, simply double-click on it. All the fonts, sounds, and some other items in the system file are listed. To remove a font from the System file, simply drag it out of the System file window. To install a file, simply drag it into the System file. (You cannot do this while programs other than the Finder are also running; System 7 will warn you that you cannot modify the System file while other programs are open, and it will give you the opportunity to close them.)

When installing fonts, you still need to be aware of the kind of font you are installing. Installing bitmap and TrueType fonts into the System file is no problem. However, PostScript fonts usually come in two parts: the bitmap (screen) font, and the PostScript font definition. PostScript font files have an icon that is generally an oblique letter A against a striped dark background. Under System 7, they are identified as "System Extensions" by the Finder; under System 7.1, they are more accurately and descriptively called "PostScript Fonts."

In System 7.0, these files need to be placed into the *Extensions* folder in your System folder in order for Adobe Type Manager or the LaserWriter software to find them.

NOTE: This font-handling mechanism is due for a change in System 7.1. Instead of placing fonts directly into the System file, System 7.1 will add a new special folder to the System Folder. The Fonts folder will be the new repository for fonts. Both screen representations (i.e., bitmap and TrueType fonts) as well as PostScript versions of the fonts will be placed into this folder.

32-Bit Addressing

Finally, System 7 provides two mechanisms that allow Macintoshes to use more memory—32-bit Addressing and Virtual Memory.

32-bit Addressing allows certain Macs to address the full range of memory that can be used by the 68020, 68030, and 68040 processors. Early versions of the Macintosh had limitations built into their ROM chips that meant only 24 bits of any addressing scheme could be used, thus limiting them to a maximum of 16MB of RAM. Reserved addresses in this range effectively limited them to 8MB of RAM.

Virtual Memory

Virtual Memory is a technique where a large file located on a hard disk can be made to appear to software to be an extension of the RAM built into the Macintosh. Virtual Memory is available on Macintoshes that have 68020 processors (as long as they also have the separate memory management hardware, called a PMMU—*Paged Memory Management Unit*—chip), 68030, and 68040 processors. Thus, though you may have only 8MB of "real" RAM in your Macintosh, Virtual Memory can make it appear to have 16MB of RAM, or more.

Virtual Memory is not a performance feature; accessing memory on a hard disk is nowhere near as fast as accessing real memory. We recommend that if you absolutely need to have large amounts of memory in your Macintosh that you outfit it with real RAM. On the other hand, Virtual Memory is great for "peak" uses—sometimes you need to make more memory available only temporarily, and that is what Virtual Memory is best for.

 # System 7 Requirements

When you are trying to decide about upgrading to System 7, the first thing you need to consider is whether your Macs are up to the task of running under it. A rundown of System 7's strict requirements, along with some tips, follows.

RAM

Technically, System 7 requires a 2MB Macintosh. Practically speaking, this leads to a Macintosh that is not very useful. Let's consider the reasons for that.

In System 6 or the earlier versions of the System that offered it, MultiFinder—Apple's utility that permitted you to run more than one program at a time—was optional. If you wanted, you could turn it off, thus saving some memory. In System 7, MultiFinder, as a name and as a program, has disappeared. Instead, the Finder is *always* running—when you launch other applications, the Finder does not quit. Instead, open applications and the Finder coexist in memory.

Beyond this, the System itself takes up more memory. Under System 7, the System itself, which includes the Finder, takes up nearly 1000K (1MB) of RAM. When other resources are added—such as Extensions and Control Panels for dealing with networks or other devices—it is not hard to have a System that takes up 2MB of RAM or more for itself.

In any case, this does not leave you much room to run your actual programs, because programs are getting larger and require more RAM for themselves.

To run System 7 efficiently, your Mac or Macs should have at least 2MB of RAM. 4MB is preferable, and 8MB is not yet approaching "too much." With RAM prices being what they are these days, it is not too onerous to upgrade a single machine. But if you have more than several Macintoshes, you need to consider the costs carefully.

Disk Storage

While System 7 itself does not take up a lot more room on a hard disk than did System 6, this is still a factor to consider. With System 6, it was possible onto actually do some work on a Macintosh with two floppy drives; that's not the case with System 7. The System itself will generally use up every last sector on a 1.4MB floppy disk, leaving no room for applications or documents.

But most Macs have hard disks, so that is not something you need to worry about a great deal. You might, though, take a look at the hard disk or disks onto which you will be installing System 7 to make sure they have enough room. When installing the system itself, you should have at least 2MB free on the hard disk, if not much more. One of the Macintoshes we use for document editing has a System Folder that takes up over 20MB of a 40MB internal hard disk!

While you are upgrading, take a look at your hard disk: does it have room for the System? Also take a look at the applications you are using. If you need to upgrade them as well, remember that storage (like RAM) requirements for applications are inflating rapidly, and costs are coming way down. If you have a 40MB disk, you should consider upgrading to a 200MB hard disk; if your current disk is 80MB, consider making the jump to 400MB.

CPU

Even with the features it adds to the Macintosh, it's surprising that System 7 is as responsive as it is. However, working with System 7—especially using TrueType or ATM fonts, or performing many of the different Finder operations—is admittedly slower than under System 6. This means that you should at least examine your current CPU or CPUs and determine if it is time to upgrade them as well. Generally, you will want to carefully consider upgrading a PLUS or an SE to a faster processor.

Potential Problem Areas

Some of the potential problem areas in System 7, such as network security, have already been addressed in this chapter. This section examines some other areas that you may need to consider when upgrading or when adding new software and hardware to your setup.

Hard Disks

Not only should you make sure you have a hard disk that is large enough to hold System 7 and its collateral files, you also should make sure your hard disk is compatible with System 7, especially if you are using Virtual Memory. At this time, most, if not all, hard drive manufacturers have updated their software to make it compatible with System 7. If you purchased your Macintosh or hard disk since the summer of 1991, you probably do not have anything to worry about (though it wouldn't hurt to make a phone call to the vendor of your disk drive). If you have an older hard disk, you should most definitely check with the vendor to see if they have released a new driver. If your drive vendor has gone out of business since you purchased your hard disk (a regrettable occurrence, but more than a few driver makers have done so in the past two years), a number of software developers have created applications that will update the drivers for nearly any hard disk.

Other Hardware Compatibility

Just as you should make sure that your hard disk is compatible with System 7, you should also do so with other devices. This includes such things as fax modems, scanners, alternate input devices (such as trackballs), and the like. If any of these devices requires some special software to work (such as a control panel or extension), then make sure that software works with System 7 *before* you upgrade.

Software Compatibility

With System 7, Apple distributes a HyperCard stack called Compatibility Checker. This stack can scan the contents of your hard disk and create a report listing the applications, control panels, and extensions that may not be compatible with System 7. Before you install System 7, you should run this program to get an idea of any possible problems with your installation.

The Compatibility Checker is by no means foolproof, however. It can become dated quickly; things change fast in the software business. Do not take its recommendations as gospel. Instead, make notes of potential problems and check with the software manufacturer to get full details.

As this is written, most application software being sold is compatible with System 7, though not all software takes advantage of all of System 7's features, like Publish and Subscribe and Apple events. A major area of incompatibility still exists with 32-bit addressing and virtual memory. *Much* older software (particularly utilities and commercially-sold system extensions) is not 32-bit clean and thus will crash your Macintosh in this mode. Some software, such as Adobe's PhotoShop, uses its own virtual memory scheme which loses efficiency when combined with Apple's virtual memory.

 # System 7 Updates

Since the release of System 7 in May 1991, Apple has released several new types of updates to the software. This section deals with those updates.

Apple's New System Software Strategy

At its Worldwide Developers' Conference in May 1992, Apple announced a new strategy for delivering updates and adding new features to its System software.

In the past, Apple has released new versions of the system software at unpredictable intervals and with much confusion. Users who have had the Mac for several years probably remember Systems 6.0, 6.0.1, 6.0.4, 6.0.5, and so on. Some of these versions were released to support new Macintosh models, and some of them were released to fix problems (read: bugs). Nevertheless, this profusion of versions was confusing: users wondered whether they should upgrade to the new version, and if so how they could acquire it. There was also the problem of getting new versions out to users.

While some of this confusion will not disappear as part of Apple's new strategy (users will still need to stay in touch with their dealers or users groups to find out about new utilities), the situation should be much more uniform.

In the future, Apple will release new versions of the software to fix bugs or add new functionality in the form of Extensions. Several of those Extensions, the *System 7 Tuner* and *QuickTime*, have been released since the initial System 7 release. At regular intervals—from 12 to 18 months—Apple will release "reference versions" of the System software, which will generally include all features released since the previous reference version. Some features, such as QuickTime and the recently introduced *Macintosh/PC Exchange* package will *not* automatically become part of the next reference version, but will remain as add-on (read: extra cost) utilities.

Remember that when it comes to Apple's system extensions, as well as all other extensions, they exact a penalty. Usually this penalty is greater RAM overhead: most extensions take up more RAM in your System. If you have a Macintosh with 4MB or less RAM, you need to weigh the benefits of each extension against this cost.

Mode 32

Soon after the release of System 7, a number of users became quite upset that Apple had apparently reneged on promises made in brochures for machines such as the Macintosh SE/30. Though equipped with the necessary 68030 processor, these machines had limitations in their ROM (read-only memory) chips that made 32-bit addressing inaccessible to them. In the fall of 1991, Apple purchased rights from Connectix Corporation to their program *Mode 32*, which enabled 32-bit addressing on these Macintoshes, and Apple essentially made it a free program. Though it is not exactly an example of Apple's software strategy, users of the Macintosh SE/30, II, IIcx, and IIx should acquire this software if they want to use 32-bit addressing. It is available from dealers, user groups, and online services. Mode 32 is *not* automatically included as part of the System 7.1 reference release.

Tuneups

Released first in early 1992, the System 7 tuners are fixes to problems with the original System 7. The first Tuneup kit, released in January 1992, had some bugs and was replaced by System 7 Tuner 1.1 later in the spring.

If you do not have the Tuneup version 1.1 (or later), and are using System 7.0, we recommend that you acquire it as soon as possible. It fixes some memory-based problems with printing and speeds file copying with the Finder. Apple dealers have the Tuneup package and should be able to copy it to a floppy disk for you. User groups also have the Tuneup kit, and it is available from online sources such as CompuServe and America Online.

The capabilities of the Tuneup utilities are folded into the reference releases of system software. Thus, if you have System 7.1, you do not need to worry about any of the current Tuneup releases.

QuickTime and Mac/PC Exchange

The QuickTime and Mac/PC Exchange packages are different kinds of system enhancements than the Tuneup packages. These are separate software packages that are sold, and will not be made part of future System reference releases. Both are available from software dealers.

QuickTime

QuickTime is a technology that provides a mechanism to allow the Macintosh to display digitized moving video. QuickTime is an Extension; it needs to be installed in the Extensions folder inside your System folder. With it installed, many applications will allow you to paste movies into them and play them on the screen. QuickTime also includes standard mechanisms for compressing still video images — notably the JPEG standard. (For a good deal more information about QuickTime and related technologies, read the MultiMedia chapter earlier in this book.)

QuickTime is available in two forms. The small form is available free from dealers, user groups, and online services. It consists of the QuickTime Extension only. The other form is the QuickTime Starter Kit, available at a list price of $199 from dealers. In addition to the QuickTime Extension, it includes utilities which let you create QuickTime movies from existing animation (PICTs) files, a CD-ROM disc containing movies, and several other utilities.

Mac/PC Exchange

This extension allows Macs equipped with the 1.44MB SuperDrive to read and write 3 1/2" disks formatted by IBM PCs. It allows you to "map" DOS filename extensions, so that, for example, a Lotus 1-2-3 file created on the PC automatically launches either Lotus 1-2-3 or Excel on the Mac when you double-click on it. This utility competes with the more full-featured similar utilities, Access/PC from Insignia Solutions and DOSMounter from Dayna Communications.

System 7.1

Throughout this chapter, we have mentioned several new features of System 7.1, due for release in fall 1992. A recap of these features is as follows:

Font Folder Fonts, including screen representations (bitmap and TrueType) and PostScript fonts, will be stored in a new Fonts folder in the System Folder.

Updates for New CPUs As mentioned earlier, many new versions of the System software have been created to support new Macintosh models. With System 7, Apple will not need to create new versions of the system for new machines, but will instead deliver Extensions that support the new hardware. This will decrease version confusion.

Language Support Originally slated to be part of System 7, a group of features will make it easier to work in multiple languages on the Macintosh. These features include a Dictionary Manager that developers can enlist for spell-checking in multiple languages, support for multiple character sets (allowing, for example, users to write using both Cyrillic and Japanese characters on a single page or even a single line), and the ability to add support for new languages and character sets with Extensions.

Beyond System 7.1

Apple has also discussed some upgrades to the System software beyond System 7.1. Here are a few facts that are known:

AppleScript

As mentioned earlier in this chapter, Apple is planning to ship AppleScript in the spring of 1993. This software will allow Macintosh users to record their actions in multiple programs, edit those actions using a language similar to HyperTalk, and save the resulting script files so they can be used repeatedly. This will mean that double-clicking a single file could, for example, open a database, extract some information from it, send that information to a spreadsheet for graphing, and finally embed the resulting graph into a report. AppleScript will be a boon to those who repeat essentially the same set of procedures over and over, and to those who must set up systems for new or largely untrained users. It will, however, require rewriting and redesign of existing software. It is hard to tell at this time how quickly that redesign will proceed.

Open Collaboration Environment (OCE)

Also an extension to System 7, OCE will provide mail and messaging services, authentication services, directory services, and digital signatures. This will allow developers to provide collaborative features in their applications. With the proper tools, various writers could work together on a document. An OCE-capable word processor could assist the writers in keeping track of who has modified or created which portions of the document. Look for OCE to arrive early in 1993, with programs implementing it coming soon thereafter.

Microkernel

At some time, the structure of the system software will change to one based on a microkernel, akin to the way UNIX is implemented. This microkernel operating system will allow for improved multi-tasking and multi-threading on the Macintosh. Slated for the same release time are the new input/output capabilities that will allow improved performance when reading and writing data to network disks or local hard disks, as well as when acquiring data from scanners.

Dealing with New System Software

Given that Apple's system software will be changing over the next several years and beyond, the question for users is how to be prepared for these changes. Here are some general hints.

Register Your Software

As Apple changes system software, so do developers change their applications programs and utilities. Registering your software is the best way to be assured that you will be notified of updates; generally, prices of updates are discounted to users of previous versions.

Beyond registering software, it is a good idea to read the newsletters and mailings developers send you. While some of them will not be of specific interest to you, often these releases are the only way you find out about such things as new versions, and you can also sometimes get tips about making the best use of your software.

Cultivate Your Apple Dealer

It is getting more and more difficult to find a good dealer, especially in an environment where Macs are sold through consumer electronic stores. If possible, we recommend purchasing from a dealer who shows a commitment to the Macintosh and to providing good service to customers. A good dealer will keep you posted about new system software updates and provide them at as low a cost as possible.

Stay in Touch with the Macintosh Community

A lot of information about new software is handled on an almost word-of-mouth level. If there is one near you, join a Macintosh user group. Often their newsletters and meetings will provide information that not even dealers know about. If there is no local user group, another good way to get the latest information is through online services. CompuServe, America Online, Genie, and AppleLink all carry a good deal of information about the Macintosh System software, and some of them make software updates available electronically.

Read the Magazines

Though monthly magazines such as *MacWorld* and *MacUser* can oftentimes be out-of-date by the time they are in print, they are invaluable as sources for information. *MacWEEK* is another good source, and it can be more timely, given its weekly publication schedule.

Index

financial modeling, 25
Find command, 423
Finder program, 422
firmware, 299
fitting, grid, 117
flat slide scanners, 168
flatbed plotters, 85
flatbed scanners, 161,
165-166
 black-and-white, 165
 color, 165-166
 gray-scale, 165
 size, 165
floppy interface, 170
flopticals, 46, 57
folders, Startup Items, 428
font metrics, 111
Font/DA Mover program,
427
fonts, 64
 bit-mapped, 64
 building, 117
 displaying, 117
 fax modems, 334-335
 hinting, 117
 hints, 68
 metrics, 118
 Multiple Master, 111
 outline, 118
 printer, 116
 raster, 116
 san serif, 116
 screen, 116
 stroke, 116
 TrueType, 112-113,
 429-432
 vector, 116
formats, file, see file
 formats, 126
frame grabbers, 160,
170-173
Freedom of Press program,
66
freeware, 280

frequency, 187
fundamental tones, 188
Fusion Data TokaMac ci
 Mac IIci accelerator, 24

G

Galaxy Plus
 Editor/Librarian program,
 214
gamma factor, 179
gamuts, color, 90
gateways, 260, 386, 378
genlock, 171
geometry, screen, 139
grabbers, frame, 160,
170-173
graphics
 bit maps, 104-106
 file formats, 180-181
 DXF, 125
 EPS, 125-126
 Paint, 124
 PICT, 126
 PostScript, 125
 TIFF, 124
 input devices, 159-160
 bar code scanners, 160,
 177
 cameras, 159, 173-175
 frame grabbers, 160,
 170-173
 scanners, 159, 160-170
 video digitizers, 160,
 170-173
 raster, 105-109
 vector, 106-109
gray linearity, 140
Gray scale TIFF, 124
gray-scale scanners
 flatbed, 165
 hand-held, 164
gray-scale images, 178-179
grid fitting, 117

grills, aperture, 138
guitar synthesizers, 210
GWorld memory, 150

H

halftones, 107
hand-held scanners,
161-164
 black and white, 163-164
 gray-scale, 164
 stitching images, 164
 virtual-page scanning,
 164
hard disk-based Macs, 36
hard disks, 36, 223
 access time, 39
 cache memory, 42
 hardware caches, 43
 software caches, 43
 cylinders, 38
 data compression, 59
 data transfer rate, 40
 defragmentation, 58-59
 directories, 43
 disk controllers, 40
 head actuators, 37
 interfaces, 40
 latency, 39
 multiple, 44-45
 organizing, 43-44
 platters, 37
 purchase considerations,
 38-39
 random access, 37
 read/write heads, 37
 removable, 45-48
 sectors, 37
 seek time, 39
 speed
 increasing, 42-43
 measuring, 39-40
 spindle motors, 37
 subdirectories, 43